THE BATTLE
FOR THE LIFE AND BEAUTY
OF THE EARTH

A STRUGGLE BETWEEN
TWO WORLD-SYSTEMS

THE CENTER FOR ENVIRONMENTAL STRUCTURE SERIES

Since 1964, Christopher Alexander and his colleagues at The Center for Environmental Structure have undertaken projects that demonstrate life-giving ways of creating our built environment. A visionary series of books has been published to put forward a complete working alternative to present-day practices in the fields of architecture, planning, and construction. The series spans forty-seven years of continuous production under Professor Alexander's leadership, and includes the following sixteen titles.

Most of the photographs of the Eishin campus that appear in this book were taken twenty-five years ago with various types of cameras, by several different members of our staff in all kinds of weather, rainstorms, and sometimes in failing light. They served to capture the process so that we could gauge our progress from day to day. Not all of the images are of high quality, but their informality conveys the relationship we had with the place and staff and faculty and students, at the time the campus was being built. Including them was an important aspect of conveying Eishin's history. The reality of the place is more important than a carefully manicured presentation.

THE

Battle

for the Life and Beauty

of the Earth

A Struggle Between Two World–Systems

Christopher Alexander

WITH

HansJoachim Neis and Maggie Moore Alexander

OXFORD
UNIVERSITY PRESS

OXFORD
UNIVERSITY PRESS

Oxford University Press is a department of the University of Oxford. It furthers the
University's objective of excellence in research, scholarship, and education by publishing worldwide. Oxford is a registered trade mark of Oxford University Press in the UK
and in certain other countries

Published in the United States of America by
Oxford University Press
198 Madison Avenue, New York, NY 10016, United States of America

Library of Congress Cataloging in Publication Data
Alexander, Christopher.
The battle for the life and beauty of the earth: a struggle between two world-systems /
Christopher Alexander with Hansjoachim Neis, Maggie Moore Alexander.
    p. cm. — (Center for Environmental Structure series; v. 16)
Includes bibliographical references and index.
ISBN 978-0-19-989807-7
1. Architectural design. 2. Architecture—Philosophy. 3. Higashino Koto Gakko—
Buildings. I. Neis, HansJoachim. II. Alexander, Maggie Moore. III. Title.
NA2750.A535 2012
720.1—dc23   2011043944

ISBN 978-0-19-989807-7

9 8 7 6 5 4 3 2 1
Typeset in Adobe Caslon Pro
Printed on acid-free paper

TABLE OF CONTENTS

On the following two pages:
The Entrance Street of the Eishin Campus, with
visitors, guests, and students,
on the day of the Annual Spring Festival, 1987. It was a rainy day.

ACKNOWLEDGMENTS

We offer our heartfelt thanks to our colleagues, partners, subcontractors, and assistants who helped during the long period from 1981 to the present. Without them, we could never have made the Eishin campus possible. Some are no longer living. They are remembered by us all.

EISHIN BOARD MEMBERS AND FACULTY: Keizo Sakaida (Chairman 1981-83), Hisae Hosoi (Chairman 1984-1986), Minoru Murakoshi, Osamu Kurahashi, Mr. Nodera, Mr. Hagiwara, Mr. Izumori, Hideo Nishigori.

CES CALIFORNIA: Chief Architect Christopher Alexander, Executive Architect Hans-Joachim Neis, Ingrid Fiksdahl-King (Architect), Artemis Anninou (Architect), Astrid Chwoika (Architect), Eleni Coromvli, Ken Petersen, Gary Black (Structural Engineering), Neville Mathias (Structural Engineering), Robert Walsh, Randy Schmidt, Jenniffer Morriss, Jeraldene Lovell-Cole, Lily Alexander.

CES JAPAN: Torashichi Sumiyoshi (Master Carpenter), Hajime Odagiri (Architect), Kohsuke Izumi (Architect), Hiroshi Nakano (Architect), Takeshi Ishikubo (Architect), Tamio Shiohara (Architect), Toshihiko Sasaki, Kumiko Sunda, Keiko Ono, Miyoko Takeda, Mr. Ishiguro (Master of kura-shikkui work — polished, black traditional Japanese plaster work), Minoru Nishida (Civil Works Manager), Noriko Isono, Nusako Watanabe.

FUJITA KOGYO CONSTRUCTION COMPANY: Kazunori Fujita (Vice-president of the Fujita construction company, Tokyo), Mr. Tsuboichi, Kaoru Suzuki, Yuden Tanaka. Toshimi Fujita was head of the Japanese crews, and his extraordinary energy, together with the energy of Hajo Neis, was, we believe, what made the project possible.

THE MORE THAN TWO HUNDRED MEN AND WOMEN WHO WORKED ON CONSTRUCTION: They worked three eight-hour shifts, round the clock, from October 1984 to April 1985, in order to complete the campus in time for the campus opening in April 1985.

OTHER CONSULTANTS: Professor Gengo Matsui (Professor of Structural Engineering, Waseda University), Mr. Iwata (Structural Engineering).

We thank all those mentioned above, together with the hundreds of students and staff who contributed their ideas and visions to the campus as it stands today.

AND WE GREATLY THANK OXFORD UNIVERSITY PRESS for supporting the preparation of this book. James Cook, our editor, helped us far beyond the call of duty, launching and supporting the practical work of creating this book. His care and concern approached the kindness of a dear friend in making sure this project would succeed.

For photo credits, please see the end of the book, page 498.

IN WARM APPRECIATION

TO ACKNOWLEDGE THE TWO PRINCIPAL
VISIONARIES OF THIS NEW CAMPUS:
HISAE HOSOI, THE MANAGING DIRECTOR OF THE CAMPUS
THROUGHOUT NINE YEARS OF CONSTRUCTION (1981 TO 1990), AND
KEIZO SAKAIDA, PREVIOUSLY CHAIRMAN OF THE EISHIN BOARD,
NOW PASSED AWAY, WHO WAS MR. HOSOI'S MENTOR AND TEACHER,
AND WHO LAID THE GROUNDWORK OF THE NEW SCHOOL'S
PHILOSOPHY.

THE AUTHORS OF THIS BOOK GREATLY APPLAUD THE
EFFORT MADE BY THESE TWO MEN,
ESPECIALLY HISAE HOSOI
WHO HAS GIVEN A VERY LARGE PART OF HIS LIFE TO THE WORK
OF CREATING THE NEW SCHOOL AND CAMPUS.
ALL PRESENT AND FUTURE FACULTY AND ALL STUDENTS AND
ALUMNI AND THEIR FAMILIES, TOO, OWE
A DEBT OF GRATITUDE TO THESE TWO.

WE PRAY THAT THE CAMPUS ITSELF MAY CONTINUE TO GUIDE
AND INSTRUCT FACULTY AND STUDENTS IN THE FUTURE AS TO
HOW THEY MAY BEST USE THIS CAMPUS, AND BENEFIT FROM IT,
AND LEARN FROM IT.

The Campus in the distance, winter 1986.

Preface

A NEW ARCHITECTURE, A NEW CIVILIZATION

Our book describes a revolutionary vision of the human environment: one which will, in coming eras, be conceived, designed, built, made, and widely understood as a necessity of emotional and social life. This will inevitably change the way we conduct ourselves in all the arts of building.

From the very beginning of the building project described in this book, we intended to show that architecture can bring life to a community — indeed, that it is necessary in order to help the community come to life. Thus, we mean to show how the physical fabric of the buildings plays a necessary and unavoidable role in the success of a community.

But in 1985, there was almost no tradition left that could support such a symbiosis of building form, social behavior, and human feeling. Building production systems did not support this kind of endeavor, and people did not even know (then or now) how to make themselves comfortable in their own environment — not in the obvious sense, and not in any subtle senses either.

———

The purpose of all architecture, the purpose of its spatial-geometric organization, is to provide opportunities for life-giving situations. The central issue of architecture, and its central purpose, is to create those configurations and social situations, which provide encouragement and support for life-giving comfort and profound satisfaction — sometimes excitement — so that one experiences life as worth living. When this purpose is forgotten or abandoned, then indeed, there is no architecture to speak of.

When we look at the decades from 1900 on, we might say that it is as if in those years, the emotional glue that held society together began to break down; and then progressively broke down after that period. More and more, it has erased the possibility of human joy. We have made less and less use of the environment itself — its geometric form — to encourage and support life-giving activity, dreams, and playfulness. In the most recent decades of newly built buildings and neighborhoods, one may say that the value of life has been dramatically and decisively diminished.

We are not raising this topic as a comment on the *technical* quality of the buildings. If we ask whether buildings, roads, roofing, or window safety, are in good order, we can assuredly say that in these areas of technical expertise, the environments being built are, for the most part, getting better. They are more sturdy, more waterproof, better-behaved thermally, more efficient with regard to energy, less likely to fail structurally, better provided with electrical outlets, the floors are more flat, more perfectly flat, the walls may also be more perfectly flat, and more perfectly vertical, the lighting may sometimes be more uniform, the telephone system may be better, the computing facilities may be more sophisticated, and the television sets may have larger screens.

But if we examine the same newly built environments during the period from 1900 to 2010, *and judge their human quality from the point of view* of our psychology, our emotional states, our social and mental well-being, our happiness, our joy in life, then we shall reluctantly be forced to acknowledge that the contemporary efforts we (as a people) are making to build living environments, are becoming **less** and **less** successful with each decade that goes by.

During this time the environments we were building became progressively more sterile, decade by decade, and rarely, almost never, provided the kind of environments in which people are emotionally nourished, genuinely happy, excited, romantic, loving, inspired, moved to tears, or deeply contented.

This gradual, steady deterioration of environmental quality has been occurring all over the world, on every continent, in every society and culture, and in every nation state.

———

The extent of this loss can hardly be exaggerated. For at least a thousand years, and probably three or four times that length of time, there was universal regard for the importance and beauty of the buildings that were made. For those who had money, the money was lavished on the most beautiful paintings and ornaments, on the magnificence of harmony and proportion. For those who had very little money, they used their own hands. Even in buildings made of mud or straw or snow, people used their own hands to make something beautiful that would be cherished.

Buildings, of whatever size and type, were loved. Care was lavished on their construction. They were admired and enjoyed, from outside and inside. In a word, they were *important.*

The *buildings* meant something to the people who lived in them and around them. The buildings represented the importance of life. And, along with the buildings themselves, the people who made them, also saw *themselves* as important. Their lives had value in their own eyes, and in the eyes of others.

By the last quarter of the 20th century, this inner human value had all but disappeared as an active process. The vestiges of other eras and other civilizations still existed as fragments here and there, but as time went by these vestiges were all that people had to remind them of what buildings had once been and what life could be. But except for these leftovers from other historical eras, the streets, buildings, roofs, staircases, and windows of contemporary construction were as nothing, and counted for nothing when judged by the standard of their human content. They were poorly built, in some cases made of disturbing or ugly materials. Even when it was high-tech junk, it was still junk.

———

Let us continue our discussion of the quality of the environment, and the ways we might arrive at methods of construction providing continuing and coherent quality in the new buildings we may be able to erect in the next, future, highly modern era.

We said, two pages ago, that quality of buildings depends entirely on the ability of any one building or group of buildings to support human life, especially in its inner, and emotional aspects; to allow human existence to have depth of meaning, to give people the fullest ability to express and exhaust the potentialities of which they are capable.

How does this work, exactly? How can buildings make it easier, or more difficult, for a person to live a fulfilled inner life? Or, on the contrary, how can buildings make it more difficult for a person to fulfill himself? What is the way in which the interaction between a building and a person, can have a positive effect on people's lives? In what fashion do buildings facilitate the inner life, or (if the effect goes the other way) how can buildings have negative effects on a person's inner life? What is the mechanism through which a building can upset or damage someone's inner life? Or, alternatively, what is the mechanism through which a building can strengthen or make beautiful, a person's inner life?

To start with, we need to accept the idea that a person's equilibrium can be upset by external events. That can happen very easily. Suppose you live on a road, with curves and corners in it, and you have the misfortune that local teenagers choose to use this road as a place where they rev their motorbikes. If the upstairs windows look out on the road, your sleep will very easily get disturbed. Or, an opposite effect can also occur quite easily. Suppose the house has a small walled garden, with trees that sway in the wind, and if you also have a fountain or a running waterfall, the sound of the water, or the wind in the leaves and branches, will soothe you, lull you to sleep, or encourage your mind to allow the formation of quiet or gentle thoughts; perhaps poetic thoughts. There is every likelihood that this house, with this small garden and a garden wall, will encourage or stimulate dreams that come by themselves.

These examples tell us, very plainly, how our ambient physical surroundings can help or hinder our states of mind and our emotions. And this leads to the conclusion that the buildings in which we live, and with which we are surrounded, must be made with meticulous care, in order, in every possible case, that the environment is made to support the fragile human system.

Stepping up these small examples and multiplying their effects on tens, or hundreds, or millions of people, this means that buildings must be conceived as support systems for human feeling and social feeling: affection, love, learning, helping, teaching, and skill. One may view this idea of an emotional support system as something that allows people, individually and collectively, to deal with their own spiritual, emotional, physical, and intellectual capacities. Such a support system must, then, engage with the largest issues, and with the smallest and most subtle conditions, which have any bearing at all on the activities which can provide sustenance for the inner life of individuals.

One cannot attempt this task without probing and understanding the most subtle feelings a person may have. Also, the conditions which will be able to support these feelings play a necessary role. It means that the quality of the physical elements in a room, or the elements and places outside the house, must work actively, to interact with mind and spirit in the people who live and work there. A seat next to a window, will be comfortable or not, according to the height of the seat, the depth, depending on the length of the back and the incline of the back. Since people come in all shapes and sizes, such a window seat may need to contain variations of dimension; yet these variations need to be so subtle that the seat remains as simple as possible.

————

To this day, eleven decades after the year 1900, our ability to make valuable, beautiful environments has not yet been recovered. Occasional pastiches or faked copies of old-time buildings stand pathetically, but fool no one, and lack, entirely, the strength, gusto, and determination of the real thing that came about in different building eras of the past. Those buildings had lightness or charm, or life, or capacity to please. But in our time, we have not repaired our baseline construction methods in ways that help, rather than damage, the fragile psyche of human beings exposed to a variety of stresses. By now, after eleven decades of deterioration, our building techniques are all damaging in the long run, and none of them are harmless.

NEW OPERATIONAL ELEMENTS

On a larger scale, we have yet to create a vigorous, new way of planning, making, and conceiving buildings which will have their own robust life, and help people be nourished by small incidents or effects that are caused by layout, materials, and details in their immediate surroundings.

To find a new way forward that moves us toward an environment and atmosphere in which all people are genuinely supported, we need something radically different from our contemporary professional activities. We need a way to break apart the elements that are entrenched in the present-day production process.

The present elements of the production system include, in one fashion or another, the following categories that are the major processes of production:

1. MASTER PLANNING
2. ENGINEERING, AT GRADE AND BELOW GRADE
3. SEWAGE AND DRAINAGE
4. COORDINATION OF DRAWINGS BY NUMBER
5. SCHEMATIC BUILDING DESIGN FOR INDIVIDUAL BUILDINGS
6. INTERIORS OF ROOMS
7. ENGINEERING STRUCTURES, ABOVE GRADE
8. PREFABRICATED COMPONENTS (SUCH AS WALLS, WINDOWS, DOORS, ETC.)
9. EXTERIOR LANDSCAPE
10. ROADS

However, these categories, as they stand, are not very helpful in guiding practice, nor are they very practical in their effects. They may have some usefulness as mnemonic categeories; but they do not help to understand, and embellish, the interlock and interaction of the different functional systems in such a way as to weave the ingredients of all these categories into a whole.

Indeed, these possibly ineffective categories tear apart systems, teams who are working in construction, and ways of creating benefit by emphasizing the way the different elements work together. The wholeness, which badly *needs* to be emphasized, is lost among the disparate and disconnected categories.

To replace these not-very-helpful categories, we have identi- fied nine new operational elements of the human, social, and creative system. These new elements are not only more practical. They encap- sulate the fundamental ways of working that will actually create comprehension for architects, laypeople, and administrators. These new elements set up nine *ways of working*, each fully dedicated to the whole, and able to support day-to-day activities that will make planning, design and construction possible in entirely new and more effective ways. They will support human beings in creating ways in which the participants can effectively contribute to the wholeness — the real wholeness — that is needed to encourage life.

If the purpose of all architecture (planning, design, and construc- tion) — the purpose of its spatial-geometric organization, the purpose of its construction — is to provide opportunities and contexts which intensely support and enhance life-giving human situations, then it must be based on a new set of operating principles that include the following:

1. Fundamentally, architecture is and must be an art of making. The impetus for wholeness guides everything, and is the driving force of all construction activity. Adaptation is a necessary aspect of design. The entire production of buildings must be an ongoing, dynamic process, alive to the circumstances that emerge day by day, and able to develop opportunities and events that come to light.

2. In support of this new production system, there will need to be sweeping changes in human organization. These changes of organization will provide for involvement and coordination among the interested people and skilled workers, and thus give a level of

deep involvement in decision-making by all concerned. Together, they will act on adaptation.

3. A new approach to the management of money will do away with the mercenary and profit-driven foundations of the building industry. Money management will need to be controlled via non-profit organizations.

4. A major focus on the fragility of human beings and whatever enhances their well-being will be respected. This will be treated as a major emphasis, and will always be considered as a source of feedback and evaluation.

5. So, too, care must be given to all animals, insects, and plants, meadows, forests, ice-floes and other natural habitats. This intense care for all living beings and systems will be a priority.

6. The land (urban or rural) — its shape, its character — will provide the context for every building project in a way that is conscious and careful. Land configurations and old buildings will provide the primary origin of buildings and new construction.

7. The shaping of buildings and parts of buildings will always be through works of craft, made by human hands (though it may include many small prefabricated components). As a whole, every effort is to be understood to be a full-fledged work of art.

8. A generative process (something like a pattern language) will always be seen as the key dynamic framework that gives generic instructions for all planning, design, and construction.

9. Something we may loosely call "spirit" will be the underlying foundation of the work of building. This "spirit" will be held in common, and because of this, the buildings we produce will be endowed with spirit themselves.

These nine operational elements (nine regarded only as a provisional number) will form a decidedly different picture of the best way to make our world. With them, we can make our world different. Improbable as these elements may seem — because they do not easily mesh with elements known in contemporary systems of production — nevertheless, by the time you get to the end of the book, you will find that they are real and necessary, and that they work.

ON REFLECTION

Of course, the deterioration of the environment has not come about deliberately. It has happened because modern life, coupled with the deadening construction processes of the environment in modern times, has been creating an enormous change in our lives, and in society. These sea changes have created a lack of comprehension among the players in the planning and production process. Architecture, planning, and construction, must all be reconfigured in order to become comprehensible once more.

There are any number of people — planners, architects, builders, engineers, etc. — who have been trying to make headway. But they often find themselves coming up against apparently unsurmountable obstacles. Perhaps, these obstacles seem to force us into producing something which goes against the grain, and we end up producing something less than we ourselves do want to make. But so many of us cannot find a way of making real architecture, given the conditions of the profession, the building industry that exists today, and the legal and stylistic pressures that persist.

Together we could choose to work toward a reconfiguration of professional standards and practices of the building industry that address both the operational and human aspects of the system of production. A daunting task, of course. Sober reflection, coupled with daring, can accomplish it. But nothing less will do the trick.

———

The battle that gives our book its name is the practical battle which incorporates these changes. It is a battle which is capable of turning the tide away from the present-day mechanical viewpoint that dominates today's society and virtually all our newly built and mass-produced, pristine places, and neighborhoods. It can achieve a worldview and a way of being, which has life, well-being, beauty, and care for the whole, as its primary concepts. It calls forth a system of production which supports these primary concepts, and has the practical means to do so, in large matters and in small ones. It points to a basis on which an overall, life-giving, environment-building process can be the foundation of our daily life.

Achieving this will be a tough battle. It will require so many changes in our idea of the world, so many revelations to become successful, that we must constantly adjust our idea of reality. Imagine a town of type "A" — a neighborhood, if you like — and allow yourself to consider that it has the quality of birds, moss-grown stones, waves breaking on a small shore, pools in which crabs and shells present themselves. Because of the depth and scope of its structure, this world is almost infinite in its richness.

Compare this imagined town with a more usual neighborhood of type "B", typical of modern property development, where there is a stale and ugly air of repetition. Even when variation is attempted, this variation does not flow from the reality of living. Rather it is manufactured variety — an *attempt* to create something interesting. But what we feel instead is something flat, without excitement, without the urgent joy of life.

These two kinds of places, then, A and B, are typically generated in two different ways. We may therefore call these two different generating systems A and B. The first system, A, whether large or small, is fresh in imagination, generated by an infinite horn of plenty. It leaves you fresh; you have the feeling that it can go on forever, without running out of ideas. That is what we call system-A. The second system, B, is oppressive. It does not go on forever — on the contrary, it seems closed in thought and scope. It leaves you tired. The light is flat. You need to sit down, because it exhausts you just to be there. The system that generates this tiredness-inducing structure, we call system-B.

To find a way of implementing the production system that we call system-A, is a subtle task. But perhaps more startling, is the fact that to implement system-A in the world, it will also be necessary to *reduce* the influence of system-B, since system-B at present, actively prevents system-A from bearing fruit.

Consequently, we have no choice but to confront system-B.

The need for this confrontation between A and B, taken together with its consequences — that is the major subject of this book. Described as an ongoing dispute between two fundamentally different ways of shaping and building our living environment, each of these two "ways" may be regarded in turn as a production system, a system of thinking, a system of how to plan and build, how to organize labor and craft, how to take care of land, and money, and how the people who live and work in the environment may nourish their relationship of belonging to the land itself. It may even be said that a civilization is ultimately defined and characterized by the way in which the environment — the world — is characteristically produced.

System-A is concerned with the well-being of the land, its integrity, the well-being of the people and plants and animals who inhabit the land. As we shall see throughout this book, this has very much to do with the integral nature of plants, animals, water resources, and with the tailoring of each part of every part to its immediate context, with the result that the larger wholes, also, become harmonious and integral in their nature.

System-B is concerned with efficiency, with money, with power and control. Although these qualities are less attractive, and less noble than the concerns of system-A, they are nevertheless important. They cannot be ignored. If we are travelling in an airplane, or a high-speed train, we shall often be very glad that this system is constructed under the guidance of some version of system-B.

System-A places emphasis on subtleties, finesse, on the structure of adaptation that makes each tiny part fit into the larger context. System-B places emphasis on more gross aspects of size, speed, profit, efficiency, and numerical productivity.

However, during the last hundred and fifty years, because of choices that nations and states have made in modern times, system-B has become the dominant production system for the environment (for land and towns and regions), largely to the exclusion of system-A. This has harmed modern society greatly.

We built the school and college campus in the years between 1981 and 1989. In order to produce a living and friendly environment for this new campus, we unexpectedly found ourselves in an almost archetypal battle between A and B, in short, between the two conflicting production systems.

Yet it has not, so far, even been recognized that A and B are in conflict. Nor has it been recognized that this conflict has the ability to create chaos in architectural and planning projects. Nor has it yet been recognized that the "business-as-usual" production system — system-B — is *incapable* of creating the kind of environment that is genuinely able to support the emotional, whole-making side of human life.

Resolution of these conflicting problems lies at the heart of our story.

————

The creativity of society, and the creativity of the environment and the way we build it, are not minor issues. They are fundamental. They go to the health and freedom of society, and to the capacity for society and environment to bring a valued and enchanting life to its inhabitants.

To bring such a civilization into being, we must arrive at a new state of affairs, in which the world's societies are able to create and re-create a healthy atmosphere, environment, buildings and outdoor places which hold our thoughts together. Places that give us a coherent picture of the world, from which we obtain nourishment, spiritual and material. We must build a civilization in which individuals are able to like themselves, to heal themselves, and to love one another in generosity.

Without that, how will we ever be able to give ourselves, all of us, and our children, and their children, a good and worthwhile life?

Christopher Alexander
HansJoachim Neis, Maggie Moore Alexander
January 2011

PART ONE

SOLVING THE PROBLEM OF ARCHITECTURE IN OUR TIME

CHAPTERS 1-6

PART ONE

It is our hope to help establish a new, life-based paradigm
for all building production in the world.

At present, any community on Earth, if it hopes for a living
atmosphere, must escape from the sterile influence of
system-B production methods. Today, that is all but
impossible. To solve the problem, construction of new
communities must be governed by other methods,
more conducive to life, and conducive
to the physical qualities of life.

These ideas rest on more than forty years of research and
practice done at the Center for Environmental Structure in
Berkeley. From 1958 to 1963, at Harvard, a
considerable amount of new theory was published and set in
motion. From 1963 to 1999, a very large body of additional
building and planning projects, backed by innovations in
practice, was undertaken by CES staff and members of
communities in many different parts of the world, with
formidable assistance given by generations of my graduate
students at the University of California, Berkeley.

In 1981, we embarked on our largest project to date:
the construction of the Campus of Eishin Gakuen in Japan.
It was the experience of building this campus that finally
woke us up to the urgent necessity for a conscious and
deliberate battle between the two currently prevailing
production systems in our society.

This needed battle concerns, above all, THE CHANGES IN
PROCESS that are required to repair the Earth.

1 THE CAMPUS OF EISHIN GAKUEN

By the early 1980s, we had already been aware for a very
long time that a crisis was occurring in
world architecture. The destructive capacity of
speculative development, mass production, and
long-distance planning had been wreaking havoc,
more and more severely, on the world.
As is well-known, this has had serious impacts on nature,
wildlife, climate, and society. But, within the
architectural profession, little had been done so far,
to establish new ways of building environments
that are genuinely good for people.

In building the Eishin campus, we were presented with
all the dilemmas and conflicts
associated with this crisis. We knew we
had to address the crisis with an
entirely new way of building.

We decided to take this challenge seriously.

In July 1981, I was fortunate to be approached by a Japanese
gentleman, Hisae Hosoi, with the request that I take charge of
planning and designing and building a new, combined college and
high school campus in Saitama prefecture outside Tokyo. In due
course we signed a contract for the work. The High School part of
the new campus was completed by the middle of 1985, followed by
construction of some (not all) of the College buildings in 1987-89.

This project was of considerable size. It was to be the working
environment for a population of 2000 students and faculty, and would
occupy nine city blocks, altogether roughly 280 meters by 320 meters,

or 8.96 hectares. In 1981, when I first saw the land, agriculture was still flourishing, with tea bushes and vegetables as the main crops. Hosoi and the Eishin Gakuen Board were then in the process of negotiating the purchase of the land. The thirty-five buildings called for were to be built for ¥2,100,000,000 yen, equivalent to about US $10,000,000. In today's dollars, the cost of this same construction would be roughly three times that amount, approximately US $30,000,000 — a full thirty million dollars. The completion of the campus, in its first functioning form, took nine years, from 1981 to 1990.

———

Between 1967 and 1981, my CES colleagues and I had already worked out most of the techniques of planning, construction, user involvement, dynamic change of design during construction, extensive involvement in different forms of budget programming, direct management of construction, use of pattern languages to help members of a community express their needs and feelings well, and attention to natural materials as far as possible coming from the earth, its rocks, soils, vegetation, and color. All these techniques have the aim of creating a living, humane environment.[1]

These techniques also depend on the spiritual or religious underpinning of daily building practice. Of course, the present-day secularized forms of religion are (by now) far from such a goal. Nevertheless, I choose to focus attention on the word religion, and its very interesting origin and purpose, because it does have tremendous relevance to our idea, and to our practice of architecture. The word "religious" comes from the Latin *re-ligare*, or re-binding.[2] Making a new world *which binds things together well* is the underlying essence of all profound techniques of architecture.

The foundations of these unifying techniques were ultimately set forth in the four volumes of *The Nature of Order*, published

1   The written and built examples of these innovations include: 1967 *A Pattern Language which Generates Multi-Service Centers*; 1969 *Houses Generated by Patterns (The Peru housing project)*; 1975 *The Oregon Experiment*; 1979 *The Production of Houses (The Mexicali Housing Project)*.
2   Wikipedia: re-connection to the divine — from Latin *re* (again) + *ligare* (to connect, as in English ligament). This interpretation probably originated with St. Augustine.

2001–2005. However, the four books were already circulating, in draft form for fifteen years before the actual start of the Eishin project. Furthermore, the entire effort of our layout, planning, building design, construction, overall conduct of the project, and day-to-day practical administration — all of this was governed by the teachings described at length in the 2000 pages of *The Nature of Order*.[3]

When Mr. Hosoi first came to see me, these techniques of ours had already been used on a considerable number of modest, experimental building projects in different countries with the aim of creating a living architecture. But they had not yet been used to generate the architecture of an entire community.

The Eishin Campus, as it has now become known, represents a large, achieved conclusion, which demonstrates many of the techniques and ideas in *The Nature of Order*. It is, so far, the largest project in the world that has been built using these techniques, demonstrating and verifying the rich and complex theoretical ideas presented in that book.

It has become clear to us that the focus on the system of production and its production processes, are decisive. To be understood, the **processes** have to be seen through the details of the complex story we have lived through and experienced. Since the mid-1990s, I have come to realize more and more clearly that the battle which gives this book its name must ultimately be used as an example that illuminates and demonstrates the collective worldwide problem of environment-building that all human beings share. Whether in urban or in rural settlements, our story demonstrates that practical means at last do exist to solve this problem of creeping technological uglification.

Although many planners and architects and developers, in many countries, have been trying to build more hospitable settle-

---

3 The four volumes are *The Phenomenon of Life* (2001); *The Process of Creating Life* (2002); *The Luminous Ground* (2004); *A Vision of a Living World* (2005). All four books are published by CES Publishing, The Center for Environmental Structure, Berkeley, California. The books make these ideas available for practical use and study: the ideas are explained in a way that can be followed, copied, and improved.

ments, their success has been limited. That is because fundamental
and deep-seated issues have not yet been embraced or understood
as a necessary part of all building production.

As time went by, we began to see that this book (a detailed
record of experience) can stand as a model presenting what needs
to be done for architecture, planning, and the environment on a
global scale. It is a model that shows what system of actions can be
effective and practical in healing human communities, large and
small — perhaps even all over the world.

Above all, it shows that a new way of organizing building production, fundamentally reshaping the very nature of production, is
the necessary key to the renaissance of a physical architecture suitable for our time. This new architecture is beautiful and generous,
and it is of benefit to people and the lives they lead. By the end of
the book we hope to have set out, in paradigmatic form, how the
lessons of the Eishin Campus may provide a broad view of the
production of *all* environments.

1981: The land in Iruma-shi, on which the new campus was to be built. The area of land is about nine hectares mad
up from fifteen farmers' separate fields, assembled to provide a single site. At the time this photograph was taken, the
land was still under agricultural cultivation. The flags visible in the picture show the very roughest, early marks for
possible campus precincts and buildings, as we first began to think about placing them. By the time we were done, th
configuration of flags was dramatically changed.

2 THE CRUCIAL IMPORTANCE OF LOCAL ADAPTATION

An environment or community will not come to life unless each
place, each building, each street, each room becomes unique, as a
result of careful and piecemeal processes of adaptation.

This is a quality not acknowledged or valued in the history of
modern architecture.

That this process is the foundation of a living architecture
is a significant discovery.

Paying attention to this pervasive kind of adaptation throughout
our project required mental, artistic, and procedural tools.
We had to develop these tools so that adaptation could be
a constant focus in each place,
at many different scales,
all over the Eishin Campus.

There are, loosely speaking, two types of building production. Type
(A) is a type of production which relies on feedback and correction, so that every step allows the elements to be perfected while
they are being made. This is not unlike the way a good cook tastes
a soup while cooking it, checking it, modifying it until it tastes
just right. Type (B) is a type of production that is organized by a
fixed system of rigidly prefabricated elements, and the sequence of
assembly is much more rigidly preprogrammed. This type became
commonplace in the 20th century, and is still widely used.

　　All in all, building is a continuous process. Even small buildings
take years to grow, and often take centuries before they reach their
peak. It cannot be hurried. Even the small gate of the Eishin
Campus has taken years to grow, and years for its subtle harmony
to show up among the welter of different processes that cause

adaptation, leading to successive approximations of maturity and harmony. On these pages you see two photographs of the entrance street of the Eishin Campus, both showing the small gate, through which one enters from the outside world. In the photograph on this page, you see the gate as it was in a photo taken 26 years ago, in 1985. This is what the small gate and the entrance street looked like on opening day, showing the first visitors arriving in ones and twos. The gate is visible, complete, but not yet fully finished, not yet fully integrated or harmonious.

Next, we may also note the rudimentary state of its exterior and of the Entrance Street, on that day in April 1985. On page 21 we see the same entrance street in 2010. It has now been polished and refined by a quarter-century of care, reaching what we may hope to be something near its final state.

Twenty-five years later, the entrance street, has been modified in many ways, and has a calm and peaceful atmosphere. The small gate is plastered white now, not gray. The workshops on the left are

April 1985. The Small Entrance Gate as it was first built.

April 2010. Looking through the archway of the Main Gate, we see the Small Gate, in the distance, at the far end of the Entrance Street.

very helpful, being practically useful, and making a more densely inhabited space.

The white surface on the outer wall is more harmonious, too, and the people who made it white had better judgment than we did twenty-five years earlier, probably by virtue of the fact that they walked through it every day for years, and therefore knew more deeply what had to be done to make it better.

BIOLOGICAL ADAPTATION

The idea of adaptation originated in biology, especially in relation to evolution.[1] It found a firm basis in Darwin's *Origin of Species*, and has become a major theme of 20th and 21st century thought. The idea is that a certain type of organism reproduces itself over and over again. Characteristics set by the genetic material in the organism move gently, and step by step, so that qualities beneficial to that organism will occur more often or more prominently, thus gradually serving the organism, and improving its performance over time.

By definition, then, this kind of adaptation is a systematic morphological variation, happening by chance, under the pressure of selection, in such a way that the organism becomes better adapted to its environment. This notion of adaptation is strongly functional, since the process thus set in motion creates a gradual improvement in the organism's ability to survive in that environment.

The same thing can happen as a result of human action — for example, in the evolution of a certain type of Formula-1 racing car. The car is built repeatedly, over time, and improvements are made in each new phase, by modification of an existing car. Once again, the adaptation occurs gradually. The car is rebuilt again and again, with an opportunity for the engineers to observe its performance, modifying some physical component or configuration, making these modifications accumulate, and thus creating better and better adaptations over time.

ADAPTATION IN BUILDINGS

The "adaptation" I shall now refer to — in buildings — is very different from the adaptation that is typically observed in biology. Indeed, we shall use the word 'adaptation' in a way that is pervasively present in all architecture, urban issues, and ecological issues. But it differs, entirely, from the standard use of the word in evolution-

---

1   Darwin, *The Origin of Species*; Richard Dawkins, *The Blind Watchmaker*; Ross Ashby, *Design for a Brain*; Christopher Alexander, *Notes on the Synthesis of Form* (Cambridge: Harvard University Press, 1964).

ary biology. It therefore needs to be very carefully explained, to be sure this novel terminology does not cause confusion.

A small part of the process of building adaptation, like evolutionary adaptation in biology, works by modifying the genotype. This happens when a familiar pattern (for roof construction, say) evolves with discoveries of new roof surfaces, thicker insulation, and some collecting of solar radiation in panels built into the roof surface. This process is exactly parallel to the appearance of a modified or mutant gene which finds its way into the gene pool. Thus, in biology a successful gene is soon copied again and again, thus changing the typical, or "normal" organism. And in building, the new idea or mutant gene becomes the typical way roofs are built now, thus slowly adapting to conditions of weather and climate by using more effective methods to protect us.

––––––

This kind of adaptation is in some degree similar to biological adaptation, but it is not coded through the genes. It is purely functional, and it is driven only by functional pressure. It is also driven by geometrical considerations of coherence.

Suppose, for instance, that we build a small wall outside a house, to enclose the front garden from the public street. Very often the wall will get modified over time. A gap in the wall may be made narrower or wider, to permit an opening in the wall, or installation of a gate or doorway. This wall is not a genotype, which then evolves. It is a single particular wall, in a particular place, which gets improved over time.

Later, the owners of the wall may decide to build a certain kind of coping along the top, made in such a way that small wells in the coping are filled with soil, and flowers may then be planted along the top of the wall. In a particular sunny spot along the length of the wall, a bench might be built by extending the brickwork. This brick seat will be shaped to be comfortable: and the wall, gate, flowers, and bench will gradually become more and more unified: a coherent unity will gradually be formed, and thus happens as a result of repeated incremental acts of construction, which make the place in question more and more lively, or pleasant, or useful.

It is true that these adaptations are practical, and happen in time, and in response to circumstance. But there is no evolving genome; it is the unique and individual thing itself, the actual physical wall and place, which gets improved over time. And above all, and most strikingly, it is a geometrical process.

In a typical square mile, of farmland or of city, this kind of *direct* adaptive process occurs hundreds of times every day. This is the process by which the geometric construction is made effective and harmonious. That is the exciting and marvelous thing — wonderful in its effect. But such a geometrically adaptive process is missing altogether from the contemporary production processes of society. And that robs the environment of all subtlety, of its flavor, of feeling, of poetry — of pleasantness and utility in the most ordinary sense — the sense of being comfortable on a bench by the wall on a sunny day.

————

It is this geometrical-adaptive process that drives much creation. Design, as a drawing-board process is said to be creative. But it is not, because it cannot take in the impact of feeling, human experience and judgment, that which matters most to the life of the environment.

An environment can only be made healthy, and good for human life, if the process mobilizes vital adaptations at many scales, and thus generates the intricate geometry and structure that are needed to support life.

These characteristics all depend on subtle adaptations between neighboring systems. The systems must contain a hierarchy of nested processes, and place emphasis on the wholeness of each step that is taken, at every scale. In short, the production process is finely graded. It has a hierarchy of nested processes, and each place and element is shaped and adapted, by virtue of these processes, to become fine-tuned to its context, and gently fitted to the peculiarity of the particular place where it exists.

In order to understand this idea fully, we have to pay attention to the *geometry* of spaces between buildings, the *geometry* of the buildings themselves, and the *geometry* of the elements and the spaces between the elements — since it is after all this mutual co-adaptation between elements that brings unity to the living system. Since the co-adaptation, almost by definition, involves irregular and unpredictable modifications of the detailed geometry at almost every turn, it follows that a well-adapted system contains vast numbers of these minor irregularities. This is (of necessity) the overall geometry and physical character that must come from a living process. It is focused on adaptation; it helps each place and each element in every place; it makes sure that each one is minutely sized, shaped, and adapted to its context.

These kinds of subtle, fractal, and organic adaptations are entirely different from the typical geometries of the architecture, planning and development in the 20th-century machine age. One may say that the cold, often sterile geometry of 20th-century buildings is the hallmark of the 20th-century process. If this was indeed the natural result of 20th-century production processes, we can be fairly certain that these processes will never, and cannot — as a fact of their *nature* — create the kinds of environment that have the needed adaptations.

———

It is very surprising that during the 20th century — the century of the so-called modern architecture — the architecture itself, the physical structure, was rarely examined or criticized from the point of view of its geometry. Rather, as we all have good reason to know, the architecture of the last seventy years has often been stark, homogeneous, boring to a degree that is almost frightening, very often entirely without delight, and — most important — absurdly lacking the functional co-adaptation between parts that would mark it as living.

I believe that this has arisen because during the 20th century, the production process itself — the step-by-step acts that bring a building into being — were largely modeled on Taylorian notions of time and motion and efficiency.[2] This led to a widespread assumption that in the name of economy, or simplicity, or cost, we need to accept the poverty-stricken geometry of buildings, and to believe that there is no viable alternative. However, such a lemming-like chase over the cliff of Taylorian thinking had no rational basis, and it certainly did nothing to accommodate the shapes and physical adaptations that could make spaces and buildings truly comfortable.

––––––

Drawing on a biological analogy, let us imagine that we are going to plant a hedge. We would plant one-year old seedlings, a few feet apart, following the line of the hedge. The seedlings themselves are all different to begin with. They become more different as they grow, and they interact while they are growing, thus pushing the growing plants to adapt to one another and to the surroundings. While this is happening, the stems, trunks, branches and twigs are growing, each one different; the leaf shoots grow in places that have good sun and rain conditions; as the twigs from neighboring plants grow toward each other, the boundary is forced to shape itself to accommodate to the conditions of the next-door plants.

In the case of nature this hedge-growing process is a production process which arranges all these needed local adaptations. As a result the majority of hedges are successful, and birds, insects, grasses, worms, all find their places. Of course, in the case of buildings, we can hardly expect that the buildings will literally be grown, biologically. For the moment that remains in the realm of science fiction.[3] But the production system, *as a human organization* backed by suitable materials and technology, can generate buildings which have the same kind of variation, delicacy of detail,

––––––––

2   For discussion of the impact of Taylor's thought on building production, see *The Nature of Order*, Book 2, pages 515-530: "The Influence of Frederick Taylor," and following pages.
3   Some recent scientific studies, as well as occasional works of science fiction, have in fact portrayed such scenarios. A recent issue of *New Scientist* (a few years ago) ran an article discussing how some semi-realistic proposals for growing buildings have actually been made, and even tested in principle.

fine-tuning, and adaptation of one structure to the next. In principle, we know that this is technically feasible. We know it because many traditional cultures actually had production systems which worked, in old-fashioned ways, exactly like that.

There is no reason why highly modern, ultra-modern production systems, should not be capable of supporting and providing this intricate kind of adaptation in plans, in structures, in window positions, in doors, in interlacing, mutually co-adapted building volumes, heights, access ways, and gardens. Of course, these subtle variations will not be chosen arbitrarily. They will be created by on-the-ground, human-inspired changes, and by detailed shaping of elements according to context. They will become possible because of changes in human organization, lines of communication and control, which permit creation of a more organic, more subtle, more intimate, and more nourishing environment.

That is, in principle, what an adaptational production system might be able to accomplish, and what it *did* accomplish on the Eishin Campus. Let's take a look at a few of the buildings on the campus, and focus on the geometric qualities of these buildings and the quality of the spaces that appear between the buildings when subtle adaptations shape them.[4]

THE ENTRANCE STREET AND THE MAIN GATE

In the first picture, on page 28, students are coming to the entrance of the campus on a festival day, first approaching the small gate, then the main gate. The path to the main gate is gently curved, in an irregular curve — and the width of the curving path space tapers from one end to the other. The process of laying out this curve is described in some detail, as it actually happened, in chapter 11. It results in a non-rigid, more fluid geometry. In the distance beyond the main gate, and to the left of it, we see the end of the Administration Building.

---

4   Analysis of these types of spatial adaptation is discussed in *The Nature of Order*, Book 2, chapters 2, 6, and 9; and again in *The Nature of Order*, Book 3, chapters 3-5.

Approaching the Campus along the entrance street.

THE ADMINISTRATION BUILDING

The diagonal trellis of fine concrete splines that forms the outer wall of the building is both ornamental and structural. The very slender concrete members which form the trellis, contain fine steel wires. They both ornament the surface of the building and strengthen the building against shear forces. Within this structure, we see examples of minutely subtle geometric adaptations, where the cells of the trellis meet the windows. The spacing cuts off; it is not perfectly symmetrical in its joining, and this must happen, if the windows are placed carefully to begin with and are to satisfy the position of the upstairs window openings in each of the rooms.

Administration building: the second story wall is a trellis of fine concrete splines, with the spaces between the splines plastered in white.

Thus the slight irregularity at the window corners is needed to allow each window to be just in the right place in each room.

TWO PICTURES OF THE CENTRAL BUILDING

In the first picture of the Central Building (page 30), you see it without people, looking down the middle of the hall. What is unusual here is the subtle curving of the trusses, made with hand-carved and shaped wooden arches. Here the adaptation process required a model, made in 1:50 scale with balsawood. The full-size arches were made from Douglas fir. During the process of making the model, one could see the most harmonious jointing angles, which were then carried out by hand on the full-sized wooden members. The subtle curving of the trusses, were made with hand-cut, jointed, and assembled wooden arches.

As you can see in the second picture (page 31), people fit into the alcoves in many, natural, easy ways. Students were dancing — what used to be called break dancing. The alcoves are shaped and

The Central Building, emptied of people to show off the beautiful curved wooden trusses.

Break dancing in full swing, in the Central Building. As you can see, the alcoves are spacious and comfortable. You can also just see the alcoves along the sides of the hall, in the left-hand photograph.

sized so that people can talk, sprawl, slump, gather and fill them. It is a student's gathering place, protected from weather, at the very heart of the campus.

NEXT PAGE: THE LAKE, WITH THE GREAT HALL ON THE FAR SHORE

The lake has an irregular curve that follows the contour of a certain low-lying level in the land, thus meeting the land in a natural way. When we built the lake, we made sure the bulldozers did as little grading as possible, treated it as very sensitive work, and kept every nuance of the land as it was before we started. While the bulldozers and backhoes were digging, we made sure that

The lake and bridge, and Great Hall.

every shovel and bucket of earth was placed gently, where the land felt natural and carefully made: that is what produces the natural quality of the land that we created at the lake edge.

In this picture at the top of this page, the Great Hall lies behind the bridge. The ducks live on the lake.

A COLONNADED STREET ON THE CAMPUS

Here is an interior street on the campus, with an arcade opening from the back of the classroom buildings. The arcade steps up as the street goes along the slope. Because the natural contours of the land are preserved, the arcade jumps up, in small increments, as it goes along. Steps are inserted where needed; and in plan, too, the arcade follows a gentle series of curves and bends, following the natural character of the land. This aspect of a street is not usually present in large construction projects, which typically destroy the natural character of the land. This aspect of the street is not usually present in large construction projects, which tend to start with a blank "page" that has been created by perfect grading and flattening.

This place, rather, preserving the trace of the land from which it started, has life. Even when no people are there, you can feel its humanity because of the multiple adaptations shaping the street and columns with regard to land forms.

Interior, colonnaded street within the campus.

AN ARCHED OPENING WHERE THE INTERIOR STREET PASSES THROUGH A BUILDING

Here, at twilight, is an arch at one end of the colonnaded street, looking toward one of the walls of the Great Hall. Two lovers appreciate the privacy. The idea that a small street might pass through a building is very useful, as well as charming. Yet it is something that would be ruled out by too stringent a type of "functional" or administrative thinking. Though unusual, it gives another example of local adaptation.

Two lovers in the passageway under the administration building. The archway looks directly towards the Great Hall.

A DENSE, THRONGED, URBAN STREET ON CAMPUS

On the page opposite, you see the easygoing casualness of another interior street. It has an irregular placement of buildings, making a really nice, comfortable, and relaxed space between them. On the left, the faculty building, made entirely of wood, reflects a more thoughtful and reflective atmosphere, and distinguishes its character from the uniform materials of the many classrooms. In this part of the campus the bright sun, deep shade, and bustle have the atmosphere of a small city.

The atmosphere of a small city.

A SMALL BRIDGE CROSSING ONE OF THE LAKE CHANNELS

Here below, on a bright day, students walk about the campus along the edge of the lake. You can see that each classroom building has its own ornaments, cast into the concrete wall. The students walk purposefully, reflecting, talking.

It seems to be *their* place. It *belongs* to them.

Students casually walking about by the lake.

MISCELLANEOUS ORNAMENTS IN POLISHED TERRAZZO, BEAM ENDS IN THE CORNICE, WINDOWS SHAPED IN WOOD

Ornaments on one of the College buildings: cornices, beam ends, carefully shaped windows, and a diamond frieze. The black and white diamond-frieze was made in two colors of terrazzo, ground to a finely polished surface.

HAND MADE CONCRETE AND PLASTER ORNAMENTS

A row of handmade ornaments, made of cast concrete, and hand-filled with white plaster. We see how these ornaments enhance the human quality of the buildings as shown on the previous page.

BALANCED INTERMINGLING OF NATURE AND BUILDINGS

In another place, we find a big tree, a fence, and a relaxed arrangement of buildings. They are placed where they need to be, without anyone superimposing an artificial, formal pattern.

The big tree, grown up amongst the buildings; the tree grows big because the space between the buildings allows it the room to flourish.

INTERIOR GARDEN BETWEEN THE FACULTY BUILDING VERANDA, AND ONE OF THE COLLEGE BUILDINGS

On this page, seen from the veranda of the faculty building in springtime, a garden is visible between the faculty building, one of the college buildings (on the right), and the Judo Hall (to the left). Two students sit looking at the garden, and in front of them, there are trays of seedlings that other students are preparing to plant. This place is actively concerned with adaptation of the trees and bushes.

A one-time student, the woman near the camera, Keiko Ono, has a look on her face, a patient look of pleasure, absorbing what she sees. She is profoundly engaged with the place. I well remember the look on her face as I took the picture.

Students sitting together on the veranda of the Faculty Building, with seedlings being planted out.

THE CURVED PEDESTRIAN BRIDGE CROSSES THE LAKE

The bridge leads toward the cafeteria, giving glimpses of the college buildings, the high school classroom buildings, and the gymnasium. Outside, ducks, evening light, people walking on the bridge, gentle breeze on the water. The bridge was made gently curved, lifting people above the water, and allowing a view of the buildings through the bridge structure.

Ducks on the lake.

THE AVENUE OF TULIP TREES

Here, spring flowers and tulip trees line the path that leads up to the ridge that forms the basis for the college part of the campus. The tulip trees are no less important than the Judo Hall. Walking past these trees, faculty and students are made physically aware, every day, of the philosophy that lies at the core of the College teaching program.

Toward evening. The Campus and the partially built College precinct, with the Judo Hall on the right.

THE CHARACTERISTIC NATURE OF A WORLD THAT IS FULLY SHAPED BY LOCAL ADAPTATION

In the pictures presented in this chapter, we have seen glimpses of a physical world which embodies — in its physical character alone — something quite different from the normal architectural products of 20th- and 21st-century capitalism.

In this campus, most of the elements were shaped over time, in relation to the contexts which surrounded them. This allowed a form of adaptation which was common in traditional building methods, but is virtually unknown in modern protocols.

Looking at these photographs of a world made from the land itself and from the buildings that we built there to form the environment, we may see the hint of a new society, a new kind of social life, a new attitude to feeling, a new attitude toward the human being. There is a fusion of man and nature. There is in these buildings, a new kind of human possibility — a way in which people may see how the environment, the physical world we construct around ourselves, tells a story about our attitude toward ourselves, our attitude to life, even our attitude toward the universe. All this is a result of the production process we initiated, to make the buildings, and the space between the buildings, and the details of both buildings and exterior construction.

We succeeded in all of this by paying attention to the thousand-fold, minute adaptations between places, trees, views, buildings, and people, in creating a new form of mental and spiritual life — something that allows human feeling to exist on an intimate and personal level in a newly built community, now at last taking over from the familiar mass-society that we have known. This was our aim.

The first, and most directly important thing about the adaptations illustrated, is that they create freshness and uniqueness wherever they appear. That is already a huge step beyond the rigidly mechanistic components of a typical 21st-century building project.

But there is a second, even more important feature of the campus that came as a result of the adaptation process: *the wholeness and unification accomplished by multiple, mutual adaptations.* Suppose that element A is adapted to some other element B. This adaptation forms a relationship between A and B. Suppose then, that we draw a diagram of all the thousands of elements in the campus complex: small, middle-sized, and large. Let us, in this imaginary diagram, draw a line between every two elements which are adapted, one to the other.

There will then be hundreds of thousands of pairwise, adaptive linkages. And the effect of these multiple adaptations, is to create a widespread net of unification across the whole campus. The effect, then, of the process of adaptation, is to forge a solid, powerful unity among the many campus elements. This draws the whole place together, just as a living organism is also drawn together and unified by its internal linkages. The campus is not merely an assembly of loosely placed buildings, but a coherent and complex organism — living indeed, not as a metaphor, but living *in fact* — as a result of the adaptations that have been achieved.

At this moment, people everywhere on Earth are looking for methods, frameworks, and practical steps to heal the environments in which we live. We hope that a new adaptive process, oriented toward the kind of environment we have built on the Eishin Campus, can help us with our difficulties, and provide a new way of thinking about remaking our global environment at many scales. That, we believe, will require understanding of some fundamental issues that we — as a society — have not yet understood. This understanding requires new forms of thought and new forms of action, in which shaping, organization of space, human awareness and consciousness, the process of adaptation, the living fabric of water, plants and animals, and thoughtful interaction of human beings all working together to make each place whole. In future, these kinds of actions must all be happening daily.

We of our generation *must* find a process of environmental production, which can make these interacting actions happen continuously — planned, shaped, built — to keep the environment living, daily, as a whole.

3 SYSTEM-A & SYSTEM-B: A NECESSARY CONFRONTATION

System-A is a system of production in which local adaptation
is primary. Its processes are governed by methods that make each
building, and each part of each building,
unique and uniquely crafted to its context.

System-B is, on the contrary, dedicated to an overwhelmingly
machinelike philosophy. The components and products are without
individual identity and most often alienating
in their psychological effect.

The pressure to use such a system of production
comes mainly from the desire to make profit,
and from the desire to do it at the highest possible speed.

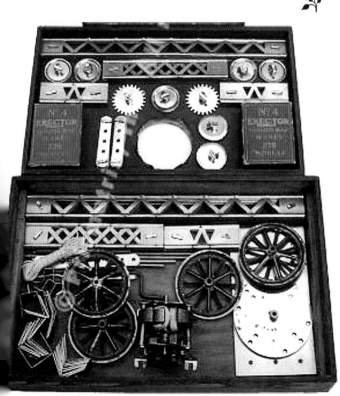

Child's erector set, manufactured USA, 1913.

Mass production began in the 19th century. In the 20th century it became all the rage, and the dominant fact of modern life. It was so much a fact of life, that this children's erector set (left), first sold in 1913, soon became commonplace. From an early age children grew up believing this is the way you make things. Living in the midst of the pervasive shift that was occurring, how would they know anything else?

By 1940, under the pressure of World War II, vast numbers of planes and tanks and guns were being fabricated. Mass production began to dominate 20th-century thinking and manufacturing. This hangar in Seattle, where

*Mass production of **B-17 bombers, under construction at the Boeing plant, Seattle, in 1942**, just one example of a type of artifact produced this way, by mass production. After World War II, cars, machinery, cornflake boxes, clothes, wall panels, prefabricated wall surfaces, windows, and machine-made ornaments, prefabricated bathrooms, and toothpaste tubes were all produced by mass production.*

B-17s were being built for the war, virtually stands as an emblem for the first era of mass production. It was a dramatic shift of focus for building production, too. One must say it was a catastrophic change in building, which now dominates the field of architecture, and makes adaptation almost impossible. The discipline that we've come to know as architecture has gone through a massive surge in the direction of prefabricated assembly and component building. It has now gone off the rails with huge momentum. Starting around 1930, the attempt to build buildings was swamped by the use of mass-produced components. Today, with current construction practices, **buildings no longer have the possibility of local adaptation. Nor does the assembly process permit an element**

of a building to become unique according to its context and position in the whole.

I am sure that many people would see mass production as a great blessing. It is not only going to give untold wealth to the factories who make these things, but it's going to be clean, efficient, and cheap. All that enthusiasm is somewhat overdone. But nevertheless, that is what has overtaken the whole field of architecture.

Architecture is now only transmitted *through drawings*. The typical architect does not personally know how to make anything — not buildings, not windows, not floors or ceilings. He or she draws drawings. Some other organization then produces buildings from these drawings. We are, by now, so deeply enmeshed in this way of thinking, that it doesn't sound like idiocy. It sounds like a very practical thing to do. But it is, in fact, idiocy. Mass production has turned architecture on its head!!

The organization of nature is not modular in the sense that modern architecture has been made from prefabricated modular components. Someone may ask, what about atoms, what about molecules, making the false assumption that electrons, atoms, and molecules are modular and identical. But this is altogether mistaken. The discipline of quantum mechanics established many decades ago that the quantum field sets up special, effective conditions that make each atom become unique under the influence of its quantum field. Hence, any two electrons are different, according to time and place, thus always depending on their context.

What is more to the point is that the reality of things — what I call the reality — comes from the structure of something which *at every level* is highly complex and unique. The idea that buildings can be made successfully by assembly is too-simple an idea which just does not work. It follows from grade-school chemistry, but it is not accurate in its physics. It is simply an idea which has swelled and expanded, buoyed up by a naive shift in modern thinking and an economic imperative.

From a structural point of view you can either have this assembly of prefabricated parts — which to many architects seems appropriate; **or,** from a different view of the world, a more realistic view, you can make buildings as they are made in nature. Let us ask ourselves what is the true difference between nature, and the things we consider to be "man-made."

If we look at the blooming hawthorne blossoms on this page, it is plain to see that the blossoms themselves do not have the perfectly regular shapes of the modular components we find in modern buildings. Instead, they grow! On the other hand, things that are fabricated, serving as components in buildings, machines, cars, enormous engineering structures with their precisely made repetition of bays. All these are highly regular, and most often repeat exactly.

As we have seen in chapter 2, the natural way for things to be shaped is according to the way they fit together. This simple requirement has the effect that the elements are not regular in shape, not geometrically perfect.

What is the essence of this difference? In order for things to fit together, these "things" must have the freedom to fit together — not in a straitjacketed, hyper-regular format, but in irregular configurations. They have the capability to appear comfortably, in an almost endless

Hawthorne blossoms in green bud

Some in bud, some half open, some in full bloom

The blossoms in full flower

range of geometric ways. This means they cannot be cubes, for example, because the huge variety of possible three-dimensional configurations can *not* be made consistent with the arrangements that take up grid-like, cubic formats.

From chapter 2, we have an understanding of the way local adaptation works — how it works day by day, during construction and after construction, to improve the shape of buildings and the spaces between buildings. But the present system of building production and environment creation makes it all but impossible for this process to occur. Bluntly, adaptation — so necessary for the life of spaces and for the life of buildings — is not presently available under contemporary business conditions. In effect, our present production system dooms our tracts, our business parks, condominium developments — indeed virtually all new construction. These places cannot be given life, because it is not possible to give them life within the constraints and means at our disposal! Building freeways; building acres of repetitive, low-cost social housing; building prefabricated children's playgrounds; building offices and workspaces by the square yard — all these lack the quality of life in fundamental and important ways.

Repetition of relatively few different components and objects has a further deadening impact on the assemblies created from these collections of mass-produced components. In the early years of the industrial revolution, the components were very small — screws, bolts, washers. Later they became larger — identical pressed bricks, concrete blocks, prestressed beams, whole bathrooms, and whole kitchens. And later still we met very large components — whole houses, whole roofs ready to drop in place by helicopter, prefabricated swimming pools, multistory parking garages, and so on. This assembling of giant modules robbed the entire urban landscape, and the rural landscape, too, of its uniqueness and identity.

From factory-based production, you get a very small number of *types* of components, but very large *numbers* of components that are identical or nearly identical. It is the fact that they are identical which makes them deadly! These isolated components are unrelated to each other, and unrelated to ourselves.

You cannot create real adaptation, unless there is a process at work which permits, and *encourages*, the active placing, sizing, and shaping of each element of the environment. This is what makes it unique, and able to be loved.

Our lands, and our buildings, need to have a structure that is created organically. A piece of land embodies *relationships*, not blind replication of components. So we need a production system that is capable of producing thousands and thousands of overlapping *relationships*. That is the main thing a living environment is — a system of nested, overlapping relationships. The production system MUST therefore have techniques at its disposal that will enable it to create multiple relationships, without undermining the multiplicity, complexity, and individuality that make a place living!

Suppose that on a particular piece of land, there are 1000 key relationships which have to exist among its elements. We can, in general, only do one at a time, and we shall soon run out of possible configurations. Perhaps we have accomplished no more than 100 of the needed relationships. The number of relationships you can cram in will depend on the order in which you take them. There may well be a sequence which allows you to get 200 or 300 of the relationships in. A creation system which works, will, in some fashion, optimize the total number of densely packed relationships in that piece of land.

From the outset, we must therefore be ready to initiate a process which follows the mutual adaptation of roads, trees, buildings, courtyards, rooms, windows, paths, and flowerbeds — including also nails, hinges, wall-caps, door frames, and edge tiles of a roof. This is the foundation of any adequate environment-making process. Each element gets shaped to be unique, each time that it occurs. As in nature, the way the components fit together will never be exactly the same twice in a row.

This discovery, once accepted (and *if* accepted) will be momentous for the field of architecture.

SYSTEM-A AND SYSTEM-B: TWO ARCHETYPAL SYSTEMS OF PRODUCTION

In **SYSTEM-A**, creation and production are organic in character, and are governed by human judgments that emanate from the underlying wholeness of situations, conditions, and surroundings. This is the primary driving force of every action, and every decision. Small or large, this driving force will be applied continually, to every process. The quality of wholeness which defines what is to be done, comes into play at every moment of the long drawn-out production process — whether it be planning, conception, design, fabrication, modification, or completion. The process of creation goes forward, from one moment to the next, depending on the wholeness that is there, and whatever particular step can be taken to reach more wholeness in the next configuration.

In **SYSTEM-B**, the production process is thought of as mechanical. What matters in system-B are regulations, procedures, categories, money, efficiency, and profit: all the machinery designed to make society run smoothly, *as if* society itself was working as a great machine. The production process is rarely context-sensitive. Wholeness is left out. Or, if it is considered at all, it is left far behind those mechanical considerations that are regarded as primary. Ideas of wholeness and harmony, as guiding features of the production process, have hardly any place at all. Certainly none that has useful, practical effect.

Of course, the A and B categories do not cover all the differences which can exist among different systems of production. Identifying these two categories, simply helps us sharpen and clarify the range of differences among ways of creating the environment that exist in different societies, economies, and cultures. And the two categories do serve to identify a dimension of great importance: the dimension that runs from **more** life-giving to **less** life-giving. We shall use "A" to refer to the **more** life-giving systems. They are those which are based on wholeness and adaptation, where elements are formed under the influence of the whole and in the effort to enhance the whole. We shall use "B" to refer to the **less** life-giving systems. These are the ones which are based on relatively rigid mechanical processes, both in regard to their administration and with regard to the types of physical design they can produce.

Extensive empirical studies by many architects, builders, and scientists, working over the last twenty to thirty years, have shown that the difference between more life-giving and less life-giving environments can be measured by a range of indicators. Most of them correlate with considerable reliability. Perhaps most important of all, is the fact that these indicators correspond to environments where people feel well, and where they *are* well. They also correlate with physical health, mental health, ecological health in the environment, and the way that people are treated socially in these environments.[1] Other studies have shown that the physical design of places and buildings — and especially the geometrical character of these places, together with their social character — also correlate to the health and mental health of people living and working in those environments.[2]

Research in the field of architecture has established that the quality of housing almost always depends on the ***process*** conditions through which the houses and apartments ***are produced***. A successful community organized and built by Shlomo Angel in Bangkok, was helped by the quality of its processes.[3] Buildings built by Kyriakos Pontikis[4] in Cyprus, and by Nili Portugali[5] in Israel, have also followed similar regimens of process-inspired design. In *The Nature of Order*, too, numerous extensive discussions present studies and results which show, unambiguously, how human well-being depends on particular configurations in the environment. This occurs, not because the bricks and mortar affect human

1   Studies of this kind may be found in works of Herb Gans, Amos Rapaport, *House Form, and Culture*; Clare Cooper Marcus, *Housing as If People Mattered: Site Design Guidelines for the Planning of Medium-Density Family Housing* (Los Angeles: University of California Press, 1986) and "Design guidelines for high-rise housing" (Reprint / Institute of Urban & Regional Development, University of California, Berkeley).
2   See, for example, *The Nature of Order*: Book 1 pp. 366-402, Book 3 pp. 260-282, Book 4 pp. 50-72.
3   Shlomo Angel, *Housing Policy Matters* (Oxford University Press, 2001); and Shlomo Angel and Zilla Phoativongsacham, *Building Together: Issues in Mutual-Aid Housing* (Bangkok, Human Settlements Division, Asian Institute of Technology, 1981).
4   Kyriakos Pontikis, *Construction of an Apartment Building* (PhD dissertation, University of California, Berkeley, 2002).
5   Nili Portugali, *The Act of Creation and the Spirit of a Place: A Holistic Phenomenological Approach to Architecture* (London: Editions Axel Menges, 2006).

well-being directly, but because certain benign configurations encourage certain forms of social interactions and certain kinds of positive emotional states in people. These in turn have direct healing impact on human well-being.[6]

The systems A and B are, in part, systems of human organization. But what we mean by human "organization" is something broader and deeper than the organization chart of a company. It includes the informal rules that govern people's actions. It includes feelings, attitudes, techniques, and practices. It includes processes and procedures that are operational, well-defined, and can be followed. Above all, it includes new types of action that provide clients, architects, builders, subcontractors, and planning officials with an understanding of the reality of land, human needs, environmental needs, and opportunities to repair damage.

We may say that system-A provides a new organization of production processes that routinely open the door to successful, built environments, densely packed with needed relationships. In our experience, system-A generally works well to create living environments. This comes about because of a general awareness that everything that is shaped or made, must be shaped by its context.

System-B does not do so well, because it is not focused on the subtlety of needed relationships between elements, only on number of elements produced, and their cost. That is not enough to provide the rich, relational structure needed for a living environment.

BLUEPRINTS: THE GREAT WEAKNESS OF SYSTEM-B

We do not know exactly when blueprints were first invented — perhaps about 200 years ago. Today they still exist in what we now call CAD drawings — a computer version of the old blue ammonia prints, where the information existed as white lines on the blue. In any case, I am referring to the kinds of machine drawings that were used for engineering. They were easy to reproduce, so that prints could be made, with the technical details which gave exact dimensions and the details. This allowed a master craftsman — working in wood, or

---

6   *The Nature of Order*, Book 3, pp. 25-66; and Book 4, pp. 262-300.

brass, or steel, or tile or brick, or cast bronze — to pay attention *only* to the dimensions and connections of the part he was making.

The oddest thing about these blueprints, though, was that the drawings did *only* convey the size, shape, length, angles, etc. It was possible for a machinist to replicate the geometry that was laid out on the blueprint. But the blueprints had a deficiency: there was really no information on the blueprint that would explain how the thing worked, nor even what its purpose was.

An example. Let's compare two lamps, lamp-A and lamp-B.

Lamp-A is a standard lamp, five to six feet high, with a very large lampshade, made of translucent silk, stretched over a wire frame. There are loops and tassles at the bottom of the shade. The silk is stretched on the bias, alternating, on adjacent segments of the wire frame. At the top and bottom, there are ornamental silk loops. The lamp shade is supported on a brass standard, a tubular brass leg, and at the bottom, three feet splayed out, acting as a tripod.

Lamp-B is a much simpler lamp — a conical shape, on the end of a coiled-wire, bendable stem. The shape itself would typically be painted black on the outside, white on the inside. It is a type of lamp that is very cheap, and is supposed to be "functional." It casts a cone of light in the direction coming from the cone mouth.

Both of these lamps are made to be used with a single 60- or 100-watt bulb. The A lamp has a soft illumination, something a little like the natural light that you get under a canopy of translucent leaves in a birch forest. The B lamp is very hard and harsh, by comparison. It produces glare at the hard edge of the cone, where bright light and strong darkness are right next to each other, without a gentle transition zone. It is not comfortable for your eyes if you are reading, nor especially comfortable for the overall light quality in the room.

Let us say that blueprints were made for these two lamps, and sent out to technicians, who were able to read the drawings, and had the necessary skills to make the lamps according to the blueprints. Unfortunately, though, the blueprint itself gives no information about the lamps themselves, how useful they are, or whether they work well or badly. The blueprint in no way establishes the likely use, or the likely behavior of these two different lamps.

What does this signify? It comes to the very essence of system-B. The blueprint does nothing to tell the maker anything about lamp A or lamp B, not any practically useful judgment — not even what are the good qualities of the lamps, or the bad qualities. The design, *in the form of the blueprint,* tells people nothing significant about the relative quality or value or usefulness of the two lamps.

In system-A, the maker acquires broad practical knowledge about the way the lamps work. The meaning, usefulness, and purpose of the lamps are essential aspects of the lamps themselves. System-A considers the lamps as part of the whole world in which they exist. But in system-B, the evaluation of the lamps is absent, the lamps are treated as artifacts without meaning. They exist without being woven into, or concerned with their relation to the people and the world around them.

In a very minor way, even the essentially harmless conical lamp, with its very harsh glare, can exist only because the makers, sellers, and tradespeople who have anything to do with the conical lamps, have entered a mental and emotional world unconnected from positive value. That is the world of system-B! It is the world of mass-produced, unrelated parts.

Blueprints lead to the making of things that are abstract, not always based on reality. Once something becomes abstract, it breeds disconnectedness — separation and the inability to connect with our surroundings. People buy houses from blueprints, but then don't like the actual house: "What on earth is this? I had no idea it was going to be like this . . . etc." As the use of abstract blueprints grows in society, emotional separation gradually becomes extreme without us being aware of it. Without compunction, teenagers throw bottles onto cars speeding under freeway overpasses. We live with crime and fear, and retreat to homes we try to protect, unable to escape alienation and antisocial behavior. Carpet bombing from 30,000 feet is similar. The bomber crews are so far away from the people they kill, that they do not experience the real fact.

System-A finds the "real." System-B replaces the real, and does not so easily allow us to evaluate things on the basis of the reality of feeling. Instead people make abstract judgments. The abstraction cannot evaluate or predict how people will use the made thing, not even whether it corresponds with their needs. So, they don't relate to B, or enjoy B. In system-A, we overcome this massive deficiency by making mockups to test our ideas and hunches about how a made thing will feel when it is finished. Even when a mockup is rudimentary, a maker or client can see and feel its relevance to living, and makes a connection to one's own life as it is lived.

THE CHARACTER AND CONTRAST BETWEEN SYSTEMS A & B

Now consider the character of modern building production. What about on-site fabrication, the construction of tract-built developments of offices or houses, not actually taking place in a factory, but nevertheless managed by organized crews who work according to precise rules and procedures? It is not literally mass production in the old sense of the word. Carpenters still walk about with a tool belt, and a hammer slung from the belt. But the work of the group is organized in the form of a machine. It does repetitive actions, controlled by blueprints. The whole organization of a field crew, working in that manner, is nearly identical to the smooth running of a machine. The production system is rigidly regulated by tightly controlled step-by-step processes that are immune to feedback.

Yet it is obvious that the character that a truly living world requires, if it is going to work well for us, cannot be the character of a machine. What is needed is something much closer to biology and closer to the psychology of nurturing.

People, in their social aspirations, seek relationships and fluidity of expression. The order that can guide such relationships and help them forward, must be based on the daily work of building a whole world of relationships — relationships between people and land, between houses and their gardens, between ways of moving around; a world in which color and water and trees encourage and remind us of visions of a loving future.

The means of creating buildings (modern-day building production) are still almost entirely based on system-B, and our late-19th-century ideas of efficiency. We are not yet sufficiently conscious of the quality of our environment when we go into a McDonald's, or take a three-year-old to play in a fabricated environment of rolled steel bars and pipes called a "playground," that then causes the enjoyment of play to be vehemently stamped out with the character or psychology of a die-casting machine.

No wonder then, that our children are not always able to find a way to grow and become whole. The world does not provide a place where people can become whole. We feel comfortable that our roads, sidewalks, windows, rooms, and sheetrock, are made up from modular processes — which inevitably, then, leave their mark on the world we live in. But this is not a mark which is appropriate. Indeed, it is deeply inappropriate. We should not feel comfortable in such a world.

The ministers of our national governments are themselves well-used to such machine-inspired playgrounds. Small wonder, then, that there is only the slimmest chance that a child's life can take its shape in the form of relationships activated between people and mechanical devices. What kind of environment might help to set things straight, and make clear that the opportunity for play comes from love? Perhaps, in our era, life, beauty, spontaneity, and depth of intent can come into a newly made physical world as rich, in its way, as the flowing lines of a Matisse nude, the rhythms and harmonies of an African tribal cloth, a Greek frieze, or a 15th-century Turkish carpet.

This is what we must ultimately be aiming for in our production system. The approach to building that my colleagues and I have been practicing (and writing about) since the 1960s *requires* that important and difficult changes must be made in our present-day, worldwide system of building production.

This new approach to the production of outdoor space and indoor space and buildings — what is, in short, a new approach to architecture — can only be successfully defined by constant emphasis on the real feelings of human beings, and by a wide variety of new creation processes that are powerful enough to replace the currently chaotic and severely limited construction methods that were typical of 20th-century production.[7]

The needed changes are potentially difficult. Although we at CES have managed to implement these kinds of changes again and again, in many countries and districts of the world, these projects have rarely been larger than a neighborhood. The criticism has (perhaps justifiably) been made that these small projects are not large enough to provide a "proof of concept." To succeed in establishing the feasibility of new techniques and processes so that they that can be scaled up for widespread use in modern society, is fundamental to their ultimate acceptance. Small neighborhoods and individual building projects can be accomplished by *ad hoc*, seat-of-the-pants methods. But when a project becomes large, there must be explicit, well-understood, sharable processes for bringing life to these projects in reliable and predictable ways.[8] The Eishin project shows that this can be done successfully, and paves the way for more and more sophisticated ways of doing it in the future.

THE CLASH BETWEEN THE TWO WORLD-SYSTEMS

Of course, we cannot pretend that it was easy to make these changes in a thirty-million dollar project (today's dollars) — being run according to entirely new rules, new contracts, new involvement of the people who would live and work there, different kinds of financial management, and different approaches to design, different approaches to craft and materials, different approaches to construction management. The job was, in addition, required to meet a ferociously demanding construction schedule (more of that later)!

Slowly, the clash became more and more evident as our project moved forward. Two systems so dramatically opposed were bound to clash. And indeed they did. We undertook and accepted the conflicts

7   These required changes or adjustments have been described in two volumes of *The Nature of Order* (Books 2 and 4); in a recent paper entitled *Generative Codes*, published in a collection of essays published in April 2008; in a forthcoming, parallel volume in the present series called *Sustainability and Morphogenesis*; in a paper entitled *Harmony-Seeking Computations*, published as a monograph in the *International Journal of Unconventional Computing*, 2012.
8   See, for example, Christopher Alexander, Brian Hanson, Michael Mehaffy, Randy Schmidt, et al., *Generative Codes*, published in Tigran Haas, *New Urbanism and Beyond* (Rizzoli International, 2008), pages 14-29.

between the operating assumptions of these two production systems for a powerful reason. We wished to make it widely understood that, using the techniques we have developed, the task of creating living environments can be achieved.

What we actually did was not reliant on any specific qualities of Japanese culture. It merely happened to take place in Japan. In Japan, as in any other modern country, there was a strong mix of highly modern technology and techniques, coupled with the dying embers of historical and craft techniques. The giant contractors, and the highly technocratic assumptions which have been considered as natural and normal, worked and behaved in just the same way in Japan as their counterparts in California, or London, or the outlying districts of Paris, or in the reconstruction of slums in Bombay. These system-B methods are all essentially the same in their mode of operation: they are based on profit. It is these assumptions that must be challenged and refined to open new ways of undertaking building projects.

A NEW FORM OF PRODUCTION

The role of architect is diminished by system-B. Architects of our present era are so preoccupied with *design* and *drawing* that they have, in the last century, rarely thought about the needed building processes, and the human organization needed to create a living world. So they have continued working with their pencils, and have mostly missed the more vital point — namely, that within the framework of present-day operational assumptions, good buildings, and good communities can hardly be made at all.

It is not worth wielding a pencil or computer mouse, if the most fundamental assumptions that affect the making of buildings are mangled, or left out. Stated more directly, we may say that we will **not** be able to make a living world, unless we put in place entirely new kinds of human organization and new operational assumptions, which will encourage beauty, health, and genuine humanity to be achieved.

The approach we used to conceive (and build) the campus of

the Eishin School depended on a new system of production — one that was explicitly guided by the feelings of the faculty and students. It was guided by close adherence to the emotional character and feeling of the land, in every detail. It was explicitly oriented toward craft and construction which aimed at loving details that give joy to ordinary people. It aims at the idea of supporting and healing the wholeness of people, animals, and plants that live there. It depends on temporary field workshops at the site, so that craft and the making of special purpose building elements, are produced to support local wholeness, setting the context for each piece of building work, thus allowing it to become beautiful.

THE OPERATIONAL DEFINITIONS OF SYSTEM-A AND SYSTEM-B

We have used the letter A because we consider the A system to be older, and more essential to everyday life. And we use the letter B for the system of production that has been in use for the last two- or three-hundred years or so, using B to mean that it is *less* essential to everyday life — *if the word "life" is deeply understood.*

However, system-A itself, as we describe it and think of it, is emphatically *not* a re-creation of any past era. It is something entirely new, a production system made today. In its present form it exists now for the first time. It relies on a new kind of humane organization of building and creative processes, and is carried out in a highly modern, even avant-garde form, acceptable for our time, and congruent with the technical marvels we have come to expect as everyday. Its essence lies in the focus on human experience — on feeling, on well-being, on the possibility of living a deeply contemplated life.

Within **SYSTEM-A**, all decisions are made, and governed, by attempts to see the underlying wholeness in a situation or event or thing, and then we act accordingly. That is the primary driving force of every act, and every decision, small or large. Everything else is put in second place.

Within **SYSTEM-B**, ideas of wholeness, harmony, and wholesomeness have hardly any place at all, certainly none that has practical effect. What matters in system-B, are regulations, categories, money, efficiency, and profit: all the machinery designed to make society run smoothly, *as if* society were indeed a great machine. Wholeness is left out. It is left far behind the primary considerations that originate from system-A.

In concrete terms, system-A, in the modern form we have put forth, will be defined by the processes described from chapters 7-25. The cardinal rule of our new system-A, will be "**Always try, at each moment, in every policy, and in every action, in every line and every shape, to do that thing or take that action which increases the life in the buildings being made — and increases the life in the place, in the people, and in their environment.**"

This means that one reveres the land, does one's utmost to grasp the overall form and structure as it is, and then tries to make all actions support and strengthen that structure as it is. More loosely expressed, one might describe this as a state of mind which takes the land as holy, and tries to extend and increase that holiness, in every act. This is not concerned with religion, but with the present beauty and structure of the land, its animals and plants and people, and with the task of supporting them as far as it is humanly possible.

Of course, to some degree system-A is an idealized system, which may, in our minds, exist only in some far-off, imaginary, golden age. Perhaps it really did exist in the proverbial traditional society. Possibly it exists in perfect form only in our minds. However, we are interested in it, *now*, and we are guided by it, *now*, and we wish to work in it *now*, not so much as a historical precedent, but as an ideal target for our own time, a source of wisdom, a guiding ideal for the future.

This source of wisdom is achievable today, based on practical ways of behaving, thinking, doing, building, repairing, and embellishing. At the same time it is a way of evaluating whether the production system we are using is acting wisely, and accomplishing what we want it to do for us. It is a way of looking at our daily lives, a way of asking if this is the kind of life we want, day after day.

It is reasonable to say that any useful change in society must show us how to generate life, how to provide the foundational conditions which will enable life to flourish. This will start, in all cases, by our looking at everything both as a very practical thing and as a thing that is connected to everything around it. It does not start by looking at the market value of a commodity; a commodity with exchange value and use value. Indeed, it deliberately pushes those monetary considerations away, in order to make room for these other, much more significant considerations.

The primary terms of system-A are *not* the primary terms of the market economy. System-A starts by looking at a thing, a house, a building, a bench, a stone, as something made, or to be made, so that it has the capacity to support life, very practically and going into considerable depth about the way that people really feel: what they experience as human beings, what they experience spiritually, what is worthwhile for them, not in monetary terms (their salaries), but in felt, human terms involving creativity, fellowship, the experience of being of service to the world, and the experience of love and affection.[9]

The built environment with its thousands of acts of design and construction is finally a made thing with its own process of life and making. If the making process is dead (as it cannot help being in system-B), the resulting product, too, will *inevitably* be dead. If the process of making the environment is living *as a process* (as in system-A), the results, the generated forms and places, will then have a very good chance of being alive.[10]

We hope that by now the reader will understand that the battle between system-A and system-B is not merely a clash between two competing theories of architecture. More profoundly, it is a clash between two competing systems of thought, human organization, and social activity. The two worldviews differ about the ways human society should be organized, about questions of ultimate value, and about the ways in which our social and emotional life may typically be arranged.

---

9   See, for example, the discussions on feeling and awareness in *The Embodied Mind*, by Francisco Varela, Evan Thompson, and Eleanor Rosch (Cambridge, MA: MIT Press, 1991).
10   See the discussions on feeling in Book 1, *The Nature of Order: The Phenomenon of Life*, pp. 297-402. These four chapters are chapter 7, "The Personal Nature Of Order;" chapter 8, "The Mirror Of The Self;" chapter 9, "Beyond Descartes: A New Form Of Scientific Observation;" chapter 10, "The Impact of Living Structure on Human Life." These chapters go a long way to establish the connection between human feeling and the objective condition of wholeness.

When this distinction is understood, it will indeed be seen that there *must* be conflict between the two world-systems. We need this confrontation in order to heal ourselves, and our communities.

The connection between human feeling and the wholeness of the world is profound. The activity of using this connection in service to the world is something that can be regained and *must* be regained. And in our search for wholeness, the presence of profound feeling in the hearts of human observers is the most sensitive, most reliable measuring stick.

During the positivistic era of the 20th century, the concept of wholeness was hardly ever accepted, and many architects (and some scientists) were in the habit of asserting that there is no objective way of estimating or measuring degrees of wholeness, nor indeed, any objective way of judging the presence of wholeness at all. In recent decades, however, this 20th-century superstition has been superceded by experimental ways of measuring wholeness. This has happened because feeling and degree of feeling, have at last been recognized as legitimate phenomena. Many ways of estimating or measuring degree of feeling, are nowadays widely accepted.

Wholeness is both an objective structure in the world, and a subjective feeling, experienced by different individuals. What we call "positive feeling" as described and analyzed in *The Nature of Order*, is the subjective talisman by which the presence of objective wholeness makes itself known. This is the foundation of the battle which begs for common sense evaluation of positive environments, buildings, and urban landscapes.

The following system-A projects, in which we sought wholeness, were built, drawn, or described by CES during the forty years 1961-2001. You will find them referenced in *The Nature of Order*, Book Three, *A Vision of a Living World*. The page numbers listed below, (page 62) give you the page references in Book Three. The Book Three page numbers are listed in boldface.

Further references are given in books and articles, and are also marked by boldface type.

1961-India, State of Gujarat, Bavra: village elementary school and new village plan near Mehe-medabad, population about 600 people, pp. *526-527*.

1967-New York City: design of Multi-Service Center, Hunts Point, The Bronx, *A Pattern Language which Generates Multi Service Community Centers* (Center for Environmental Structure, 1968).

1969-Lima, Peru: houses built of block, Bamboo-urethane beams, canvas, two courtyards per house. Single-family houses, two stories high. The families laid out their own house designs, then they were built by construction workers supplied by the United Nations in 1973. Location of the project is at kilometro onze, 11 kilometers north of Lima on the Pan-American highway. See *Houses Generated by Patterns (Center for Environmental Structure, 1969)*.

1975-Eugene, Oregon: Master plan for the University of Oregon, still growing and active today. *The Oregon Experiment* (New York: Oxford University Press, 1975).

1976-Mexicali, Mexico: houses and community center built with residents; *The Production of Houses* (New York: Oxford University Press, 1983), a detailed description of an unusual form of construction and production. *Book 3 pp. 10-11, 334-336, 446, 464, 479, 493-495, 551-555*.

1981-Linz, Austria: public cafe, built by CES as part of the Forum Design Expo, 1982. *The Linz Café* (New York: Oxford University Press, 1981), *Book 3 pp. 428-431, 441, 621*.

1981-Berkeley, California: the Sala house, 3-story tower, red/gray concrete, pp. *240-241, 534-537*.

1984-Whidbey Island, Washington State: the Medlock House, pp. *254, 409, 417-420*.

1984-Fresno, California: the Fresno Farmer's Market, heavy timber structure, pp. *501-505*.

1986-Berkeley, California: the Upham house, pp. *254, 459, 598-599*.

1986-San Anselmo, California: Potash/McCabe house, including hand-painted large-scale frescoes and furniture, pp. *623-626*.

1988-Moshav Shorashim, Galilee: neighborhood plan, pp. *349-351*.

1989-Tokyo: Tokyo Int'l Forum, Conference Ctr. and Auditorium, competition entry, pp. *115-118*.

1990-Santa Rosa de Cabal, Colombia: 76 houses, led by CES with a generative process, each house then built by the family who designed it, laid it out, and finished it over a period of years, pp. *398-408*.

1990-San Jose, California: the Julian Street Inn, shelter for homeless people, 100-bed accomodation, built by CES and Steve Oliver, pp. *120-125, 211-223*.

1992-Austin, Texas: Back-of-the-Moon neighborhood, five houses on Lake Travis, designed and built by CES for individual families, pp. *82-85, 366-371, 371-381*.

1984-1988-Martinez, California: complex of workshops, pp. *433-458, 617-620*.

1984-Sapporo, Japan: Sapporo Building, 10 stories, pp. *224-227*.

1985-San Francisco, California: the Fort Mason Bench, three-tiered bench, cast concrete, with extensive ornaments inlaid into the concrete with white and green marble, pp. *352-360, 586-588*.

1987-Tokyo: Downtown five-story apartment house, 20 apartments, pp. 166-173.

1987-Napa Valley, California: the Berryessa House, pp. *159-165, 434-437, 628*.

1988-Range of office furniture for Hermann Miller, pp. *386-397*.

1988-Katmandu, Nepal: Buddhist monastery for 200 monks, pp. *151-152, 475*.

1989-Mountain View, California: Mountain View Civic Center, pp. *13-14, 112-115*.

1990-San Francisco: De Young Museum, gallery of Alexander carpets discussion include interior construction, color, lighting, and installation and hanging of the carpets, pp. *425-427*.

1992-Nagoya, Japan: Chikusadai neighborhood in Hazama, reconstruction, pp. *166-267, 382-384*.

1993-Guasare, Venezuela: neighborhood plans for new town of Carbozulia, pp. *340-347*.

1993-West Sussex, U.K.: West Dean Visitors Centre and gardens, pp. *486-489, 544-545*.

1994-Portsmouth, U.K.: Mary Rose Museum (New York: Oxford University Press, 1994). *Book 3 pp. 132-147*.

1995-Berkeley, California: the Sullivan house, pp. *412, 424, 472, 584-585*.

1995-Frankfurt, Germany: designed community of Hoechst, pp. *86-92*.

1996-Progresso, Ft. Lauderdale, Florida: reconstitution of an urban neighborhood, pp. *284-303*.

1996-Eugene, Oregon: University of Oregon, student housing, 20 units, pp. *182-186*.

1999-Brookings, Oregon: community of houses, *Master Plan and Process for Harbor Peak near Brookings, Oregon* (Center for Environmental Structure, 2005).

1999-San Francisco: Bay Bridge, Eastern span design, p. *469*.

2001-Athens, Greece: studies for the Grand Concourse of the Athens Opera House, pp. *563-565*.

2005-Strood, South East England, Rebirth of a working Community, using a generative process. Strood was designated for redevelopment very much in the system-B model. We offered, instead, an alternative process shaped by a system-A model; this process was highly enlightening.

4 INNER ASPECTS OF THE TWO PRODUCTION SYSTEMS

The effects of the clash between A and B can be found
in each one of us, and the clash still drives our inner conflicts.

With the march of history, and the fluid underpinning of
rapidly evolving cultures, the fluid underpinnings of system-A
were gradually overtaken, and replaced, by the harsh,
mechanical demands of system-B.
Direct human judgment became impossible.
We were now truly imprisoned.

System-B constrains our psyche, and makes a mental prison.
System-A frees us mentally, when we are allowed to use it.
It provides us, in our inner lives, with food and forms and
sustenance, and the language of the soul.

Even so, the spirit of directly making houses, gardens,
furniture, and windows, has mostly
been taken away from us by system-B,
and, even now, we are still tortured.

How, and when in our history, and why, did we move away from
a conscious connection to wholeness? The further we look back in
history, the stronger was our ability to make things with wholeness
as a foundation. Understanding what happened, and recovering
our capacity to work with system-A, makes it possible to find the
configurations that heal, both inside ourselves and in our physical
environments. We can find ample evidence and examples to show

that people once acted out of a coherent connection with their world, and made beautiful, functional places and buildings that enhanced their well-being. For them, it was the natural thing to do.

This photograph shows a panel factory in South Australia. It is utilitarian, aimed at enclosing industrial space, cheaply and efficiently. Yet, in spite of its usefulness and practicality, this panel is cold and unfeeling. If one wants to be more frank, one can say that it is ugly and unpleasant. As such it will do nothing to enhance the environment. Although it will be utilized efficiently by system-B, its use will *not lift our spirits* or make for improvement in our surroundings.

What we achieve in shaping the environment will depend *entirely* on the production systems we enable and support. It will always be through the mouths of those production systems that our buildings will have spoken.

System–B. Factory production of building components,
Laing and O'Rourke, Australia.

THE SPIRITUAL AND EMOTIONAL CHARACTER OF THE ARTIFACTS OF SYSTEM-A

System-A is that system of production which comes direct from the interior of a person, from the interior of a people. The original system-A is, if you will, something akin to what lies in the aboriginal people of Australia, or the long-gone carvers of the spirals on the stones of Carnac in Brittany, and their cousins the stonecutters of Ireland. For these people, there was not much of a gap between the interior life they led, their interior feelings, and the direct *making* that they brought into the world.

In a preliterate era, the inner nature of a people, and their psychic life, came entire. It was the ocean in which they swam. It was, quite simply, part of them. There was a massive significance in such a connection. It did not need to be questioned. As a result, their consciousness flowed in them, and from them. It was an awareness, which defined the place and nature of their life.

The most ancient of these carvings, drawings, and paintings hearken back to forms of magic, ancestor worship, and a complete integration of life and belief with the rock painting below. For example, portraying a spirit, or a ghost, and uniting the artist and

System–A. Work by hand: Aurochs cave painting in Lascaux, circa 17,000 BCE.

System-A: Prehistoric, spiral carvings, Newgrange, River Boyne, Ireland, circa 3000 BCE.

any onlooker with a nether world of the unknown. Focused as it is on the whole, system-A comes directly from the interior of a person — from the interior of people. The four pictures printed on pages 65 to 68 show what happens when there is a deep connection between the maker and the made, and the conviction that the human soul is something real.

The rock painting on the right (page 67), estimated by archaeologists to be as much as 50,000 years old, was found in a cave in Western Australia.[1] It depicts a shaman, with a head-dress, and the shaman's paraphernalia — altogether a magical and forbidding figure. The freedom of drawing, and the abililty to show an utterly relaxed quality is evident, down to an easily visible, musical walk. This painted character is undoubtedly felt to be a living character, and

---

1   The estimated date comes from the archaeologists who look after this most ancient painting, now protected by the Bradshaw Foundation, in the Kimberley Collection of Aboriginal Art, Broome Historical Society Museum.

System-A. An aboriginal rock painting in Western Australia, estimated to be about 50,000 years old.

without doubt also has a spirit quality. It carries a profound sensation of the unknown.

Concretely, to help you decipher the shaman drawn on the wall of this ancient cave, it will be easiest to pick out the head, the two arms, the two legs, the items the shaman is carrying — things that hang from the arms, a long stick with a totemic head. Most particularly, think of the shaman, carrying all these things, walk-

System-A. Bronze mask with gold leaf, China. Late Shang dynasty, circa 1200 BCE.

ing perhaps with a swinging step. His head, above the shoulders, is dark. You can see his eyes, his forehead, his mouth, the ribbon tied around his head flying loosely in the wind. The anatomy in the drawing is very realistic: feet, ankles, thighs, shoulders, hair, knees are all carefully drawn.

Even in shamanistic or primitive situations, a person's actions were inevitably modified to a large degree by their culture and society. But the departure from the most ancient archetypes, would, at first, have been relatively minor, as perhaps in pre-Hellenic Greece, or Bronze-Age China. Then, by the time of the European Middle Ages, another thousand years later, socially accepted standards of action were still congruent with the inner feeling (the depth psychology that people really had). Society still supported the inner feelings that people had pouring out of them. The beloved, great cathedrals were instances being built in medieval Europe. The Potala in Tibet, the Casbah in Marrakesh, Machu Picchu in the Andes were examples in other parts of the world.

Gradually, though, a shift occurred. As time went forward, culture and society became more complex, and social norms were no longer carrying a public form of the inner feelings that people actually had. Instead, people's actions became less rooted in true feeling, and more and more were shaped by other — outside — sources, concepts, and habits.[2]

As a result, people would have begun to experience something like a war within themselves, a conflict between their own personal impulses, and the guidance of external laws and norms and attitudes. What came from their own psyche, and what came from outside, began to be at odds. In such a period, people could no longer say that their actions were "pure," from the heart. Rather there was one inner voice representing what was in the belly; and another inner voice embodying a social or political construct, influenced by power, by money, by force that one felt, for whatever reason, one should adhere to.

There was now one inner voice that came from the heart, from a person's instinctive reaction to the fields and furrows, or to the behavior of a boat and sails. And there was a second inner voice, generated or shaped by social forces, which actually came from outside a person, was planted in their minds by social constructs, and by social institutions like the army or the bank. But this second type of "instinct," this second voice, became so familiar that it appeared to be inside them.

It is these two voices which gradually became embodied in what we, in this book, are calling system-A and system-B.

System-A comes from inside, from the human psyche, and its archetypes and from human culture. System-B comes from the laws, the institutions of society and, ultimately, from the mass

---

2   George Herbert Mead, *Mind, Self, and Society* (Chicago: University of Chicago Press, 1934).

production of the industrial era.

One might say, at first blush, that system-B is the product of industrialization, and came from that origin. But this change in human consciousness is only partially entangled with the industrialization that started in the 18th century. It is a much older, broader process, which has taken thousands of years; and over that long span of time has been responsible for the gradual evolution of the human self.[3]

By now, in modern society, people are genuinely confused about their inner feelings, because it is hard to separate the feelings that are manufactured through television and advertising, from those that are more instinctual and come from deeper sources in the psyche.

What is especially important, though, is the fact that artists, builders, farmers, and creators were once able to rely on their instincts about materials, location, physical structures. In the primitive period, these instincts were reliable, and were, above all, good for the land. People had a direct connection with the land as their source of livelihood, so their own wholeness (the wholeness of the people) and the wholeness of their environment were not at odds.

Now, as the modern era has unfolded, people's instincts are more often shaped by external sources — fashion magazines, telling people what they should think about housing, food, clothes, accessories, cars — all focused on selling goods. The inner voices, also now shaped by these exterior forces, have therefore become less reliable in terms of well-being, less capable of discerning wholeness, and ultimately less good for the land.

System-B, as a system of production, has become focused on efficiency in selling goods and making money, while system-A has struggled to create well-being — but too often in an inhospitable social environment. As these two systems vied for position in our daily lives and in our minds, all of us have become, to a mild or less mild degree, crazy. Mind and body seem to have been severed. The human being is rarely, now, intact — no longer a unified being.[4]

---

3   George Herbert Mead, *Mind, Self, and Society* (Chicago: University of Chicago Press, 1934).
4   Clinically established criteria provide a firm basis for claiming the breakdown of the organism's unity. A major scientist, Kurt Goldstein, The Organism, MIT Press, 1995, was one of those who

However, during the late 20th century there was a general process in which the old forms of society were giving way slowly to a new form of society — arising from computers, from the internet, and from wider, freer types of communication, in which human community, depth of feeling, and depth of spirit, were becoming relevant and worth fighting for. It was a fascinating time — an inspiring development — no matter how small it seemed at first.[5]

The Eishin Campus described in this book is one case of such a transformation of human existence. This project, and the events it brought in train, made visible the vivid contrast between system-A and system-B. We believe this was a significant event in the gradual change which was taking place toward the end of the 20th century, and which is now, in the beginning of the 21st century, expanding.

The progress we have recorded had a great deal to do with the formation of the physical environment, the construction of physical buildings, and physical public spaces that formed the landscape of that place. This progress had to do with architecture. But at the same time, new ways of thinking about human existence were introduced — new ways of thinking about society, new ways of thinking about individual responsibility, new ways of thinking about how to undertake human problem-solving and problem resolution, educational philosophy, and the care of the individual. All this became embodied in the architecture.

A CONFLICT OF WILL REGARDING THE INNER NATURE OF SOCIETY

What took place in Japan during the period from 1981 to 1989 really was a battle between the two world-systems that have been described. It was a conflict of wills; a conflict of ideology; a conflict of understanding regarding the nature of a human being; a conflict of understanding about the nature of the human spirit; a conflict about the nature of human society; and a conflict about the way that nature and human beings should interact. It was even, implicitly, a disagreement about the nature of the human soul.

---

first put this forward.
5   This is also related to modern positivism, and the liberal ideas emanating from the 1960s. By the 1980s, though, it had not yet jelled to consolidate in postmodern forms.

Such a depiction of this rift between system-A and system-B is not overstated. The distance between the two is by now immense.

For this reason, we hope that the impact of this battle may be remembered, for the force of the shock, and for the clarity of the result; and we hope, too, that it can become a signpost to a more wholesome civilization in the future.

Of course, a change such as the recovery of system-A characteristics can never happen suddenly. It is a slow change, all across society, but an upheaval nonetheless, an immense giving way of all the basic assumptions about life and work, and a replacement of old assumptions with other assumptions. In real, practical terms the changes require an upheaval ... an immense force ... something like a cataclysm. As they happen, we feel the basement shaking.

In the course of ancient history, changes as big as these were often marked by battles. They marked events in which the issues of the change were puzzled out, thought out, fought over and gradually, then, for one side or another some ground was made, some ground lost.

This, we believe, was such a battle. Slowly, system-A and system-B moved apart from each other in our changing, tumultuous contemporary society. By 1981, when the Eishin project was conceived, 20th-century methods of architecture and development had too often produced artistic sterility and ugliness and spiritual death. The developments which they created were too often money-oriented, alienating, cold, phony, facile and unpleasant, marked by endless repetition, lack of differentiation, very cheap materials, unsuited to the conditions or the landscape.

CAPITAL DEVELOPMENT AND FINANCIAL DEVELOPMENT

You may view the settlements pictured on these pages 73-76 as extreme examples. Neverthless, it is true that "modern" cities around the world are now composed of "developments" that are built to make money, not to serve communities or to support the well-being of inhabitants. They are commodities built for money by *developers* and their supporters (banks, local governments, etc.) — those who hope to gain profit by building them. And this

System-B. Prefabricated shacks, Soweto, South Africa. This was typical in the post–World War II era. The prefab houses were identical, rectangular boxes, the same roofs, the same windows, the same placing of the only door. The one human touch was the paint, people did their best to transform the hundreds of identical boxes. By splashing color the boxes were transformed by their inhabitants. System-B was trying to become system-A.

approach to building cities is condoned by governments almost everywhere in the world, and accepted by people who want houses, roads, and workplaces where they can live and work.

The *spirit* of men and women and children is rarely found in these places. Developments of this kind did not, in the 20th century (and do not now) reflect our dreams, our aspirations — the essential qualities of profound life. Instead they are packages of material, dressed up to seem good on the banker's spreadsheet, packaged for their images, made for the money aspirations of their developers, with an appearance of usefulness, style, and a small dose of function sometimes thrown in by architects — who are, sadly, almost all part of the same development package.

It is true that various noble efforts (those of the New Urbanism group, for instance), have tried hard to make needed improvements in these standardized developments. But their improvements have

System-B: Kalinin Prospekt, the main shopping street of Moscow (at night, 1967).

still focused only on the outward shape of the architecture, and as a result did relatively little to change the underlying social and human situation — the very thing which most urgently needed repair.[6] They *could* only *aspire* to creating visual copies of old living communities, because the underlying production process was still that system-B development process which *cannot* generate living community. Only the outward form was changed. There was too little connection to the human inner core, too little relationship of flesh and blood to dreams, and sweat, and money — a person's own money. These more essential relationships were unregarded and unchanged, and therefore nothing really did change. Buildings, neighborhoods, and communities are today most often considered

6   Andreas Duany, and a considerable group of dedicated people working with him, and under his influence, have done their best to make this work. However, the nagging failure to deal with the issue of appropriate uniqueness, and the failure to show, *practically*, how uniqueness arises out of a healthy social structure, have made it unlikely that this can succeed as presently put forward.

as commodities. They are made to be bought and sold and hired out.

Almost nothing that was done had the explicit aim of uniting people with their land. Throughout the late 20th century and during the first years of the present century, there has been a soul-destroying quality to most modern development, to the apartments, schools, shopping malls, and office complexes which our society was and still is able to produce.

And that is all they *could* produce. The same problem exists in the United States, Japan, England, Egypt, Russia, China, in every modern society. Buildings in typical development projects, whether in Jakarta, Tokyo, Los Angeles, or West Berlin share the dead quality inevitable in a built environment conceived primarily as capital, an income-producing machine. Essentially all these products are the result of focus on money, and ways of dealing with money.

System-B. Developer's model for Nirvana-Gurgaon-Escape, New Delhi, 2007.

The use of money to make money, which "inspired" Western society in the 20th century, and which has quaintly been called "democracy" and euphemistically "the market economy," did produce great wealth for a few. But not for most people. And it has ravaged our environment. None of it unites people with the land they love; indeed, most often the land that is left, cannot be loved.

This problem is of our time. It is of our own making. And it is largely dominated by the banking-investment policies of system-B, which are deeply separated from ordinary people's wishes. Except for minor differences, the rules of system-B are almost unrelated to the different cultures, ethnicities, climates, social systems, ideologies, and beliefs of the various groups of people on our planet. This bizarre circumstance will remain unchanged as long as our planet's development policies continue to be governed by system-B.

System-B: Downtown Dubai, 2010: pretentious, flashing its money, and ugly. And indeed, it is a Waste Land. The spaces are not shaped for human beings, nor can they comfort anyone.

5 THE WASTELAND IN OUR HEARTS

A civilization is marked by the buildings, and roads, and forests; by the crossing of rivers; by the usefulness of a lake shore. It is marked, too, by the kindness with which we regard each other.

But do not think that a broken city will recover automatically, of its own accord. If we smell the dust of a crumbling society, we need to face up to our necessary task, to rebuild our civilization, and to do it well.

Everyone knows — in their bones, anyway — that a civilization cannot exist, unless the physical landscape of each city is a civilizing landscape; unless the buildings are beautiful and individual; unless the streets and rivers, the gardens, the front doorsteps, the great windows and the small, all play their part. That is indeed, part of the definition we carry in our minds when we use the word "civilization." But, of course, the cities we are presently building do not have this quality.

Collectively, we do not even know how to make such a city. The processes we use, to conceive and build, are inadequate to such a task. The engineering developers who raise up buildings, the financial developers who have an eye on money as the core of their aims — they have almost no regard for the human qualities which might flourish there. And certainly a civilization will not grow in a wasteland.

The building processes which are now accepted as normal drive out our humanizing inclinations, with every form and every piece of paper. We are dried out by these papers; our buildings make little room for love, or children, or old age. The work of building up a civilization again, giving it renewed life, is not different from the work of building up a physical environment that can be regarded as civilized. We must be able to live — to *live* — with dreams that can be realized, with experiences from which we can make more of ourselves. Deep in our hearts we have almost given up. The task seems hopeless. We hardly dare to believe that there is real hope of re-establishing a living civilization.

> *What are the roots that clutch, what branches grow*
> *Out of this stony rubbish? Son of man,*
> *You cannot say, or guess, for you know only*
> *A heap of broken images, where the sun beats,*
> *And the dead tree gives no shelter,* ... [1]

Yet we still want something to believe in. In recent years, architects and builders and politicians have been running in droves to build sustainable communities. But what they have in mind, and what their hope clings to, are technical achievements, devices which can recycle water, clean the air, and irrigate the soil. These things are well worth aiming for. But technical achievements of this kind are not enough to rebuild our hope.

We need the kind of courage that is the most difficult of all — the courage to dare to be human, the courage to come back from retreat, to dare to do the very things which seem most difficult and are most frightening, to search unflinchingly for those things that have a chance of making us whole in ourselves.

I am a hard-bitten realist. I know how hard it is, and I know the huge obstacles that, to many, seem insurmountable. But we have written all this down, because we believe it must be done.

For a few decades now, it seems that people have been lamenting some sort of loss — a loss of *something*. There is an emptiness inside us, as we live in and regard the world around us. What causes this feeling? Is it an unsavory nostalgia? Is it foolish-

---

1   T.S. Eliot, *The Waste Land* (London:Faber and Faber, 1922), lines 19-23.This chapter contains several very brief passages from this very long poem.

ness? Is it an unwillingness to embrace the present and the future? Could it perhaps be nothing but a hypochondriac oversensitivity, treating a stomach-ache as if it were a dread disease? Or is there really something vital that has gone wrong, that has been lost along the way? And if it were so, what might that something be? What could it be that has been lost? What is in the way of building the beautiful world we wish for?

It is tied, certainly, to the machine-like and impersonal operation of system-B, acres of identical, repeating houses and apartment buildings, freeways, and office blocks. It could be tied to lack of trees, and grass, and animals.

> *Unreal City,*
> *Under the brown fog of a winter dawn,*
> *A crowd flowed over London Bridge, so many,*
> *I had not thought death had undone so many . . . .* [2]

But it comes, too, from the disrupted network of social relations and communities. Families are scattered nowadays to the four winds, often miles apart in different states and different countries. The connections of the family, and the extended family, are breaking down, in some degree have already broken down. That makes us anchorless — at the very same time that it comes to many with a certain feeling of relief that family quarrels do not need to be confronted and healed. Ironic or not, this could be lurking in our souls as an underground cancer, a terrible loss.

The living world of animals and plants is damaged, too. Even the most ordinary animals are going missing. Red squirrels, badgers, butterflies — the Small Blues, Red Admirals, even Cabbage Whites — are all seen less often than they used to be. And we are getting used to it. Often we go through a whole day, even a whole month, or year without once missing them. That is a depressing

---

2   T.S. Eliot, *The Waste Land*, lines 60-63.

thought, but true. Our brothers and sisters in the world of animals are dying off and leaving us alone. Instead there is a world of free-ways, motels, apartment towers, which, as physical substance in its own right, seems to give very little back to us.

The grim, concrete form of building apartments over half-open carports, ignorant of contact with the Earth, is based on shallow forms of practicality. But what is it really? The practicality is mundane, at best, while the damage that it does to us is sharp and persistent, an invisible abrasion to our self and our feelings. It is, at best, an architectural analogue of iron rations: something that gives you minimal calories and vitamins, but not much more.

The wasteland in our hearts does not come only from the breakdown of society. It comes, in equal measure, from the breakdown of the physical environment. More and more buildings, and roads, and parking lots have accumulated, in heaps, nihilistic worlds, where there is little that can be loved, among the enormous tracts of land developed into office parks, tract houses, and public children's parks — all indeed necessary; sometimes very vaguely pleasant, but more often dead and abstract. It is hardly possible to experience a profound relationship with these places. So the landscape of our era has become, and contin-ues to become, a wasteland.

T.S. Eliot's great poem, *The Waste Land*, describes the psycho-logical wasteland we have made of Earth, and at the same time evokes a wasteland of the spirit. The two are tightly linked. When there is a wasteland of the spirit, the physical Earth is also laid waste. When there is a wasteland in the physical things we build on Earth, it soon breeds a wasteland of the spirit in our hearts.

Eliot was the first to describe this quality in our civilization. He was the first to be direct about the pain that a crumbling civilization inflicts on us; the first to be direct about the frightening possibility that the loss of civilization may not be recoverable; possibly the first to know the fear and heartache that follow from the pain we feel before we know what it is that hurts us.

This observation that something is badly wrong has been gnawing at the bowels of modern human beings, for a very long time. There is a history of 19th- and 20th-century writings on the subject, extending back at least to the beginning of the 16th century, and forward to the present. All these writings depend, one way or another, on some version of the visible contrast of two kinds of system in society: those that seem (and are) healthy in some degree (systems of type A); and those that seem (and are) damaged (systems of type B). This vast and subterranean, unseen struggle that occupies our minds, and often our psyche and our dreams, our unconscious preoccupations, has been explored by writers of the 19th and 20th centuries — poets, novelists, and essayists, as well as historians and philosophers. Aldous Huxley, James Joyce, George Orwell, and Kafka have seen the absurd, and horrible, flavorless and colorless emotional landscape, and they have described it. Dramatists and moviemakers, too. Bertolt Brecht, Strindberg, Chaplin, Fellini, and Renoir show the face of system-B.

All these writers dwell in one fashion or another on a surging underground battle, never far from us, gnawing at our vitals all the time. It is a battle between the instincts of individual human beings, following, if they can, the dictates of their hearts, and the oppressive system, which constrains and nobbles our human passions, and forces us to live within a mechanized society that is imposed on us. It is a perpetual conflict between a healthy system-A, (innate in us, interior to us, a part of us) and a damaged system-B, (exterior to us, created by society, ultimately thus created by ourselves, leaving us caught and damaged by the social mechanisms of our own creation).

These powerful writers, with many others, have drawn attention to the destruction of human solidarity, the grinding of the human spirit in the gears of a brutal, machine-like society.

Their writings illuminated the 20th century, because there was no other light than knowledge to be had, and these anti-utopias at least awakened us to our condition, and shed light on our grim way of life. This was a powerful, artistic and humanitarian achievement.

But, beyond waking us up, this achievement still did relatively little that was practical to help us create a better condition in society.

> *. . . I could not*
> *Speak, and my eyes failed, I was neither*
> *Living nor dead, and I knew nothing,*
> *Looking into the heart of light, the silence. . . .* [3]

Indeed, among these writings that explore the darker sides of human society, it is rare to find any that gives a concrete, realistic description of the positive conditions — practical, physical, and fiscal conditions — which would be able to transform system-B into something closer to system-A. That is not to say that people have not historically made experiments, or made powerful changes in society to better the human condition. They have, of course. The Utopian movements of immigration to the United States sometimes had this practical quality. The Shakers, for example, were successful for a hundred years and built communities which worked, which developed a particular form of house construction and furniture building. They gave us an example, though probably too dry for most people as a model of daily life.

But writers have been far less successful when trying to conjure up the conditions that will rescue or create an entirely new society. Few of these writers have drawn attention to our problem from a positive perspective. They identify, depict the capacity of human beings to create machine-like, social cages, bound by rules that can hardly be escaped. Those writers who attempt to describe positive utopias to show the bright side, or a way out of this misery, have too often been unable to go beyond a milquetoast antidote, a feeble kind of social engineering, which does not inspire, and rarely convinces. Nor can it still the inner wars between A and B, as they occur in people every day.

Of course, life in one sense has become vastly better for many millions of us in the modern age. Many of us have basic shelter,

---

3   T.S. Eliot, *The Waste Land*, lines 38-41.

food, water, electricity, roads. Many of us have the right to vote; television sets bring every imaginable play and film and opera into our houses; audio-systems can play the most wonderful music for us; medicine can help us and our children survive the most terrible diseases and accidents; education, nowadays free to all in most countries, opens people's minds and gives young people untold choices and opportunities. Houses grow bigger; cars are more efficient and safer; we can travel to distant places; we have clothes to rival the opulence of the Arabian nights. These are not only material benefits. They are real benefits, and there are few among those who have these benefits who do not thank their lucky stars. We tempt fate if we mock them, and we mock them at our peril.

And yet! ... and yet! ... the more we have, the more we become aware that there is a growing wasteland in us and around us. In the United States it is reported that as many as 20% of all teenagers have some form of mental illness.[4] Hunger and poverty and homelessness are on the rise for hundreds of millions. Those who see such things happening are inevitably distraught by them, sometimes unhinged. In London there are knife crimes every night. The wars of the 20th century killed more than a hundred million people, 50,000,000 people in the first half of the century, and 50,000,000 people in the second half of the century.[5]

At the same time, many disciplines have moved us in a positive direction. Psychology, anthropology, sociology, political theory, ecology, botany, zoology, engineering, music, dance, and many others, have brought profound and lasting benefits, helpful to the needs of system-A. In 19th-century psychology, Jung and Freud and William James began to detect, and then describe, profoundly troubling phenomena in human beings. Another group of discussions on the topic of system-A and system-B is to be found in anthropology. In this regard, the generation of anthropologists who began work about 1880 — Boas, Malinowski, Benedict, Mead, Bateson — made efforts to give various small

4   Statistics from *Mental Health: A Report of the Surgeon General*, online, 2008.
5   Figures from Niall Ferguson, *The War of the World* (London 2006).

societies — be it in Samoa, or the Cameroun, or the Mongolian Steppes — their freedom to live in their own chosen "way" and to have protection for their cultural individuality.

Similar studies have arisen in political science. In the mid-20th century, the political theorist Theodor Adorno took the formation and maintenance of values seriously, and began describing and analyzing the aspects of society which must be studied and evaluated, thus ultimately leading to an active search for social change. Adorno was famous for what became known as critical social theory: namely, that one cannot merely observe without judging, so that evaluation then became a necessary part of observed truth.[6] In Adorno's work, and in that of his colleagues, under this impetus, a new view of ethics came into being. After the Third Reich had gone so far into the horrific during the Second World War, the necessity of arriving at a view of truth which would help to generate benign social conditions in society could no longer be avoided. Adorno's work may be regarded as one of the foundation points of the emerging recognition of a modern system-A.

All these innovations originated from underlying observations of system-B as dangerous and harmful. The damaging consequences of system-B were observed by sociologists like David Riesman and Herbert Gans who pioneered ways of observing system-B and its problems from a sociological point of view.[7] Many disciplines like psychology, ecology, medicine, engineering, zoology, botany, are now beginning to direct attention to the work of discerning how and why the positives of system-A are necessary to life, and how the negatives of system-B can be identified and overcome.

As architects, we try to make things. Making is essentially a positive activity. So, when I began to encounter these huge and very problematic social issues, I did not want to dwell on the negative.

---

6   Stanford Encyclopedia of Philosophy, *Theodor W. Adorno*, by Lambert Zuidervaart, special attention to the section entitled *Ethics and Metaphysics after Auschwitz*, 2003.
7   David Riesman, *The Lonely Crowd* (1950); Herbert Gans, *The Urban Villagers* (1962).

But it was impossible not to observe negative phenomena, even though I rarely spoke or wrote about them. I gradually began to understand what was wrong with architecture, . . . learned that buildings and neighborhoods had suffered at the hands of clever 20th-century horror-mongers, much as society itself had done. I do not blame architects exclusively for this, but also those bigger players, the sources of investment, government restrictions, industrial production, and an overarching sordid approach to money; clever manipulators of wealth and public opinion who prize the game of making money over the health of society, so that simple qualities of the environment were destroyed.

Architects did play a role, of course, in the deterioration we all felt. Many were seduced by these fiscal and political changes. They pandered to the people who had the money. Inevitably, then, good qualities in buildings and in neighborhoods, in streets and parks, became scarcer and scarcer.

We builders have suffered immensely from this loss. Against our better judgment, we have been contributing to the wasteland, even when we do our best. Starting in the 1950s and 1960s, I began trying to work out what attitude to our environment might help to make the world alright, what kind of simplicity would take us in that positive direction, not the other. Simplicity of concept, simplicity of means. I have devoted my life to trying to find ways of rescuing architecture and society, but especially the small things in every circumstance which can bring a smile to people's faces, without giving in to the depredations of self-important rascals. I have tried to find out how things can be done in a simple and straightforward fashion, so that it may be worth calling myself ar-chitect, and might help to make a world fit for others, too, who also want to call themselves builders or makers, not always architects.

The gradual, damaging process which crept up on us during the last 150 years, and caused the emptiness we feel — this loss that al-most all of us experience in some degree, hinges on fragmentation. We lie in fragments. Our social order lies in fragments. The physical order of our lands and towns lies still more horribly in fragments.

You might say that the one is not more horrible than the other. But what is true, in any case, is that the fragmentation of our emotions and personality is relatively invisible, while the fragmentation of our streets and cities, and of our urban and suburban landscape, is violently visible all around us. It is as if the physical fragments we see all around us, display the fragments in our segmented, empty, and fragmented inner lives.

> *The river's tent is broken: the last fingers of leaf*
> *Clutch and sink into the wet bank. The wind*
> *Crosses the brown land, unheard. . . .*[8]

One of the main purposes of this book is to demonstrate that the *physical-ecological* and the *mental-emotional-social* cannot be separated. They can only be healed together. That means, effectively, that we can make ourselves whole, only when we make our lands, and towns and villages, and our environment whole as well.

The project described in this book is perhaps one of the first times in modern history that a comprehensive and coherent process for creating real community has been described and activated, and has begun to show success.[9] Our results were achieved by using the human relations that existed, and the simple goals which our communities aspired to. To create and establish a geometry of life — a geometry that supports living, growing, and achieving, as well as honoring our community and the ecology in which it resides. The acts of building in this manner provides countless opportunities to initiate repair. It provides a model through which we can directly influence the wasteland — and then, the basis for the actions which will gradually *replace* the wasteland.

---

8   T.S. Eliot, *The Waste Land*, lines 173-175.
9   An early example of such a venture was the famous Peckham Experiment, a community health center built in 1930 and run until 1950. Pearse, I. H., and Crocker, L. H., *The Peckham Experiment.* (London: Allen and Unwin, 1943) and http://en.wikipedia.org/wiki/The_Peckham_Experiment.

6

WHOLENESS AND
THE WHOLE

If each of us is to engage in the very personal journey
toward wholeness, and thereby heal our communities (the
only way a community can be healed at all), we must keep
wholeness at the forefront of our thinking and our activities.

We seek to create coherence in the physical realm, the
ecological realm, the emotional realm, the spiritual realm;
and perhaps, above all, in the realm of art — that spiritual
realm of art and of creation, where
we are able to find unity.

How do we make intellectual sense of the enigmatic word "wholeness," which is the opposite of wasteland? It promises so much,
yet falls so far short in precise scientific meaning, that one almost
throws up one's hands. Even so, of the words I know, it is the word
which best describes that ideal world, that system-A, that core of
society's production which stands in opposition to system-B.

Years ago, in *The Timeless Way of Building*, I introduced another phrase, "the quality without a name." That was very helpful
and inspiring.[1] But it evaporates too easily in the mind to guide
practical effort.

Wholeness speaks of the oneness of all things. It suggests a
vast understanding of things in their entirety. It speaks to us, encouraging us to try and see things in their unity, perhaps for those
of us who accept such a formulation even in their unity with God;
certainly in their ecological health (potentially a scientific concept,
but one that has not yet been clearly defined); and certainly in

---

1   *The Timeless Way of Building* (New York: Oxford University Press, 1979), especially chapter 2.

some sort of social communication and coherence. The relative beauty of different buildings — now also beginning to be accepted as an objective concept — also speaks indirectly of wholeness.[2] How can we tackle the task of making good sense of this intuition of unity and wholeness?

First, wholeness is a structure, and can be understood as such. This means that when we try to find the wholeness of a particular thing or place, we can point a finger at that structure, and so make it possible to share our idea of what the wholeness is.[3]

Second, the thing we call wholeness — the feeling or the intuition, of what the wholeness is — *always extends beyond the thing in question*. If we speak of the wholeness of a person, we may be confident that this wholeness is felt through that person's connection with the world. It is not possible to be whole by being isolated from all that surrounds you.[4]

Third, there is also the fact that somehow, any wholeness we want to point to, or think about, seems to elude comprehension. That is why I sometimes call it "wholeness, the intangible." The intangible comes from the fact that every thing that has, or maintains wholeness, is always unique. This means that words and concepts almost always fail to encompass it perfectly; only the wholeness itself can point to what it is.

Fourth, there is, too, the presence of unity. What we refer to as wholeness, is a quality of being one, being glued-together, interlaced, being *unified*. It is, also, somehow at peace. Even if it is a raging storm at sea where we experience wholeness, somehow, in some sense and some fashion, it is peaceful, because it is exactly what it is, and nothing else.

Fifth, each wholeness contains and is composed of myriad

---

2   Roger Scruton, *Beauty* (New York: Oxford University Press, 2009) has recently published a book which uncompromisingly asserts the objective nature of beauty, and manages powerfully to make his case.

3   See Book 1 of *The Nature of Order, The Phenomenon of Life*. Detailed definitions of the structure of wholeness are sketched in chapters 1-6.

4   Ibid. The extension of the wholeness beyond the immediate thing, is partially captured by some of the fifteen properties in chapters 5 and 6, especially the property of not-separateness.

other wholes.[5] This last is something that is describable. There are specific geometric qualities and properties that come into play, These tell us what kinds of relationships between smaller wholenesses and the larger ones, are doing the hard work. They are always there, and must be there, in order to create the wholeness of the larger thing.[6]

Sixth and finally, the idea of wholeness encompasses the idea of *healing*. When something is whole, we consider it healed. If we wish to heal something, we seek to make it whole. The middle-English word *hale*, lying as it does halfway between whole and heal, gives us a sense of this connection. Healing is making whole; that which is healed has a stronger wholeness than that which is not healed.

Wholeness can only be understood in the act of grasping it and moving into it, creating it and experiencing it. Much as we might like to have a crisp definition, it simply is not possible. We can reach understanding of wholeness only when we see the objective wholeness in the thing or place, and simultaneously experience the growth of wholeness in ourselves. These two must go together. That is the nature of the phenomenon.

This definition of wholeness, then, can be extended into a procedural definition: that is, a general specification for a process that is capable of increasing wholeness in a domain, and particularly in the physical domain where something, some place, some part of the world is being conceived, or built, or repaired.

―――――

Let me suggest how the nurture and creation of wholeness, with all its human and ecological benefits, may be introduced into

―――――

5 The vision of these endless wholes and beings is most magnificently expressed in *The Avatamsaka Sutra* (The Flower Ornament Sutra), one of the great, possibly the greatest, of the Vedic scriptures. It is an immense book, more than 1600 pages long. Even if you only have stamina to read a few pages, I most strongly recommend it. It is a visionary platform to stand on, and will help you understand *this* book. The endless hierarchy of levels, and wholes within wholes within wholes is captured in chapter 5, especially the property of levels of scale. (It is also discussed in Book 4 of *The Nature of Order*, *The Luminous Ground*, especially in chapter 4, where discussion of multiple beings in a given wholeness is rather detailed.) Edited and translated by Thomas Cleary, published by Shambala, 1994.
6 The wholeness is dependent on the fifteen properties, see chapter 22.

the unyielding, massive, stiff, resistant clay of modern commercial architecture, planning, and construction. When a group of people make their environment for themselves, this has enormous, healing consequences. In the act, they bring forth the real content of their own existence: this has a huge transforming effect on their consciousness.

The nature of this process is not yet well understood. But if people are "given" an environment built by others, whether out of commercial interest, or from patronizing motives that attempt to do good, then it effectively means that the environment is getting built for quite different motives. And this in turn means that the transforming, healing process does not take place, people remain as ciphers in society, their consciousness is not awakened, and their lives are stunted, less able to bloom.

The opportunity to blossom is a necessary part of a person's awakening. But in the modern world, this process of awakening cannot easily happen of its own accord. Circumstances are too complicated. The processes which might allow it to happen, and which can support it and sustain it, must first be put in place. This is precisely the meaning of system-A, as we experienced it ourselves during the making of the Eishin Campus, and as we now describe it in this book. It is the procedural environment of processes which allows self-awareness to arise, and freedom to exist. And this in turn then creates great riches, beauties of an ordinary, humble kind, a world in which the maker and the made coincide and coalesce.

This book describes how the life of a community, and the lives of individuals in that community, may interact both with the structure of what lies in their hearts, and with the way that stones and trees and buildings, too, are shaped to be in harmony with that structure in their hearts. The whole community becomes an emotional-ecological system that maintains itself, intensifies its own life, and can enhance the lives of individuals.

One of the most important forms of life for us is the life of cities, towns and villages — the social, physical, and ecological life of our communities. All of us citizens have a tacit obligation to enhance the life in our communities. The way that works, in its manifold aspects, is yet again through the activity that we call system-A.

But it is difficult to bring it off, because in today's society the creation of cities and towns has been given over to mercenaries (stating it politely), who choose to make communities into things, buildings into objects, and people into pawns of financial and political forces that they cannot even see. That is the destructive activity that hides in system-B. We believe that these attributes of system-B in large part exist unintentionally. It is nevertheless a hugely destructive activity that undermines and destroys the healing action of system-A.

In spite of that, because these issues have not been brought adequately before the public, the process and mentality of system-B has, currently been accepted — as a matter of fashion, especially among architects — and by others, as normal and commonplace. We have written this book to counteract that accepted norm.

The book tells of a necessary struggle against certain forces which pervade society and which unwittingly make the processes of system-A almost impossible to reach. It describes a new kind of process that makes it possible to support just precisely those activities which are capable of making true community occur, and it describes the battle, which must inevitably follow. It is always wholeness that is at stake. Wholeness cannot be reached within a society where system-B pervades. It can be reached only in a society where in some measure, at least, system-A pervades. That is why a battle came about, and had to be fought — to allow wholeness to emerge and to give it room to breathe.

From 1981 to 1987, beginning with the creation of a pattern language in which the community played a major creative part, we and our colleagues worked to establish the life-giving system-A in one college campus, where we fought to protect and make living the social groups and stones and paths and trees and buildings. This was the basis on which it became possible to establish a community in which people could live their lives well, and could then together sustain the fragile structure that had been started in the stones and paths and trees.

OVERLAPPING, INTERWOVEN, KNITTED, NESTED, FLOWING ENTITIES AND CENTERS THAT ARE SLOWLY STITCHED TOGETHER

Let us discuss some spatial images, to show how wholeness comes about *physically*. We have explained that wholeness, in the large, is created by many smaller wholes, at a wide variety of identifiable scales. Each of these smaller wholes is, in a manner of speaking, stitched to other wholes. If the wholes are of different size, then we may say that the smaller one will be nested in the larger one, or woven into a larger strand. The overlapping, smaller wholes form a nearly flexible, connected and coherent tapestry, much as a patchwork of bits and pieces form a quilt. If each patch is attached to at least two other patches, the quilt then has a flexible but coherent quality, since the individual wholes cannot spin or move too freely. They remain coherent and whole — even when they are moving. A similar kind of quilt or tapestry is formed by rings that are interlocked, and because of their spatial interlocking, make the tapestry entire, even when it remains flexible.

In the example of the church on the right-hand page opposite, this is a tapestry of space and stone. These very simple images of structure, do give us some idea of the way that wholeness is made of smaller centers and larger centers, linked together, thus forming a tough but resilient tapestry of space and stone. Individual wholes, of whatever size, may all be characterized as "centers." For example, the simplest kind of centers are made "center-like" by their geometry: An archetypal church is typically formed by six squares (nave, two transepts, choir, tower, chancel). The arrangement of these squares (themselves already centers), creates a striking center, of greater power, indeed of mighty power, by the configuration which appears in the larger whole. If you look carefully at the different entities in the plan drawing, on page 93, you see how centers appear, again and again, large, sometimes larger still, medium sized, small, often also showing many, many very tiny centers, helping to give the church its presence as an overall center of real power.

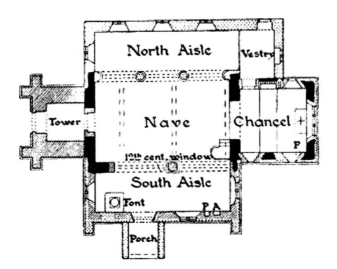

Plan of Cocking church, West Sussex.

Cocking church, seen from the south.
The view of the church is the same as the orientation of the plan. The tower is on the left end of the church; the massive roof starts high, over the nave, and comes sweeping down toward the porch.

Interestingly, this power is felt, and is visible, from the careful assembly and growth of low-key, small objects like the plain gate in the flint wall, and the memorial cross nearby, engraved with the names of soldiers who died in the Great War.

The centers are piled on, slowly, one by one, very carefully placed. And they are very humble, not ostentatious. But the overall fact is that real presence, real power, is created by these humble artefacts and structures. What we refer to as the stitching together of smaller wholes, creates the quality and depth of such a place.

NATURE'S WHOLENESS

The wholeness that is accomplished in the world, occurs most vividly, throughout nature. A waterfall, a forest, an ocean beach — each teeming with millions of centers ranging from the tiny to the very large, all intricately interwoven and shimmering with life. But of all the most complex wholes in nature, one of most deeply complex wholes that comes to mind as an example, is a human being. Consider a human hand. There are smaller wholes (fingers), and even smaller jointed groups of wholes (knuckles), and inside, the cells, organelles, and molecules. But if we ask wherein the wholeness of a human hand actually lies, we might point even more readily to the extended tendons, and the extended branching systems of nerves which give the hand its capacity to grasp, hold, write, draw, and cook, taking their direction from the brain.

The hand is remarkable, too, because it can take so many spatial positions, each with its special purpose. It is specifically the wholeness of your hand, and its wider linkage to your body as a whole, that illustrates what wholeness means in the case of the hand, and what this wholeness *does*.

HOW WHOLENESS COMES INTO BEING

The largest driving force in the whole-making and wholeness-enhancing process is the step-by-step process which demands that at each step the configuration be made more coherent — as far as possible. Repeating this process will gradually lead to a condition

A baby gerbil, held in a person's hand. A human hand can do almost anything, and reshape itself to millions of tasks, configurations, and unfamiliar situations.

where the whole is not only geometrically coherent — but also emotionally coherent. It is this coherence of feeling and function that holds everything together.

Unless this is the process being followed, there is almost no hope that a built place will sustain people emotionally, and little hope, either, that the place will create feeling in people's hearts.

For emphasis, we would like to repeat the reference to the *Avatamsaka Sutra*. We cannot ever claim to have achieved what that book describes. However, the ideal embodied in the *Sutra* comes perhaps closest to what wholeness means and what "the whole" really means. The *Sutra* does not give a definition of wholeness that would satisfy a Western scientist. However, it does convey a compelling vision of the way that thousands and millions of wholes are nested in each other, interlocked, and interwoven. As a vision and as a beacon, it is unforgettable.

And it is, above all, a practical way of working which gets results. The knittedness is not merely a metaphor. It is a practical way of understanding how matter and space can be interwoven, can be interlocked. We find ourselves thinking of this knitting process, which focuses our attention on the ways we can knit, and thread, and interlock, so that the actual material fabric of a town and its buildings is slowly stitched together.

The nature of wholeness is very difficult to grasp, in practical and material terms, but it is not mysterious. Creating wholeness is a practical matter, which comes about only when small wholes are twisted and threaded into one another. Buildings and environments need to be made this way. Difficult as it is, it is above all practical, and arises from having the right understanding of the way that wholeness works geometrically.

———

During the construction of the Eishin Campus, this repeating process led ultimately to the symbiosis of the human community and its environment. The constructive interaction of the people and the buildings took hold. As a result, in some measure, we may say that we did succeed in creating life. What we had to do to make it happen, is the story told in parts two and three.

PART TWO

RUMBLINGS OF A
COMING BATTLE

1982-1983

CHAPTERS 7-12

PART TWO

Hosoi and I began by looking for a new way of thinking, about the people, about the community, about high school and college education, about the buildings, and about the land.

Part Two of our book demonstrates a way of conceiving a new community, a new way of building, and a new way of living — altogether a momentous undertaking.

1982. One of the many occasions when Hosoi and Chris went together to study the site.

7 HOSOI'S DREAM

As Hosoi expressed it in his own words,
"All we wanted was just to find out the normal way through
which ordinary school buildings are built in the most sensible
and ordinary fashion."

Hosoi's dream for the future of education in Japan stood
in sharp contrast to the then-prevailing approach to 20th-
century education and architecture — system-B.

Indeed, system-B altogether undermines the
possibility of doing things that people have dreams about —
even today. That is why Hosoi came to visit me in 1981.

To begin telling the story of the conception, design, planning, and construction, let us now go back to the way Hosoi began his work in 1981. It stemmed — all of it — from his aims and visions, both as an educator and as a man who wanted to change Japanese society's view of education, and as someone who knew ahead of time that the buildings that would be built had to have new qualities.

This was Hosoi's dream. At root, he had a burning conviction that the people who lived and worked in the school would put all their knowledge — individual knowledge about myriad circumstances — into the design process. He and his colleagues, the faculty, also wanted the

Hisae Hosoi, Managing Director of the Campus, on the way
to his office in the morning. This was one of the first campus
buildings to be built and used.

school to provide a *culture*: a human, social, and emotional context in which learning could take place. And when it came to the college students, Hosoi believed firmly in a humanistic education along the lines of John Dewey's thought and writing. That is, an education based on familiarity with the great literature of the last 2500 years.

There was a further part to his dream, which appeared only gradually, as we learned to work together. He believed in craftsmen. He had in his mind a rough conception that was essentially his own version of what we are calling system-A. He believed in this with a passion, and was ready to back it to the hilt.

In order for system-A — real life, that is — to exist in any project, Hosoi felt it to be essential that the clients (the people controlling the project) have a real vision of life in buildings as a possibility, and also have a clear understanding of the difference between system-A and system-B.

In our era, system-A can only exist in a conscious way, as a deliberate and intentional effort, deliberately set in opposition to system-B. Sadly, you cannot succeed in getting life in buildings if you believe that it can be done in system-B. You also cannot succeed in getting life, if the client wants life, knows it cannot be achieved in system-B, but still tells you to do it within system-B, because he doesn't have the courage to face system-B and make it change. This need for courage is a real requirement. It is absolutely necessary as a practical matter in the world we live in today, because key obstacles must be overcome to make system-A succeed.

Thus, a project can only succeed in getting life if the client has the courage, and the wisdom, to understand that system-A must be injected into the prevailing system we now have, and is willing to face the necessary battle, and ready to absorb the emotional cost in hours of effort, sleepless nights, struggle, and heartbreak.

The particular events which took place in Tokyo and are recorded here, begin, as this suggests, with a very unusual client, a man of infinite patience, a quiet soul, and a steely determination to succeed. And he is, and has always been, unfailingly polite. This project would not have happened without him. And probably, such a project could not succeed in any place without another person of the caliber of a Hosoi.

As managing director of the Eishin school — a private high school in Musashino-shi, toward the west of Tokyo — Hosoi had been given the task of developing an entirely new campus for the school — a campus which was to combine the existing function of the Eishin high school together with a new college yet to be created on a single campus, both institutions on one campus.

Complicated educational questions were raised by the high-school-university combination in Japanese law. In addition, because of the school's fundamental policy of "involvement" of teachers and students in decision-making, and because of his own beliefs about the inhumane nature of late-20th century society, Hosoi had an instinct, I believe, that these questions would not get answered unless the space and spatial organization of the campus were subtly fashioned to cope with this complexity. This required an unusual kind of architect. As a result, around 1980 Hosoi began trying to find an architect who would work *with* the school's teachers and students in the process of creating the design. He had just this one fundamental request: that the architect must be willing to work *with* the users and inhabitants in the creation of the new campus.

He first spent about a year trying to find such an architect in Japan. The Japanese architects' response to his request was simple and surprising. He interviewed many Japanese architects. All of them *just refused*.

Hosoi explained that he was willing to pay extra for this service, since he recognized that some time and trouble might be involved. "No," he was told by the directors of Yasui Architectural Company (one of the largest design companies in Japan), ". . . just give us the space requirements and leave us alone to create the design for you. We cannot cooperate in your request to work together with the teachers in the creation of the design."

This was the battle cry which finally exhausted Hosoi's patience, and launched his determination to succeed in some other way.

TRUE DESIGN BY USERS AND INHABITANTS

It should be said that the extraordinary arrogance of the Japanese architects' response to Hosoi's request was unusual in its honesty. In the United States or England in 1981, many professional architects would have accepted his request — with their lips.

Superficially they would have agreed to and undertaken a series of meetings in which the teachers' requirements were noted, taken into account, and then gradually incorporated into the design. However, the users' true desires would, in all probability, still not have been allowed to help much in the creation of the design. Rather, the users would typically have been passive observers, allowed to state their requests, but without creative influence on the design.

Yasui, though gross in their arrogance, and unusual in their honesty, not only reflected the attitude of most Japanese architects in the last decades of the 20th century, but also reflected the underlying reality of attitude which was at that time prevalent among professional architects throughout the world.

Confronted by this fact, Hosoi began a lengthy search, lasting more than a year, looking for a group of architects who would *genuinely* — not with lip service but with sincerity — ***desire*** the involvement of the teachers and students in the creation of the school's design. At some point in his search, Hosoi came across *The Oregon Experiment* — one of the earliest books in the Center for Environmental Structure series, and one which deals with a novel planning process in which students and professors take part, year by year, in the ongoing development of the campus.[1]

As a result of reading the book, Hosoi wrote from Tokyo to ask if he could meet me. Unfortunately, I was lying in bed with a back injury, unable to move, so my wife wrote to let him know that I was confined to bed and would prefer to wait. To my great surprise, in spite of my wife's letter, four or five days later he telephoned, from San Francisco airport, not Japan, and asked if

---

1   Christopher Alexander, Murray Silverstein, Shlomo Angel, Denny Abrams, Sara Ishikawa, *The Oregon Experiment* (New York: Oxford University Press, 1975).

he might be able to see me in my bedroom. I was startled and charmed by his gentle persistence and invited him to come. I was to learn more of his gentle persistence, in the years that followed.

Hosoi came, and for two days sat by my bed, telling me about his dreams for his project, his feelings about necessary changes in society and architecture, and — altogether — about his attitude. We hit it off, had a wonderful time, and talked and talked and talked and talked.

Towards the end of the two days, he asked me if I would be willing to design the site plan and outline of the buildings, and then hand these sketches to Yasui Design Company to complete the details. When I heard this, indeed the very moment I heard this, I realized that we were now about to plunge, headlong, into a subtle but dramatic issue that had to do with the subterranean battle between system-A and system-B. Hosoi, listening to me, was in his mind simply being practical. How would we get the project built in practice? How would we make up for the fact that I did not speak Japanese? and so on. But I knew something that Hosoi did perhaps not fully appreciate, namely that the kind of buildings Hosoi had let me catch a glimpse of in his poetic verbal descriptions, the kind of buildings he *wanted*, were in a mental universe far, far from Yasui.

I knew this because I could surmise what Yasui stood for. From Yasui's categorical unwillingness to agree to do user-design, I knew that they would be utterly incapable of making the kinds of buildings that Hosoi wanted and was dreaming about. I knew this in my belly, in my soul, because I had grasped the essence of what Hosoi was hoping for, and I knew, intimately, what would be required. It would require a process in which buildings could come into being from the act of making them; something that could not, ever, be captured by any mechanically executed set of working drawings.

So I was shaken when I heard Hosoi's request, and I knew that I must tell him the truth, exactly as it was. I told him his plan was very unlikely to work — that the work with the users would indeed help a great deal — but the actual physical material and substance of the buildings would determine the final feeling completely. It would be useless to get the preliminary design from us, then go on to complete the buildings with Yasui. To do what Hosoi had in mind, we would have to work in system-A. But Yasui would almost certainly be working in system-B. It was therefore virtually inevitable that there would be a profound clash, because from the two viewpoints of system-A and system-B, our two companies would see the world quite differently. Between us, every single fact, line, instruction, and problem, would be interpreted quite differently.

The great beauty of Hosoi, and his immeasurable contribution to this battle, was that though not so experienced in the world of architecture, he himself had a very clear picture of the battle between system-A and system-B, in its larger social meaning. During the several years that followed, each time he heard that there was a potential conflict between A and B on the project, he unfailingly (and when possible, immediately) did his best to take whatever steps were necessary to support and implement system-A.

So, after hearing my explanation, he immediately withdrew his idea that Yasui might carry out the details of construction. He proposed instead that Yasui could do it under our direction.

Privately, I was almost certain this wouldn't work either. But it was too early in our relationship for me to confront Hosoi with a second refusal so quickly. Instead, I said that I would agree if Yasui would accept, in writing, the idea that they were going to work for us, under my direction. I felt almost certain that they would refuse, and in a sense I hoped they would, since I knew that if we were tied together in such an unholy union, the conflict of the two world-pictures would cause endless trouble — and thus ultimately lead to failure.

In any case, to my great relief, Hosoi wrote to me a few days later from Japan, saying that Yasui had refused. We then made plans for the Center for Environmental Structure to do the architectural design for the project in full, and Hosoi made arrangements for me to come to Japan to negotiate the contract.

———

During the times we gradually got to know each other, I learned things, which may make it easier for the reader to understand the compelling vision Hosoi had, the earnest — not fanatical, but passionate — determination to change the state of Japanese society, and to change a little bit, the direction the world was taking altogether.

He told me stories about his life on the barricades during the student riots of the late 1960s.

He had a passionate, yet gentle way, of righting wrongs, small wrongs that occurred between people. If a misunderstanding occurred, created some discomfort, or if there was even a momentary hiatus in a human process, he would go to almost any lengths to sort it out. He would sit with the person or people who seemed to be entangled in some way, until the situation solved itself.

He also had a favorite expression that he used whenever troubles or difficulty showed up, "Let's go whistling through the dark . . . let's go whistling under any circumstance." He believed that a happy demeanor, and a tune on your lips, could chase away any demons in the dark, and keep things stable in the project. And he encouraged me to join him in this attitude, and indeed, when times got tough, we used to whistle together, as a joke, to fight troubles away. He always assumed that everything was for the best, and that events which at first seemed dire, in fact only needed a little light shone on them, and some gradual talking together.

In extreme cases, he even flew from Japan to California, staying only one night to talk something through that he felt might be going off the rails. In other cases, he and I would move around Tokyo coffee shops, sometimes all day long, moving every two hours or so to another one for what he called "a change of scenery." All this time was spent talking through the human details, discussing them, until we saw what might be the problem. It was a fascinating way of working in human society, and tremendously effective. I learned an enormous amount from him. He cared about everyone, and he was very careful.

He in turn, had learned a great part of his attitude to education from Keizo Sakaida, Chairman of the Eishin Board at the time the school contracted with CES. Mr. Sakaida was the source and origin, I think, of many of Hosoi's ways of thinking and working.

Hosoi is a very dear man, and within a few months of the start, we became the closest of friends. His dream was deeply inspiring to me, and to many of his colleagues with whom he worked. But it became clear that the dream would be challenged in many ways before it took shape in the campus that we built.

ANOTHER SEARCH FOR A JAPANESE REPRESENTATIVE

There still seemed to be a necessity for us to have *some* Japanese architect working for us as an anchor in Japan. So I promised to begin looking for someone. Hosoi did the same. However, although we did not know it then, the simple task of getting a Japanese architect to work as the executive architect for the Eishin project was to become a battle in itself.

This battle had nothing to do with any conflict between cultures, nor with any conflict between the American way and Japanese way. It was a problem which would have existed just as strongly, if we had needed to find an American architect, to act as the executive architect for the project. The essence of the issue was this: What needed to be done in system-A could not be understood by *any* architect who was working in system-B, no matter what part of the world he or she came from. Perhaps 97% of the world's architects, at that time, in the last decades of the 20th century were still working in system-B. So the task of finding a "friendly" architect was as difficult, and as inevitably headed for battle, as the basic conflict between system-A and system-B itself.

Shortly before my first visit to Japan and the Eishin site, Hosoi wrote me a letter explaining the arrangements he had made to welcome me, and to get the project going. In his letter, he also introduced the architect Masamitsu Nagashima and his team, whom I was supposed to meet and work with. However, Hosoi still did not fully understand that there could be a big problem in trying to create cooperation between architects working in system-A and architects working in system-B. Although he was dimly aware of the general rift between A and B (and he was certainly aware of it as a general division between two modes of action in society), he had not yet understood clearly how massively this rift was embodied, at that time, in the practice of architecture. We shall see in the next few pages (110-117) how deeply system-A and system-B are irreconcilably opposed.

Mr. Nagashima was at the airport to meet me, with Hosoi. Almost from the first few minutes, he created a slightly strange atmosphere, as if he intended to control the project forcefully, but without saying so. It is possible that this was a natural expression of his hope to be helpful and involved in the work. However, in my eyes his behavior became the first visible manifestation of a battleground between system-A and system-B.

He told me that he had arranged an itinerary for me. It included, very early, a visit to a recently built project of his — a school — together with visits to several other existing high schools in the Tokyo area. He had also prepared a chart outlining our work in the first few months. The format of this chart was unsuitable, since he could have no way of knowing how I intended to organize the project.

I did appreciate his kindness in showing me his own recently built school. It was a pleasant building, of a higher quality than other schools being built in different countries at that time. However, I did not understand the purpose of his proposed visits to other existing schools. He took it for granted that I would want to visit them, and that it was *necessary* for me to visit them. I tried to let him know that there would be virtually nothing to learn from visiting them. He could not understand me, and insisted on our schedule. I had to refuse very strongly, when I discovered his inability to understand the problem.

I told him that I wished to spend the first few days having some serious and deep talks with faculty members, about their hopes, dreams, and visions of the school, and that I also wanted to spend many hours by myself sitting on the site. I explained to him that these two things — especially the talks with teachers — were the only two things I wanted to do, and that they would tell me a hundred times more than all the visits to the all the existing high schools in Tokyo. He did not want to believe this or could not understand it.

After a while, I became mildly offended by his attitude. He did not seem to grasp that it was not only true that the architecture of existing schools would *not* help me, but that it would be a waste of time, because it would create a stale and deadening state of mind in all of us, which would — in the end — give little or nothing to the project.

Perhaps even more important, he failed to grasp, intuitively, that the process of becoming friends with the teachers, and really understanding their hopes and dreams, was of fundamental importance. This blindness, similar in content to other architects' arrogant refusal to allow participation by teachers, which Hosoi had already met in Yasui, troubled me, and made me very cautious about further contact with Nagashima.

About a day later, he did a very strange thing. Hosoi had asked that I explain to him, and to some other teachers, how the pattern language method was going to work in practice. In the course of a formal meeting with teachers — in fact in my *very first* formal contact with them — Nagashima began arguing with me, and trying to devalue the whole purpose of this method, *in front of our clients*.

I was astonished. The fact that he, who had been clearly designated as my assistant, would take such a step (in *Japan* of all places, where formal hierarchy is so clearly defined and understood) revealed a level of impoliteness in his behavior which had many implications. Of course, he gave lip service to his appreciation of the work that we were doing. Yet, at the same time, from the very first day, he began undermining its real meaning.

This is when the battle between system-A and system-B really had its second, concrete confrontation. Mr. Nagashima — a well-established member of the architectural hierarchy of system-B in Japan — directly confronted and tried to wipe away system-A, even though he had been invited to work for me by the client. The underground clash between A and B was so powerful that it dominated his behavior, and made him do things which — by normal standards of politeness, and by Japanese etiquette — were absolutely unacceptable.

I want to make it clear that this comment does not imply disrespect toward Mr. Nagashima. Mr. Nagashima is an honorable person, and by the standards of 1980 an excellent architect. I do not feel now, and did not feel then, that he was intentionally impolite, or intentionally aggressive. He was honorably and conscientiously carrying out his task, *as a careful and competent architect working within system-B*. Any sense in which he was guilty of a "bad" action was surely unconscious, and not intended. It was caused only by his social milieu, and by his desire to act correctly. The trouble is that he was acting *correctly according to the canons of system-B*. From the point of view of system-A, his behavior was inappropriate and antagonistic. And indeed it was. It was *objectively* antagonistic. Further, and to me more worrying, was the fact that he was not interested in Hosoi's dream; Hosoi had given him some definition of his desires, but somehow they did not register with him. Yet even then, I believe that there was no evil intent in it. It was simply an unintended battle between two utterly different views of the world, and between two utterly irreconcilable attitudes toward society.

I am pretty sure that even to this day, he would not be aware of the true meaning of his own behavior during that week. Probably he recognizes that he acted strangely, since that fact was finally pointed out to him, both by me and by Hosoi, and explained in detail. But I do not believe that he knew then, or knows now, that his behavior was an outward expression of the deep-lying war between these two systems, A and B. In my view, he acted unconsciously as a soldier of system-B, and was unable to grasp the nature of system-A, as soon as he felt that system-B was being threatened.

Finally — and with considerable discomfort — I had to tell Hosoi that I felt the situation with Mr. Nagashima was becoming impossible. I knew, after these experiences, that if Nagashima continued to work for us, he would be fighting against us, perhaps without meaning to, *every* day of the project. The situation was therefore impossible. Hosoi understood me at once, and very clearly. I asked him how far he wanted me to go, and he told me that he wanted me to go to whatever lengths were needed to make system-A become practical. I asked him what he would feel if I needed to reject Mr. Nagashima as my assistant. Hosoi said that he would understand completely, and had only one request: he asked me to be kind and polite in making the dismissal.

So, with sadness, I had to explain to Mr. Nagashima that he would not be needed on the project. He could not believe it. It took three or four days to convince him that it was true. He tried and tried to persuade me, and Hosoi too, that he would be able to work for us. I knew that he would not be able to, and there was nothing further to say.

Without any special words, Hosoi had grasped the whole situation profoundly. My level of respect for him increased, and my affection grew. I began to recognize that our friendship was already growing deep, and touched the roots of his dream, and mine.

A few days later, Hosoi and I signed a contract for the Center for Environmental Structure to take sole responsibility for the project, and we began our work.

HOSOI'S PRESS CONFERENCE

As we have said earlier, Hosoi's name for system-A was "the ordinary way." In his very first press conference about the Eishin project (in May 1982, the night of the signing of the contract), we had dinner with several members of the press in Tokyo. After the dinner, Hosoi then quite formally explained the meaning of the project in his mind, and his idea of replacing the present, contorted, way of making buildings and towns with something new that he referred to as "the ordinary way." The following is the text of Hosoi's statement to some of the major newspapers of Japan.

"Since I dropped one important fact so far, I would like to make an additional comment, which may be extremely subtle to you, though. The unexpected part about starting this project was the response of the people I met, who showed a very strange feeling about my idea of employing Mr. Alexander for this project. People I met in chorus told me and showed a strange feeling about my act as if we are doing an unusual behavior, which is totally beyond my comprehension.

"Probably, if we only wanted User Participation we might have been able to get some other people who could use the method of User Participation in the design. However, after discussion with Chris, he explained to me that pattern language is one aspect of people's involvement and its realization is rooted in the deeper level of culture. This was the more confirming point from which we were convinced to go ahead with him. In terms of this point, when reconsidering how to approach Mr. Alexander, all we wanted was just to find out the normal way through which ordinary school buildings are built in the most ordinary way.

"I repeatedly told Mr. Alexander about the necessity of all 84 faculty members' involvement. However, it was too natural a thing to ask for. It may not be necessary for me to repeat it so many times; but this request was ignored so often by architects that I could not help mentioning it again and again. I really did not know the fact that such repetition is not necessary.

"I heard a very interesting story from him, which probably would be an English proverb, which says 'Buying a pig in a sack.' We are the customers who open up the sack before buying, so that we can check what kind of pig is in it. Probably the sellers of bad pigs will always try to persuade customers to buy pigs in the sack. But we are *determined not to* buy a pig in the sack until we are allowed to see the pig.

"In addition, User Participation is so normal a thing that we do not have to take the trouble to argue about it further. To do an ordinary thing in an ordinary way leads and necessitates us to go and ask Mr. Alexander for help. It is neither the result of theoretical conception we sought, nor some intentional challenge to do some special things in particular procedure. The most ordinary thing to do in the most ordinary way has eventually resulted in this attempt. Please understand this point. Of course, to get public attention is not too bad for our school since it is a private school, but this is definitely not our main purpose.

"I would like to mention here one thing I was really happy about as a client. It goes like this. Since we got the annex building built 4 years ago and some sports fields in Tokorozawa, through these experiences, there is the one thing those professional architects have not done at all. Two days after the day of his arrival here, Chris got some clay. I was wondering what he was intending to do. The day after he visited the site, he told us he needed a map and an aerial photo of the site. We happened to have such stuff ready from a long time before that.

"At that point, I could not make it out what was his intention. Four days later, I found a small site model was being built in his room, which well represents the subtleties of the site contours. It well represents even a house at the corner of the site by using contour lines.

"Tomorrow, he is leaving Japan with this site model. We have encountered so many people who, even though they had plenty of time, never attempted to build a site model before signing the contract. He was the first who did this. This may sound a little funny for you, and may be actually an unfortunate thing to mention. If the ordinary thing is to be done in the ordinary way, no word is necessary. All we need is the person who will just start building a site plan, and which is the most happiest experience the client may have of all. So please understand the situation and get to the point that our behavior is not merely odd but straight enough to do a straight thing. Merely just as a client, I was happy to find the best and direct response to me by his act of having built this small site model."

THE ARCHITECTURAL CONTRACT

The beginning of the project, and Hosoi's dream, cannot be fully described without mentioning Igarashi. Igarashi Takayoshi, was a close friend of Hosoi's, a brilliant lawyer, and a well-known writer in Japan. His enigmatic character and mysterious actions, and his final betrayal of his friend Hosoi, played a big role in the greatest difficulties of the project.

However, at the beginning of the project, his role was entirely positive. When I first went to Japan and proposed to Hosoi that I would only be able to do the project if I had sole responsibility — after experiencing the initial problem with Nagashima — it was only Igarashi's advice, which made it possible for such a far-reaching and radical contract to be signed.

There was a level of human trust implicit in the first contract, which was quite beyond the ordinary. Neither I, nor the Center for Environmental Structure, had (at that time) ever built such a large project. There was no reason to assume that we could do it. Many advisors had warned Hosoi that we would *not* be able to do it. And the project was a very risky one, precisely because of the confrontation between system-A and system-B — a confrontation which was clearly visible and known to all parties even at the beginning.

And in addition, here I was asking for total control of the project — a non-Japanese architect in Japan. Hosoi had every reason not to sign the contract. It was Igarashi's influence and help which made it possible. Igarashi helped to draw up the uniquely informal contract, with few details, and based mainly on trust. It was his legal mind, and his ability to confirm the legal possibility of what we were doing, that made the contract workable.

Toward the last days of my visit, there were often doubts about whether the contract could be signed at all. When the key phrase was introduced by Igarashi — the phrase which forced me not only to have sole authority, but, also, to accept sole legal responsibility for the work — my heart was in my mouth.

At first I refused. I asked him, for example, what happens if we fail to get the cooperation we need from Japanese engineers? What happens if the Japanese engineers make a mistake? How can I myself take responsibility for that? But on this point Igarashi and Hosoi were intransigent. If I wanted total control of the project, it was fine, they said, and they could see that the project might be impossible in any other way. But I *must* also accept total and sole legal responsibility for the project.

Finally I agreed.

It was a gamble, of course. But without this gamble, the whole thing was meaningless, and my life — finally given this chance — would also have become nearly meaningless. Besides, it was just true and commonsense; it did not make sense for me to wish to escape it. So I accepted, and agreed to sign the contract.

Only later did I realize the full extent of what I had taken on. That happened a few weeks later, when Igarashi told me that it was the first time in Japanese history that such a contract had been signed . . . and that he was thinking of writing a book, *just about the signing of this contract.* The importance of the contract and the full weight of my responsibility were reported in an article in *Nikkei Architecture* in June of 1982. We here record our thanks to Igarashi and recognize that without his help the project might not have started at all.

In summary, Hosoi's dream — his dream of a pure and *straight* process, and his support as client — gave us the foundation of what we were able to do. It was indispensable to the proper work of system-A.

Hosoi fully recognized the importance of his own position in the success of the project, when he wrote a paper in 1986, called *The Client: Villain of Modern Architecture*.[2] The following quotation comes from this paper.

"If the clients do not have a clear view of the issue of life in the environment, do not move towards the demands of life and living structure, and do not lead the way in moving away from fashionable images, there can be little hope for the project. Much of the bad architecture of the image-ridden magazine architecture of today is created by clients who want that image stuff, and who then support the kinds of architects who will produce it. Ultimately the lack of real life in the cities of today is caused by clients, as much as it is caused by architects, or contractors, or banks.

"The importance of the client, and the absolute need for the client's wise vision, is fundamental to every project and to its success."

---

2   Hisae Hosoi, "The Client: Villain of Modern Architecture," 1986, published in a privately circulated manuscript.

CREATING LIFE IN THE ENVIRONMENT

It is immensely hard to help people tell you what they want.
Even in the simple practical issues of a building, its
entrance, its rooms, its gardens . . . people cannot easily
formulate their vision or their desire.

Since we wanted people to have their heart's desire, we must
help them and teach them to see their own visions, drawn
out by our words and by their own words.

If we learn to do this well, we will help their dreams to
materialize. Their dreams will take concrete, outward form.

In *any* environment we build — building, room, garden, neighborhood — always, what matters most of all is that each part of this environment intensifies life. We mean that it intensifies human life, animal life, emotional life, the life of storms, the life of wild grasses and lilies, the life of fish in a stream, the life of human kindness in a rough place where it may not be easy to find.

We may say that this is the object of *all* architecture. It needs to be the source, fountain, and origin of everything we think about, and do, as we shape our world. Indeed, it has by now, become well-known that the underpinning for successful work in architecture will almost inevitably depend on some kind of generative system, or system of rules, or patterns, which give the key elements of the architecture their shape and organization.[1] This idea has a long history, with roots in traditional and vernacular architecture,

---

1   See the extensive literature on pattern languages and generative systems, to be found in Hajo Neis and Gabriel Brown, Fall 2009 International PUARL Symposium: Current Challenges for Patterns, Pattern Languages and Sustainability (PUARL Press, 2010, School of Architecture and Allied Arts, University of Oregon).

with roots in classical architecture of various kinds, and most recently with roots in our modern era in the sophisticated theories of pattern-formation that have been developed over the last fifty years.

In order to make buildings and their surroundings have this kind of life, we must search for details of life as it is lived — as it is experienced. That can only come from the intensity of our own observations. Only when we notice, and pinpoint, those features of a classroom which are likely to activate life, then will we be able to build a place that actually propagates, or generates, life for the teacher and the students in that room. Then we can focus especially on those details and aspects of things which evoke deep feelings of life for the people who are living there, working there, enjoying themselves, touching each other, looking at each other's eyes, seeing the beauty of animals and clouds and rain, and making people aware of their precious moments of life. So the job we want buildings to do is to enhance this sense of life, and increase the feeling of life at every moment.

We want aspects of the environment — both in their parts, and as a whole — to stimulate the thoughts, actions, and feelings, also sensations, to support our own sense of life. We are not interested in making an *image* of life; only in creating conditions that will activate and intensify life itself in any given place.

To accomplish this, we must always begin by creating a pattern language — a word-picture that describes the wholeness of a place. We may create it from scratch, or we may modify an existing language and tailor it to serve our needs. However we get it, it must describe what the place can become, and also how it can become. Each pattern describes a certain element, or piece of the built environment, or a relationship between such pieces. The patterns range in scope from very large to very small. In other words, the piece of the built environment with which a particular pattern concerns itself might be large, small, or somewhere between. So a pattern language always contains patterns at a variety of scales, working together, typically arranged with the patterns nested from large to small.

The most essential thing in a pattern language *is that it works as a whole* — that it actually generates holistic structure for a specific place from its specific nature. This means the pattern language is capable of generating the large-scale and small-scale configurations, and those added relationships between these configurations that will bring life to the place.

————

Our work on the Eishin project began, as promised in the contract, with the construction of a pattern language. We spent four to five months engaging students, teachers, and administrators in creating this new pattern language, which would spring from their hopes and dreams as well as from the land itself.

The very first thing we did was spend two weeks just talking to different teachers and students, to get a feeling for their hopes and dreams. These talks were one-on-one and often lasted about an hour, for any one interview, during which we asked questions, talked, probed, explored dreams of an ideal campus, and tried to understand each person's deepest visions as a teacher, or as a student. We asked people about their longings, and their practical needs. We asked them to close their eyes and imagine themselves walking about in the most wonderful campus they could imagine.

This was not easy to do. It required much of both the interviewer and the person being interviewed. From the interviewer, it required love, compassion, and joyful acceptance of every person interviewed. Each question had to be steered by affection, or by a strong wish to see that the person's desires (no matter whether idiosyncratic, brilliant, or boring) materialize in the school. Our efforts in these conversations were to try to help each person reach the deepest place in their own hearts and to help them bring this material out into the open. We were looking for the spark of ideas that would generate a better place to learn than they were accustomed to. By loving and respecting each person as a collaborator, we supported the search.

For the person being interviewed, getting to their deepest desires required a break from system-B. As you might expect, if you ask a person what is wrong with his classroom, or what kind of classroom he would like, he will probably give you an answer which is very similar to what he has already. In his mind, there is no way of escaping from what he is used to, and he is trying to be helpful within the framework of the system-B version of a classroom, as far as he understands it. Thus he is already making the tacit assumption that system-B is inevitable.

If you ask him, instead, to close his eyes and imagine that he is in some kind of heaven, and that he is teaching, or learning, for the first time in his life in a place of perfect beauty that is ideal for the task, this question invites him to escape from system-B. Even so, he may refuse this kind of question by saying, "I don't know. I don't really have any idea. I am not quite sure what kind of thing you mean."

In addition to holding the people being interviewed in very high regard, it was necessary to insist that they leave the constraints of what they had experienced so far in the classroom, and get to their deep feelings. As they became convinced that we were truly interested in that, they relaxed and began to tell us their dreams. They entered another world where their feelings were the main thing, where love of human reality and human feeling is a governing force. When that happened, their answers were profoundly useful. Probing with this kind of insistence is difficult for the interviewer, particularly if he himself is caught in the effects of system-B.

It was difficult for many teachers to give a description of an ideal campus. At first, they stared blankly, or said something general about classroom size. In the context of present-day Japan, where most schools are massive concrete boxes, with an asphalt playground on one side, it was hard to overcome this difficulty. Even the old Eishin School in Musashino-shi, where these talks with teachers and students took place, was that kind of place. It was almost impossible for teachers to say anything they really felt about the matter, or to take seriously the fact that they were being asked. System-B was so deep in their blood that it was hard for them to imagine a world in which their own feelings might be taken seriously, or might have a legitimate place. Such is the effect of a built environment that does not support life.

In any case, I always gently insisted. Often I would try to help them by saying something like, "Please close your eyes. Just keep your eyes closed and dream . . . imagine a place . . . the most wonderful school you can imagine, a kind of fairytale school where everyone is happy. The students are happy, you are happy teaching, the teaching is going very well, and it is a pleasure to work there."

In answer to this kind of gentle invitation, most people would begin to say something. Reluctantly, hesitatingly, often with some embarrassment, they would begin to describe their feelings about things — shyly, as if it was not allowed, or as if it was crazy for them to attempt it. They began to describe true dreamlike atmospheres. For example, one teacher said something like this to me: "I imagine walking by a stream, small streams and islands, perhaps bridges, and trees hanging in the water — a place where I can walk quietly and think about my class, or collect my thoughts as I prepare to teach."

We shall see that many of these shyly presented, hesitating thoughts and feelings, were deeply true. They represented a real truth, which was demonstrated empirically once the school was built. But although these kinds of thoughts and feelings are indeed the very stuff of system-A, in system-B these things are trampled on, disregarded, discouraged. In system-B people are made to feel small and ridiculous for even having such feelings. We tend to overlook the violation of people's feelings because it happens every day, and we have become accustomed to it. But this *is* a violation of people's feelings. When these true things about their experience are forced into hiding, like some dark secret, because the world of system-B has created a fictional universe in which these things are portrayed as unimportant or even downright impossible, damage is done.

PRACTICAL EXPERIMENTS

These kinds of down-to-earth experiences and experiments provide the deep origins of the battle which now began.

EXAMPLES OF PEOPLE'S DREAMS

Hosoi, although dimly aware of these problems, emphasized the positive aspects of our endeavor in these words: "When we started the work in establishing 'Pattern Language' in this project, the first question Professor Alexander gave the faculty was 'What is the most holy place in the school?' I was very much pleased and felt some indescribable joy when I listened to this question from him. He shot the target very exactly. It was a clear sign which meant we had just begun to trace our ordinary way in reconstructing a picture about 'What is a school?'"

We began by writing down a crude first pattern language, which was just a rough intuitive amalgamation of their dreams. We then sent this first very preliminary language to the teachers, with the following letter:

MEMO TO TEACHERS, MAY 1982

Dear members of Eishin Gakuen:
    In the first phase of our work together, to design the new school and university, we must build up a verbal picture of the school and college, as we imagine them in our minds. To do this, we shall describe them by a list of "patterns" — which are the essential elements, out of which the school will be made. When this list of patterns is complete, it will contain a nearly complete description of all the essential elements that are going to appear in the project.
    After talking with a few of the faculty and students (about fifteen people altogether), we have created a very rough, first draft of this list of patterns, for your comment. Please understand that this first draft is extremely far from the final one, and is meant only to stimulate discussion among the faculty. Especially, we want to apologize to those members of the three main committees whom we have not yet met. Time ran very short on my first visit, but I am very much looking forward to receiving your comments when I come back.
    We ourselves are working on this list, even while you are reading it, and already have ideas about how to change it for the better. We expect that you will also have reactions to what it says and that from your comments, discussions, and suggestions we shall together make a second draft, which is a closer and better description of the school which we want.
    Please read this, and discuss it, with a flexible mind. Do not assume that it is fixed; be ready to receive changes, see a better, or deeper way. Also, most important, there are certainly many things which have been left out of this first list. Please dream freely to find things which we have forgotten, so that we can include them in the second draft.

Please remember that the thing we want to reach, most of all, is the deep feeling which will make this school successful. The deep feeling is carried by concrete realities which appear on this list; and the list will be most successful when the concrete realities which it contains, carry a very deep feeling indeed.
That is our intention.

Christopher Alexander

Here are a few examples of the dreams of teachers that, with many others, formed the base for our first rough Pattern Language draft.

"The main entrance is critical to the character of the whole campus, its placement on the edge of the site must be done with great care. I see the main entrance as a gate, where I can greet students and teachers in the morning."

"I see the new campus surrounded by some fence or wall."

"There is one essential center, where the sun shines on the buildings, and which catches the spirit of the whole school. It is an open place, where very important buildings lie . . . Something is there, do not know exactly what, that makes this place catch the spirit of the whole school, and stays in the memory."

"I see a main assembly hall that in particular symbolizes the overall community of high school and college. It is the locus for major events such as the fall festival, or lectures for the college."

"I see white walls, wooden columns, and heavy wood."

"I see an inner area of the campus, where most of the daily life of students and teachers will take place. It is the place for meeting and interaction."

"The heart and most important center of the college is the research center and the library."

"Each college building should have its own garden for quiet study."

"I see the high school separate from the college, but also connected, do not know exactly how this is to be done, yet."

"The homerooms of the high school should be organized in relatively smaller freestanding buildings, each of which may contain anywhere from 2–6 homerooms."

"There should be a lawn for rest and taking lunch."

"Somewhere I see a pond, possibly close to the college area."

"The student house should be a freestanding building by itself."

School members who contributed to these dreams and to dozens of others, and the discussions that followed them, included Mr. Suzuki, Chairman, Board of Directors; Mr. Sakaida, Board of Directors, Education Committee; Mr. Hosoi, Managing Director; Mr. Kurahashi, Principal; Mr. Aida, Head Teacher of high school; Mr. Murakoshi, Head Teacher, junior high school; Mr. Hagiwara, Japanese Language, College Committee; Mr. Nodera, Physics, Building Committee; Mr. Izumori, Mathematics, Education Committee; Mr. Suzuki, Music, Building Committee; Mr. Tokuoka, Sculpture, Building Committee; Mrs. Suyama, Japanese History, Education Committee; Miss Osawa, Student; Miss Tamura, Student.

MAKING THE FIRST SKETCH OF A PATTERN LANGUAGE

As our grasp of these "dreams" and suggestions became good and practical, we were able to write down a rough overview of what the sketch would contain. It went like this:

1. *The new campus will consist of an outer precinct with all the sport fields, gardens and outer buildings, and an inner precinct with all the buildings, high school and college activities.*

2. *The inner precinct of the school is made up of seven major entities.*

3. *The entrance street, which connects the outer boundary to the inner boundary.*

4. *The main yard, which contains the great hall.*

5. *The ta-noji center, which contains two narrow crossing streets, all the communal functions, and the college departments.*

6. *The home base street, which contains the individual home base buildings, and the common space for high school students.*

7. *The college cloister which contains the library, and the special college functions such as research center.*

8. *The lawn which is shared by the high school and the college.*

9. *The gymnasium, which stands at the end of the home base street, and forms its head.*[2]

It should be strongly emphasized that this very brief and rudimentary pattern language was not created by sociological "research," nor was it done by making a list of what people spoke about. Rather, it was a poetic vision, crude but potent, which tried to flesh out in architectural language and in three dimensions, a physical world whose inner meaning corresponded to the meaning conveyed to us by teachers, staff, and students, and by them to one another, as discussion of the nature of the school began. This language was made and polished by us, the architects. But it was made, more essentially, by the teachers and students from the raw material and work and expressions of intent that they first gave to us.

The numbered paragraphs gave us a key group of nine patterns that defined the global structure of the campus. Moving on from them, the campus, in its gross physical structure, could be pinned down as we started trying to see more detail.

Many teachers made beautiful drawings which showed what the language communicated to them. These drawings were immensely helpful to us in judging the overall structure and form of

---

2   As it turned out in the event, the gymnasium was placed on the lake, not on the home base street. In the evolution of a language, contents do sometimes change.

the school.[3] They also gave the teachers a way of checking their understanding, and telling us what they thought might still be missing from the language, or still needed to be modified.

MAKING A FIRST DRAFT PATTERN LANGUAGE FROM TEACHERS' COMMENTS

We then began making this rudimentary pattern language physically coherent. A pattern language is not just an expression of the needs and desires which people feel. It is above all an active specification of physical structure. This means, it must have the ability to *generate* a coherent physical structure.

So we took the first nine-point, crude language on page 123 and worked on it until it began to express and generate a physical structure which was coherent. To do this, we tried to generate different campus plans with the language — not yet for the actual site in Iruma-shi, but for other imaginary sites of roughly similar size. We were, in effect, testing the way that these patterns could cope with a variety of unknown conditions. Since, at this time, the actual site had not yet been bought, we could fully concentrate on the archetypal structure of the pattern language.

By tests of this kind we were able to ask ourselves where the language was problematic, inconsistent, or incoherent. During this work, we also asked the teachers themselves to use early versions of the language to generate physical campus plans, in image form — again independent of any actual site.

What followed from that work was the second version of the pattern language. You may see a drawing of a possible campus plan, as sketched by Mr. Hagiwara. It is reproduced on page 136.

THE COMPLETENESS OF THE LANGUAGE: SEVEN PRINCIPLES

• **RELATIONSHIPS.** Each pattern establishes certain relationships which should exist in the finished campus. The sum total of these relationships, expressed by the patterns in the language, acting together, define the possible configurations which this language generates.

---

3   Sadly, the folder containing most of these beautiful drawings was lost some twenty years ago.

• **SPATIAL.** A given pattern contains, or defines, certain spatial entities. The relationships are defined among these spatial entities.

• **RELIABILITY.** The essence of these relationships is that they must be reliable, and true. They cannot be arbitrary relationships (as they might often be in a single person's design). They need to be sufficiently true, so that we can trust them, and would want to find these relationships present in any version of any campus that might be generated by this language.

• **CONSISTENCY.** It is not necessarily easy to define a system of patterns which is consistent. For example, if one pattern asserts a certain relationship between two entities, and another pattern asserts a further relationship between the same entities, but one which is inconsistent with the first, then that system of two patterns is inconsistent, and can only, with great difficulty, work to generate real physical configurations.[4]

• **INCONSISTENCY.** From time to time, two patterns which are physically inconsistent may be refreshing and life-giving. This happens because the contradiction generates vigor and opens new ideas.[5]

• **COMPLETENESS.** A system of patterns is complete if it contains sufficient relationships to allow a well-formed configuration to be built.

• **COHERENCE.** A system of patterns is coherent if the relationships specified among the patterns tend, most of the time, to generate easily graspable geometrical configurations.

In mathematics, these concepts are, typically, well-defined. In architecture, however, as in painting, the kinds of relationships that can exist in two or three dimensional configurations are less easily pinned down, and inherently richer than those of mathematical logic.

Some of them may be generated easily by sequential processes. Others may be discovered only with difficulty, or by chance. In

---

4 The topics of completeness and consistency played a huge role in the mathematics of the early 20th century, and were extensively studied by Hilbert, Gödel, Peano, Church, Turing, and many others. See the entry on Hilbert's program at the Stanford Encyclopedia of Philosophy, and the Wikipedia entry on David Hilbert.
5 This should only be encouraged if there is genuine need for such a contradiction, and there is a strong likelihood that some entirely new invention will be forced into the open because of it.

a system of architectural patterns, the ideal kind of simplicity is one in which the geometrical configuration can be constructed by following certain sequential procedures that will always lead to a coherent configuration in a small number of steps.

REFINEMENTS OF THE LANGUAGE

Once we had the language working to the extent that it could generate coherent plans, we then began a series of meetings with the school's Building Committee to discuss and refine specifics of the various patterns. This committee included Mr. Kurahashi, then principal of the school; Mr. Hagiwara; Mr. Nodera, the chief science teacher; Mr. Suzuki, chief music teacher; Mr. Tokuoka, the chief sculpture teacher. It also included Mr. Murakoshi, the vice principal.

The discussions which took place in these meetings were fundamental. Typical topics of discussion included:

1. The degree of separation or integration of high school and university.

2. The existence of separate buildings.

3. The meaning of the homeroom street.

4. The meaning of the tanoji center.

5. Walking around in the rain, and how much cover to have.

6. The number of buildings which would be shared between the college and the high school.

7. The material of the buildings.

8. The degree of difference and autonomy of different class-room buildings.

What was remarkable was that the teachers understood the specific details of the pattern-language at a practical and concrete level. These discussions did not have any feeling that they were abstract. On the contrary, it was clear to everyone, that we were discussing the coming reality of the school **in the most concrete way**.

Shortly after these committee discussions, we also started a second round of discussions with the teachers. Hajo, Ingrid, and Hiro (CES staff) spent a month talking to all eighty-four faculty, all staff, and about twenty-five students as promised in the contract. In this final level of discussion participants were asked to express their views and dreams of the new campus and to provide the details for the larger patterns which had been established so far. Items involved here included such things as storage for classrooms, size and shape of rooms, exact facilities provided for athletics, and so on.

On the one hand the work was very enjoyable. Many teachers, staff, and students were able to express their dreams and needs quite successfully. Others had problems expressing themselves, and needed help to relax and bring their dreams to the foreground. A few did not believe in this process at all; they believed that they had nothing to say anyway. And another group of teachers expressed desires which were out of scale, bombastic, or not quite appropriate.

Nonetheless our task was to listen to them, help them, and try to accommodate them as far as possible.

HERE ARE SOME EXAMPLES OF THE KINDS OF DISCUSSIONS WHICH TOOK PLACE AT THAT TIME

INTERVIEW WITH CLINIC ROOM TEACHER

The clinic room teacher approached us in the corridor and wanted to talk about the health room. She had a copy of *The Oregon Experiment* in Japanese on her desk and was quite prepared to talk to us.[6] Her main concern was sun in the health room. The current room did not have any sun. She also expressed details of the health room she wanted to have in the new school.

MR. HASHIMURA, POLITICAL ECONOMICS AND SOCIAL STUDIES

Homeroom very important. Tight relationship between students and teacher is preferable. Decrease number of students, increase number of teachers. Directors disagree. Ideal classroom: Not big or wide. See each student's face clearly. Little bigger

---

6   *The Oregon Experiment* was translated into Japanese in 1977.

desk with containers. Much light, clear windows. No plastics. Traditional materials. Calm. Wood.

HIROYUKO AJIRO, PRESIDENT OF STUDENT BODY

He likes the homeroom and he does not want to lose it nor the homeroom teacher. His teacher is like his mother. Not all students like the teacher, maybe 5 out of 45. These students are too self-centered. Most students get along fine regardless of hair style. Some weak students are treated very rough. There are too few women students in the school. He thinks that the stairs in the existing school are grotesque, too dark, too hard, so he wants to have some more fun stairs in the new school.

MR. IIHAMA, CHAIRMAN OF BUDGET COMMITTEE

The most important point for the new school is that students can walk around barefooted, so that the foot can touch the ground directly, with grass, flowers, and earth. Education should be more related to nature not to the city. Water gives a fresh atmosphere. The buildings should be half-hidden. There should be some facilities for high school and college together, but there also needs to be some clear separation.

MR. MOCHIZUKI, CHAIRMAN OF PERSONAL LEARNING

He is very keen on a large gymnasium. Sometimes the present gym is used by three classes at the same time. He feels that the gym should fulfill a multipurpose function, and it could be 2–3 stories, perhaps partly underground. He does not respond positively to the suggestion that some sports could take place under just a big roof. He wants the gym at least twice the size of the present one, horizontally as well as vertically.

MRS. TOMIZU, CHAIRWOMAN OF BASIC LEARNING

There should be a delicate entrance. Maybe there should be several gates, but one main gate. The way from the gate to the buildings should be not straight but winding. This entrance way should have some trees alongside, particularly trees with big leaves which fall in autumn, change colors. Wants to see the change of seasons in these trees.

There should be no car parking on the campus. Safety from traffic is needed.

MR. SUZUKI, MUSIC TEACHER AND BUILDING COMMITTEE

Use as much wood as possible, because the most important aspect of a music room is acoustics. And it should have a high ceiling, possibly a stepped room. He needs two music rooms for 1200 students, now there is only one. The music room should be on the ground, perhaps a building by itself, should feel like a little music hall.

MESSAGE FROM THE PRINCIPAL, MR. KURAHASHI

He would like to talk to us, because he is worried that teachers will say too many different things which do not fit together.

MRS. IWAMOTO, PHYSICAL EDUCATION

She would like to incorporate the new gymnastics for females into the curriculum. And she would like to have a small gymnastics room with a large mirror on the wall, so that one can see oneself while dancing.

MR. KAJIYAMA, JAPANESE LANGUAGE, HOMEROOM TEACHER

For the new school it is quite important to have a good library with many books. The library should be a special building, but close to the classrooms. Even a tatami room may be nice. The atmosphere is quite important. He does not like the atmosphere of modern types of buildings, he likes the feeling of the old buildings. Buildings should be no higher than 4 stories, 3 is fine. The color of the building should be subdued like an ivory white.

MR. TAIRA, PHYSICAL EDUCATION AND HEALTH EDUCATION

The most important thing for him is a spacious sports field and a spacious gym. This is very important because at the present they teach two classes of sport at the same time in a very limited space.

YOSHIKAWA AND KIKUCHI, STUDENTS

Kikuchi is going to become a public official and Yoshikawa an auto-mechanic. For both of them it is very important to meet other students. They both would like to have a nice coffee shop in the new school, preferably two.

———

Conversations like these took place over many weeks. The materials were collected, synthesized, sifted, discussed further, and synthesized again, and so on, until we felt we had a sense of what the place — the campus — was to be.

A Pattern Language for the Community

Once we have learned to take a reading of people's true
desires and real feelings, we can then describe the
patterns that are needed to generate a profound campus
environment.

The system or "language" of these patterns can give the
community the beautiful world they need and want, the
physical organization that will make their world practical,
beautiful, life-enhancing,
and truly useful.

After the many points raised in the previous chapter, we were able
to put a pattern language together for the Eishin Campus. This pattern language is a list of key centers, each of which contributes some
essential quality to the campus. The list was established long before
any design started. Each of the patterns, defines an essential aspect
of the project, which will contribute to the life of a school, college,
campus, or community. Each pattern can be thought of as a center
that defines one aspect of a way of life for a school or community,
which, in this case, was entirely different from any way of life recognizable or existing in Japan in the late 20th century. [1]

As we created this list of centers, we (together with teachers
and students) could see, and feel, merely by reading the names of
the centers and their descriptions, that what would be going on
in this new school was to be very different from the typical 20th-

---

[1] The concept of a center is defined in *The Nature of Order*, Book 1, *The Phenomenon of Life*. It is
an organized zone of space that is a discernible whole. When I use the word center, I am always
referring to a physical set — a distinct physical system, which occupies a certain volume in space,
and has a special marked coherence. For example, a human head, or ear, or finger is a discernible
whole. It is also both visually and functionally a center. A pattern is a center, made up of centers at
many levels of scale. Altogether, the centers that form a pattern take care of some recurring problem
or opportunity in the life of the community.

century, asphalt-jungle school. We could also see this new way of life as a complete structure. The way the campus was to work was captured completely by the list of centers. Thus in all important aspects the life of the new school was encapsulated in these centers very early in the project.

Once again, it must be emphasized that this pattern language is a work of creation, like a poem, created by the architect, but nourished and inspired by the dreams of the users. The poetic coherence of the list defines the seed of the architecture which will follow its use. Of course, it should not be an idiosyncratic vision, peculiar to the architects. In the case of the language for Eishin, it was a vision which, as far as possible, embodied the real feelings of the people of Japan, and in particular of these people who formed the staff and teachers and students of this school.

It had to be so, so that when the language was used later, as a basis for laying out the school, what would emerge would then become a concrete reality — one that could succeed in embodying the true life of the people of the campus and their desires.

The Eishin Campus pattern language is included here to show how the stage was set. As many details as possible have been included so you can see how the pattern language felt. The names of students and teachers who contributed to the inspiration of these patterns are also listed.

1. GLOBAL CHARACTER OF THE CAMPUS

1.1 An outer Boundary surrounds the Campus. A white, 60 cm wall serves as the base for a wooden fence. The fence varies in material and character. There are high, wooden, closed parts; at other places there are bamboo and climbing plants; and there are openings to look through. At other places a boundary will be formed by the landscape. The fence is punctured by gates at important points, perhaps with a darker concrete or stone foundation. Several buildings will be set into the outer boundary, connecting the school with the surrounding community.

Tomizu, Igarashi, Hosoi

1.2 Contained by this Outer Boundary there is an Outer Precinct. The Outer Precinct surrounds an Inner Precinct. A second wall, far inside the first, surrounds the school itself, and forms a second zone between the first and second wall. The zone between the two walls can be used for various activities and sports. The inner wall is not continuous. Instead it creates a feeling of enclosure, but leaves the precinct open at many spots, where it opens directly to the outer precinct.

1.3 The Inner Precinct is a densely built area where School and College have their major buildings and activities. It is the place where the daily life of students and faculty occurs. It is a place for meeting and interaction, a dense area with streets, yards, small gardens and courtyards, which includes all the major buildings for high school and college, and where intense activity of learning happens.

Oginawa

1.4 The Outer Precinct is an area for relaxation, sport, outdoor activities and recreation. The area between the inner and outer boundaries contains sports fields, tea fields, natural vegetation where the students can get away from the pressures of school. The area also contains some special classrooms, located in various places between the fields, such as art studios, lab buildings and workshops.

1.5 As a whole, the Campus is given its character by stone foundation walls, natural concrete walls, wood columns, white plaster surfaces, some green surfaces, wide overhanging roofs, dark roofs, stones and grass and pebbles on the ground. In addition, white walls; heavy wood; roofs overhanging; natural bushes and trees; paving with cracks between stones; sliding doors and windows; slate, dark tile perhaps; wooden gates; overall, materials with natural color; post and beam construction; buildings made to improve with time; materials that are easy to maintain.

Toruoka, Hosoi, Taketsu (student), Katsamatu (student), Nodera

2. THE INNER PRECINCT

2.1 The Entrance Street to the campus is a highly visible pedestrian Way. It begins at the Outer Boundary of the Campus, and ends at the Inner Precinct. This Entrance Street is vital to the character of the whole campus. There may be other openings in the outer boundary, but it is this one entrance which everyone will pass along, once or twice a day.

Kurahashi, Tomizu

2.2 The Small Gate marks the outer end of the Entrance Street. It is a small, imposing building, which has height and volume.

Hosoi, Nodera, Suzuki

2.3 The Entrance Street is flanked with walls and trees. It is extremely quiet. The street is on the order of 60 meters long and 15 meters wide. It has tall stone walls or trees on both sides, interrupted by occasional smaller buildings and openings. The street may be paved in the middle, and have planted strips along the sides.

Kurahashi, Oginawa

2.4 Where the Entrance Street meets the Inner Precinct, there is a second, much larger, Main Gate. It is three stories high. Both Small Gate and Main Gate are ceremonial in character; each one is a building which makes you feel you are entering a place of learning and education.

Kurahashi

2.5 Beyond the Main Gate, there is a Public Yard. Opening onto this public yard, there is an immense building, the Great Hall. The Great Hall shapes and forms the Public Yard.

Kurahashi

2.6 Beyond the Public Yard is the Tanoji Center, the Core of the Inner Precinct. This Center is the meeting place of College and High School. This essential center is reached through several layers, and it contains further layers of quietness within itself. The sun shines on the buildings, and catches the spirit of the whole school.

2.7 The High School consists of two main parts. The home-base street, where most of the morning classrooms are located; and the gymnasium where small meeting rooms and public functions are located.

2.8 The College. The college also consists of two main parts: the buildings around the tanoji center, which form a great space, surrounded by continuous arcade, with continuous gardens and small classrooms where the teaching happens; and the **Library cloister,** which is the main part, that contains the library and the central intellectual heart of the university, where teachers hold seminars and discussions among themselves.

2.9 The Tanoji Center, geometrically the center of gravity of the Campus, unifies College and the High School, and connects all the other important functions of the inner precinct. It has the rough form

of a cross — formed by crossing paths. **Because this cross resembles the Japanese character "ta," the school has named this place the Ta-noji Center.** It is an intricate space. First of all, it is a cross of two very wide streets of about 15–20 meters each. In the four corners of this cross, the area behind the streets, the five departments are located as squares around gardens.

2.10 At the crossing of the streets and paths which form the Tanoji Center, there is a smaller center. This is the Kernel of the Tanoji Center. The hub of the school has the form of two intersecting streets, which are lined by the communal and lively functions of the school, with the college departments, located in the areas behind the streets, surrounding interior gardens. At this most lively place, the middle of the Tanoji Center, one of the most active functions should be located. It is likely that the student house will find its appropriate place here.

2.11 Opening from the far side of the Tanoji Center, is a higher and most peaceful place which we call the College Cloister. This is the inner sanctum of the College, and the most peaceful place of all. The **Research Institute** for higher learning is located here together with the campus **Library**.

This college cloister aims to represent the holy of holies in the school, and to be the special territory of the college. It is essential that the college has, at its core, a seminar, or institute of seminars, where senior and junior faculty, and invited professors and scholars, maintain a continuous discussion of major issues about self-government, politics, religion, etc.

Sigihara, Igarashi, Hosoi

2.12 Also opening directly from the Tanoji Center, is the Homebase Street. The Homebase Street is a wide, lively, sunny street — formed by the Individual Homeroom Buildings, where the high school students have their classes. In the old school (in Tokyo), the most intense places were the corridors during the recess time. In the new school the long and wide Homebase Street with individual classroom buildings will provide an intense physical place which permits release of students' energy.

The core components of the high school are the homerooms, where the students receive their most intense academic training, and also establish their stable daily peer groups. The basic education is concentrated in the four early hours in the day, during which all of the 1200 high school students have a shared territory. This represents an extreme amount of pent-up energy. It is our contention that this pent-up energy must be taken seriously for the academic instruction to have a chance.

Iihama

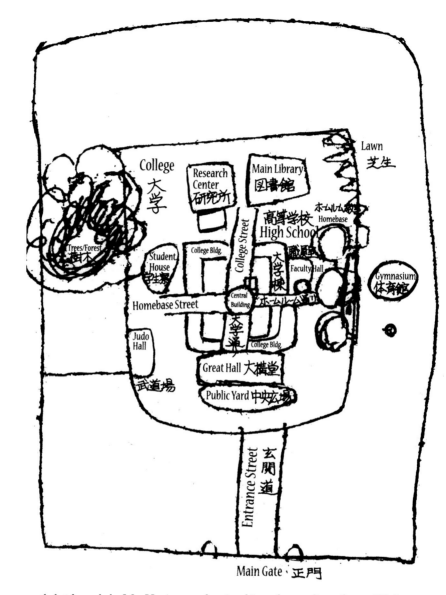

田

This is the
Japanese
character
that is pro-
nounced
"ta."

A sketch made by Mr. Hagiwara, showing his understanding of a possible layout for a campus community, one that would include the general structure, and major details, as he understood it from the pattern language.

2.13 Opening through gates on another side of the Tanoji Center, is a lawn. This Lawn, especially for the college students, is close to the college buildings, and leads directly to the Lake. A wide lawn, perhaps 100 meters x 50 meters, surrounded by college buildings which open onto it. This green is a place for resting, lying, sitting. It is important that the different spaces around the green open into it directly, with sliding doors, so that surrounding interior spaces communicate with the central green effectively.

Tokuoka, Hagiwara

2.14 The lake is a peaceful place to rest. At the lowest point of the land, there is a lake, with grass and trees along the edges, placed so that the lawn, and tanoji center, and cloister all communicate in some way with the distant lake. It is a large lake at the north end, and at the low point of the site, which is capable of holding all the drainage from a heavy rain on the site.

Hosoi

3. THE BUILDINGS OF THE INNER PRECINCT

3.1 The main building of the Campus is the Great Hall. This great hall is a long hall with seating for 600 people, surrounded by rooms and galleries, so that it can seat a full congregation of 1200, for important meetings.

The Great Hall is the building that symbolizes the overall community of the campus. Rather than seeing this building in the middle of the hub of the activity, we see it as the most public building, and the building that one confronts as an entity by itself, in the space that you come into when you have entered the school. The building should be imposing, with a beautiful roof, and faces the entrance broad-side.

The Hall is the natural locus for major events such as the fall festival. It is also where larger scale lectures are given in the college, and where all larger forms of assembly take place.

Aida, Murakoshi

3.2 The second building of the Public Yard is the Eishin Museum — a small house, which explains the place and its philosophy to visitors.

3.3 The buildings which comprise the College are the College Departments. These are organized so that one feels the college as a whole. They are placed around the edge, so that one feels the college as a whole, whenever one walks through. The college departments are located in the quadrants of the tanoji center, around gardens. To the streets there are arcades, so that one can always get a glimpse of the gardens from the streets.

**3.4 The College is made up of the following five departments:
A. Financing and Budget   B. Local Government Administration
C. Public Enterprise and Public Utilities D. Local Cultures E. Local Government Studies.**

Hosoi, Oginawa

3.5 Each of these five College Departments has its own garden.

3.6 Also, at the very core of the Tanoji Center is the Student House: a building three stories high, which stands exactly at the axis of the crossing paths. The student house is a building which contains space for high school students, and college students, and space for student government, and places where students can meet informally.

3.7 In addition, there are other buildings, shared by college and high school, which form streets and centers inside the tanoji grid. These buildings include the judo hall, a small gymnasium, clubrooms, small classrooms and lecture halls.

3.8 The main buildings which form the homebase street are the Individual Homeroom Buildings. Each of these buildings is two stories high, and has one classroom on each floor, the upper one with its own private staircase leading to the ground. The identity of each homeroom and homeroom building should be as strong as possible. The space between homebase buildings will be pleasant in character. It is here where stairs will lead to the upper classrooms, at various places bathrooms will be located, and occasional openings will lead to the lawn and outer precinct.

Hashimura

3.9 The center of the Homebase Street is the Large Gymnasium, which stands at one end of the street, and shapes the street. This building is large, has a beautiful shape, and forms the head of the high school, in a very prominent position, at one end of the homebase street, all the time visible for everybody. The roof will be totally different from the standard modern gymnasium roof in Japan. Spectators will sit on bleachers, or in a gallery along one side of the building.

3.10 The secondary center of the homebase street is the Faculty Building, which stands near the middle of the street, as easily accessible to all the homerooms as it can be. All high school faculty offices will be in this building, including the principal's office, close to the students, and homerooms, at the center of gravity of the homebase street.

Kurahashi, Tanaka, Tokuoka

3.11 The College Cloister is the home of the Research Institute. Its buildings are the research buildings for the college faculty. These are buildings where intensive discussion about the problem of local government, and research, take place. It is the academic center of the college, a very important place. It provides senior and junior faculty with the facilities for pursuing research; and it provides the ambience, where continuous discussion of major issues about local government problems, politics, economics, and law, can take place.

Igarashi

3.12 The Campus Library is the center of the college cloister. It stands three stories high, with the main reading room on the second floor. In the university, a place of very great importance, a main place, quiet, and with quiet walks and gardens near it. A beautiful, main reading room, on the second story, large, quiet, with floor to ceiling shelves, forming alcoves with big windows, where there are open tables and comfortable chairs. More dense stacks at one end, or on the ground level. The whole building raised on columns which are open, so it is possible to walk through underneath.

Kajiyama, Oginawa, Tomizu, Sato

4. THE STREETS OF THE INNER PRECINCT

4.1 The Public Yard has a gravel surface, with stone paths crossing it. It is informal and quiet in character. In some ways the yard is like a forecourt to a major building. Yet the term yard is more appropriate, since we imagine that the ground is hard-packed dirt or gravel, and not paved.

Also we imagine that the building is sitting among larger trees which makes it feel sheltered and appropriate, the way large farm buildings are surrounded by trees in the middle of wide open fields. There are also other trees in the yard, and may be some grassy areas. There may be quiet, out-of-the-way spots among the buildings.

4.2 The Homebase Street is the widest street, even wider than the streets of the Tanoji Center. The Homebase Street is the forum where the high school students sense themselves as a large group, and where the liveliness of this mass of teenagers can have a chance to unfold. It should be surrounded by a roofed walkway, that connects the buildings and that provides shelter on rainy days. Similar walkways should occasionally cross the street, and some suggestion of respective territory for the different grades may be suggested in this manner, if judged desirable. This could also take place by distinctions in the terrain. There are trees in the middle, and the street is flanked by raised terraces, along both sides, where the buildings stand. The buildings are colorful and spontaneous.

Tsurumaki, Honda, Hashimura

4.3 The Tanoji Streets are wide with a stone surface that form a Cross. At the central point of the cross itself there is a space which is the crucial busy center of the high school and the university.

4.4 One half of the Tanoji Center is more public and more busy. It is the place where students are moving every day. It is also the place where graduation ceremonies pass.

4.5 The other half of the Tanoji Center is more mysterious. It is the part, towards the college cloister, perhaps behind the student house. This part is glimpsed through gateways, or through columns and arcades: but it is quiet and unreachable for high school students. The glimpses they have of it, give them a longing for the part of their education when they will be studying in the College.

4.6 The College Cloister is extremely quiet. It is raised, perhaps with a lawn or garden in the middle, and an arcade around the edge.

4.7 The Lawn leads down to the water of the Lake. It is relaxed, and pleasant and informal, a place where students can lie in the grass and have discussions.

4.8 A System of Arcades. Within the inner precinct, especially in the tanoji center and the homebase street, there are Many Arcades — open structures of roofs and walls and columns, where people can walk and stay dry when it is raining. These arcades are placed so that even if you want to cross the campus, you never have to go more than a few feet in the open rain.

4.9 In addition, there are many subtle level changes according to the rising and falling of the land.

4.10 The Homebase Street has three zones, at slightly different levels, corresponding to the three grades of the school. These zones are only subtly separated, by a slight change of height, or by a low wall, or by an arcade which connects the two sides of the street.

4.11 Somewhere, very important in the Homebase Street, there is a special terrace, surrounded by balustrade or sitting wall, where students often meet. On this terrace there are one or two concrete ping pong tables, shielded from the wind.

4.12 Opening onto this special terrace is the High School Dining Room where the high-school students meet and eat their lunch. There is enough space for students to meet, and with a place immediately outside it, where the students can sit and eat sandwiches, meet their friends. Possibly, there is an ice cream shop, also near the outside. This is the place

to talk and rest in recess; possibly a place where faculty can go as well.
Osawa (student), Suzuki, Tamura (student), Oginawa

4.13 The College Students also have their own eating place, a Cafe, which is part of the student house, at the heart of the tanoji center. A place for university students to sit, talk, eat ... Possibly equipped with enough of a kitchen so meals can also be served there — especially for faculty. Should have a terrace, and an outdoor feeling.

4.14 Within the inner precinct, all connections between buildings, and public spaces, are marked by Wooden Gateways — less imposing than the main gateways, but small and nicely shaped. The inner precinct contains a variety of different buildings and open spaces, and the transition between these should be marked by gateways. The repetition of these gateways will strengthen the coherence of the whole.

4.15 Around the tanoji grid, but inside the inner boundary, there is an additional passage, a very quiet passage, with small doorways leading to the open fields beyond.

5. THE OUTER PRECINCT

5.1 The Wall which surrounds the Inner Precinct is quite irregular, and follows the buildings, and paths, and terrain. It is similar to the inner wall of a great Japanese castle. This wall may not be continuous but in various places may be open. It includes many buildings and may be heavy at times; at other places it may be similar to the outer wall.

5.2 Outside this irregular Inner Wall, is the outer precinct, which surrounds the inner precinct, and is made up of alternating sports fields, gardens, and important out-buildings. The outer precinct is divided into a series of roughly square pieces of land, each with its own character and purpose.

The path around the site joins each building and each piece of land, forming a band of discrete places that surround the inner precinct: courts for playing tennis and volleyball, laboratories for science experiments, gardens for sitting and thinking, studios for painting and drawing — every activity and every building fitted perfectly into its place on the site.

5.3 The alternation between sports fields, gardens, and outbuildings is done in such a way that each one of these things always forms a separate and distinct entity by itself. Thus for instance: volleyball, basketball, baseball, tennis, pingpong, golf, soccer, rugby, handball... also athletic sports, track, running, jumping . . . also judo and kendo . . . also swimming . . . even such things as zen archery and gateball (a form of croquet).

5.4 This means that each sports field is always standing by itself, not next to others, and is instead surrounded by a hedge, wall, separated from the space next to it by a free-standing building, or otherwise surrrounded and made distinct. Thus: An interlinked system of small sports fields, each one for a particular sport, each with some slight sense of enclosure, near the next one, but not quite adjacent to it, and with some small buildings in between the different fields, and slightly separating them from one another.

Nodera, Osawa (student), Iwamoto

5.5 In addition, every Sports Field is always attached to some building, which has nothing to do with the particular sports function. Thus, for instance, the tennis courts, may be next to the art studio, and placed so that people entering the art studio, are just at that place where the tennis court is most enjoyable to watch.

5.6 The different sports fields, gardens and outbuildings, make up a chain of Alternating Spaces.

5.7 There is an Orchard, tended by the students. A formal garden of fruit trees, useful to the students, and part of their studies to keep it alive, and a good place to go.

Yoshioka

5.8 There are the Science Laboratories, mainly used by high school students, but also open to those college students who wish to continue scientific work. For high school use the building should contain a physics and a chemistry lab, each of which should have a preparation room. In addition there should be a small lecture room, for student groups of 30, for lecture and demonstration purposes, which would be shared between the labs.

Nodera, Kojima

5.9 There is a Soccer Field. We will provide a minimum soccer field (min. 45 x 90, perhaps bigger if possible), with bleachers and adjacent baseball diamond. The field may be grass, if this seems feasible to maintain. Otherwise earth. In case it has to be earth, we will surround the field with trees, so that earth is screened, and does not disturb the pleasant feeling of the project. Baseball probably cannot be provided separately, since there will probably not be enough room. If possible, we will put a softball field, on one side of soccer field, with diamond, or anyway plate and catcher, outside the field.

5.10 Carpentry Workshop. There is a carpentry workshop, where various kind of tools and equipment are available for students to make things. A place where students may learn carpentry. To be used by both college and high school. Also a place where students (and staff) may use the tools to make things for themselves.

Suyama

5.11 There are two Tennis Courts, preferably on grass. Tennis games are both beautiful and exciting to watch; they are not noisy, the sound of tennis is pleasant. It seems like the courts for tennis games should be located in a very integral fashion with quiet or dignified outdoor activity. This kind of unusual adjacency of functions can give great vitality, and enhance both functions.

5.12 There is a Music Studio. This music studio, should be behind the Great Hall, somehow, so that musicians have easy access for practice and performances. The use of the auditorium for musical practice or for special events may be very fruitful for classes and activities associated with music. It seems very likely that also college students may want to participate on an extra curricular basis, in musical activities.

Suzuki, Mochizuki

5.13 There are several Small Fields of tea bushes left from the present agricultural state, and still farmed by local farmers. A tea field, usually on a sloping site, has rows of tea bushes, planted, with walks between them, all parallel, the bushes are about 1 meter high, and the spacing between rows of bushes varies, from 30 cm to about 150 cm.

Hosoi

5.14 There is the Art Studio, which has space for painting and sculpture. A separate building, possibly with a forecourt, where art and studio classes are held outdoors. This can be shared between high school and college.

5.15 There is a Swimming Pool, in a place that is fun to watch, and fairly close to the inner precinct.

Kurahashi, Taira, Anzai (student), Sunaga (student)

5.16 There is a Small Museum and Maintenance Center, which contains the record of the construction of the project, and is the shop from which ongoing construction and maintenance are done. Museum with workshop. Inside: whole history of how school was built; process of construction; pattern list; material for each stage; records of persons, panels; materials used for buildings; tools construction method; samples; exhibit of natural and social involvement of community increasing involvement.

Hosoi

5.17 There is a volleyball court.

Nishimoto, Mizoguchi, Sekine

5.18 There is a Covered Sports Area, about 12 x 30 meters, with a roof, and open sides, where students can play active games in rainy weather. If the site area allows, there could be a roofed sports area for use during rainy days, and also to supplement the other sports facilities generally.[2]

5.19 Somewhere there is a Quiet Area, with benches, trees and ponds. This quiet area might most naturally be at the far side of the college lawn, so that it creates a destination for people who cross the lawn. One area,where there are benches, trees, and ponds . . . a very quiet place, where classes, and students can peacefully talk, walk . . . There may be a system of ponds which connects to the lake, but is not the same as the lake, and has some kind of sequence to it . . . There may be a students' garden . . . a dream corner . . . an adventure field . . . It is a place with a lawn, wide swings, simple shelter-like summer house, half enclosed.

Nodera, Mrs. Shoji

5.20 There is an open air Basketball Court. There will be one open air basketball court, preferably close to the high school street, a paved court, and there will be some bleachers at one side.

Sekine, Mizoguchi, Taira

5.21 There are Handball Courts, or Squash Courts, with walls and roofs.

5.22 There is a building which contains clubrooms for sports. The building is located in a place which makes it clear that this is student territory, possibly slightly hidden.

5.23 Somewhere there is a Wild Garden. There is a sort of a wild garden, a pure piece of nature, where nothing is added by the human hand, a wild forest.

Okahara

5.24 There is a Gardener's Shed, for storage of tools and equipment that are used by people who look after the grounds.

---

2   This is now known as the Central Building, the core of the Tanoji Center.

5.25 And finally, there is a Path, which goes all around the Outer Precinct of the Campus, near the outer boundary, passing from one thing to another, tying them together, in such a way that it is possible to take a pleasant walk by walking all around the outside. A path around the site, with gravel on the ground, for walking and informal jogging . . . it will follow the outer boundary, often directly adjacent to the wooden fence. The path will connect all the functions of the outer precinct, and it will connect smaller paths coming from the inner precinct.

6. FEATURES OF THE INNER PRECINCT

6.1 Inside the inner precinct, the buildings and exterior spaces are placed in such a way that there is a subtle, indirect path, passing through the school, and always reaching places which are more indirect and more private and more secluded, with changes of direction, and subtle barriers.

Tokuoka

6.2 The buildings themselves continue this feeling, in their inner structure. All the buildings are organized internally, to produce a rather intimate collection of larger rooms and smaller rooms, entirely without the formal corridors and stairs typical of modern schools and universities.

Tokuoka

6.3 The College Departments, arranged around their gardens, each contains about 6 seminar rooms, individual rooms for professors, and common rooms where students can read and study.

Hosoi, Kai, Hagiwara

6.4 The High School Homeroom Buildings, are two story buildings with one classroom upstairs, and one down, and a stair going directly to the ground from the upper classroom.

6.5 The Faculty Hall contains a common room for faculty, with rooms for group discussions grouped around it on the first floor, and individual study and discussion rooms upstairs. Its heart is a common faculty lounge, with all the smaller faculty offices grouped around this very comfortable space. These offices should be in one building, at the center of gravity of the homebase street. The building should contain one common room (lounge); then three rooms for three grades, perhaps on the same floor. Then individual study rooms, where teachers can prepare their work. Then there should be some small alcoves, for two persons, where teacher and student can have comfortable and private talk (small rooms might be upstairs).

The office of the principal will be part of the hall of faculty offices.

Tokuoka, Kurahashi, Tanaka, Taketsu (student), Sunaga (student),
Katsumata (student), Ohwaki

6.6 The Library, also a two story building, has a large quiet reading room on the second floor, with shelves, and tables, and carrels, and beautiful windows. The most important space in the library is the large reading room. It is located on the second floor, and is a rectangular space with a row of tall windows along both sides. The ceiling is 16–20 feet high. The stacks are on the ground floor, and along the exterior walls are work carrels. Also, in the library building will be located 2–4 small classroom/seminar rooms to be used jointly by high school and college, and a special research room with work desks for high school faculty.

Kajiyama, Oginawa, Tomizu, Sato

6.7 The Great Hall contains a central space, which is a long narrow hall, with pews that seat 600 people, surrounded by raised rooms, with sliding screens, which can be removed to seat a total congregation of 1200 people. The great hall contains seating for 600 people, in a format that is relatively long and narrow, and very high, with a stage for performance. Seats will be quite narrow, like church pews, to save space. In addition, there will be raised smaller rooms at the two long sides of the hall. The walls of these rooms can be removed, so that additional space for seating can be provided. Together with the narrow hall and narrow seating, there will be seating for 1200.

6.8 The Homerooms are small, for 30 students each, and with a very private character. The single factor which has the highest correlation with good education, is the student-faculty ratio. When the number of students per instructor is low, the quality of education is high. When the number of students per instructor is high, the quality of education will be low.

It is essential, to improve quality of education, and feeling of concentration of students, that the homeroom have a maximum of 30 students.

Sakaida, Kuharashi, Inagaki, Nishizono

6.9 Twenty-four smaller Classrooms, suitable for seminars and individual learning, will have a special character by three different room sizes, and also by the specific subject taught. For individual learning in the early afternoon (1–3 pm) there are 126 courses offered right now, of which 75 deal with academic subjects, 25 deal with sports and 25 deal with cultural subjects, mainly arts.

Kurahashi

6.10 There are two different kinds of Clubrooms for high school students, 10 rooms for sports clubs, and 10 rooms for cultural clubs.

Nodera

6.11 For college students there are special Clubrooms, where they can discuss philosophy, politics, arts, and local government problems . . . these clubrooms are highly visible. Club activities are even more important for college students than for high school students. The Eishin philosophy, when extended, will require more extensive use of development learning for college students. Typical of college students, that they discuss endlessly, philosophy, politics, art, etc. We suggest therefore, that the clubrooms, as physical places, should be highly visible in the college.

6.12 The Science Lab Building contains a Physics Lab, a Chemistry Lab, Two Preparation Rooms, and a Small Lecture Room. Basically the science lab will consist of one chemistry lab and one physics lab, there will be two preparation rooms, and a small lecture room which is stepped. The college does not seem to have a natural science curriculum, but physics and chemistry may be taken as electives by college students. In other words, science laboratories will be used by high school students as well as by college students.

Tomizu, Kojima, Nodera

6.13 The Music Studio contains two music rooms, wood panelled, with two smaller classrooms, and practice rooms.

Suzuki, Mochizuki

6.14 The Judo Hall contains two areas of fifty mats, surrounded by galleries and open space for people watching.

6.15 The Small Gymnasium contains wall bars, equipment for dance and gymnastics, and long mirrors on the wall.

6.16 The Administration Building contains administration for both high school and college in a single building.

Sakaguchi, Takabe

6.17 Two Examination Halls, have space in them for lectures to a hundred students, or for showing films, also for formal examinations. These examination halls might be quite special places, perhaps upstairs, light and memorable. There is need for two of these lecture halls.

6.18 The University Cafe contains a dining room for university students, a dining room for faculty, a kitchen, and a small public

coffee shop. The university cafe will be part of the student house in the middle of the tanoji center. The coffee shop will be a special place, which can be used by college students as well as high school students. The dining room for faculty and college students will be located adjacent to the coffee shop.

6.19 Opening off the Entrance Street, there are bicycle sheds to hold 70-100 bicycles.

6.20 There are various small spaces for storage and other miscellaneous functions. Audio visual room, Dressing and shower rooms, Broadcasting room, Guardhouse, Facilities for fire, House phone system.

Takabe

6.21 There is a Calligraphy Room, with tatami floor, and traditional interior, at some point in the grid, looking out over one of the internal gardens of the quadrant. Special rooms, with tatami on the floor, raised platforms, take off shoes at entrance . . . for calligraphy.

Suyama

6.22 Somewhere in the school, perhaps outside the Calligraphy Room, there is a Small Exhibition Space or Gallery, where student works can be displayed. This space will be located in such a way that people who just walk by can see the displays without having to go into a special room.

Honda

7. SPECIAL OUTDOOR DETAILS

7.1 The approach to many of the buildings is indirect, and passes through a green area, bushes, gardens and fences. The approach to the buildings is more like traditional approach to traditional Japanese buildings perhaps a gravel approach way . . . with changes of direction, passing through different courtyards.

Suyama

7.2 There will be stone paths, particularly in the inner precinct, following the main lines of movement. The homeroom street has paved terraces along both sides, with an earthen street in the middle where there are trees — maybe gravel on the ground.

7.3 At gates between the outer precinct and the inner precinct, there will be a shallow water trough for cleaning outdoor shoes. Since the outer precinct will contain many muddy areas, which will easily contaminate the areas inside the school, it has been suggested that at each place where muddy outside paths, come to the paving of streets of inner precinct, there is a water trough: wash bottom of shoes in water trough, then dry shoes, then pass onto relatively clean surface of inside paving.

7.4 Planted throughout the school there are Keyaki trees, enough of them to line the many public spaces, and to give shade in summer. Right now, there is a group of Keyaki trees with very hard wood, and small leaves, which are growing on the site now, in a nursery, and can be replanted to form avenues, or squares, or other formations.

7.5 Somewhere there is a small carp pond, with very ancient fish in it. Old fish swimming slowly in a circle, under bushes, and in a way that allows people to sit and talk and be quiet near it.

7.6 In the grounds, there is a traditional Japanese tea house, with an outer garden, and an inner garden. A traditional Japanese tea house, placed with an outer garden, and inner garden, a fence separating the two, and a stone path leading through the outer and inner gardens to the tea house itself.

7.7 There is also one garden, so secret, that it does not appear on any map. The importance of the pattern, is that it never must be publicly announced, must not be in site plan; except for a few, nobody should be able to find it.

Hosoi

7.8 Flowering cherry trees, where they are very visible in spring, are placed at particular locations where they please the eye.

Hosoi

8. INTERIOR BUILDING CHARACTER

8.1 The interior character is warm and subdued: wooden columns, floors and walls in places; pale yellow wall color, comparable to golden chrysanthemums, paper or silk; near white sliding screens and ceilings. Wooden columns, often visible; Wood floors in classrooms; Passages and more public areas, floors of soft red tile; Wooden walls, dark; Pale, not white, yellow wall color, comparable to yellow chrysanthemum paper or silk; Ceilings, off-white, bamboo or cloth; Wooden windows; Near white sliding screens.

8.2 Floors of many buildings are raised, slightly, off the ground. We will raise the floor off the ground, thus giving each building an extra two feet of height . . . and helping to make the whole thing a little more stately.

8.3 Classrooms have polished wooden floors or carpets on the floor, and shoes are off inside the classrooms. The classroom has a single floor, no teacher's platform. Students sit on cushions, not chairs, and have a low desk in front of them.

Since many buildings are separated, it is inevitable that people will wear outdoor shoes to move between buildings. They can keep these shoes inside in certain places, like Great Hall, cafe, dining room . . . However, they must take them off in classrooms.

Izumori

8.4 All homebase classrooms will have big windows facing south. If possible, the glare from these windows may be modified by the existence of a gallery, about 1 meter away from the window. Sliding screens, translucent, run parallel to window.

Izumori

8.5 Many rooms have traditional gallery spaces to one side, where light comes in beyond, and shines through screens.

Tomizu

8.6 The classrooms and the rooms are furnished, with very solid, massive wooden desks, which several students share.

8.7 In the larger buildings, there are many mirrors, where students see themselves. Especially in high school, small, as well as big enough to see whole figure. Teenagers like to see themselves often in the mirror, more often than we would expect. Close relationship between children and mirror, deep, close, it is not meant to be seen as a way to make children behave themselves; it is just important for teenagers to be able to see themselves. There is a mirror now in the corridor in front of Hosoi's office: 70% of all students look at themselves when they pass this mirror. 100% look at themselves when they walk by alone.

Mr. Hosoi was quite surprised at this, felt that there was significance in the mirror . . . the mirror has a value to the students.

Hosoi

8.8 Outside, next to the buildings, there are often flower beds. Looking after flowers and plants is one of the main things which the students in the school are taught to do. A large part of the new school consists of either gardens, trees, outdoors, or agriculture. Since the school is not a palace, there is no way to pay for gardeners to look after all this, and keep it in good shape, except maybe for one farmer's family, who will devote themselves to the place.

It is required, therefore, that the process of maintaining, growing things, looking after plants, and having responsible attitude to the place, becomes part of the curriculum, so that students learn to do these things, and become helpful in keeping the place in shape.

Tamura (student)

8.9 Inside, here and there throughout the Campus, there are surprising soft highlights of color, shining out among the subdued colors of the rest ... A figure painted pale in kingfisher blue ... In one place ... A golden yellow iris in another. For the most part, the school is composed of materials with beautiful, subdued, natural colors; wooden columns, plaster walls, wooden floors, stone paths. But occasionally, and only where necessary, highlights of lively colors are used. These places with bright color are not harsh or garish, but give the campus the same sort of life that wild flowers give to a meadow in the spring.

BUILDING COMMITTEE DISCUSSION AND APPROVAL

The list contains 110 essential patterns, each describing a generic kind of center, and itself made of other centers. As they are defined here, these 110 key patterns, completely govern and define the life of the school. Even before we have any idea about the physical configuration of the buildings, their shape, or design, or the way these centers are made real in space, it is already obvious that the school is given its life to an enormous degree, merely by this list of patterns.

One of the remarkable things about the pattern language, and about the members of the existing Eishin School, was the concreteness and pleasant feeling of our discussions about the language. As we have said, a committee was appointed by Hosoi, to oversee the project. This committee, which included Kurahashi, Suzuki, Tokuoka, Nodera, Murakoshi, Hagiwara, and several students, met fairly often in the main meeting room of the old Eishin school in Musashino-shi.

Once we had a realistic draft of the language, we then began a series of discussions with this committee. The discussions were fascinating, because the description of the new school and college, as embodied in the language, was completely real to everyone in the committee. We had discussions about deep matters of content, in which the relation between curriculum and space was understood by everyone. This became the substance of some of the most interesting discussions we ever had.

One was about the relation of the high school to the college. Originally Hosoi had made it clear that the two were to be strongly sewn together. But since the college didn't yet exist, most of the committee members were staff of the high school. As a result, there was a tendency to keep the high school separate, in its present form. This had to be discussed very thoroughly.

To reach this agreement and approval, and to help steer the process of criticizing, changing, and approving the pattern language, the following memo was sent to the Building Committee.

July 6, 1982
To the Building Committee
    1. A joint committee of building committee, high school committee and college committee will make decisions about the final pattern language with the architect.
    2. All faculty will have a chance to give feedback and opinions about the pattern language, but will not have power of decision.
    3. Building committee will coordinate comments, and modifications proposed by faculty, and it will be the responsibility of this committee to obtain these reactions before July 18.
    4. Building committee will also coordinate the decision-making process of the joint committee. Several meetings must be scheduled, during the next two weeks, to discuss major points, and reach agreement about these major points.
    5. Building committee has special responsibility to understand the intention of the present draft pattern language very well, so that they can explain its meaning and purpose in the most profound way to College committee and High school committee, and obtain serious discussion of the most important points.
    6. We should like to have a final pattern language — that is, final agreement on all major patterns — by July 24.
    With best wishes, Christopher Alexander

On July 24, 1982, there was a meeting of the whole school in the school auditorium. The Building Committee had made copies of the final pattern language, and had circulated it earlier so everyone could see it.

The committee, then, together with the full audience, had a discussion lasting about one hour. They then took a vote. The pattern language was adopted.

I sat watching and listening, very well pleased about the way the members of the school had taken this responsibility.

The final pattern language was accepted at a full faculty meeting of the school, in September of 1982.

10 THE CONSTRUCTION BUDGET

As a matter of common sense and practicality,
we next provided the clients of our
community with the means to check the cost of the
environment that was to be built for them (and by them).
We did this by arranging for a sober discussion of a very
practical matter.

Many people, on reading the pattern language, might feel that that the emotional language, and the issues that are raised, go almost too far into the realm of dreams. How can something like the cost or budget be made practical? How can you even be sure that such a large project can be built within the budget?

The answer to this last question is of fundamental importance. It was after all possible that members of the faculty — while agreeing to the poetry of the pattern language — may have differing ideas about the relative sizes of the different areas, and different kinds of construction, different kinds of educational spaces. In this case, the layout might thus be harboring hidden conflicts which no one knows of. When the early work starts, and they meet the inevitable constraints of space and money, the seeming harmony of the pattern language might then give way to a series of quarrels about expenditure.

To solve this problem (before it even has a chance to *be* a problem), we finish the pattern language phase with a serious analysis of space and money. It is done right away, so that any hidden conflicts are visible, and can immediately come into the open to get resolved. This procedure was straightforward and was demonstrated by the steps we took at Eishin.

First of all, we made a record of all the spaces and areas which were defined by the pattern language — adding up, pattern by pattern, the total outdoor space and total indoor space. In our case, the analysis showed that the requested numbers were too large. The site had an area of only 6.7 hectares (67,000 m²), compared with the 84,286 m² requested by the faculty when the pattern language was first constructed. Likewise, the most up-to-date estimate of available funds for construction in 1982, led us to calculate that it would be financially feasible to build 13,204 m² of indoor space, but this was the highest number of square meters we could afford. However, faculty requests for indoor space, when added up, summed to a grand total of 17,990 m² of indoor space — more than 4.79 hectares above what was manageable. It was going to be necessary to trim the areas, so that the expressions of demand in the pattern language could be maintained in principle, yet modified to fit the maxima of available space and available budget.

Second, as the simplest way to trim all space to our available budget, we made an average percentage reduction for all items, one figure for trimming indoor space; and then another for exterior land area. Each item was trimmed by a similar (but not identical) percentage. Those areas requiring *land* were reduced by a percentage to make them all add up to the size of area which we actually had available on the site. Those areas requiring *indoor* space were reduced by a uniform percentage to make them all add up to the dollar figure we could afford in the total volume of buildings that could be built for the available money. As you see below, the reductions were 73.4% for indoor space, and 79.5% for outdoor space.

AREAS REQUESTED BY THE FACULTY			
A. Built Space (indoor space in square meters)	First guess requested	Available 73.4%	Renegotiated, finalized
Public Yard Buildings	945 m²	693 m²	750 m²
Buildings of the Tanoji Center	7583 m²	5566 m²	5604 m²
Cloister (research center)	1350 m²	991 m²	1150 m²
Homebase Street buildings	5680 m²	4169 m²	4300 m²
Buildings in the Outer Precinct	2432 m²	1785 m²	1400 m²
Total	**17990 m²**	**13204 m²**	**13204 m²**
B. Coverage Of Land (outdoor space in square meters)	First guess requested	Available 79.5%	Renegotiated, finalized
Total	**84286 m²**	**67000 m²**	**67000 m²**

Third, we then asked the faculty to re-allocate the spaces, keeping the same trimmed totals, in order to conform to the available resources. The rule was simple: they could increase some, but must then decrease others, so that the total areas remained as they must remain. This required a careful process of comparison, judgment, and balancing of numbers. We and the faculty, together, played with the system of numbers until it worked. With the following memorandum, we involved the faculty in the process of making these adjustments.

September 11, 1982
To all faculty
This memorandum contains the raw material needed for a thorough discussion of space, required by the pattern language, and feasible within the available budget. It is our intention that thorough discussion in the first two weeks of September, will lead to a revised set of numbers, similar to those presented, but now feasible within the available limits.

The architects wish to emphasize, that even when this revised space budget has been defined, it must be completely understood by all persons, that the budget always remains flexible, and is always nothing more than an approximation. The process of laying out the site, and the process of laying out buildings, have their own laws. Careful attention to the wholeness of the situation during these processes will certainly require modification of the numbers we agree on in September.

Christopher Alexander

In order to give the process of discussion a baseline for comparison, we showed three columns in the tables presented to the faculty and students for discussion (the worksheets we used are shown on pages 157-159). The first column showed the area ideally suggested by their definitions in the pattern language. The second column showed the area available if all areas were reduced by a uniform percentage, to bring the totals within the stated limits. The third column was left blank, so that faculty involved in the discussion could make their own proposals for raising and lowering areas in specific line-items, so as to reach the most balanced and fitting overall distribution. This would then allow us to begin the site layout.

FURTHER RUMBLINGS FROM SYSTEM-B

Problems about space were natural enough. Of course these discrepancies had to be discussed, and had to be resolved. And the democratic form of government of Eishin School allowed the teachers to face these problems in a rational and pleasant fashion. Everyone had his say, and resolutions were reached by agreement.

Nevertheless, once again, as these matters were approached, and finally resolved, the underground fight between system-B and system-A became visible, and finally became *clearly* visible.

In system-B, the mechanistic world, things which affect feeling are considered relatively less important. Things which are mechanical, and can be formulated arithmetically, are considered more important. It is not surprising therefore, that the conflict between system-A and system-B began to show itself, just at that moment where the allocation of square meters and amounts of money to different functions had to be resolved. When you can count the money, it is easy to argue about it.

In particular, in our case, the argument started over football. Some teachers had hoped for a football field on the new campus. That in itself was understandable. Every teacher, in a high school, knows how important it is for young teenage men and women to take exercise, and that the healthy body is a necessary partner to the healthy mind. In the old school, students had to travel almost an hour to get to a distant football ground. No wonder that one of the dreams of many teachers — and students, too — had been a football field right in the middle of the campus.

A few teachers went further. They wanted a football field, and a baseball diamond, and an athletics track. But when you look at the numbers, this one thing — an athletics track — requires an enormous area. It would have been virtually impossible to have it, unless one sacrificed the subtlety of all emotionally satisfying space that could exist throughout the campus. If you want water, gardens, paths, bridge, platforms, small gardens, small tennis courts, terraces, gardens for classrooms and so on, then you cannot also have a standard athletics track.

But of course the athletics track is more tangible, in its definiteness, than all these other things prescribed by the pattern language. So, which choices should we make?

LAND COVERAGE

Figures in all three columns represent square meters. The uniform reduction factor for the figures in the second column is 0.795.

	desire	reduced	final choice
Inner precinct	15000	11925	*
Entrance Street	900	716	*
Buildings in the Outer Precinct	1972	1568	*
Out-buildings with roof only	460	366	*
Lake	7000	5565	*
Orchard	1250	994	*
Area w/ Benches, Trees, Ponds	4000	3180	*
Paths	3500	2783	*
Gardens	5000	3975	*
Soccer field (45 x 90)	4050	3220	*
Tennis courts, 2 @ 16 x 40	1300	1034	*
Basketball	700	557	*
Volleyball courts, 3 @ 288 m²	864	687	*
Space around sports fields	6000	4770	*
Open space next to buildings	3000	2385	*
Swimming pool	1000	795	*
Parking, 50 spaces @ 25 m²	1250	994	*
Bicycle Sheds	40	32	*
Land that was unusable	7000	5565	*
TOTAL LAND AREA m²	**84286**	**67011**	**67011**

*The asterisks in the third column, indicate that relevant faculty should choose numbers that sum to 67011 m², the same total that is shown in the last row of the second column. These faculty members should work together to discuss how best to apportion the areas assigned in different rows to make the best use of the total available area.

System-B says we must have an athletics track, because convention requires it, without regard for its impact on the other more subtle features of the environment. The disproportionate physical size of the athletics track must be broken down, or distributed in smaller places. The monolithic oval of a big running track was just too dominant physically to be accommodated, and it would inevitably throw the atmosphere of this campus out of balance.

System-A says we need the subtle and beautiful environment filled with a lake, and gardens, and paths, and small outdoor places for the spirit of the students who are growing into adulthood. Let us then have all kinds of smaller sports fields and sports facilities in the outer precinct as defined in the pattern language, and have the athletics track somewhere else, or get one later, when we can afford more land.

BUILT INTERIOR SPACE

Figures in all three columns represent square meters. The uniform
reduction factor for the figures in the second column is 0.795.

	desire	reduced	final choice
1. THE PUBLIC YARD AND ITS BUILDINGS			
Great Hall	900	661	*
Eishin Museum	45	33	*
Subtotal	**945**	**694**	**694**
2. COLLEGE BUILDINGS / TANOJI CENTER			
Five College Depts	4000	2936	*
Student House	270	198	*
University Cafe (college and faculty dining)	275	202	*
Subtotal	**4545**	**3336**	**3336**
3. HIGH SCHOOL BUILDINGS			
Coffee Shop	70	51	*
Administration	473	347	*
Judo Hall, 100 mats	180	132	*
Small Gymnasium	190	140	*
Two Lecture and Examination Halls @ 150 m²	330	242	*
Small Classrooms	840	617	*
Six College Clubrooms, @ 20 m²	140	103	*
Cultural Activity Clubrooms (High School)	100	73	*
Calligraphy	40	29	*
Miscellaneous (storage, toilets)	300	220	*
Arcades, 150 x 2.5	395	275	*
Subtotal	**7583**	**5565**	**5565**
4. RESEARCH CENTER AND CLOISTER			
Main Library	800	587	*
Research Institute	550	404	*
Subtotal	**1350**	**991**	**991**
5. HIGH SCHOOL HOMEBASE STREET			
Homeroom Buildings, 20 @ 140 m²	3080	2261	*
Gymnasium and small gym	900	661	*

Hall of Faculty Offices	500	367	*
Dining Hall	300	220	*
Misc storage, toilets	300	220	*
Arcades 240 m @ 2.2	600	440	*
Subtotal	**5680**	**4169**	**4169**
6. BUILDINGS & FACILITIES IN THE OUTER PRECINCT			
Art Studios	310	228	*
Science Labs	405	297	*
Cooking/Sewing Workshops	250	184	*
Music Studio	290	213	*
Gardener's Shed	60	44	*
Carpentry workshop	150	110	*
Swimming Pool & Changing	100	73	*
Handball Court	125	92	*
Caretaker's cottage	70	51	*
Small Museum & Maintenance	100	73	*
Sports Clubrooms	100	73	*
Tea House	12	9	*
Main Gate	60	44	*
Bicycle Sheds	40	29	*
Covered Sports	360	264	*
Subtotal	**1973**	**1784**	**1784**
TOTAL BUILT INTERIOR SPACE m²	**17990**	**13203**	**13203**

*The asterisks in the third column, indicate that relevant faculty should choose numbers that add to 13203 m², the same total that is shown in the last row of the second column. These faculty members should once again work together to discuss how best to apportion the areas assigned in different rows to make the best use of the total available area.

This problem was difficult to resolve. Superficially it appeared to be a dispute between the sports teachers and the other teachers. At a deeper level, though, it was a manifestation of a more serious underlying disagreement inherent in the difference between system-A and system-B.

One way to look at the difficulty is to point out that the school had voted to adopt the pattern language, thus implying a consensus about the use of many small exterior spaces with different functions. But the sports teachers who wanted an athletics track would perhaps have argued that at the time of the vote it was not sufficiently clear what they were agreeing to. That is very possible; and illustrates the great concreteness of a pattern language, and the way that people need to be clear, from the beginning, that this is not an idle game, but a serious decision-making process.

WHOSE REALITY SHOULD GOVERN?

Even though the preparation of the language was enjoyable work and went rather smoothly, already there were a few signs of the coming battle. While the request for larger sizes for the sports facilities is a clear example, the next example is more subtle by far; not at all obvious on first view.

The first pattern language already contained some reference to color in the very last pattern: highlights of color. Right away, some teachers objected to the inclusion of the pattern about color. They claimed that what they called "gorgeous colors" had no place in Japan, and asked us to remove this pattern from the language.

Politely, we had to refuse. The reasoning which led to our refusal was this. The peculiar fear of color, which existed throughout the west in the early part of the 20th century, was itself a product of system-B. All over the world, fear of the emotional aspects of color created, at the end of the 20th century, an architecture almost devoid of color — marked by gray buildings, white walls, and neutral colors.

In Japan, with its long tradition of the use of natural material like stone, paper, and wood, this tendency naturally had also gone quite far. But many traditional buildings in Japan exhibit subtle color.

Some of our teachers, captured by system-B, then claimed that the use of color was un-Japanese, and unsuitable in feeling. But factually, this was inaccurate. Throughout the history of Japan, artists have enjoyed the use of brilliant and subtle colors in silks, in pottery, and in painted screens. The kimonos and textiles of the 16th and 17th centuries are wonderful examples. Tea bowls with gold leaf, painted screens with shimmering blue and gold, scrolls, paintings, cloths, banners, armor, all show the Japanese love of color, and their intensely subtle use of it.

However, the importance of color is a *living* thing, not a historical thing. Color is important, because it is in color, above all, that the deepest feelings manifest themselves, in the creation of art. So we *could not* abandon use of color. It is through color, above all, that human feeling would most definitely establish itself in the school. Color was essential — central — to the reality of system-A. Thus, our reluctance to accept the teachers' wishes about color was our concern with the objective nature of emotional reality.

We paid attention to the teachers' wishes, whenever we could, and so long as the wishes that they expressed were consistent with the truth of their own cultural heritage. But when the teachers began to express wishes, or opinions, which were inconsistent with their own cultural and emotional realities, we had to reject their judgment.

Of course, this is a dangerous thing to think, or say. If a group of architects set themselves up as ultimate arbiters of truth, and refuse the wishes of the users, in the face of the users' own statements, in what respect is this different from the fascist and totalitarian disregard for users, which was at that time typical of many architects in system-B? After criticizing system-B so strongly, is this not an example where, like any other 20th-century architects, we, too, just used our own judgment in defiance of the people's wishes?

But system-A does not, above all, have to do with people's wishes or opinions. It has, above all, to do with a zen-like reality — with "the all" or the Whole, as far as it is possible to reach it — and with the truth and facts of human feelings. While the truth and facts of human feeling come most reasonably from users themselves, and while we must therefore give great weight to the judgments and the opinions and feelings which users express, we cannot, in the end, take into account the judgments of the users as final absolutes when we know only too well how drastically system-B has influenced and manipulated society in the 20th century.

In order to come to the truth, we were forced to use judgment about the users' feelings, just as we must also use our judgment and feeling for reality. Even the respect for users, if pushed too far, or made into a dogma, would interfere with this reality, and would then interfere with our ability to establish system-A.

To make a balanced judgment, we felt it must always be reality which governs. System-A comes closest to just that process, which allows reality to govern. In our reluctance to accept the teachers' skeptical statements about "gorgeous color," once again the project showed a faint rumbling of a far-off, coming battle between system-A and system-B.

11 FLAGS: THE REALITY OF THE LAND

We are now, at last, going to make an imprint on this land
— the first dramatic act that changes form, and establishes
the shape of space.

The chapters 7–10 you have read so far have been
explaining and deciding, in principle,
what *kinds* of things are going to happen — what the social
processes are that will stir the people, and stir up the land.

But now, this thirty-eight-page chapter 11 will create an
unforgettable and archetypal form in the site,
creating the organization of the campus itself.

When you are finished with this chapter,
you will have witnessed the birth of this archetype. We shall
see how the actions we took in the twelve months of 1982
changed the shape and character of the place, deeply and
powerfully. By the end of this chapter, the land was to be
marked with a living footprint.

The site plan was to be pulled from the land itself, and the
land was to deliver up its secrets, so that what was built later
would come decisively, and uniquely, from the land itself.

**SECTION 1. SITE LAYOUT IN SYSTEM-A: THE JOY OF LAYING
OUT THE SITE PLAN ON THE GROUND**

The essence of site layout in system-A, and the way in which it
fundamentally differs from making a site plan in a planning office,
lies in the fact that one physically draws the site plan out from
configurations that may be seen because they are discernible *in the
land*. Thus the site plan is not an abstractly conceived, or designed, or
invented figure, but a figure pulled out from the features of the land

itself. This activity comes from the root nature of system-A. It is based on the use of feeling that allows you, and shows you how to judge the wholeness of a configuration. It is a feeling-based estimation of the degree of wholeness in a piece of land, and whether large or small in scale, it is a dynamic, ever-changing process, constantly monitored by feelings and sensitivity to details which seek harmonious results.[1]

In system-A, it is always the wholeness of the place that matters. To intensify the wholeness of any place — whether it consists of existing buildings in a town, or of virgin land that is largely unbuilt — proposed construction and buildings must be decided, and that means "felt" and thought through on the site itself. It is really not possible to do it any other way, since the relationships which exist between the buildings and the world around them are complex and subtle.

On a drawing or a plan, one simply does not see enough. The drawn plan does not give enough information. So trying to make decisions by drawing on a plan is doomed to failure. To produce a plan that has reality, and to bring the actual place itself to life, decisions are made gradually, on the site itself, under circumstances where one visualizes the situation as the whole it really is. Step by step, this brings building positions to life in the mind's eye — and so, in imagination, one conceives the buildings literally, in their full size and volume as they are really going to be.

ACTUALLY CREATING THE SITE PLAN, WHILE WALKING ON THE LAND

Let us say right away that the method we, at CES, have used for years, and the method in common professional use today, are two entirely different processes. Here the differences between system-A and system-B come sharply to the forefront, in dramatic fashion.

In system-B, making a site plan is something generally done

---

1   These concepts are discussed at length throughout the four volumes of *The Nature of Order*, beginning in Book 1: *The Phenomenon of Life*, pp. 297-444. In particular, see chapter 8, pp. 313-350. The process of this activity, is indeed anchored in feeling, human feeling. It rests on a kind of feeling which may be verified. It is not feeling, as people sometimes use the word to refer to an opinion which they hold. It is a feeling that in large measure can be shared and will be shared. But it will only reach that status when it is judged, or perceived, by a person who has learned to discern wholeness. System-A is dependent on this use of feeling as a reliable form of measurement.

Faculty members and staff members sitting on the south ridge, a place from which we could see the layout of our land — all seven hectares of it, and the important places on it. We studied the land for many hours at a time, over a period of many weeks.

on paper. It is an abstract process that happens in an office. But system-A is a real process — physically and emotionally real. Making the site plan is almost like making the buildings themselves. It is done on the real site, with stakes or blocks or flags. As you do it, you have the sensation of building the real place, bit by bit. Emotionally, you feel as though you are literally creating the actual physical school itself. You feel it, even at this early stage of creation, as it will be felt when it is built and finished.

The process can be nerve-racking, because the difficulty of working out what steps to take is hard and sometimes punishing. When you do something wrong, it feels wrong immediately. You can change it; and then you feel you have to change it. You cannot avoid changing it because the wrongness is so clear.

And when you do something right, it is exhilarating. You feel the same joy, mildly, that you will feel in the built buildings later.

The changing arrangement of flags, as our work on the site went forward. Each flag denotes the corner of a building, c *corner of an important part of space. This was an early arrangement, and was provisional. It took a long time to get* *final flag positions exactly right. See final flag positions on page 189, as shown in the take-off from the positions of the*

Most of all, the process is physically exhilarating. You enjoy the fresh air, the rain, the sun, the wind. You have the real bushes and plants and trees around you. You are dealing with living things and build-ings, in the most real way possible. Once you have tasted it, you are unlikely ever again to go back to the method used in system-B.

BEGINNING THE LAYOUT OF THE SITE PLAN

We began work on the site in September 1982, as soon as

the pattern language had been approved by the faculty. Hosoi made arrangements with a group of farmers near a village called Iruma-shi, west of Tokyo, to sell various small pieces of agricultural land, so as to make up a contiguous area of about 8.4 hectares.

Knowing the overall configuration of this land, we had already been thinking about the way the pattern language might generate a layout on that particular piece of land, given direction of access, orientation, wind, views, slopes, and so on. As the content of the pattern language became clear, we were trying to understand the site, and trying to imagine the global structure of a possible campus layout that would arise naturally from the structure of that land.

Each time I went to Japan, I went out to the tea fields in Iruma, and walked and walked, trying to see how the prescriptions of the pattern language could come to life there. Sometimes Hosoi went with me. Once Ingrid King, another CES colleague, went with me. Once Hajo went with me. Others, of course, went by themselves, as well. Each time we were out there, we sat for hours, trying to absorb and understand the structure of the situation. Sometimes we sat there all day. All the hard work was done on the site itself. There were, also, many group discussions with teachers and students. One of the discusssions is seen in the photo on page 165. Sitting on the ridge, we were looking at the whole site, reflecting on what we saw, trying to imagine how to do it right.

Hosoi and Chris in discussion

SECTION 2. FINDING THE TWO FUNDAMENTAL SYSTEMS OF CENTERS

To make the creation process clear, it is first necessary to decide, *in general*, what it is that has to be done when a site plan is made with a pattern language. In any building project, before the site plan can be created, we must identify two different systems of centers.[2]

(1) There is the system of centers which is defined by the pattern language. Pattern-language centers define the major entities which are going to become the building blocks of the new project. In our case, the case of the Eishin project, the language defined the main building blocks or centers from which the new school and university were going to be made. They included, for instance, the entrance gate, the entrance street, the Tanoji Center, the homebase street, the main square, the back streets, Judo Hall, and many others.

(2) Secondly, we had the system of centers which existed in the land. This system was created by the land forms, the slopes and

---

2   The concept of a "center" is defined (and used) throughout *The Nature of Order*, Book 1, and is also described in the context of real projects throughout Books 2 and 3. It is also discussed from the point of view of the deep nature of what centers are in Book 4, pp. 50-134.

Evening light is coming, after a long day's work.
Hiro Nakano, Ingrid Fiksdahl-King, and Chris, are looking at flags, judging and discussing together. They are seen here, marking key positions. We were transfering positions, angles, lines of sight, using the flags, and recording the configurations directly from the land and flags onto the rough working topographic maps we took with us.

ridges, by the roads, by directions of access, by natural low spots, natural high spots, and by existing trees and existing buildings.

It must be emphasized that these two systems of centers already existed at the time one started walking out the site plan.

The first system consists of **patterns** (created notions or entities that exist in people's minds). These patterns exist in a loose and undeveloped form in people's minds, even if they have not explicitly built a pattern language. When the pattern language *is* explicitly defined, it is more clear and makes a more powerful system which will get better results, especially because it comes from the feelings of people themselves. See patterns on pages 131-152.

The second system exists in the form of **places** on the site, discernible places that can be seen and felt on the site, if you have sufficient sympathy with the land. You can make this system explicit, by making a map of the centers, and paying attention to their structure. Each of these two systems is real. Together they provide the raw material from which the community is going to be made.

DIAGRAM 1: A DIAGRAM OF THE MOST IMPORTANT CENTERS GIVEN BY THE PATTERN LANGUAGE

We may see the pattern-language centers in summary form, in a diagram made by one of the teachers, which puts the patterns together, geometrically. This diagram does not indicate any one arrangement on the land.

1. The **ENTRANCE STREET.**

2. The entrance street leads to a big square element which we refer to as the **TANOJI CENTER.**

3. This was to be the core of the college, and the center of gravity of the **FIVE COLLEGE BUILDINGS.**

4. Leading out from the Tanoji Center, in some direction, is **THE HOMEBASE STREET,** the core of the high school.

5. INDIVIDUAL CLASSROOM BUILDINGS open along the **HOMEBASE STREET.**

6. THE GREAT HALL and **MAIN SQUARE** next to it.

7. THE LIBRARY AND RESEARCH CENTER, to one side.

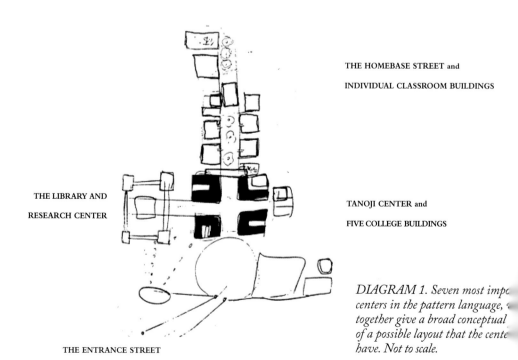

THE HOMEBASE STREET and

INDIVIDUAL CLASSROOM BUILDINGS

THE LIBRARY AND

RESEARCH CENTER

TANOJI CENTER and

FIVE COLLEGE BUILDINGS

DIAGRAM 1. Seven most impo
centers in the pattern language,
together give a broad conceptual
of a possible layout that the cente
have. Not to scale.

THE ENTRANCE STREET

DIAGRAM 2: A MAP OF THE MOST IMPORTANT CENTERS AND THEIR POSITIONS AS SUGGESTED BY THE LAND FORMS

These were the dominant and strongest centers which existed as "natural places" in the land.

1. NATURAL ENTRANCE POSITION. The most important among these centers was the location of the main approach. This was in the southeast corner, partly because of a bus stop in Nihongi village, and partly because of the feeling of one's natural desire about how best to approach the site.

DIAGRAM 2. The seven most **NATURAL** *centers in the land, which, together can lead to a basic possible layout that the centers can have. in their* **LOCATIONS** *in the land.*

2. THE RIDGE, running along the south of the project site. A beautiful spot, with breeze, sunshine, view . . . a very delightful feeling. This was the high point in the site, and it was on this point that we sat and looked and sat and talked, until we began to see what was really there to be seen.

3. THE SWAMP, where vegetables used to be grown, the low point in the terrain — a kind of swamp — that later became a lake.

4. A NATURAL PLACE FOR LARGE BUILDINGS, a zone in the middle, running the way the contours ran, from north to south.

5. MINOR ENTRANCE POSITION, the northwest corner — a natural high spot, from which to view the site, also a natural point for a secondary entrance.

6 & 7. EAST AND WEST ENDS OF THE RIDGE, the two ends of the ridge, which formed natural high points, and at each end, the feeling of a terminus, along the two ends of the ridge.

These seven centers in the land could only be discovered by observation, intensive walking about on the land itself, looking, looking, and seeing. The diagram shows how we identified their rough positions in the landscape. Repeated visits to the site, by different members of our team, consistently confirmed the reality of these centers and their positions.

However, as we can see in the two plan diagrams (below), it was difficult to find a way of arranging these crucial elements in the relationships given by patterns, **and** in a way which made sense on the site. Restating the same idea, we ourselves found it very difficult to find an arrangement of the key centers in the pattern language that preserved their relations to one another, and also coincided with the arrangement of the key existing centers in the land.

In all the cases shown in these early diagrams, the arrangement placed the pattern-language centers in key positions which were quite different from the positions where the real existing centers of the site occurred. For example, in **Test Plan 3**, the homerooms are along the entrance street, too early after entering the campus, and the Great Hall is on the ridge which does not make the most of the linear shape of the ridge. In **Test Plan 4**, the homerooms are along the ridge, the Tanoji Center (shown as a square in plan) does not make use of the uphill line of the procession from the Great Hall to the ridge.

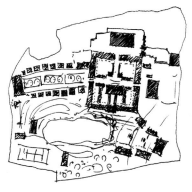

Test Plan 3

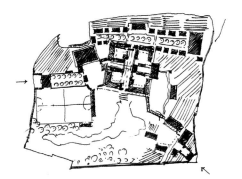

Test Plan 4

Our attempt to preserve the structure of the site, at the same time as introducing the new structure needed by the new school, was essential. It was only in this way that we could work toward the wholeness of the land. When we started, in September 1982, we still did not yet have even the beginnings of a coherent idea of how to place the major elements of the pattern language on the site. We knew that if we could not find a way to resolve this dilemma, we would surely fail.

COMBINING THE TWO SYSTEMS OF CENTERS

What has to be done in creating a site plan for a community or an institution, is to bring these two systems of centers together. We have to hunt for a single configuration which springs from both systems, and integrates the qualities of both. We must find a way in which the system of centers defined by the pattern language can be placed, so that it enhances, preserves, and extends, the system of centers which is already in the land. It is a kind of healing process, which uses the new centers given by the pattern language, to heal the configuration of the old centers — those that exist in the land.

In some cases this is very hard to do because the two systems of centers may not coincide on all points. That is why it takes serious intellectual and emotional effort. In many architectural projects, this is the single most difficult phase of the work. The Eishin Campus was no exception. Including the time taken during the work on the pattern language, it took from May 1982 to January 1983, about nine months of continuous effort, to get the site plan right. When it was finally done, the site plan was a *discovery*, a real achievement, which came from constant study and experience of the site itself.

We composed a memorandum on this topic to help the teachers and students understand what we were struggling with, and what we all needed to resolve, which included the following proposal.

Sept 13 1982

The possible defects or problems in the present pattern language, cannot be improved by thinking about the language any more. Any further thought about the language, without reference to the site, will only continue the slightly problematic

feeling which the language has. We will solve all these problems, and reach a deep
structure suitable for the project, when we begin the work of finding the right
structure of centers for the site.

It is my intention, then, that we shall undertake this task in two phases, which we will
do together with the members of the education/building committee who wish to
participate.

Step 1. First, we shall spend some time at the site, very thoroughly understanding
its feeling, trying to identify good places, and bad places, and trying to discover its
structure together. This phase may take a few days.

Step 2. Then, when we have a clear idea about the structure of the site, and the
way it speaks to us, we shall begin the task of trying to place the major elements of
the school, in appropriate positions on the site, so that together they form a whole.

Step 3. Then, later, when we have a clear picture of the large organization of the
site, and feel satisfied with it, we will develop the detailed layout of paths, positions
of all buildings, and complete the master plan.

The main thing to realize is that this process is a very flexible one, which is based
on the reality of the site, and its structure, and its messages to us. In the process of
understanding the site, and reaching a structure which is harmonious with it, it is
inevitable that the patterns we have defined so far — especially the very big ones —
will be transformed and modified quite strongly by the site. This is perfectly all right,
and is consistent with the intentions of the pattern language. It is important that
all of us who are using the pattern language, continue to understand it in a flexible
and open fashion, and do not get trapped by a rigid interpretation of what it means.

Helped by this memorandum, we (all of us, teachers, staff,
students) went back and forth from the old school in Musashino-
shi to the new site in Iruma-shi, always trying to find out how to
solve the problems of reconciling the two systems of centers into a
single coherent whole. Again and again we visited the site in Iruma.

But, as yet, we could not solve it. We all continued to search
for an answer, analyzing carefully how the campus would be used.
To show the kind of activity which was involved, we provide this
memo on the main entrance, written for faculty, staff, and students,
enlisting their help.

MEMO ON POSITION OF MAIN ENTRANCE

October 1982

The problem of determining the best main entrance for the school, is a complicated one. It is necessary that we begin to develop a clear idea about the position,
WELL BEFORE we try to start laying out the school in October.

We cannot begin the layout until the positions of the main entrance is clear. It will
take several weeks of careful thought to decide the best place for the main entrance,
and this work must begin immediately.

Another moment in the daily process of placing flags — looking at the land, evaluating the position of each flag, looking at them, studying them, thinking about the spaces which the flags define, moving them.

The issues are the following:

First, arriving students will come to the site in three main ways.

1. By bus which arrives in the village below the site.

2. By school bus, shared with girl's college, which will probably drop people along main road above the site.

3. By special Eishin school bus, which will take students from local station, to position of main entrance.

Second, locations.

1. If entrance is on south side (on side where village bus arrives) it may be necessary to buy extra land: either the "useless" mouth-shaped parcel in southeast corner; or, a strip of land giving access to main tea-bush hill on south slope.

2. Access from road along north side is very bad.

3. Access on east side is not good, since main feeling of site is very far towards west side.

4. Access on the west side might be quite good — but this conflicts with position of bus stop in village, which suggests arrival up the east road from village.

Third, feeling of architecture.

In order to give the school a deep feeling, it is necessary that the sequence of arrival be quite profound. This sequence is not easy to create, and happens to be quite exceptionally difficult, with the constraint of the given conditions. It is essential for the good of the project, that this problem be solved in a profound way. In order to resolve the problem posed by these various considerations, I suggest that we adopt the following procedure:

1. Get a clear idea of approximate percentages of students who will be arriving by the three methods outlined in first paragraph.
2. Get a clear idea of any basic desires felt by clients, about position of entrance.
3. Visit the site, with some members of building committee, in order to obtain a preliminary discussion of the issue.
4. Also discuss possible feasibility of obtaining extra land, towards the south, in either of positions defined in second paragraph, clause 1.
5. Try to find a tentative solution, or range of solutions to the entrance problem.

  I should like to make some preliminary progress on this question, before leaving Japan, this visit.

Christopher Alexander

After the distribution of this memo, we and the teachers together made several visits to the site. We were looking, to start with, for certainty about the best place for the main entrance of the site. Working our way into the site, from the entrance position, we then started looking for the best line and positions for the entrance street, and the location of the public square where the Great Hall would be. We gradually became sure about the centers which existed there by an intuitive process, more than by an intellectual process.

Our work went on like this for weeks, from day to day, each day raising new or old issues, some days bringing solutions to positioning and placement. This required constant attention and deepening understanding of what the land would support.

USING THE SMALL MODEL IN BERKELEY

In order to make it possible to think about the problem of the overall plan form, while away from Japan, we made a series of accurate topographic models of the site. We had a large one in our office in Japan, at a metric scale of 1:100. And we had two in our Berkeley offices in California — one made at a scale of 1:200, the other was made at 1:500. This last was very small, and therefore very helpful, because it allowed us to judge the configuration *as a whole*. Larger models show details very nicely, but you lose the drift of the gestalt, as it sits in the land, and reflects the land.

In order to use these models, we recorded on them the seven most important facts about the land, which we had identified during our many visits to the site. The seven were these:

1. One experienced a natural desire to enter the site on the southeast corner, and to walk towards the northwest.

2. The natural position of the lake was given by the swampy low-lying area in the middle of the site, and we therefore knew its position, just from the contours.

3. There was a natural spot, somewhere near the low point and the lake-to-be, where the main square might be.

4. There was also a natural walk, from this low point to the ridge — a walk from north to south, slightly uphill, and slightly curving. This was also inherent in the site, and could be felt by everyone.

5. The ridge along the south edge of the site was the most beautiful spot — it was the spot everyone went to most often, and loved most, because of the view of the distant hills (even including Fujiyama, Mount Fuji, far away in the distance) and the coolness of the breeze in summer. One felt an inspiring freedom there.

6 & 7. The two ends of the ridge also seemed to be natural centers, or more colloquially "good places."

These facts seemed irreconcilable with the key patterns because there seemed to be no natural way of arranging the college precinct *and* the homebase street (as we had them in the pattern language) in a fashion consistent with these seven "facts" about the land. Finally, though, after all our efforts in Japan and in Berkeley, and after all the work on site by everyone, and so many months of frustration, the problem did get solved.

It was solved, oddly enough, in Berkeley. Following one of my visits to Japan, all of us in the Berkeley office spent several days playing with the 1:500 model. We had pieces of balsa wood, cut roughly to the size and shape of buildings, or building-wings — pieces which (at scale) were about 3 meters high, 5 meters wide, and of various lengths. Also lots of small scraps.

We placed them on the smallest site model, toying with the same variations we have shown in the diagrams, trying to reconcile the pattern language with the seven key facts about the site. It still wasn't making any sense. All the time it still felt wrong. Our frustration was considerable, and I began putting down pieces of balsa wood onto the site model (made of modeling clay with accurate contours) in a way — any way — very rapidly, to let the blood flow, and to reach a result that seemed intuitively congruent with what we saw in front of us.

Now all of a sudden a new point emerged. The fact that the homebase street would be more powerful as an *approach* to the Tanoji Center, than as something *hanging off* it. This was hard to see, at first, because it implied reversing the main sequence of the pattern language. But when we tried it, it was clear that the sequence almost instantaneously "jelled" with the land configuration. After playing with it more, we confirmed that it was indeed much better. The sequence of the pattern-language elements which we had taken as fixed, was suddenly reversed.

Instead of this:	We now had:
1) ENTRANCE STREET	1) ENTRANCE STREET
2) MAIN SQUARE	2) MAIN SQUARE
3) TANOJI CENTER (COLLEGE)	3) HOME BASE STREET
4) HOME BASE STREET	(HIGH SCHOOL)
(HIGH SCHOOL)	4) TANOJI CENTER (COLLEGE)

This reorganization seems almost minor. But it dramatically affected the situation. A few days later, we reached the second crucial breakthrough. All the time, we had been imagining the Tanoji Center as square. It had appeared this way, from the time of our earliest diagrams, and we had continued to imagine it like this.

But the main center on the site — the most beautiful spot — was *not* square. It was the ridge along the south edge of the property. Suddenly we realized that this long narrow ridge could actually *be* the Tanoji Center *on* the ridge.

The moment these two breaks in perception were made, the puzzle fell into place. Goaded by frustration, and by the mental energy of our group situation, we rapidly rearranged the bits of balsa wood into a new configuration. The speed and freedom of our movements, *inspired us to act freely and to be free.*

Everything now seemed to find its place. We had the rudiments of an idea. The model with its rough bits of balsa wood, and

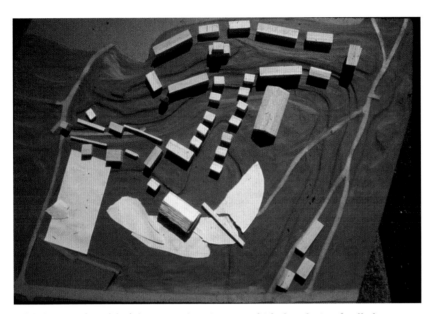

The small balsa-wood model of the site, scale 1:500, on which the solution finally became apparent.

the precarious configuration we had come across, was kept for more than a year. It had immensely subtle relationships, curves, lines, caused by the blinding speed and freedom of the moment. They were very hard to draw. But they inspired us. After a few days, we were sure that, at least on the model, everything seemed fine.

I took the next plane to Tokyo. Now, of course, we had to go back to the site, to see if the site itself told the same story as the small model we had been working on. I remember getting on the plane to fly to Japan to check it out . . . with a great deal of fear. Would the site confirm this vision? Or would we have to start all over again?

I got to Japan on November 1, 1982, and hurried to the site. It was clear very quickly that, in principle, *the new idea of the site plan we had seen for the first time on the Berkeley model really did resolve all the major problems,* and did create a combined system of centers in harmony with the existing centers of the land and site. I telephoned the staff in Berkeley to let them know the good news.

This balsa-wood model was carefully and preciously guarded, even though the configuration was not glued or pinned down. I knew that if the pieces were moved even a tiny bit, the precious configuration might disappear, or it would slip out of our minds, and hands. The configuration, so specific to the millimeter, could elude us in a minute if an unwary move was made. We made certain that it would remain fixed in our office, and everyone was given careful instructions not to touch it.

The spirit of this configuration spoke louder than us all. It was the first hint of the green animal spirit that could be made, like an archetype, to have its own life, and that in that spot we could rely on it to be there forever.

SECTION 3. FLAGS v. SYSTEM-B AND MR. MIURA

Now events moved on quickly. We reached an important skirmish of the larger battle — one that sticks in our minds until this day. What started with an apparently minor argument about flags, turned ultimately into a pivotal physical and emotional event.

We have already made it clear that nearly all our work on the site plan was done on the site itself. Whatever we did on models, we used the models as if they were the site itself — and relied on feelings that we could feel in the model, imagining that it was the site itself. This was made necessary by the huge distance between California and Japan.

As one works on a site and the plan gradually emerges, it is necessary, of course, to leave marks — sticks, stones, markers of various kinds — to fix the position of the different things which have been decided. On the Eishin site, this was more important than usual, because the site was covered in tea bushes. These bushes were three to four feet high (deep). In a few places there were mulberry bushes which were even higher. A marker therefore had to be about six feet high, even to be seen at all.

So we used six-foot-long bamboos. But even they could not be seen at a distance among the tea bushes. To see what was happening — to grasp the evolving site plan — one had to be able to identify key points from distances of several hundred meters. We therefore tied different colored ribbons and cloths — white, yellow, red, blue — to the ends of our long bamboos. These were our markers — our *flags*.

We had started making these flags quite early in the process. Even in July of 1982, as we began to get an idea established about the entrance position, we marked it with three or four of these flags. They were very effective. One could see them from a long way off. They looked beautiful. **And they made it possible to visualize the evolving site plan, truly, because they were real**. They also created a tremendous sense of drama that we all enjoyed.

When I came back to Japan after the breakthrough in November, we took about two hundred of these flags to the site, and began planting them in the ground, starting to make a realistic version as opposed to the very rough-and-ready diagram we had made so far. At this stage, now dealing with real positions and dimensions on the land, we brought true feeling to the land itself. It was visible on the ground.

But now we faced an unexpected problem. Mr. Nishigori, Hosoi's assistant, suddenly asked us if it was possible to make the flags inconspicuous. I explained the physical problems just described, and said that by nature of their function the flags had to be conspicuous: they had to be, because we had to see them clearly, and also needed to relate ourselves to the spaces they marked, as if we were walking about among the finished buildings.

Colored flags, to identify various special purposes and areas on the land.

Then Nishigori asked if they could be temporary. Could we place them, and then take them away again. I explained that this, too, was very difficult. The whole reason for using flags, and for making the site plan on the real site, not on paper, was that very subtle relationships are achieved — often critical to within a meter or even fifty centimeters — and that the positions, to this accuracy, never get recorded correctly on paper — even with the most sophisticated modern survey techniques. It was therefore necessary to leave the markers permanently on the site, and gradually fine-tune their positions — but always leave them in position, right up until construction starts — and then use them when construction starts, without going through the intermediate stages of paper, plans, or surveys, which always introduce inaccuracies and loss of crucial detail.

Now Nishigori and Hosoi explained something of the difficulties inherent in this method. The land was still being farmed. The flags would get in the farmers' way. I countered with some obvious proposals to solve this problem. Then Hosoi explained a more serious matter. The land, although it had been bought, was still, officially, under negotiation. Transfer of ownership had not yet taken place. According to Japanese law, land sales are very complicated, and the process of determining a fair sale price is always mediated by the government. It is a very lengthy process. In this case, even though the agreement to sell the land was complete, the final details of price had not yet been fixed and would not be fixed for several months.

Hosoi and the land-development company involved as broker in the land sale, were very worried that the presence of the flags would somehow stimulate the farmers to ask a higher price than they would if there was no evidence of our work going on.

This was a serious obstacle indeed. I explained to Hosoi that there was no way of developing the site plan without using the flags — and that if we were going to stay on schedule, the flags would have to be placed right away.

He agreed, and we then worked out a compromise. The flags

A pouring day. It poured and poured and did not stop. Of course, we all wore raingear. Here Hajo and Ingrid are looking for a place to get dry.

would be placed for brief periods, and the cloth at the top of the flags, and certain less essential flags, would then be removed temporarily, whenever we were away from Japan. Only a few main flags would be kept in position.

After reaching this compromise, we went off to the site, with our 200 flags in the back of the van. We began placing them and pounding them in.

During the next few days, the site began to seem like a medieval battleground. Hundreds of tall, multicolored flags, paraded all over the site, by various people, determinedly carrying the flags, with the wind blowing and the flags streaming. It looked like nothing so much as a feudal, samurai pageant.

In this respect it was also, once again, immensely enjoyable. The feeling of this pageantry inspired us in our work. It made the project come to life. It was intensely real for us, and for the teachers. It introduced a new level of blood and energy to a process which had, so far, only been carried out on paper, and on a human level.

Suddenly it had become physical . . . real . . . thrilling. It was highly visible. The bowl-shaped site, filled with flags, the flags streaming along the ridge of the tanoji center — inspired everyone who saw them. Something real was happening here. There was no doubt.

And then disaster struck. At three o'clock one morning, asleep in my apartment, I got a rude awakening. The phone rang. Hosoi was speaking from the site. There had been a riot among the farmers. He had to see me right away. He would be at my apartment in one hour. At four a.m., he and Nishigori rang the bell.

A long and complicated story followed. Somehow the farmers, incited or inspired by the flags, had indeed started talking wildly about the project. Negotiations had broken down. The real-estate broker, Mr. Miura, had finally gone by himself — at midnight, without anybody's permission — and had ripped out every one of our two-hundred flags.

The site plan we had produced with such care, was gone. The delicate physical relationships we had identified in the land, the stakes which marked the key positions with accuracy, positions which had been produced and fixed so precisely during the past three or four days, had been lost and fatally damaged. Emotions were at a boiling point.

There seemed no possibility of putting the flags back again, for several weeks. And how could we remember where they had been? A few days of angry talks passed. Only gradually was the *absolute necessity* of using the flags, now established as a fact. The compromise solutions in which some markers, without flags, could be left, and in which we would work as fast as possible, were all threshed through again.

Finally, we got back to work. But now, as a result of these violent or semi-violent incidents, the drastic difference between system-A and system-B had truly asserted itself. The difference between system-A and system-B, was visible without doubt. It had asserted itself fully and dramatically, for the first time.[3]

---

3   It should be said, that the wild situation created by Mr. Miura in suddenly removing the flags, was by no means crazy. The land for the campus was built up from individual sales by some fifteen farmers, contributing separate parcels. This was a delicate operation, as all land assembly is. It is possible that at the time we began setting out the flags, there may well have been one or two holdout farmers who were trying to get as much money as possible for their land. From Mr. Miura's point of view, the image of splendor to come that was created by the flags, must have looked like a promise of wealth for the farmers, and could only have encouraged efforts to further jack up prices of the remaining parcels. In that sense, the dramatization of this event as a battle between system-A and system-B might be regarded as grandstanding. Mr. Miura was simply trying to protect the interests of the school. This is undoubtedly true. It is only common sense.

But it is nevertheless also true that the obsessive use of the language of money as a basis for

DEEP FEELING v. STALE BUREAUCRACY

In theory, of course, the whole incident seemed easy to explain. The land negotiation was going on. Visible signs of progress would hamper the negotiations. It was necessary to keep a low profile. Not much more than that.

But the conflict between system-A and system-B was evident here, at a deeper level, at a level far beyond coincidence or inconvenience. The essence of system-B is that it works with abstractions. Plans are abstract. Money is abstract. The process of construction is abstract. Negotiations are abstract. Reality itself is abstract. There are no feelings, no truly human events, only calculations, ink, and paper.

The essence of system-A, on the other hand, is that it is *real*. It deals with reality of people's feelings. It deals with real people as flesh and blood. It deals with feeling itself. It deals with the three-dimensional reality of buildings, in all its force, with land, and soil, water, and trees.

In our allegiance to system-A, we had (from the point of view of an administrator) committed an unforgivable sin. We had made visible an unavoidable reality. The reality of those flags hit people as hard as if the buildings themselves were already there. Feelings were created. Passions were aroused. The pretense of our site-planning as a polite (and neutral) paperwork could no longer be maintained. And so system-B (in this case, in the form of Mr. Miura, the real-estate broker) had moved in to wipe out system-A. System-B, at its root, could not tolerate the reality of human feeling that was visible in the flags, and was directly experienced in the strong emotions of system-A. So, at midnight, on the 20th of November, 1982, full-scale battle began with the stealing of the flags, and the destruction of their positions — an act hardly less violent, no less hostile and destructive than the capturing of flags in a battle between samurai — as it pertained to the creation of the Eishin campus.

The purpose of the flags was practical, reasonable and straight-

decision-making, rather than the wholeness of the land, was indeed, under the surface, **precisely** what created this physical skirmish between system-A and system-B.

forward. They were placed so that we and the students and teachers could all feel and experience the large building complex, as it was really going to be built. This was something almost unprecedented in the annals of 20th-century planning, and it was aimed entirely at the well-being of the campus. Yet the real-estate people ignored its practical importance, and treated it as if the flags (actually little more than pieces of cotton cloth wired to the top of long bamboos) had been unfurled as flags of war and had to be destroyed.

It took months to solve the problem and make up for the damage that had been done. Worst of all, the positions of the bamboos, placed with care and sensitivity, had been lost. Now, a new series of half-hearted compromises were made. We were supposed to use the flags, and then take them down at night; use flags which were not too big; and use flags that could easily be removed. Anything to avoid the possibility that awful reality, with its real feelings, could contaminate the abstract process of system-B.

But we agreed to make these compromises, simply so that we could get on with our work. This meant that once again we placed flags, walked about, studied the feeling, moved the flags, and went on like this until we felt the whole plan was once again coherent, and had the valuable and harmonious feeling with the place, that we had achieved before.

SECTION 4. THE FIRST HARDLINE DRAWING MADE FROM THE LAND & FROM THE POSITION OF THE FLAGS

The hard work of fixing detailed positions on the site, and recording them, now began. By this stage, we had a rough idea of the site plan — the one which was made on the model in Berkeley, and then checked out roughly with the famous flags. But now that we had experienced the layout of the buildings, approximately, and knew that they were more or less correct, we had to begin the long slow process of getting all positions and dimensions right, in detail. This work was arduous, and took a further six months to complete. The work demanded that we gradually build up a picture of the general site plan we had already sketched out, now fixing each building in just the right position, and getting every space to feel exactly right, in position, orientation, and dimension.

Up until now, the Japanese office of CES had provided general support for our activities. But we had not, so far, had any one of our own Berkeley team living permanently in Japan. I asked Hajo if he could move to Japan, and he began to stay in Japan for rather longer periods. During these periods, he did an immense amount of hard work, adjusting, fixing positions, modifying drawings, modifying the model in the Japan office, and so on.

The various kinds of work which we shall describe now were done between September 1982 and June 1983, at various times. Sometimes the work was done by Chris and Hajo on the site, sometimes by Hajo and Hiro Nakano on the site and in the office. There was one very enjoyable time with Ingrid, Chris, Hajo and Hiro all working together in a day of nonstop, pouring rain. In any case, it was a slow process, and required a lot of patience.

By October, we had a rough idea of the site plan, and had staked it out. In system-B, the normal procedure, would now simply be to make the drawings of this plan more precise, in a drawing office using technical drawings or (as it would be now) using computer drawing programs to do the same: working out details of access, drainage, boundaries, building locations and so on, and then making a formal drawing which could be submitted for a civil works building permit.

In system-A it is quite another story. Each building is intended to be placed in a position which *feels* exactly right, where it has an immediate, felt, harmony with its surroundings. Each space, each line of movement, each axis, each boundary, is also supposed to be something which comes directly from the real place itself, fits the land perfectly. Every detail must arise out of the reality of the land.

The animal-like figure of the building complex was now consciously being sought. Every nuance was examined, accepted, or rejected. We knew we were playing for high stakes, and we had to pay attention to the process by which the animal spirit would reveal itself, to us, and become substantial. Everyone had

to make a shift in orientation to the project: stop thinking about this as a building project, and start thinking of it as a living thing. Together, we found ourselves searching for the living animal.

Compared with this ideal, the first site plan we made, though also an overall positioning of all the elements and their relationships to one another, was not yet fully precise to the level needed for foundations. That required yet another pass, to add still further precision to the points that had been set. The positions had 90% accuracy. Now they needed 100% accuracy, give or take a few inches. Each point, each center, and each corner, had now to be fixed finally, once again by appealing to the real feelings of the real place. To succeed in this, each building had to be staked out with real stakes, examined, reexamined, felt, watched at different times of day, and in different weather.

This process is, *in its effect*, similar to building slowly in a traditional society. It is what would happen naturally, as a farmer, or a traditional master mason built a farm or a small village, over a series of decades, and took his time, gradually, to get every detail right. But, in Eishin, because of the conditions of modern site planning, all this had to happen, on the land, over a period of no more than a few months.

Rather early on, for instance, we had to fix the position and size of the first (small) gate. At that time there was a patch of mulberries, right where the entrance street is now. But we could not be sure of the small gate's position, without also being able to visualize the entrance street. So we got a few very long stakes, about five to six meters long, long enough to stick up out of the mulberry bushes. We placed stakes to try and get the edges of the entrance street just right. Then the small gate itself was placed. Should it be eight meters wide, or nine meters wide? Seven meters? How far from the road along the east side of the site should this small gate be? We first imagined it right on the boundary, then a few meters in from the boundary, and so on.

It should not be understood that there is some systematic way of trying many alternatives. The process is more intuitive than that. We would begin by placing the thing where it felt right. This was by pure instinct, a kind of primitive, almost animal-like action. Then, since there were often two or three people involved, we would try variations which seemed as if they might be better; then gradually eliminate them one by one, until finally, we had a version of the most instinctively right place that felt just right to everyone.

Often, in the later stages of such a process, the members of the faculty were involved. We would bring them out, and ask them if they too felt that this or that was right. Especially in difficult cases, we consulted them many times over, to be sure to get it right. Sometimes, the same thing would be done, repeatedly, two or three times, each time becoming a little more certain, each time a little more deeply related to everything else that had been decided.

In the case of the entrance street, for instance, by the time we settled it, the mulberries had been picked, the bushes then cut down to the ground for winter, and then grown up again a second time and become dense again, just before the civil works began. Only when cycles of season and cycles of social change had been experienced, could we feel sure that we had examined the conditions sufficiently.

The drawing on page 191 is the first and only hard-line drawing we *ever* made of the site plan. This means that we had never, up until that moment, tried to make an accurate plan drawing on paper. All the content captured on this drawing came from our tramping around on the site, recording the information we got from the site, and doing our best to keep making subtle adjustments — because of what we felt in reality, and then keeping records of the positions and markers we had used. This was in the hope that the feeling which had guided us, would be accurately enough transcribed to the drawing, so that it could preserve the sensitive and precious feelings we had brought to life in the land.

THIS PARAGRAPH IS VERY IMPORTANT

In this particular project, it happened that the beautiful rows of tea bushes, made our work very much easier. As you see in the drawing on the next page, the lines of the tea bushes were surveyed by an aerial photograph, then transformed by photogrammetry. When we then placed flags, by counting rows, and measuring the distance from the end of the row to the position of the flag we had placed, we were able to keep an ongoing record of the flag positions.

SECTION 5. GETTING DETAILED BUILDING POSITIONS

The main gate was especially important, and also very subtle. Its exact size and exact position had great effect on the feeling of the approach. If we made it twelve meters wide (across the building face one sees as one approaches it), it created *one* feeling. At fifteen meters wide, it created quite *another* feeling. Even the difference between fourteen and fifteen meters was enormous and felt like two different creatures. The same was true of its depth. We tried it at five meters deep. Fifteen meters deep. Ten meters deep. Each one was entirely different in feeling.

And, of course, the exact line and position of the entrance way itself had a surprising effect. Indeed, the entrance way when staked out at five meters wide, and at six meters wide, created two different feelings in the way that the inner area beyond the gate revealed itself.

Using the flags, one could judge the angle of the gate's surface to the line of travel (it was not always ninety degrees). The angle of the gate to the axis of approach had a big effect on what one could see through the opening as one approached it. We used four stakes to mark the actual space of the entrance way itself. It is hard to explain this in a book, but the amazing thing is, that if one moved one of these stakes by twenty centimeters, it made a crucial difference. You can see the subtle angle that was achieved, in the sketch and photograph of the main gate on page 191 and 192.

Imagine the two stakes which create the front plane of the main gate. This is the face toward the entrance street. If we move the left stake forward or back by twenty centimeters, it completely changes the angle of the building, the axis of the entrance way, and the view of what one sees as one walks through the gate — so the feeling is entirely different. And of course you have to check and look from all sides. For example, the opposite face from the entrance street forms the main public square with the Great Hall and other important buildings. So it was critical that the facade of the main gate had an absolutely positive impact on the space of the public yard.

Again stakes were moved, angles checked, until the position, width, and opening felt completely right, not only from the entrance street face but also from the public square face. And the same thing happened again when we checked the main gate from the other two remaining sides. In fact, the building somehow got its form and exact size largely through our efforts in defining the spaces surrounding it. All volumes and spaces were thus defined in a way that they became thoroughly intertwined, together making positive spaces and positive volumes in the larger whole.

SECTION 6. RECORDING THE SITE PLAN ON PAPER

During this period, we were thus placing stakes, and recording them, to a level of accuracy which had to be exact to within twenty or thirty centimeters — on a site that is more than 280 meters across, in each direction. While we were working on the site,

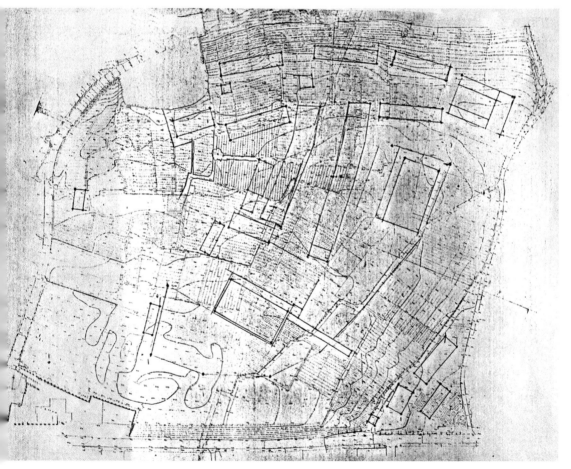

The first precise, hard-line site plan, derived from flag positions, calibrated and measured according to the tea-bush rows on the land, visible here, and as given from an aerial photo.

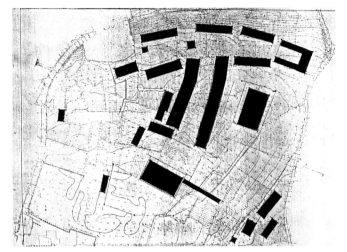

*The same measured
drawing, taken
from the tea-bush
stakes on page 189.
Here the important
buildings are
shown in black.*

*Laying out the entrance street walls, turning through the few
degrees needed to line up with the main gate. In the black
drawing, above, we can pick out the small gate because it is
the furthest to the left. At a similar angle, but further to the
right you see the footprint of the main gate. The main gate is
about two lengths of the Great Hall away from the small gate.
On this black plan, the footprint of the main gate is too thin,
compared with its breadth. This happened because we were not
familiar enough with its shape. As soon as we began building
models, the Main Gate shape soon put us right. See photo
below. The thickness of the gate is about one half its width.*

 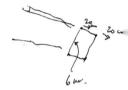

*If you consider the rectangle as the main gate plan,
and if you push the top right-hand corner of this
rectangle by 20 cm outwards, you can rotate the
gate by any amount, until it feels just right.*

*The main gate, as it could be seen later, from outside the entrance street. In this picture, the
entrance street runs behind the wall (from left to right), going toward the gate, then under the
gate, and on to the edge of the lake and a view of the dining hall.*

Ingrid and Chris discussing our early working model of the project, in our Tokyo office, scale 1:100. At this stage, we were studying the relative positions of the Great Hall and main gate, but at this early stage we had not yet modelled the actual shapes which would, later, be given to these two buildings. On the next page, we see the actual frame of the Great Hall, about fifteen months later.

we also had, in our Tokyo office, a 1:100 model of the whole site. The main gate model was only cardboard, but rather accurate in regard to plan position, with all contours, nearby buildings and so on, all carefully shown.

Every day, when we had finished working on the site, we went back to the office, and made marks on our 1:100 model, and made adjustments in the physical positions of things, according to whatever we had determined on the site that day. In many cases, we built rough test models of a particular building, only to change it again a week later as our understanding of the buildings developed.

By now we already had approximate volumes for the buildings. Of course, these could not help being approximate, since the detailed design and volume of the buildings were not yet known. But there was enough known about each volume, so that we could keep pace with the daily work from the site in the 1:100 cardboard models on the site model. Then, each time we made new decisions about the position of a building, or its dimensions, or its axis, we would immediately modify the model in the Tokyo office to keep it up-to-date with the latest decisions that were being made on the site. But the sheer problem of measurement itself, was immense. Indeed, conventional methods of surveying were inadequate for recording decisions of such precision, where twenty centimeters mattered.

It is very hard to realize the immense work of going back and forth, between the site and the office, recording these minute details, for every building, and for every space, and then finally transferring them to a perfect, final plan. Hajo, with his background in the military, working with military exactness, was able to do it right. He played a major part in this enormous task.

This photograph is about the same view, from the same direction, of the Great Hall and main gate. We are using it here to illustrate the stakes, and poles, and ropes, which allowed us to mark the position of the entrance street. In the picture we see several of our crew laying out the detailed position of the entrance street, with the long stakes and ropes, all the time judging the shape and position of the space of the entrance street as it was developing.

SECTION 7. REFLECTING ON SYSTEM A AND SYSTEM B AS TWO WAYS OF LAYING OUT A BUILDING SITE

The reader may possibly have noticed, especially in the last few pages, that to some extent the process seems haphazard, seeming to be done almost without premeditation. For an engineer, or for an architect trained under system-B conditions, this haphazard quality is likely to seem foolish, possibly irresponsible, and not sufficiently in touch with obvious practical questions of space allocation. Yet you can see how beautifully the long buildings lie on the land, and in the land, how comfortably they are grouped, how eloquent the variation of building length is, as one compares building to neighboring building. It is precisely this placing of the buildings on the land, by the visceral process described above, which makes the finished buildings lie so comfortably in the land (see photograph on page 196). Indeed, the lack of concern, for detailed building design, at this early stage, is entirely appropriate. It means that one judges the comfort and harmony of the buildings first by intuition, and by eye. Then, and only then, is it appropriate to finely tune the areas in each building.

It is simple and appropriate to make these calculations as the buildings get settled more and more firmly in their position in the land. It is this which allows the buildings to form a harmonious enclosure for the college.[4]

In fact, the very life and wholeness which is aimed at by methods of system-A are achieved by a more relaxed state of mind. It is not sloppy, and the calculations and costs do not suffer. Instead, this atmosphere of work in system-A allows the buildings to find their place, their proper and harmonious existence, and so make beauty appear in the buildings and the land.

The exaggerated precision typical of system-B, often done at inappropriate times, can kill the spirit of the buildings. Just so, many other aspects of system-B, too, can kill the spirit of buildings and their human essence.

---

4 The concept of *positive space*, is fundamental to the nature of wholeness. A piece of space is positive, when it is felt from the inside outwards, and thus is capable of being embodied with "being." Definitions of these concepts may be found in all four books of *The Nature of Order*.

The long, white buildings perfectly curved in synchrony with the land contour, thus expressing the natural formation underlying the positions we gave to the edge of the ridge.

In marked contrast to that system-B approach, consider this. Years later, Hosoi was making a public statement of our experiences during the months of the site-plan work and the placing of the flags. This is what he said of the flags: "We could see . . . the actual buildings . . . standing there." He said this very slowly, with pauses and emphasis, as if to insist on the huge impression this had made on him. I can still hear Hosoi's voice today, saying these words. "We could actually see . . . the buildings . . . standing there."

He meant it literally. When he walked around the campus, at the time when there were only flags standing there, he had already begun to visualize the buildings, and walked around them, and looked at them, and showed them to his friends.

SECTION 8. CREATION OF POSITIVE SPACE AND SPACES

We come, now, to what is perhaps the most important, single issue that comes up in all land planning and building layout! When we think about buildings we asssume, naturally, that the buildings are the most important entities and we assume then that if we place them well, that will be the end of the problem. **BUT THIS IS NOT THE CASE.**

When we were walking about on the land, long before it was a campus, we naturally felt inspired to walk, and stand, and sit, in certain places.

The white entities represent space (viewed as if each chunk of white space was a solid material), created and surrounded by the black material in the drawing which represents the solid buildings made of stuff of space.

The open space, the white stuff and its organization, is the most important and significant aspect of the campus.

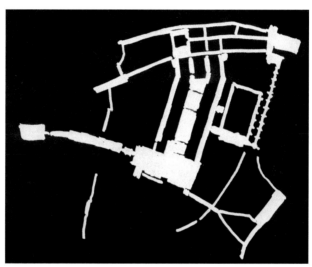

Other places did not encourage us to go there, did not cause us to have positive pleasure, did not make us feel, in our hearts, that we had arrived at a place which we very definitely wanted to inhabit, and wanted to stay there.

These places — which may be noticed and joyfully enjoyed — are the places which must be marked, and furnished with enclosure, and views and furniture. These are the kinds of places which mean something to us, and which — ultimately — become the important places of the campus. It is these places that we call positive space, or positive spaces.

It is the positive, outdoor spaces above all, which give us pleasure, and which give us our attachment to the land.

SECTION 9. THE GREEN CREATED ANIMAL — THE NEW REALITY THAT WAS FINALLY ACHIEVED

These spaces are formed *by the buildings*, it is true. But these spaces which might be regarded as accidental, or lesser, are actually the most important treasures of the campus. The life of the campus, and the lives of the students and teachers, will always depend on the extent to which these outdoor places are positive and are made up of positive spaces.

After months of hard work, skirmishes, and battle, it was a great moment when the final site plan was in front of our eyes, on the land, with white, red, yellow, and blue flags, measured and visible for all to see. It was amazing to see it; now it was completely real. The bowl-shaped site was filled with flags: blue flags which formed the lake, yellow flags which formed the paths, red flags which marked important centers and spaces on the site, and white flags which formed the buildings. It was fascinating to see the flags forming the entrance street, marking the main square, then climbing up the homebase street, and then continuing to form the outline of the tanoji center and college along the ridge, marching finally toward the research center and the library. Almost everybody who saw it was inspired.

The core of the "created animal" — the site plan which results from all the efforts depicted in this chapter — *lies in the positive space which establishes the gestalt of the site plan as a whole*. The white drawing on the black background (see page 197) shows the space which is experienced, and made by the buildings. The twofold sense of (1) order, and (2) roughness showing the life that comes from the way this place is being consciously and continuously made and remade. This production of positive space, that arises from the living experience as we shaped the space by walking around in it, is visible in purely graphic terms. This rough sketch, based on the original trace in the tea-bush fields also gives a quality not unlike the best examples of oriental calligraphy. It is rough, but it is full of life.

And this trace transmits its feeling to the actual space in and among the buildings. We hope that this quality will also be visible in the buildings that were made subsequently (see chapter 12), to fill out and shape each space, thus passing this quality on, from the outdoor rough spaces and their organization, to the physical and material details of the buildings themselves. On a smaller scale, we hope the same quality will be visible — and experienced — in the rooms and interior details.

For people who visited the site for the first time, it was easy to understand these beautiful spaces, just by seeing them and walking through them, because the whole — the space as a whole, as it was created on the campus by the buildings — was so utterly harmonious and real.

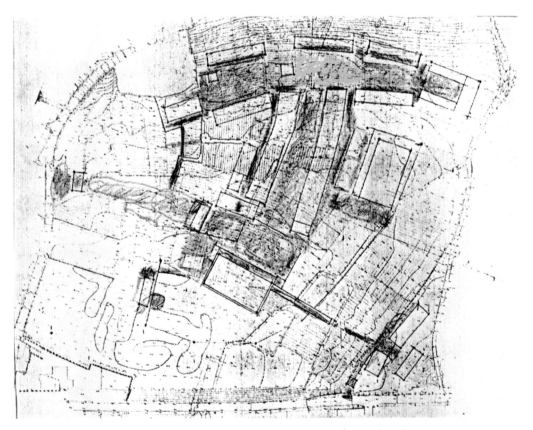

The green spaces in this drawing represent pedestrian space (viewed as if it were a solid material). These green entities, the green organization, the paved outdoor areas — all that is of the essence. It is the most significant aspect of the campus.

It brought about the feeling of a living entity, an animal with its own right of being there, providing breath for both students and teachers, and for craftsmen, and for carpenters and plasterers, and for those who made the concrete and plaster ornaments.

It was alive. The place was alive, because we had struggled, worked the stones, and spent the strength of our bodies to shape every part just right, knowing then, that the animal would have its spirit. The animal we had been looking for — the spirit of the place that we had worked so hard for, for such a long time — had finally arrived.

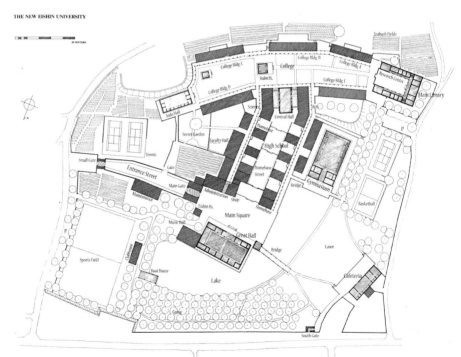

Scale site plan of the Eishin Campus at the scale of approximately 1 cm to 28 meters. A few buildings are not yet built, including the three college buildings on the south side of the ridge, the Library and the Research center complex, at the west end of the ridge. A larger drawing of the campus site-plan, may be seen in the final end paper of the book.

12 SYMMETRY, SIMPLICITY AND GRACE

In chapter 11, we laid down a conception of the campus plan as a whole. Because of the creature-like quality of its morphology, we spoke of it as a "living animal." Although this phrase may have seemed clumsy, it led us to a practical, animated group of buildings, emerging and forming together, a new kind of living whole.

In chapter 12, the buildings now take on a more massive and solid, three-dimensional form. This happens in such a way that the relation between people and buildings, and walls and doors and windows, takes on a quality in which the stuff of the built material becomes directly related to its solidity, its geometry, its ornaments, and to the relationship between the people and the building **space**, and the building **mass**. As a result, people have a tangible relationship to the matter from which any of the campus buildings are made. The outdoor rooms and spaces are made from surrounding "walls" — which are actually the buildings of the campus.
This is fundamental.

We aim to create a direct relationship between the built forms of the buildings and the people who will live and work there; direct, in that the built forms evoke feelings of belonging, self-esteem, and nourishment. Particular geometry, ornaments, materials, and space then form this very special environment where we have in our mind's eye — all the time — just what it means for buildings to have symmetry and simplicity.

Changing the Way Architecture Should Be Done

ASPIRING TO A BETTER ARCHITECTURE

We began by expressing to one another, our desire to reach buildings of some artistic and spiritual worth. We hoped to achieve this arising from simplicity and nested symmetries — easygoing, geometrically profound — laying down a way of conceiving and erecting buildings as solid constructions. The initial manifestation of the campus, which started with the flags, now became more solid and would now be three-dimensional.

Walking about the campus, visiting the different buildings and the spaces they created, in our mind's eye we could imagine an outline of the finished campus as a whole, and the volumetric disposition of the buildings, in detail — without even a single brick actually being laid.

With the site plan more or less complete, and already including a rough volume envelope for each building, we continued work on the design of the individual buildings. This arose out of the careful work we had done with the pattern language, the site, and the placement of building volumes with stakes and flags. We began to experience the buildings as structurally real — as things made, of concrete, plaster, tile, wood, and stone, not cardboard images.

At once, when we take these matters into account, we find that the process of designing buildings and building them is entirely different in system-A than in system-B. In system-A, each building arose, in a natural way, from the specific conditions of its location, by extending the configuration of the site (landscape, buildings, slopes and views). It also arises from the cooperation and layout of the people who are going to use it. And it gets its physical character, its actual material substance, from a process of thinking how to make it. All this sounds commonplace.

The professional, contemporary, architectural rhetoric of system-B — as it has been in the architect's professional attitude from 1960 to about 2010, with the beginning, now, of some signs of abatement — likes to claim that a building gets its form from similar considerations. But in system-B this is most often only rhetoric. The real situation is more likely to be that a building still gets its character, first as an image, drawn on paper, by an architect's fantasy, a simulacrum which is then physically built in cheap and flimsy studs and sheetrock, concrete panels, cardboard — or in whatever conventional system of construction the contractor has to hand.

Sadly, this is where the dull, lifeless, and stereotyped character of buildings in the 20th century mainly came from. It is also, at the same time, where the wild and fantastic egotistical shapes of the present era come from. They are conceived and carried out as images, not conceived and built as beautiful material things which are to be made as extensions of the wholeness of a place. The word "beautiful," here, effectively means that it is a picture of the human soul. You cannot flinch from this word, and expect to succeed. System-B still maintains this recent modern habit, and still fails to extend the wholeness which is there. In system-B, most buildings are conceived as images or part-images, not as built, **solid**, **made** works. These papery, system-B things are not conceived and made for the sake of their material reality. The feeling one gets in the presence of these buildings, does not fill the onlooker with the beauty or the presence of the material substance.

We were determined and intent on overcoming the dullness of contemporary building methods. And we were intent on the task of putting life into the elements and components as we made them.

THE SIMPLICITY OF RECTANGULAR, SYMMETRICAL SHAPES

Let's roll up our sleeves, now, and tackle the buildings themselves! The thirty-odd buildings on this campus are plain, sometimes almost severe in their simplicity, rectangular in plan, dominated by a symmetrical structural section, and thus depend on a single axis of symmetry, based on the simplest structural form. With the exception of a couple of sheds, the roofs all have symmetrical pitched roofs. Yet the buildings are all different, and are given their charm and profound character by their purity of structure. Within the simple shape that gives birth to all of them, there are variations and complications that arise directly from necessity, as you will see when we describe the process of designing and constructing several buildings. The simple shapes are capable of carrying enormous variation, and rich ornament, and majestic interior space.

There are no fashionable shapes, or exaggerated shapes. The appearance of symmetry in nature comes about because there is a symmetry of the conditions where the thing in question exists. In most cases the symmetries occur because there is no good reason for *asymmetries* to occur. That is why raindrops are symmetrical. That is why trees are roughly symmetrical. That is why volcanoes are roughly symmetrical.

The raindrop meets the same conditions all around, while it is falling. That is why any axial, vertical slice through the raindrop looks the same. Horizontal slices are the same, too. The drop has circular symmetry. A tree has, roughly speaking, equivalent conditions, no matter from which side you look at it; though the differences of sunlit directions and shaded directions will cause differences in plan, so that the plan view is symmetrical with a circle symmetry.

With buildings it is much the same. Most buildings have characteristics which generate similar conditions inside according to symmetrical positions inside the building. Most traditional and ancient buildings have a structural plan which is symmetrical, (other things being equal), because it is the simplest thing to do, and the most satisfying, and structurally the most stable.

As a result, the sensible and natural rule of thumb for building shape is that buildings will, in most cases, have at least one axis of symmetry in plan, sometimes two axial symmetries at right angles to one another. Floors will be similar, except for a natural gradation from ground floor to roof, usually made necessary by differences of light and ease of access as one goes upward from the ground.

That is why buildings have a partial translational symmetry as one moves upward, from floor to floor.

There is, therefore, an overwhelming reason why the buildings in a group of functionally related buildings look similar. It is because they share the fundamental ground conditions, which will produce roughly similar, and internally symmetrical, shapes and sizes, and organization.

These elementary considerations make it highly unlikely that there should be any need for wild variations of shape, configuration, or articulation. There will be some, of course, when called for; but modest, not exaggerated.

That is why churches used to be symmetrical, because it was the simplest and therefore the most profound condition. That is why the Parthenon is symmetrical. That is why the buildings of Angkor Vat are by and large internally symmetrical. And that is why the Japanese traditional architecture, and the traditional Norwegian architecture, and the traditional Russian architecture, all have a vast and overwhelming use of connected symmetrical structures, with minor variations from one to another, according to the specific and detailed needs that may vary.

They are the simplest way to build things. They are most elegant. And the simplicity of the external envelopes, provide immense scope for decoration and ornamentation which follows from the internal symmetries.

So, for all these reasons, we began **each** building on the campus with the assumption that it started life as symmetrical within itself, and was kept very simple.

CHOICE OF MATERIALS AND STATISTICS OF MATERIALS, SUPPLEMENTED BY A CAREFULLY CHOSEN STRUCTURAL SYSTEM FOR EACH BUILDING

The first thing we did, when we began the design of any one building, was to discuss the materials of its construction. The pattern language already gave some hints about materials. But now we had to begin thinking clearly about the physical structures themselves. We studied various large complexes of buildings — historical ones from different countries — to find out what quality their materials had as a whole and in the large.

Immediately, we made a very striking and surprising discovery. The most beautiful and most harmonious groups of buildings always have a subtle and complex variety of materials. There is almost never one single material of which everything is made. Instead, there is a range of materials, for different tasks, and these harmonize subtly, and profoundly. The feeling which exists in these places clearly comes from this interplay of materials.

One of the clearest examples of this quality was visible in a photograph of an ancient Chinese monastery we found in a library book. Throughout our work we kept a copy of this photograph on the wall of the office, to inspire us. The photograph is fascinating. It shows just one very small corner of a huge complex of buildings — near the main entrance. But in this one small corner, we already see stone, brick, wood, plaster, roof tile, clay, and wall tile. And there is a feeling of perfect grace and harmony. No feeling at all of clutter, of any kind of over-rich combination. Just perfect ease.

Our experience, studying many complexes of buildings which are remarkable for their beauty — both famous ones and others not so well known — was that this rule was confirmed, time and time again. The grace they have comes from subtle combinations of materials, which use the many different materials *in different quantities*. Although this observation may seem obvious, it is surprising, because, as an empirical fact, it so strongly contradicted the dogma of 20th-century convention about building complexes. The most famous complexes of modern times were essentially made of a single material. Le Corbusier's monastery of La Tourette: concrete. His Marseilles apartment block: also concrete. Mies van der Rohe's Lake Shore apartments: black steel and glass. Alvar Aalto's Saynatsalo town hall: almost entirely brick. In general, in the mid-20th century, it was widely supposed that the unity and integrity of these projects would come from the so-called purity — usually meaning the uniformity — of their material.

Labrang monastery, Western China

It is therefore surprising to find — as an empirical fact which anyone can check for themselves — that the buildings which most profoundly communicate subtle harmony are composed of a complex mixture of materials, with the overall amounts of different materials jumping in a calibrated cascade — typically, according to a power law.[1] And we made a second observation; namely, that the relative proportions of materials — the statistical distribution of materials by quantity of total visible area — is critical. It is this specific distribution, not just the mixture, which creates depth of feeling.

---

1   Zipf's law, named after the Harvard linguistic professor George Kingsley Zipf (1902-1950), is the observation that frequency of occurrence of some event (P), as a function of the rank (i) when the rank is determined by the above frequency of occurrence, is a power-law function Pi ~ 1/ia with the exponent **a** close to unity (1). For a similar rule, see the table on page 210.

We therefore began a series of experiments, to discover the best distribution of materials for each building in the project, and for the project as a whole.

We already had a feeling that the project would include concrete block, concrete, wood, and plaster, and roof tiles. We therefore set out to find out what mixture of these materials — what percentages — gave rise to the most harmonious feeling.

Our first experiments, usually full-size mockups, were done in our Berkeley construction yard. We used concrete blocks to represent concrete block, cardboard painted with gouache to represent plaster, wood for wood, and concrete for concrete. In addition, we included, in these experiments, the possibility that the plaster might have several different colors. The accompanying photographs show some of the mockups.

Test 1. Black plaster below, plaster and concrete ornaments to separate the upper from the lower wall, then light green plaster above, and natural concrete on the right.

Test 2. Natural concrete below, plaster and concrete ornaments to separate the upper from the lower wall, then black plaster above.

Test 3. Black plaster below, plaster and concrete ornaments to separate the upper from the lower wall, then dark concrete above, and a pale green pilaster on the right.

The photographs on page 209 emphasize the fact that even at this very early stage, before any buildings had been designed, we were already looking for detailed information about the physical balance of color, light and shade, texture, material, and breakdown of quantities of materials on exterior surfaces, so that we could see, and grasp physically, the quality of the buildings we were going to make.

The deliberate effort to create overall statistics of the different surface materials in a large project is a basic, essential thing to do. It is common sense, yet few architects do it, and virtually no system-B architects do it. As soon as you begin, it is clear that some combinations and distributions are more harmonious, and others are less so. You can notice this in your own experiments, and begin to appreciate the difference between abstractions and real feelings.

Variations and mockups in our California workshops. Multiple materials, in natural combinations, generate a touching variety. Test 1 is above; tests 2 and 3 are below.

Please remember, we were not, at this stage, looking for any details of arrangement — only for the relative percentages of the different built materials in the project. After several days of experiment and careful observation, we came to the conclusion that a distribution along the following lines — a hierarchy of different quantities — would usually be helpful:

EXAMPLE DISTRIBUTION[2]

Concrete	42 %
Plaster	28 %
Wood	18 %
Tile	12 %

Also, the plaster (black, white, gray, or green) could be mixed randomly without changing the statistical effect; but it was generally better if there was some mixture of these colors, rather than a single color. Most important was the principle that different materials, when measured by visible surface area, should have different perceived amounts, so that the contrast and hierarchy of materials is backed up by a measure that also speaks of the contrast.

To verify the principle, we then began to check these proportions with similar mockups on the site in Japan. The results were surprising. The soft light of Saitama, often with a light mist, is extremely bright. White plaster, especially, does not work well in large quantities. The light is so bright that the gray quality, or better still, a soft gray brown, is most harmonious in the light. We therefore revised our percentages, reducing the plaster, and increasing the concrete.

About this time, too, Hosoi visited our Berkeley workshops and commented that he was worried about concrete block — that it might have a dead quality. We took him to see two beautiful buildings in Berkeley which were built, many years ago, with an entirely different kind of concrete block. This material was poured.

---

2   Another example of a series of numbers which follow a version of Zipf's law.

The small bits of stone and silica and mica in the aggregate are visible, not covered with paste as they are in any concrete block made in a normal mould.

We began experiments to see if we could, ourselves, produce a block with this kind of beauty. These experiments went on for several months.

We also made experiments to test a green alabaster-like surface, which we produced by pouring lime, plaster, and pigment, against a perfectly smooth surface. It was translucent, and shone with a deep grayish green. Unfortunately, we could not find a way to smooth it to the glassy texture we wanted, nor could we find a reliable way to make it waterproof.

For the sake of convenience, we now shifted our mockups to the yard outside our office in Musashino-shi (part of the old school in Tokyo), where we were able to keep daily contact with our experiments. We built a project workshop in the yard. There we tried a variety of different trusses, different plastered surfaces, previously untried surfaces for ground materials using mixtures of cement and gravel and sand, and so on. It was a wonderful place, and we enjoyed our work enormously. Many other experiments were going on at the same time.

HARMONY, VARIETY, AND THE UNITY IN DIVERSITY THAT ORIGINATES IN SYSTEM-A

Meanwhile, we began the work of coming to grips with the design of the individual buildings, together with the individual construction detail of each building, included as something valuable in itself. One of the most striking things about the campus, if we compare it with other recent projects of comparable size, is the variety of the different buildings. Although each building is a rectangle, each one seems like a thing unto itself, a force in its own right. There is no uniform style or system of details, which carries on throughout the project. And yet, there is a reasonable unity, a comfortable way in which the different members of this group of buildings seem to belong to a single species. All coexist to form a harmony.

This is the typical — one might even say fundamental — outcome of the production methods of system-A. The character of harmony in variety is vitally important. It is quite different from (and stands in stark contrast with), the uniform, homogeneous, undifferentiated buildings that we became used to in the aggregate of late 20th-century buildings and building sites as they were produced by system-B. The geometric character and quality of the buildings include the following features:

- One senses harmonious physical and stylistic relationships between the different buildings, even though the individual buildings are all different.
- One sees that the buildings form beautiful and pleasantly shaped outdoor spaces that together give the community its home.
- One sees that each building is related to the place it occupies, so that the uniqueness of every area of the campus is confirmed and celebrated by the particularity of each building.
- One sees that the buildings are connected to one another by strands of building tissue, like gardens, paths, gates, wings, stairs, and terraces, so that the building groups form practical and intelligible wholes that invite emotional participation by students and teachers in the course of their daily life.

INCREMENTAL SHAPING OF POSITIVE SPACE, STEP BY STEP, ALL OVER THE CAMPUS

One cannot consider the buildings without also thinking about their position and interlock with positive space around the buildings, which is also space surrounded by buildings. The outdoor spaces of importance are staked out, flagged, and then formed by the buildings as if they were walls.

These outdoor spaces are of the greatest importance, and are (almost) more important than the buildings themselves, as defining social spaces and gathering places. The creation of positive outdoor space, as we walked out the spaces, and tested them for length and width, is described at length in chapter 11. This process is of immense significance in the layout and connection of the outdoor spaces. It is this which gives the campus its very positive feeling and success. Without these exterior spaces, the community (viewed as a social system) would hardly work at all.

- A positive space is an outdoor space without a ceiling. The perimeter of such a space may be enclosed by walls, or partially enclosed by walls. It may even be enclosed by a few markers — columns or trees — and the rest of the perimeter is open.
- Through model building — a dynamic, active process (not mechanical, passive transcription of a plan drawing) — one finds by intuition, shape, size, degree of enclosure, height of perimeter walls, number of openings, extent of views enabling people to look out, and quality of material (masonry, foliage, flowers, height of low solid wall, and so forth).
- The model is built up, step by step, considering the creation of space as a series of experiments, testing variables and continuing to make judgments about the life and pleasantness of the space as a place that is really nice to be in.
- The model is built up as a three dimensional volume, and it is this model which is ultimately best achieved by a physical mockup, using bamboos, ropes, sheets of cloth, possibly sheets of paper or cardboard.
- The process of building up this mockup is, necessarily, gradual.
- If it is impossible, for practical reasons, to make a full-size model, it is still likely to be useful to make a small model, roughly to scale. In this case, it is essential that the model makers look at the model by putting one's eye to the ground, and then looking to see height, distance of views, overall sizes of any opening, and its impact on the space. Make sure there is no claustrophobic feeling (if a perimeter is too close, too high, etc.).

- This is an experimental process, and at each step you must allow yourself to be guided by the pleasantness of the sequence of the spaces, one to another, and the pleasantness of the various views in different directions, establishing a truly wonderful experience.

It must be remembered that the creation of positive outdoor spaces happens gradually, one space at a time. In effect, a tapestry is being created, and the thought that should be in your mind as the "next" space is being shaped and created, is that the sequence of spaces and the living nature of the connections, and the ways that these spaces enter one from the next, will ultimately be guided by the question: Is this arrangement a pleasant sequence of movements and experiences?

Each space, as it is being made in the model, should be viewed as a building just like any other building, except that these outdoor spaces will only rarely have ceilings, or partial ceilings.

THE ARCHETYPAL GENERATING PROCESS FOR THE CAMPUS BUILDINGS

The starting point for every building is a rectangular prism, with a symmetrical pitched roof, as shown in the sketches below. To create these sketches, we simply answer the following questions for each building. The first six questions and the last two (on page 216), are the most critical, and are sufficient to pin each building volume down.

- Width (meters)?
- Length (meters)?
- Number of stories?
- Height (meters)?
- What is the roof slope?
- What is the exterior wall height (meters)?

- Where are the entrances, and in what direction do they point?
- What is the building's main axis, or axes, with respect to the land?
- What direction is the axis pointing?
- How big is the largest interior space?
- If there are major centers, which of them provide the major focus of that particular building?
- Is there a hierarchy of spaces in the building, and in what sequence should they be experienced?
- What is the natural repeating bay-size for structural columns?
- What are the structural bays?
- How big are the main columns, and the smaller columns?
- How many windows are there, and what size and shape are they?
- What main interior spaces are given?

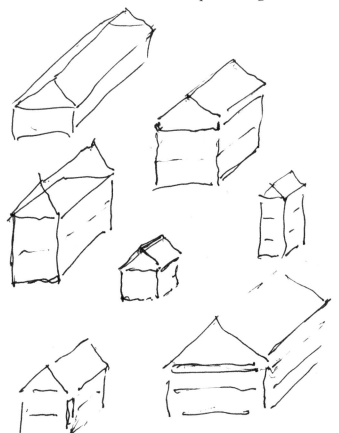

Examples of the generating prism for various different campus buildings. The diagrams represent (clockwise)
1. *Carpentry shop*
2. *Central building*
3. *Main portion of library*
4. *Three story student office/ clubhouse*
5. *Small gate*
6. *Two-story homeroom building*
7. *Great Hall*

- What additional subsidiary volumes are attached to the main volumes: terraces, porches, galleries, arcades?
- Interior gardens associated with homeroom buildings, and fully enclosed by walls?

After that, the work always ends with a very small thumbnail sketch, which captures the essence of that particular building and allows a rough model to be started.

All in all, there are thirty-six different buildings on the campus. You can see them on the campus site map, on the end paper at the back of this book. Twenty-nine of them have been completed. Among these buildings, there are fifteen similar homeroom buildings, and two similar college buildings. The remaining buildings (sixteen of them) all have unique features, and are all different in kind. However, all the buildings, all thirty-six of them, share similar features, which make them have family resemblances, and gives them a loose and discernible familiarity. Of the full complement of thirty-six buildings, seven are yet to be built.

DESIGNING IN THREE DIMENSIONS, BY MAKING, USING, AND TESTING MODELS

During this early phase of the building design work, our office was literally covered with models. In our offices, both in California and in Japan, there were three or four whole rooms, entirely filled with models — dozens and dozens of them. All these models were in a constant state of growth, change, cut and paste, scissors and paint . . . worked at and worked at, until we felt completely comfortable with them. Once again, the reality of this process tended to make the buildings unique and particular.

Building a large model in this way is very similar to the process which we normally follow in construction. While you are building a building, you look at the real thing day after day, and keep making mockups, to see what will be most harmonious, as the particulars unfold during construction. Years of experience have shown us that this kind of work, on a site, is the only way to get real character, and real harmony, into the building — because the details, the detailed organization, then really come from human feeling, are guided by human feeling, and are guaranteed, by this method, actually to have true human feeling in the result.

The use of large models, during the design process, had the same effect. We worked with a medium where we could actually see what we were doing. We could feel the real relation to various exterior details (which must always be part of the model). We could feel the real effect of subtle changes in height, forms, and outline, and we could feel the real character of different interior spaces, and the feeling they produce.

Even our preliminary drawings were drawn at 1:50 scale — an unusual procedure by typical architectural standards. We did this because this was the scale of our smallest models, and because it gave us better understanding. Afterwards, we then reduced our drawings photo-mechanically for the client — because of course, being preliminary drawings, they still contained too little information about the details of construction.

We then began to evolve a special system of construction for each building. For example, in the library, we had to find a type of frame which was very efficient for a heavy load on top (the stack floors had to take a dead load of 500 lb./sq.ft), a large span near the top, many columns, and close spacing of beams near the bottom of the building. We invented a frame which had just the right behavior for this unusual section. We also spent a great deal of time working out the details of the library structure, on the entrance floor, making sure that the massive, closely spaced columns would create beautiful spaces.

Some 200 models were used to build Eishin. They convey the range, size, roughness, and charm of our models and their ultimate accuracy — yet the models were all made rapidly, sometimes in minutes, never more than hours.

It should be said, finally, that there was an immense interest and excitement, from the construction of the models, on an on-

Mr. Murakoshi (standing), the one time principal of the school, and Mr. Izumori, the former mathematics teacher, squatting comfortably on the working model, while discussions were going on.

going, daily basis. In the accompanying photograph, we see two of the senior faculty studying our model and feeling very comfortable in their relation to the model. Students were also allowed to come and look, so that for them, too, the model provided an absorbing interest, making vivid the laying out and coming to fruition of the campus itself.

Many of the drawings that were made for these buildings appear in the Appendix (pages 489-498). **They were made only after the details of each were roughly known, and after the models had made the physical and geometrical organization precise.**

Discussion of the Buildings and the Building Groups

Let's start, now, to examine the detailed issues, which give the buildings their shape. Every one of the following issues has been established as an important and deep practical matter in the previous chapters (chapters 1-11). All these issues are now going to be applied to the buildings, thus making the shape and geometry of the buildings resonant with the quality already established in detail and in the global pattern of the whole. Now the buildings take their shape from the same key principles.

Each of the elements in the following list were essential to the creation of every space and every building at Eishin.

- The way each building relates to its surroundings, as well as the ground on which it stands.
- The geometry directed by its position in the whole and its function.
- Working with people who will inhabit the spaces.
- The immensely detailed use of models and experiments.
- The search for beautiful materials and ways of making the buildings that should stand there.
- The careful use of money in a manner that reflects the values of the endeavor.
- Creation of positive space, at every turn, and every scale.
- Placing materials between other nearby materials that are similar, and wedging harmonious materials in-between.
- Interlocking spatial links forming a two dimensional sheet of courtyards, buildings, and openings.

These considerations, and nothing less, allow us to make wholeness within system-A.

Entrance street, the small gate and carpentry shop at rush hour.

THE MAIN GATE, THE SMALL GATE, AND
THE ENTRANCE STREET

To get the ball rolling, we begin by showing the entrance street, and the small gate. This is the point of entrance to the Campus. The small gate is a very straightforward rectangle (in plan), with an arched space piercing through it. That is all. You approach on the eave-side, not, of course, through the gable ends.

On page 220, the morning rush of students enters the campus, coming through the small gate. The entrance street runs from the small gate to the Main gate. We see the early morning shadows lengthened by the early hour.

With deliberate care, in the 1980s, we planted flowering cherry trees close to the main gate. When they were first planted, they were very thin saplings, as you see them in a photograph on page 192. Ten or fifteen years later, we see the older students leaving the campus at the end of the day, through the main gate (as seen on page 221). The cherry trees have grown, and are in bloom.

A bus brings students from another school to a sports competition event being held on the Eishin Campus.

Students leaving the main gate, the cherry trees, and the campus at the end of a day of lectures.

The main gate with checkered diagonal terrazzo surface, made of cement and marble dust, ground to a polish. We planted several cherry trees next to the gate, giving us a beautiful display of blossoms every spring.

THE GREAT HALL

The Great Hall has a special place on the campus. It is the highest building on the campus, and the largest. It is the only place that could hold a conference, or social gathering for more than 1200 people. It is the most visible building on the campus.

All in all, one might portray the Great Hall as a kind of mother hen, with a brood of chicks under the mother hen's skirts — these chicks being, metaphorically, the brood under the care of the mother hen. We see the Great Hall from almost every angle, so that both artistically, and socially, and emotionally, it holds things together.

GREAT HALL MODELS

Close to the small gate and the main gate, is the Great Hall. The Great Hall is the largest building on the campus. Because it is so important, it took a tremendous amount of effort to get it right. We made many models, looked at them, played with them, tried to judge which of them had the magnificence that was demanded of this building.

Significantly, the Great Hall was the first major building to be started, and the last to be finished. That happened, of course, because there was the most work to be done: it is the most complex and elaborate structurally. And it is the building which has the most complex and beautiful ornamentation.

If you look at the photograph of the Eishin Campus in the winter (Front matter, page ix), you see how the building stands out against the snowy landscape. It holds things together, and the atmosphere of cohesion is immediate, and compelling.

However, it was not easy to **find** the shape for this building. One of the first models we made (see page 225) shows what a weak shape that first model had — and would have had, in fact, if we had gone ahead and built it in that form. It took many more studies in three dimensions before we found a building shape

The Great Hall, end view, looking across the lake, with the main gate in the distance.

...n early Great Hall study model, 1:20 scale, was made to help us imagine the quality of light inside the building, and to test different thicknesses of columns compared with the width of the openings in the bays.

that was simple, and majestic, and could hold its own. The interior study model shown above was primarily built to study light — and we were surprised by this model because, before we built it, we were trying to make a dark interior, with mystery. However, the large hall, even filled with massive, thick columns, let in far too much light. To get the result we wanted, we had to close the openings as you see in the interior — see page 226 to see the much more mysterious effect.

We had progressed from this model to another one that had more widely spaced columns, and much less light. This was built, then, and you may see (on page 226) that the space was indeed mysterious, even haunting. And here, to the left, we see an unsatisfactory, early study model, at 1:100 scale, from the early days, when we were still trying to discover how to achieve a feeling of tranquility and majesty in the building as it was going to be seen from the outside — but as you can see, we were failing.

The later shape of the actual building, as built, is shown on page 224, and does partially, and finally, achieve this majesty in some degree.

First stage of columns, beams and capitals, finished in white shikkui. This state existed for the period from 1985 until 1988. Then the finishes in colored shikkui were applied, and from then on the Great Hall has remained in this state until the present day.

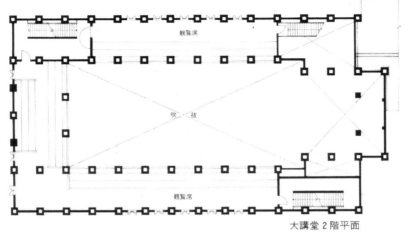

観覧席

吹　技

観覧席

大講堂２階平面

Great Hall plan, as built.

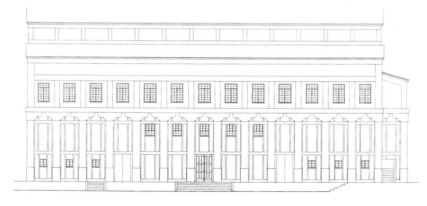

Great Hall main front elevation, as built.

Upper gallery of the Great Hall, with hanging lamp (first stage of white shikkui finish).

Interior of the Great Hall. The plaster work is made from "kura-shikkui," or black plaster with ornaments carried out in red plaster and white and gray highlights. This design was first worked out on a small model where the giant columns were only about one inch in diameter. To double check colors and dimensions, we also made a full-size mockup, on paper draped over the actual columns (see photo on page 410). The plasterers who carried out this work were eighty-six year old Mr. Ishiguro and his son. The surface of the plaster was hand-polished some thirty times to reach this lustrous finish.

A formal concert given in the Great Hall.

The intimate and beautifully worked surface designs, create an intimacy on the stage (pictured here) that contrasts with the grosser and almost massive scale of the bigger columns in the nave and auditorium (seen on the left-hand page).

Raining: In this picture we see the Great Hall at the lower end of the Home Base Street. Students are lining up with their umbrellas. They are standng in the Home Base Street, flanked by wooden galleries from each homeroom building.

THE HIGH SCHOOL
AND ITS HOMEBASE STREET

On the left-hand page, we see the Home Base street for the first time. In this photograph we see students and some visitors looking down the street, with the broadside view of the Great Hall. The first sketches of the homeroom buildings appeared in the margin of the pattern language. When we had the idea of a homeroom street, we also began imagining the homerooms themselves as small pavilions, along both sides of the street. At that time we imagined them as red and brown.

When we reached the actual building design phase, we began in-depth consultation with the teachers. The teachers who had been assigned to work with this problem were Miss Tomizu, the chemistry teacher, and Mr. Izumori, the mathematics teacher. We had two long sessions with them to discuss the ideal layout of classrooms. In these sessions we discussed the best size and shape for the classrooms. We had our discussions in the old school. Slowly and carefully, we tried to find the best possible shape for a classroom, the best possible layout of desks, the best direction of the light, and the best position of the entrances.

As the discussion developed, using actual school furniture, we made full size mockups of the proposed layouts, simply by using chairs and desks from the old school, in one of the art studios that was big enough to hold a complete imaginary classroom, plus sheets of plywood to stand for walls and partitions. After two sessions of this kind, we had fixed the "ideal" layout for a class. It was extremely specific.

This floor plan was the model for all the classrooms. Sunlight was essential in it. A discussion had been held by the teachers, and they had come to the conclusion that they very much wanted sunlight in the classrooms. It may sound obvious, but we had been unsure, since traditional Japanese buildings, with paper shoji or indirect light, tend to have a soft pearly-gray light in them, not direct sunlight. But the teachers clearly wanted sunlight.

Homeroom buildings along the lake.

Once we had this ideal floorplan, we went back to our models, and to the problem of the street, and the volumes of the buildings, and the space of the gardens between the buildings. We made a series of 1:50 models of the buildings and the street. It now became clear that the pavilions we had first conceived did not create good positive space between the buildings. Also, from the discussion with the teachers we knew that the upstairs and downstairs had to be somewhat similar — just because they contained the same classrooms.

Most critical of all, we found that the actual size of the street, on the land, was rather short. There was a shortage of space, especially when one took into account the need for the gardens to be there, and the need for sunlight to get in over the roof of one building and into the ground-floor windows of the next. Gradually, from our models, we got a simpler form of the buildings. Also

Here you see the quality of the positive space inside the Home Base Street, and the actual space shaped by the Homeroom buildings and their galleries. In the distance, we see the Central Building.

from the models, we got other essential features of the buildings.

1. The galleries along the homeroom street itself.
2. The arcade along the back street, below the buildings.
3. The fences which formed the gardens.
4. The exterior stairs.
5. The benches facing south, inside the gardens.

These points are very important because they illustrate the way that building form arises — often, from careful attention to the outdoor space. And, what is perhaps more important to realize, we learned to recognize these problems in the exterior space from the activity of making models. The models we made always had the exterior space in them, and as many local details of the site and nearby buildings as possible.

We first put the galleries in because we began to see the real

Students and visitors passing the Homeroom buildings and walking along the planted gardens in the middle of the Home Base Street.

danger of a lifelessness in the homeroom street. The upstairs roof above the galleries (accessible from the classroom stairs), and the galleries themselves, created the likelihood of a continual watching of the street, by students, watching one another, meeting, waving, forming small groups . . .

We put the small gardens in, because we saw the formlessness, and lack of usefulness of the space immediately next to the buildings. Unless the gardens became intimate and coherent, private for each class, and each one with a positive shape, their usefulness would be compromised. And we put the arcades in, partly because we began to appreciate the need to make the back side of the buildings "something" — and partly because the teachers

Homeroom buildings and gardens in the snow.

emphasized the problem of rain, and the fact that they wanted to be able to move around the site without getting wet.

The homerooms themselves, as buildings, also required an immense amount of thought when it came to the construction. We had decided, early on, that we wanted to make the buildings out of concrete. But we had a problem with cost. We needed to build a concrete building, but the budget we had available for these buildings was limited, and very low.

At first we thought of using dry-stacked block, with some wood, and some plaster. But after trying this out, we found the concrete block had a rather dead character. The quality is caused by the way the mold is pulled past the block: it smears the cement paste across the surface, and makes something which is emotionally quite flat. So we had to improve the physical quality of the wall. But we also knew how limited the budget was. At this stage, when we were still laying out the buildings, we had detailed cost sheets for each building. We knew that we had no more than 20 million yen to spend on the walls of the homerooms, a cost of about ¥9000/m².

While we were trying to solve this problem, we remembered two famous buildings in Berkeley. These buildings, which were built more than fifty years before we started our work, were built in concrete block. But the walls have all the life and harmony of stone. One feels the same ruggedness, the same depth of feeling, as in an old stone wall.

How was this done? The blocks were only 1.5 inches thick, with tongue-and-groove connections. But the crucial thing is that the blocks were *poured*. This made their surfaces quite different. The surface is what one gets from the poured concrete, lightly washed. It was beautiful. We made many experiments, with different aggregates, and different methods of washing. For the time being, we had reached the stone-like quality of the walls for the homerooms.

Sadly, however, in the end we could use these special blocks only for the material of the main gate, not for the homerooms, and made all the homeroom walls out of concrete, by pouring them *in situ* into steel panel forms. We then worked for months with a Japanese manufacturer, to get this kind of block made in large quantities for the main gate.

We also intended to plaster all the exterior ornaments — in white shikkui. But, we couldn't decide whether to plaster the upper half of the building, or just the cornice, or both the cornice and the column-like ornaments. The debate about this went on and on, for more than a year. It was impossible to settle the isssue, and we didn't finally settle it until the last moment when the buildings were being built, and we could see exactly what was best to do.

THE CENTRAL BUILDING

This building, which finally turned out to be one of the most successful and beautiful of all, started life as an afterthought. We simply needed an open space, a place where students could fool around in the rain, an outdoor gathering place with a roof. Probably its relaxed and simple character came from a certain carelessness which was permitted by its lack of importance.

Anyway, the first thing that happened was a rough idea of the main truss. I sketched the horse-shoe-shaped truss rather quickly,

The Central Building, seen from the North.

on an envelope in the office. One of our Japanese apprentices then made a balsa-wood model, and showed that the curves — which were unusual and perhaps unwise aesthetically — in fact turned out beautiful and simple (this page shows the arch-geometry, and on page 238 the detailed geometry and a photograph of the balsa-wood model).

As soon as I got back to Berkeley, we began running computerized, finite-element models on this truss. The truss, like several others, has bending in the design. It works, because the members bend, and therefore could not have been analyzed by any method except finite-element analysis.

We had such fun on the computer. Gary Black and I started putting in the model, took

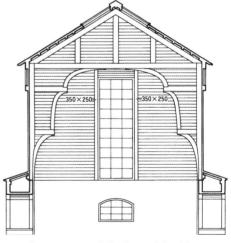

Cross-section of the Central Building.

a look to see where the overstressed members were, tried to gain
a gradual understanding of the way the truss behaved, where the
forces really are. We then made one approximation after the other,
in which we changed geometry, members, and so on, until we
had a thing which was efficient and harmonious — and worked
perfectly.

In this case the longitudinal exterior X-truss was very
interesting too — the one in the long direction (below and page
239). Wind forces in that building are extremely high. But we didn't
want to put in shear walls or diagonal braces for the long direction.

*The longitudinal X-truss, seen on the
outside of the wall, just below the roof of
the Central Building.*

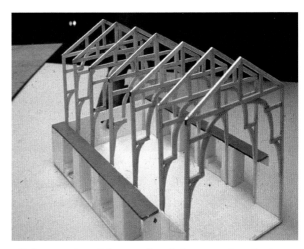

*Balsa-wood model we made to help us conceive the struc-
tural behavior, especially under earthquake forces.*

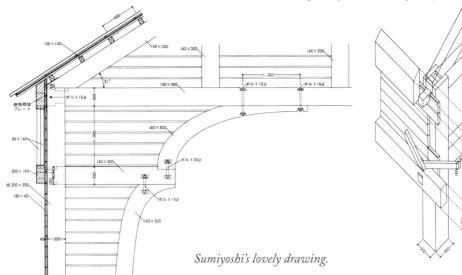

Sumiyoshi's lovely drawing.

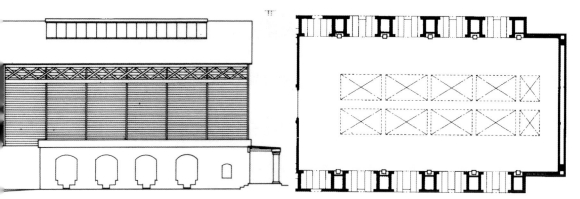

Side elevation and plan of the Central Building.

The massive concrete piers, forming alcoves, arches, and seats inside the Central Building.

We just wanted to make an X-truss which worked with moment connections. And, to make the construction simple, no tension. We wanted to make a pure compression truss.

Sumiyoshi made a beautiful set of drawings to show how the compression truss might actually be built in detail. It was his first piece of work, and one of his loveliest (see drawing on page 238).

An impromptu supper party in the Central Building.

Later, when Fujita was involved, almost everyone tried to tell us that the building wouldn't work in the long direction, and had to be modified. But Professor Sakamoto of the Kenchiku Center paid us a wonderful compliment.[3] He came to see us in Berkeley for a discussion, a tremendous kindness on his part. Afterward he went back to Japan, convinced of our common sense and sound structural insights, and asked that the buildings should be presented to the authorities *without modification*, exactly in our original conception. He felt that the original pure structural conception was the most beautiful.

This came at a time when we were having great difficulty with the problem of getting building permits. It was wonderful to get this kind of support after so many months of dealing with engineers who were not sophisticated enough to understand the subtleties.

---

3 The Kenchiku Center, known in Japan as "the Earthquake Center" is the central, all-Japan, clearing house where sophisticated engineering problems were studied and resolved. Professor Sakamoto was a senior engineering professor at Tokyo University. His word was law.

As far as the base of the building was concerned — the big masonry alcoves, with their double seats and arches — we made mockups at full scale, in our Berkeley office. We got the exact dimensions from the mockup, and then never changed them.

It was the relation of this heavy masonry mass (made entirely of concrete and concrete block and stone), to the big curved trusses, which made it essential to treat the connection at the base, as a *moment* connection, not as a pin connection.

We had to fight for more than a year to convince people that a moment connection between the concrete and the wood was possible. Many said it was not. But, finally, the beauty of the building arose, *just* because this *is* a moment connection, and because the heavy masonry arched alcove and the piers between them, anchor the slender and beautiful truss at the base. If this conception had been changed, the building would have lost its beauty.

Once again Professor Sakamoto saved the day for us. System-B would almost certainly have destroyed the design. If Mr. Hijikata, the Fujita engineer, or Mr. Odagiri, the architect in our office, both working in the system-B mentality, had their way, the building design would have been changed to make the column-bases work as pin connections. It was only because of system-A, with its capacity to invent the necessary techniques to fit the mass and harmony of the building, that the building could achieve its proper form.

THE COLLEGE BUILDINGS

The main form of the college buildings — the fact that all five are very long and very narrow — came from the site plan. In order to enclose the space of the college quad, we needed a frontage of about 180 meters of building (each of the college buildings is approximately thirty to forty meters long, all five varying). And in order to form the space correctly (to make it beautiful, given the average width of the space), the buildings had to be two-stories high, not one-story.

It followed then, that each of the five buildings was about thirty-five meters long, and between six and nine meters wide. Further, the site plan had already established the need for a continuous long arcade along the frontage. The question, then, was simply how the college buildings could be accommodated within the very narrow envelopes which remained.

Each college building is slightly different. The two end ones on the south side are distinguished by the student study spaces. Hosoi gave us a vision of students studying in a long beautiful space overlooking a view, with many small desks and chairs. The room which was formed from this vision dominates the upstairs of the buildings.

Downstairs, both the south and north buildings have a group of professors' rooms, opening off a corridor which goes away from the entrance hall. In order to fit into the very narrow building, the professors' rooms are themselves long and narrow — some of them, with a small outdoor platform, looking into a garden.

Upstairs, the longer of the north buildings is dominated by the fact that it has two very large lecture halls — the only large lecture halls in the college. These rooms needed extra ceiling height. The ceiling height modified the way the entrance works, and the height of the arcade. In this one building, the roof and second- story rooms stand higher than the lower-lying arcade.

The one building which is quite different from the others is the middle building on the south side. This contains the college administration, president, dean, faculty club, and a student cafe.

Rough conceptual plan sketch of the five college buildings, arranged along the ridge. The sixth building (at the bottom of the diagram) is the Central Building, coming up from the Home Base Street.

A very rough thumbnail sketch made on the back of an envelope (south is up).

It got its main inspiration from the division into four quarters, and the very wide main stair going up the middle, to give the approach to president, dean, and faculty club a certain grandeur. Each of the buildings has some version of the same structural difficulty. We felt that these buildings needed a more beautiful character than the homeroom buildings. Wood panelling in the faculty offices. Bigger and more beautiful arcade columns and beams. Beautiful wooden ceilings. And beautiful distinctive windows.

The windows were there from the very beginning — from the first rough sketch. Later mockups of detailed window design, at full size in our office, only refined the proportions and division into panes.

FLAT BEAM CEILING DESIGN

The very unusual ceiling design is one of the most appealing aspects of these college buildings. It, too, came from a full-size mockup. We had the "fact," initially set in motion by feelings, that the ceilings in these buildings should be wooden ones. But we also knew that the buildings were fundamentally masonry, and would therefore have to have some concrete beams, to transfer horizontal shear. How to combine the two?

ize
p of a
college
w, which
de in
aterials,
ve could
best and
eautiful
ny in
pes and
Vhen
d out, we
stalled
indows
hese
ions in
college
gs.

A very small cardboard model of one of the college lecture rooms.

A roughly made model of a college arcade.

We first tried an ordinary beam ceiling: wooden plank ceiling, with white plastered concrete beams below. It sounds nice. But when we made models we found that it had very little beauty, especially when seen with these walls, small rooms, and the window shapes we had defined. The edge beam, around the upper edge of the room, was especially hard to get right.

The more we looked, the more and more clear it became that two things were needed to make a beautiful ceiling: (1) Beams that were flat and wide — the "wrong" cross-section for a beam. (2) The fact that these wide flat beams would have to be very close together — so close that beam-spacing and beam-width were almost equal. We tried small models and full-size mockups in cardboard. The facts about beauty of spacing were confirmed again and again.

One of the two lecture halls, in the northeast college building, visible from the outside in the upper photograph on p.

A corner of the college, where one college building, two homeroom buildings and the faculty building form a very pleasant enclosure

In system-B, there would have been no way to solve this problem. The usual approach would dictate either using "normal" beams, or using flat slab concrete ceilings. In system-A, the facts about feeling, which had been made clear by our mockups, then paved the way for a new structural invention.

Potentially the flat beams were very good for one thing — dealing with horizontal shear. The beams were so close together, that we found a model in which the big flat beams took the place

Northwest college building.

of a diaphragm (see model on page 244). Distortion of the ceiling plane would have destabilized if the members were not braced in the horizontal plane.

The situation was complicated by the position of the arcade. It meant that vertical shear forces were coming down the outside wall, then transferring through the arcade ceiling, into the inside wall of the arcade. But, to some extent, some moment was also taken by the massive columns of the arcade. Since these forces induced a twisting motion, we had to make a three-dimensional finite-element model of the behavior — almost the most complicated model in the project.

It finally worked very well. We put a different variation of the configuration into each building. The triumph, perhaps, of the five versions, were the ceilings of the two large lecture rooms, which needed heavy crossbeams to cope with the wide span — and we then put in stepped corbels to connect the two systems of beams, at critical crossing points where shear forces would be biggest.

Northeast college building, with two large lecture halls.

THE LIBRARY AND THE RESEARCH CENTER

The important, unique buildings already had, at this stage, a defining position in the site, and a particular, unique relation both to the land and to the site plan, or the functional layout of the campus. Each of these buildings had therefore inherited a particular character from its location — a particular spatial essence, which was quite distinct, and which could be felt, identified, and drawn upon (and which was still clearly marked by the flags we had used to mark its corners).

For example, the library was a U-shaped building, quite clearly meant to be a "quiet spot" or an "end spot" on the ridge. It was the last point in a long sequence of entering — a haven, to be reached after passing through all the other zones of relatively less and less activity on the campus. It was therefore by definition and by physical location a point of spiritual stillness, on the ridge, occupying a particular spot as an identifiable mark, a terminus, with a quiet garden in front of it.

When one imagines all of this, it was not hard to make a sketch which directly and immediately fulfilled this role, through its exterior volume and appearance. The very first sketch I ever made of this building — photocopied from my notebook — is almost exactly like the final building.

It even has the green-and-white diamonds already clearly part of it. The building — its height, length, volume, mass, and exterior character — was not given by whim. They were defined, rather precisely, by the vortex, or field, of influences which occurs at that point in the site. And of course, the influences themselves are unique. So, when given full play, and when accurately followed, they created a building which is also unique and particular.

Second, we then had the benefit of months of work with the users. In this case, for instance, Hosoi himself gave us the most detailed picture of the feeling of this Library building, as he imagined it and wanted it. This level of detail, and the precision of the feeling, naturally caused the quality already present in the first sketch to be developed further. It was not necessary to draw abstract lines, or to make mechanical gestures on tracing paper, as it so often is in large architects' offices, merely in order to fulfill the architect's obligations, or because there is not enough living substance in the architect's mind. In this case, the feeling of the interior, the detailed organization of the interior, could be lifted whole, almost complete, simply from the client's imagining. And of course, this was possible, because we had invited it, encouraged it.

Third, the detailed concreteness of the building was then made extremely solid, because we worked almost entirely at the level of models. Every single building on the campus was built several times over, at a scale of 1:50, in our offices. These models were not

My first sketch of the library.

Model of the Library and Research Center.

presentation models, made after the design was clear, in order to explain the building to another person. They were models which were made while we began the design process, in order to get a clear feeling about the precise organization which that particular building ought to have. Invariably, the drawings of the buildings followed the construction of models, once we were satisfied that the model began to capture the essence which was required, both on the site, and in its internal organization.

Sometimes, when particular spaces inside the building were unclear, we also made more detailed models of the interiors, usually at a scale of 1:20. In the case of the library, for example, we made a 1:20 model of the big reading room, on the main floor — and we also made a model of the entrance lobby, and its columns, at 1:20, because the detailed treatment of these columns and their capitals seemed so complicated and important.

The library and research center are yet to be completed.

THE JUDO HALL

During the creation of these buildings, in the process of working with the users, incidents occurred which — in retrospect — are clearly visible as manifestations of the fundamental battle between system-A and system-B.

At the time they merely seemed curious. They looked like human difficulties — similar to the difficulties which are typical of any architectural process. But in retrospect, their basic relation to the conflict between A and B is absolutely clear.

One of the most dramatic of these kinds of difficulties concerned the layout of the Judo Hall. For reasons which lie outside this project, several members of the athletics faculty were hostile to the project, and to Hosoi. Some of them had, indeed, at an earlier time in the school's history, tried to seize power in the school, and the history of that event still rankled. Perhaps because of the antagonism which remained, the athletics faculty was under-represented on the Education and Building Committees. As a result, we got too little information from them, or got it too late.

In any case, there was some antagonism. We had already experienced it at work, in the discussion of relative areas during final formulation of the space budget and site plan. The antagonism reached one of its high points during discussion of the Judo Hall.

From the time we had created the site plan, it was already clear where the Judo Hall would be placed — in a position easily accessible to both high school and college students. Its position also made it very clear that the building must have a long narrow format, and be relatively high, on a plinth. This shape was created by its relation to the cliff, which put limits on its position to the south, and by the space of the Tanoji center, which required that the front of the building be narrow, so that it could form an effective end to the space.

Its length was thus partly a function of its position and its narrowness. It was also a function of its relation to the formal

entrance path which approaches the Judo Hall from the entrance
street.

All this was known, and fixed, at the time we began the
detailed discussions with the judo instructors about the exact
layout of the interior.

The space budget specified a total area of 190 sq. meters for
the building. We, in our attempt to give the building proper weight
and prominence, had already increased this to about 240 sq. meters.
However, in spite of this increase, the judo instructors began
insisting — not in a polite fashion — that the building must be
bigger. Of course we had to refuse. We had no option, since even
as it was, we were stretching the budget, and had to work with
available funds. Our obligation to the agreements with the other
teachers made it impossible to increase the building any further.

Then the judo instructors explained that we had to make a
double square for the judo space itself — two square areas of fifty
mats each. This double-square arrangement is, in principle, very
sensible. But to accommodate it would have required a building

View of the Judo Hall, looking across the Faculty Garden.

of at least 300 square meters — far beyond our budget limit. We therefore began negotiating with the judo instructors, trying to get a reasonable resolution of their wishes, within the available format.

We found two things. First, they pressed us for a building which was more square in shape. We explained the facts about shape and layout mentioned above — because of the building's crucial relationship to the surroundings. They were deaf to these issues, and cared only for the interior shape they wanted. Second, when the negotiation proceeded further, they wanted to remove completely the narrow platform and walkway, around the mats.

Here we come to the crux of the struggle. Our intention, from the beginning, had been to express the Judo Hall as a place of spirituality. Budo[4] halls have, in Japanese history, always been places where the spiritual aspects of budo and kendo are emphasized, and we wanted to be sure that these qualities would be safeguarded,

---

4   Budo is a generic term for Japanese martial arts.

Interior view of the Judo Hall, a quiet, peaceful atmosphere.

preserved and extended, in a building of an appropriately spiritual dimension of its own.

However, the further we got into the dispute, the more it became clear that the judo instructors viewed the Judo Hall as a kind of gymnasium, whose emphasis was mainly on the springiness of the floor, the padding, and the excellence of the lights.

One can appreciate, even admire, the extreme practicality of their wishes. Practicality, after all, is at the very heart of zen. But their practicality was banal, not zen-like at all. They wanted to sacrifice every dimension of the Judo Hall, except the simplest practical ones. Further, it also appeared, slowly, that they were being guided by a stylistic desire for a gymnasium-like building — a kind of modernism in their judo, that was attached to 'being up to date', and the desire to impress through the exterior qualities of a super gymnasium.

We on our side, were quite unwilling to make any sacrifice which would disturb the spiritual dimension of the building, as long as practical requirements were modestly satisfied.

As the conflict increased we found it necessary to expand our research. At one point we went for an extensive interview with the

Another interior view of the Judo Hall, again a quiet, reverent atmosphere, but with quietness dominating the silent movements.

chief judo instructor at the local university in Kichijoji.

This discussion made it clear that the spiritual dimension of judo, so crucial in the past, was rapidly disappearing, and that the desire to replace a spiritual art with a kind of gymnastic exercise had become the fundamental and central aspect of judo in modern Japan. Although the judo instructor talked lovingly of the old budo halls, where indeed quietness, grace, and tranquility were emphasized, it was quite clear that he, too, was now obsessed with the super-gymnasium view of modern judo, and that the old spirituality was — in his view — no longer relevant.

We did not give up. But we now found ourselves in the absurd position of foreigners fighting against Japanese, to maintain the essential Japanese component of the ancient art. Foreigners, ourselves outside the art of judo, fighting those inside the art, to preserve the essence of the art. Ludicrous though this may seem, it is once again at the heart of the conflict between system-Λ and system-B. System-B not only perverts feeling in the environment, but also denies the spirituality of such things as judo. All in all it creates a scale of values in which temperature control and ease of cleaning are the dominant factors, while depth of feeling, sincerity, and tranquility of soul, are relegated to the position of slightly nice inessentials.

Thus, again, as soon as we found teachers — in this case the judo teachers — too deeply enmeshed in system-B, we were forced to fight them, even though they were our own respected clients, simply in order to preserve the integrity of system-A.

THE GYMNASIUM AND THE LAKE

On the next five pages, we show pictures of the Gymnasium, one of the largest all-wood buildings in Japan, or indeed, anywhere in the world. For reasons I cannot quite pin down, the photo on pages 258-259 is perhaps my favorite view of the Eishin Campus, looking up the length of the lake, and showing the wonderful, looming, dark, black-plastered exterior shell of the gym, set off by the light-red roof, all reflected in the water as one walks around the building.

Interior of the Gymnasium, building empty, lights off, windows reflecting in the floor. This, too, has a reverent atmosphere.

Interior of the Gymnasium, gymnasts practicing.

The same Gymnasium windows, from the outside.

The lake, the ducks, the gymnasium is finished in kura shikkhui (black plaster), and one of the homeroom streets is fully

...ng over the roofs of the homebase street, the high roof of the Central building may be seen in the further distance.

View of two college arcades, looking toward the Central Building.

PART THREE

PITCHED BATTLE

1983-1985

CHAPTERS 13-19

PART THREE

It would have been all but impossible to get the results we
aimed at, by making drawings and handing them to a
contractor, according to the norms of system-B. Rather, it
was the actual, direct management of craft and
construction that was the core of the whole process.
It was precisely in regard to this matter that the battle
became extremely fierce.

To win the right to build within system-A, and to succeed in
it, we had to outwit the system-B mentality again and again,
on a daily basis. Real battle as an overall, daily pattern of
action began to emerge. Unwilling as we were to
engage in fighting, we nevertheless found
there was no practical alternative.
The people who had system-B in their heads had effectively
been brainwashed.
They did not want our efforts in system-A to succeed.

Sometimes the confrontations became threatening or
physically dangerous.
The last two years of our work were not mild.
The core issues, the challenges of money, habit, human
organization, decision-making, old ways of working and
new ways of working, began more and more to
confront one another.

Commenting on the division between the teams working in
system-A and system-B, Yuden Tanaka, one of the
submanagers lent to us by Fujita, expressed it like this:
"This is war. It is incredible, almost impossible to
believe, like a scene from a courtroom."

13 DIRECT MANAGEMENT

As makers of buildings, we architects must start now,
with a fundamental change of direction.
For the last hundred years or so, we have understood
building to be an art in which an architect <u>draws</u> a building,
and a contractor then <u>builds</u> that building from the
architect's plans.
But a living environment cannot be built
successfully this way.

To achieve a successful building — one that has life — we
must focus our attention on all the crafts and processes, and
then, as architects, ourselves take direct charge
of the <u>making</u>.
We must take full responsibility
for the entire building process, ourselves.

Now we come to the core of the battle between system-A and
system-B. It lies in our overall approach to the construction of our
own physical world, our habitat of plants and animals, and above
all to the practical philosophy of the construction process and the
human organization of that process.

We may summarize this all-important feature of system-A in a
two-word phrase: "Direct Management." What this phrase means
is that the design of buildings, public space, local forms of communal space, and layout of interiors remains under the management
of an architect or engineer, who has the authority and know-how
to continue the process of design, through a series of mockups
and models. The buildings and spaces are able to take shape as
construction moves forward, and the building details — rooms,

Construction workers working on the exterior plaster of the Great Hall.

windows, doors, stairs — are gradually fitted to the buildings, on the basis of what is visible at each given unfinished stage, and are not prescribed by a detailed set of drawings that specify each detail from the outset. Thus the architect has eyes and ears, is using them constantly, and watching for potential opportunities of a positive nature, and equally watching to see if any mistakes are on the verge of happening, in time for them to be corrected without monetary losses. In short, the architect is responsible for building construction, is watching the building unfold continuously, and is making ongoing modifications as it becomes clear from each given stage, what modifications and changes should be made at each moment. And this is all to be done within a management framework that controls budget and cost very tightly.

Only this process provides the environment in which beautiful, functional, *workable,* and effective space can be made. It is likely to be a success because of the very nature of this process.

———

Consequently, the first serious concern on this project was to become absolutely certain that Direct Management would work. It will be obvious to anyone with construction experience that it is not so easy to set up a building organization that has the ability to fulfill this role. This aspect of system-A needs special skills, and must be able to rely on architectural and construction professionals who have construction experience, and know-how to make this happen. There is also the all-important issue of money. As we shall see, within the Direct Management regime, one usually gets more for one's money than in the system-B approach.

System-B produces buildings that are uncomfortable, rigid, not well-adapted to creating benign living and working conditions; they are rarely beautiful, or pleasant to be in. Dollar for dollar, system-B buildings also cost more than system-A buildings — of course, because the large general contractor takes a considerable share of the construction price, and puts it in his pocket. This is often as much as 20%, and sometimes considerably more.

This double whammy makes the whole idea of system-B potentially vulnerable to public criticism, and therefore also makes frank discussion of the monetary side of system-B construction invisible, and intentionally hidden by a cloud of secrecy. If it were to become widely known that system-A produces *better quality buildings*, and does it at a *cheaper price*, then the entire infrastructure of system-B would find itself skating on very thin ice, indeed.

All this, when it became clear to system-B construction companies in Japan, soon created a hornet's nest in our project. At the core of the hornet's nest, was a pair of meetings two weeks apart, that happened halfway through 1983, in a club in Shinjuku, when a group of men representing the major Japanese construction companies, forming a powerful cartel, offered Hosoi a very considerable sum of money to stop the system-A approach.

We shall see that it was precisely the issue of construction organization and process that reveals the dramatic differences between A and B. And what Hosoi experienced in these meetings was the harshest and most direct evidence of the seriousness of the clash between system-A and system-B.

Why are construction process and human organization so pivotal? It is because the effort to make wholeness in a place, as we have already outlined it, will depend on the flexibility of the pieces of material that play their part in the design. To make a building well, the building needs to fit the land, with extraordinary finesse; and to make the various rooms, windows, and doors well, these rooms need to be shaped, and dimensions sized, with again, extraordinary finesse. That cannot be done with materials, or components, which embody a crude modularity. Yet in modern manufacturing, the elements, materials, and even processes, all bring with them an excessive emphasis on regularity, equality of dimension, and crudity of plan. And this then comes to dominate the feeling of what can be produced.

To make a successful building out of modular elements would be impossible — it would be as difficult, or impossible, as if a regimen of rigid cubes were introduced into the flesh of a living organism. The geometry would simply not allow the variety of subtle adaptations at different scales and levels. And the apparatus of modern construction, working drawings, and purchasing — all these are in fact set up to prevent just that in the buildings which can be made.

For these reasons, a system-A approach — one which allows wholeness to be respected and enriched — is simply inconsistent with the modern system-B construction processes and management. So we face, again and again, a conflict that is the origin of the battle which this book describes — an unending conflict between the mechanical processes of system-B and the more fluid and organic system-A creation of buildings and neighborhoods which allow wholeness to govern and shape all that is made.

THE CONSTRUCTION COMPANIES AWAKEN

In the events described in this chapter and the next, we shall see the Japanese companies becoming aware, for the first time, of the fact that our intention to implement system-A might possibly have serious consequences for their own future in Japan. What we were doing, and what we proposed to do, had the potential to pose a threat to the entire Japanese construction industry.

The Japanese construction companies, as they existed in 1983, and as they exist today, are embodiments of world system-B. For reasons that we shall discuss more fully later, their form of operation was (and still is) based on methods and processes in which money and efficiency, as these are presently conceived, drive out almost every possible way of allowing human spirit to exist in buildings — and specifically to drive out the local adaptation process, described in chapter 2, and all that follows from this process.

What we at the Center for Environmental Structure proposed to do, on the other hand, was based on a worldview in which health and mental health, well-being of plants and animals, the sacred, love, affection, concern at every level for the well-being of the Earth, and the well-being of even the smallest wholes — are the main motives governing every process. This is the system of value that is embodied in system-A.

The practical consequences of the difference between these two systems become especially severe, and most clear, on the issue of construction management. If what we proposed to do could succeed on the scale of a large project like the Eishin Campus, it would totally alter the future of the construction industry in Japan — and perhaps everywhere in the world. It might also greatly weaken the dominating control of the construction companies in all construction in Japan.

The members of the cartel therefore set out to make certain that we would fail in executing system-A. Essentially, we may say that system-B took rapid and dramatic steps to crush system-A. This was not obvious to us, at first. But it very soon became obvious during the incidents of the next few weeks.

THE TOPIC OF DIRECT MANAGEMENT IS OPENED WITH HOSOI

When I first signed the contract with the Eishin school, the contract was a standard contract for architectural design. The initial assumption in the contract, though not clearly specified, was that the drawings once made, would ultimately be turned over to a general contractor for construction.

At the time of first discussing and negotiating the contract, I did not yet know Hosoi very well. I felt that it was too early to tell Hosoi the depth of my passion for actually *building* his project — even though he well knew that we were ourselves contractors in California. Indeed, I thought that if I mentioned it too early, he would dismiss me for a madman, and we wouldn't get the job. I was overjoyed to have the chance of building such a big project for the first time, and I did not want to sour the whole agreement by telling Hosoi that I not only wanted to design the whole thing, but to *build* the whole thing, too. I wanted to wait until this topic presented itself in due course, and in a natural way.

However, during the summer of 1982, after a few months of working together, I felt we knew each other well enough for me to open this subject. We had become real friends. Indeed, Hosoi explicitly told me that he wanted us to be close, and lifelong friends. He meant it.

One evening, over dinner, I told him casually — and in a way that he could easily dismiss if he wanted to — that, if we were going to make a really beautiful project, it would be necessary for us to build it by ourselves. It would be impossible to do it well through a general contractor. To my amazement, he answered calmly that he already knew that this was my opinion . . . and that it was an inevitable outcome of my philosophy.

Hosoi also told me that he himself, before even coming to see me, had already considered the possibility of having the school directly built by master carpenters, without architects. Thus the whole issue was familiar to him, and my anxiety about mentioning it was quite unnecessary. Hosoi was a more subtle man than I had realized. His only substantial question was to ask me to make more precise, what I meant when I said that we would have to build it "ourselves." Obviously, we were not going to build it with our own hands. What were we intending to do?

I answered, that *it meant we ourselves would have to manage all the craftsmen and subcontractors directly*. In order to make this idea clear, and so that he could present it to the board of directors of Eishin Gakuen for discussion, he asked me to write a memorandum explaining my idea. My answer appears below.

FIRST MEMORANDUM ON DIRECT CONSTRUCTION MANAGEMENT

July 9, 1982. In order to create the kind of construction which is compatible with the deep feeling of the new Eishin Campus, it will be necessary to use a different organization of construction from the conventional one usually used in Japan. I propose that we do not award a contract for construction to a large general contractor or construction company. Instead, I propose that we organize a construction operation, within the Eishin Campus, under the management and financial control of the Eishin School itself.

The king pin of this operation will be a manager who, under our instruction, employs the various necessary subcontractors, small subcontracting companies, and individual craftsmen, directly, and thus assumes direct day-to-day control of the whole construction operation. We will instruct this Manager, to understand our way of making buildings, and place the operational daily work in his hands.

Obviously, the choice of the Manager is fundamental to the success of this approach. And the search for this person, and the development of criteria for a successful choice, will need to take place slowly, over the next few months.

The Manager's three most immediate main functions have to do with speed, cost, and flexibility.

1. Speed. The Manager's main work will be to keep things moving, day after day, to keep schedules on time, workmen on time, to keep the flow of construction activity moving forward very efficiently.

2. Cost. His second main function is to keep all costs down to an absolute minimum, and to keep them below budget. This is essential.

3. Flexibility. The Manager's third responsibility will be to help CES achieve the most and the best quality, as determined by the architect, within the available framework of time and cost; thus being responsible to The Center for Environmental Structure, keeping track of dynamic changes and developing building designs as made by the architect, while working them through with the architectural staff.

We will need the Manager's help primarily in these three matters, and we expect to work very closely with him in achieving these aims.

Christopher Alexander

TWO TYPES OF CONSTRUCTION MANAGEMENT

The standard construction management method has been used by general contractors for many years, in different countries all over the world. The Direct Management method of construction is something entirely different. To distinguish the two, first let's review what is nowadays a typical or standard organization structure.

In standard construction management there is a separate entity called the general contractor, guided by a document called the general contract. The general contract contains precise and detailed drawings of everything that is to be built, with very detailed specifications which must be adhered to, to the last detail. The general contractor runs and manages the building works, precisely as it is laid down to the last detail in the construction contract, and takes ultimate responsibility for cost and time. For profit, the general contractor takes a profit, fixed in advance, which may be anywhere from 4%-25% of all construction costs. On top of that, provided that the buildings are built exactly to the general contract, the contractor takes every monetary surplus he can find, and puts it in his pocket. This is an additional way to make profit. To increase profit there is substantial incentive for the contractor to cut corners, costs, and use inferior materials. The more he cuts, the more money he makes. The architect only draws up the general contract. Once that is done he has no further operational role, except to supervise the administration of the contract. He has no decision-making authority while the buildings are being built.

DIRECT CONSTRUCTION MANAGEMENT

Direct Management does not include or permit the concept of profit to occur. The management is fee-based, or based as a fixed salary, and all construction costs are fixed ahead of time, and the building design is modified during construction, to make up any over-runs. The manager is not able to move money around at will, or put it in his pocket. At the same time, the design is approximately fixed, but with the understanding that it may be changed, during the evolution of the building, so that subtle adaptations can be included in the emerging building. In the Direct Management method it is the architect himself and the direct manager who together manage the building works and all on-site construction for the owner. All monies flow through an open-book system which is available to the owner's inspection at any time. The manager on-site is working for the architect directly. Any unused cash surplus that is generated in a particular building operation is added to a fixed fund, and then used, at the owner's and architect's discretion, to make the buildings better. And, in the Direct Management method it is the architect himself who has ultimate responsibility for time, cost, and quality.

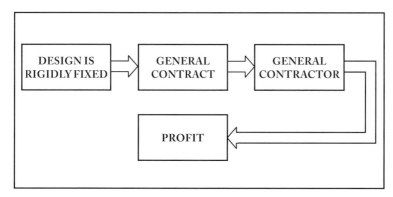

Diagram of **STANDARD** *Construction Management.*

During the months which followed, we discussed this method more extensively.

FIRST STEPS TO IMPLEMENT DIRECT MANAGEMENT

By the end of 1982, Hosoi had become convinced that we should try and use this method. However, he also felt that it might be possible to use this "direct" method in cooperation with an existing construction company, in what he called the "rent-a-network method." In this approach, he proposed that we manage the construction, ourselves, with the following things completely under our control:

1. Basic cost control.
2. Choice of subcontractors.
3. Contact with all subcontractors.
4. Day-to-day on-site decisions.
5. Design modifications and shuffling of costs and details needed by ongoing cost control.

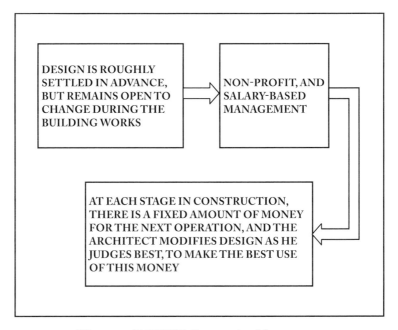

Diagram of **DIRECT** *Construction Management.*

Eishin Gakuen arranged for us to interview five top construction companies. This was done for two reasons. First, simply to explore the possibilities of involving one of them as helpers in Direct Management, via the rent-a-network idea. Second, as a back-up, in case our attempt to use Direct Management failed altogether.

We interviewed Taisei, Fujita, Sumitomo, and two other companies. In each case, we explained that we wanted to manage the construction directly, *ourselves*, and asked them if they would be willing to give us access to their network of managers and subcontractors, under these conditions.

In answer to this question, Taisei said no. Two others also seemed unwilling. Fujita and Sumitomo said yes.

It is perhaps significant that, even at this very early stage, Taisei said some things to us, which had the character of threats. They said that it would be impossible for us to run such an operation in Japan, and there was no knowing, if we tried it, what might not happen. For example, subcontractors might leave us in the middle, might walk off the job, supplies might turn out to be unavailable, etc. Although similar statements could have been made in good faith, for those of us who heard them talking, there was a not very subtle undercurrent that told us they were directly threatening us. It may seem strange that almost two years before construction started, and in a situation where Taisei was hoping to get a job, that they should make such threats. But it was a sign of things to come.

As far as Sumitomo and Fujita were concerned, they seemed willing to enter into the type of arrangement which we asked for. We therefore went ahead to ask them to introduce us to the person who would be our manager, were they to get the job. They did so, and we interviewed two prospective direct manager candidates, one from Fujita, and one from Sumitomo.

During the same period, we had also made a search to find our *own* independent manager, in order to study the case where we would run the construction directly by ourselves.

After these preliminaries, we then submitted a detailed report to the directors of the Eishin school, describing the results of our investigations. This report, which was confidential, might be described as one of the king pins in the project. It described, in a very thorough fashion, the careful analysis we did on (1) four candidates for the job of direct manager, (2) the reasons why Direct Management would be superior to a typical construction company network, and (3) possible difficulties that could arise with the Direct Management process and how they could be mitigated.

Excerpts of this lengthy confidential document are included here to demonstrate what we were looking for, and the case we made to the Directors.

CONFIDENTIAL MEMORANDUM ON POSSIBLE CANDIDATES FOR DIRECT MANAGER[1]

February 20, 1983

INTRODUCTION

At this stage, we have had an opportunity for some extensive talks with Mr. Yamamoto, a possible candidate to be an independent manager for us, and also with Fujita and Taisei and Sumitomo construction companies, who have explained their approaches to our request for hiring the direct management network.

It is now possible to draw some preliminary conclusions about the construction process we should use for the Eishin project. These conclusions very strongly suggest that Direct Management is feasible, and also very much better for the project, than the construction company network method. Since we are now about one month away from final deadline for making a decision about construction method, it is important that the client should grasp the various points involved, as thoroughly as possible, at this early stage, so that it is possible to check these points thoroughly, during the next three weeks.

Of course, as we know, both the Direct Management process, and the general contractor process, have their respective strengths and weaknesses. The main purpose of this report is to compare these strengths and weaknesses. We have suspected, all along, that Direct Management is superior from the point of view of producing better buildings. However, there have been some substantial doubts about the various dangers and risks involved in direct construction management, and there has been a widespread belief that the guarantees and security necessary to meet cost and time constraints can be provided much better by a large general contractor.

We are now in a much better position to evaluate both these general points. Briefly, our analysis is this.

---

1 To shorten this long document, we reduced a few paragraphs, without essential change of meaning. Please note, also: The confidential personnel assessments which are presented in the following pages were first written in 1983, and were kept confidential for twenty-seven years. They were shown only to a handful of members of the Eishin Gakuen, who needed to have direct involvement at that time. We have now decided that regarding this confidential information, the passage of time is sufficient to protect any sensitive matters, and we believe that no one can, at this stage, be hurt by release of these confidences.

First, the Direct Management method is very definitely superior to the general contractor method, as far as producing a high quality project, and indeed, it is now clear that there are some serious dangers to the project, if we choose the general contractor method with Fujita or Sumitomo.

Second, if we use the Direct method, with Mr. Yamamoto acting for the Center for Environmental Structure as manager, the various critical problems of time, money, security and guarantees, can be solved more easily than we previously suspected, and the apparent superiority of the general contractor method on these points, is *less* than we previously suspected. On balance, we are therefore now very strongly inclined to use the Direct Management method, and we therefore strongly wish to recommend to the client that the Direct Method should be used, with Mr. Yamamoto as construction manager.

We shall now enumerate the various points which have led to this conclusion, one by one.

PART ONE: ANALYSIS OF DIFFERENT CANDIDATES

We have now had an opportunity to interview four construction managers, three of them from large general contractors (Taisei company, Mr. Goto of Sumitomo, Mr. Tsukada of Fujita), and one independent (Mr. Yamamoto). In the following pages we shall present our evaluation of these candidates. Of course, the client recognizes that it is imperative for the success of this project, that we must have real confidence in the Manager who runs the job. We therefore begin with an analysis of the personal qualities of the different candidates, and our attitude to their capabilities.

REPORT ON TAISEI

Taisei have paid no attention to our request. They have not introduced us to a possible construction manager, and have insisted on a package deal, even though it was explained to them, several times, that we were not interested in a package deal. I assume, therefore, that we must dismiss Taisei as uncooperative and arrogant, and extremely unlikely to produce a good result for us.

REPORT ON MR. GOTO (SUMITOMO)

The written presentation from Sumitomo is the most intelligent coming from the three general contractors. It gives a really clear and precise account of the different legal structures of responsibility and division of responsibility which might be used on the job.

However, Mr. Goto is quite weak. He is a very nice person, but it is clear from all his answers to questions, that his background is primarily in *management*, to the exclusion of building skills. In answer to my question about how he would arrange production of special concrete blocks, he answered that he would ask a salesman to arrange it with some concrete block manufacturer. This was amazing to us, since the natural answer, is to contact the manufacturer directly. Again, when we asked him how he would solve problems of white plaster in-fill, and technical difficulties of shikkui, dolomite plaster, and white portland cement, he said he would call in the research division. Once again, he had no personal impulse to deal with the problem on the level of physical experiments which he himself could see and touch. In general, it was clear from his answers, that his training and experience are in pure management, and that he has very little experience or love of actual buildings themselves, or of the building process.

It would be impossible for us to work with Mr. Goto, even though he is a nice person.

REPORT ON MR. TSUKADA (FUJITA)

Fujita are very strong in their willingness, and spirit of cooperation. They have a very strong desire to do this job, and are therefore willing to extend themselves quite far, to meet our needs.

However, Mr. Tsukada, like Mr. Goto, has more feeling for management, than for actual building process. In answer to a question about how to create a good spirit on the building site, he described a kind of pep talk he gives every morning, to all one hundred workers, and then arranges that supervisors all raise their hands into the air, and shout "we will do better."

This kind of thing is typical of large corporate management, but frightening, as a description of the spiritual process needed to produce really good buildings. We are sure that Mr. Tsukada is a very efficient manager, and has a genuine desire to understand our methods. He knows more, technically, and physically, about building, than Mr. Goto. However, even so, all his answers about the building process were rather vague. He used expressions like "it must have heart," and "the answer lies in your hands"...good answers ...but somehow, he never actually gave examples which described the physical reality of construction process.

We would prefer to work with Mr. Tsukada, compared with Mr. Goto. However, he does not have a strong enough sense of physical reality to make a really good project. It is very hard to imagine him drawing on a piece of wood, to show a detail to a carpenter.

It is finally worth mentioning that the "management" orientation of Mr. Tsukada, probably comes from the fact that he was originally trained as an architect, and arrives at his present position with a "clean hands" approach. Our reason for trusting Mr. Yamamoto, more fully, is that he has grown up and learned his experience in the actual trades of construction, and is close to the feeling of trades, not at arms length.

It is almost impossible for us to work with a construction manager who has not learned his business, in actual *manual* connection with the work of building.

REPORT ON MR. YAMAMOTO (INDEPENDENT)

Of all Manager candidates we have interviewed, Mr. Yamamoto is by far the best. He is, so far, the only one who has an appreciation of building, and a concrete grasp of everyday practical reality, which corresponds to the way we work ourselves. We asked a question about plaster, and the next day Mr. Yamamoto brought a plasterer to the school, to demonstrate actual plaster mixes, and methods of plastering. We asked a question about plumbing cost, and electrical cost, and immediately, on his own initiative, Mr. Yamamoto began to make detailed cost estimates of the electrical and plumbing systems for the project.

We described a novel method of connecting shear walls (masonry), with wood columns and beams, and immediately Mr. Yamamoto began to describe the various practical aspects of this new approach, in a way that corresponded to our own.

When we asked him what he considers the most important quality which produces good results on a building site, he described the type of carpenter who can tell which kind of wood is best for a column and which is best for a beam, and the feeling of involvement in the total project. That is, he understood the carpenter's real work, in a detailed way; and he recognized that the carpenter works best when he has a total relation to the entire project.

Neither Mr. Goto, nor Mr. Tsukada have this type of understanding. When we asked Mr. Tsukada how he creates a good atmosphere on the site, he described the process of drinking and telling jokes with the carpenters. Not bad, but actually not based on any real knowledge of building. When we asked Mr. Goto how he would choose the best carpenters for the job, he told us he would ask his subcontractors to supply the best.

In short, both Mr. Goto and Mr. Tsukada, though good-hearted and nice people, have a background which is more oriented towards management, rather than building process. This is quite natural in the construction managers of large corporations. But it is also precisely this kind of corporate and managerial atmosphere which has done so much damage to modern architecture. It is essential that we avoid this kind of management feeling.

Mr. Yamamoto is the only candidate we have met so far, who completely avoids this management-oriented feeling. With him, we feel we are on sure ground. He understands building in the same way that we do, and we are confident that we can work with him.

We would like to work with Mr. Yamamoto.

PART TWO: ANALYSIS OF REASONS WHY A DIRECT MANAGEMENT METHOD IS SUPERIOR TO AN OVERALL CONSTRUCTION COMPANY GENERAL CONTRACT.

1. MORE RESPONSIVE TO DETAILS OF PROJECT AS THEY DEVELOP.

2. MORE POSSIBILITY OF MAKING CHANGES DURING CONSTRUC-TION.

We have emphasized, from the beginning, that in order to achieve really profound quality in this project, it is necessary to be able to modify it continuously during the process of construction. This in turn requires that the Manager himself, is alive to the fact that important decisions are being faced at every stage, and is aware that one of the most important things that is happening, is the evolution of the building designs, while they are being built.

We have a strong intuition that a general contractor will somehow interfere with this process, no matter what is said in advance. The reason is this. All the large general contractors we have interviewed are strongly oriented to the problem of schedule. Of course, this is one of their strengths. However, we are convinced that they are so strongly oriented to this problem, that they will ultimately kill the life of the project, in order to achieve enough management control to be able to guarantee schedule.

. . .

3. BETTER COMMUNICATION BECAUSE A DIRECT MANAGER, WORK-ING FOR US DIRECTLY, WILL BE MORE DOWN TO EARTH.

. . .

4. MORE SENSITIVE RELATION WITH CRAFTSMEN DURING CON-STRUCTION.

. . .

5. FINANCIALLY ABLE TO HIRE BETTER QUALITY CRAFTSMEN, BY AVOIDING GENERAL CONTRACTOR'S AND SUBCONTRACTOR'S OVERHEADS AND FEES.

. . . In the Direct Management method, since relatively little money is taken from budget for management, and none is taken for profit, it is possible to spend money on people who actually do the work, and thus much better craftsmen are working on the job. The general contractor method can easily damage the project in this respect.

6. MORE CONTROL OVER CHOICE OF SUBCONTRACTORS AND CRAFTSMEN.

We have already found out that the project will require a considerable number of highly specialized craftsmen, with special skills, and a special willingness to carry out unusual instructions. As we have held discussions with various possible suppliers and craftsmen, it has become obvious that the right people are often extremely hard to find, and that it is necessary to reject five persons, and choose the sixth. This is easy to do, in the Direct Management method. However, in the general contractor method, there is a very strong pressure, for the general to choose subcontractors who are already known to him, or with whom he has a previous or continuing relationship. This pressure will naturally make it more difficult to insist on choice of craftsmen or suppliers who are unknown to the general, but who happen to satisfy our requirements most exactly. This kind of difficulty can easily endanger the project.

7. BETTER APPRECIATION OF NOVEL TECHNIQUES.

The invention of novel construction techniques is an essential part of our ongoing effort to make good buildings. However, preliminary discussion with the manager candidates proposed by the big construction companies, has shown that there is a strong tendency to use standardized solutions to building problems. This is to be expected since these companies have an extensive network, and build in large volume. However, since the construction managers are not very down to earth or practical men, but more manager-type of people, they have some trouble in understanding basic engineering and construction ideas which are presented to them.

Although this can be solved, in theory, simply by resources of the large company, in practice it creates a slight strain on the process.

Mr. Yamamoto, on the other hand, has an immediate practical grasp of the new techniques we have shown him, because he naturally thinks in practical terms. As a result we are confident that he is more likely to solve the problem of technical innovations with less difficulty.

PART THREE: ANALYSIS OF POSSIBLE DRAWBACKS OF DIRECT MANAGEMENT.

At various times, during the discussions of the last few months, the following points have been raised, as possible drawbacks to the Direct Management method, since the general contractor can give a better guarantee of quality, and capacity to make good on defects during the five years after completion. We shall now see that the apparent advantage of the general contractor method over the Direct method has been slightly exaggerated; indeed the Direct method is able to solve these problems nearly as well as the general contractor method.

1. GREATER COST, BECAUSE GENERAL CONTRACTOR HAS THE ADVANTAGE OF BULK PURCHASE OF MATERIALS.

In order to analyze this problem, it is necessary to examine categories of materials rather carefully.

Wood. The single largest quantity of material is wood. We have established the very low cost of obtaining wood directly from mills in Oregon, in many cases about 50% of cost in Japan. We have also made contact with an import company who is willing to let us do business directly with his import subcontractor, so that shipping cost is extremely low (about 2%). We therefore have far better purchasing power than a typical general contractor, as far as lumber is concerned.

Concrete, cement, steel, piles. In these cases, we expect to be able to set up direct relations with some supplier, who, because of the large volumes in the Eishin project, can find a way of obtaining materials at same price as a general contractor. For example, in the case of cement, we have a contact in a cement company, who can force concrete supplier to give it to us at same price as the general contractor's price. In most cases our price will be less that the general contractor's price, since in the Direct method, there is no profit charged. We expect to develop the same technique, in all these cases.

Roof tiles, windows, concrete blocks, and other special materials. In these cases, we have established very special requirements, and special designs. This means that we shall special-order these products from small manufacturers, according to our own design. Since we are working this way, after intimate relation with small manufacturers, we will get the best possible price for special products. If we are working with a general contractor, that contractor will, in any case, only get same price as we get, from these small manufacturers, so in this case the general contractor has no advantage.

. . .

2. THE GENERAL CONTRACTOR HAS A BETTER NETWORK OF SUB-CONTRACTORS.

We have heard frequently that the large companies claim that they have better access to subcontractors. In one sense this is undoubtedly true, since they maintain a large network of connections in the construction field. However, careful analysis of the actual subcontractors used by large companies reveals a surprising weakness in their system, which is entirely negative.

Let us consider, for example, the network of subcontracting companies presented to us by Fujita. Careful examination of this list of companies, shows that very many of them are themselves large companies, which are themselves, like Fujita, essentially corporate in nature. This means that these companies themselves, even though they deal in lumber, steel, or some specific trade, are actually remote from the actual craftsmen who will do the work itself. This has two extremely serious faults.

First, it means, inevitably, that even more of the original construction budget will be spent on the overhead and profit of this second level company, thus depriving the project of money for real work on the site.

Second, and even more serious, it means that many of these companies are quite inexperienced in careful craft work, with real attention to the nature or love of the building task itself. These companies are usually organized to produce profit, by large scale organization of highly standardized construction.

In short, they are entirely unfamiliar with the task of making buildings which have deep feeling. They do not know this business, nor are they equipped to organize teams of craftsmen to perform such tasks.

. . .

It is essential, for the success of our project, that we hire craftsmen and small masters directly, and make direct contracts with them, without going through an expensive, and cumbersome system of middlemen.

3. BETTER ACCESS TO WORKERS.

During discussion, it has been mentioned several times, that the general contractor, with his existing network has access to many men and companies, and can easily assemble the necessary teams of craftsmen (perhaps as many as 100 or 150 at height of project). On the other hand, it is claimed, that the Direct Management method may have difficulty finding the necessary groups of craftsmen, at the times when they are needed.

This argument has two mistakes in it. First, Mr. Yamamoto has already made contact with a considerable number of small masters and subcontractors in the Saitama area, just around Iruma-Shi. His preliminary report indicates that we will have no difficulty at all, in finding the necessary workers. Second, Fujita explained to us, that in any case, they will ask their own subcontractors, to find grandson subcontractors near the site. In this case, Fujita would be looking for the very same people that we ourselves would look for directly, except that it would cost them about 8% more, because of the profit on the grandson relationship. If this is really true, then it is almost absurd to hire the very same people, and small subcontractors, at a higher price, through the general contractor method, as we would anyway hire directly by the Direct Management method.

4. BETTER ABILITY TO MEET THE CONSTRUCTION SCHEDULE AND GUARANTEE COMPLETION BY THE DEADLINE.

This is a very serious matter. It is especially serious, since the client has made it clear that he has a realistic danger of bankruptcy, in case the school is not ready in March

Erection of the Judo Hall in early morning light.

1985. *We must therefore treat the necessity to open the high school in April 1985 as absolute.*

It is also clear that it is easier for a large construction company to give a guarantee of on-schedule completion, than it is for our own Direct Management organization.

However, we make two observations.

First, the general contractor will only be able to give this guarantee, if he *eliminates* direct control of *all* direct management by the architect. This means, that, in order to achieve schedule guarantee from general contractor, the general contractor will sacrifice the quality of the project completely, and force it through according to drawings. But, we know this will not produce a good result. It is therefore extremely dangerous to the project.

Second, we may notice that the schedule is not as decisive as it may appear. This is due to the fact that, if necessary, we may comfortably divide the project into three phases of construction, as follows.

Phase 1. Home room buildings, Gymnasium, Faculty offices, 4,628 m² of construction.

Phase 2. Great Hall, Judo Hall, Cafeteria, Student house, Gates, Administration, 3,306 m² of construction.

Phase 3. College department buildings, Library, Research center, 5,290 m² of construction.

Absolute requirement to open the high school by April 1985, only requires that buildings in group 1 are finished by March 1985. Buildings in group 2 can be finished six months later, by September 1985. Buildings in group 3 can be finished six months later still, by March 1986. The only consequence of this extension of time, will be to increase design fees, since some members of the architectural staff will have to work for a longer period. However, this is a relatively minor cost.

This schedule is rather relaxed, and provides lengths of time greatly in excess of norms for construction of this type. I therefore feel completely confident that we can meet these construction schedules, by using the Direct Management method. We can therefore safely protect the client's urgent need to open the school in April 1985, without using a large general contractor.

5. GUARANTEE OF QUALITY, AND CAPACITY TO MAKE GOOD ON DEFECTS DURING THE FIVE YEARS AFTER COMPLETION.

This is one of the most serious potential drawbacks of Direct Management. Since the Direct Management method does not provide any existing Japanese company with stable long life, it seems as if the client cannot be protected against defects in workmanship, leaking roofs, defects in doors, etc., which are discovered after construction. The direct method apparently does not have any built-in capacity to solve this type of problem.

However, the solution to this problem is rather simple. As we know, a general contractor like Fujita, will take approximately 8% of construction budget, as profit and overhead. Of course such a general contractor normally uses part of this money to cover cost of any repairs, replacements, etc., after construction. We propose that, in the Direct Management method, we shall use the same approach. We shall create a special fund, and place about 5-8% of construction money in this special fund. This money will be left, untouched for five years, and will then be used, whenever necessary, to cover the type of things which a general contractor normally covers with his guarantee. If, after five years, this money has not been spent, it will then be available to build any extras, or special items, which could not be provided at the time of initial construction.

As far as very large-scale problems, such as structural failure, or massive damage to earthworks, are concerned, these will be covered by normal type of construction insurance, which can be provided in the case of direct method, just as in the general-contractor method.

Finally, in order to prepare to make this very important decision, we suggest that the client should obtain legal advice in order to prepare a detailed picture of the *legal* structure and organization, which may be necessary in order to carry out the Direct

Management method with full security. We request that this legal work should be done jointly by the chief architect, by the chief Japan architect, and by the client's attorney, Mr. Igarashi.

Christopher Alexander

CONCLUSION OF THE MEMORANDUM

THE CATACLYSM

Even at the time I wrote this report on Direct Management, I was aware that its mere existence might be dangerous to the project. In fact, I was so concerned about potentially dangerous consequences, that I gave instructions for the report to be placed in a locked cabinet, and that no one was to have a copy of it. I also asked Hosoi to make quite certain that the Japanese translation of it, in Mr. Nishigori's control, was also kept under lock and key, was issued to no one, and that it should be handled with the utmost care.

I knew intuitively that this document was serious enough to cause furious reactions in Japan, possible damage to the project, even perhaps potential physical danger to ourselves. At the time I took these precautions, I seemed a little foolish to myself . . . too melodramatic, like someone who has been reading too many ghost stories.

But as it turned out, my fears were justified.

14 HEAVY THREATS, ATTEMPTED BRIBES, AND DANGER

In the early summer of 1983, Hosoi told me a story.
Although twenty-nine years have now passed since the
events of the story, I cannot get it out of my mind.
It is a mystery which doesn't go away.

Although there had been many indications that the
construction industry's discomfort with CES's approach
to the project through system-A was mounting, we had
not so far given in to any pressure to conform to the
widely-practiced system-B approach that was common to
all professional construction in Japan. Hosoi was strongly
upholding his support for me, and for system-A, and for the
way we were handling the project.

Now, suddenly, the stakes got higher and more dangerous.

It started with a relatively minor event. In May or June of 1983
we began to hear that some of the big Japanese contractors were
getting interested in the Eishin Campus project — partly because
the project was, after all, big, prominent, and potentially valuable.
Taisei, Sumitomo, and other construction companies had therefore
begun low-key, exploratory contact with Hosoi. One day, Hosoi
told me that he had received a phone call from a representative of one
of these big contractors, requesting that he (Hosoi) should attend a
meeting with other related persons, in a club in Shinjuku.[1]

Hosoi agreed to this request. He did not tell me who the
people behind this request were, nor how many people were in-

---

1   A prominent district of downtown Tokyo.

volved. In fact he never told me who these people were, until the year 2009, twenty-six years later. It took twenty-six years for him to speak to me about it, or to mention anyone's name. And when he did decide to give me more details, even though he and I had, by then, become very close friends, he still did not let me in on the concrete facts of the story he was slowly telling me.

Even though I was a central player in the events of the next days and weeks, and later became still more deeply involved in serious decisions taken in the next many years, Hosoi must have felt that it was not something he could share with me. I shall never understand how he felt able to conceal information from me, given the fact that I was the most central, responsible person for the project. Nevertheless, I bit my tongue and did my best to chalk up his odd behavior as a result of an unbridgeable culture gap. I accepted his unusual way of handling this and my professional behavior and responsibilities.

THE FIRST SHOCK THAT HOSOI RELAYED TO ME

Before I go any further, I must first explain a peculiar aspect of the events which followed. When Hosoi came back from Shinjuku a few days later, he gave me a startling, and somewhat shocking, account of what he had heard and experienced in the club.

In the first version of Hosoi's story (as he relayed it to me in early 1983) Hosoi told me that he had been contacted by someone who spoke for a group of people who wanted to talk to him about the Eishin project. When he reached the club in Shinjuku, people welcomed him, and encouraged him. The atmosphere (as I recall Hosoi's telling) was mild, tense, but somewhat jovial. However, as the discussion with this group unfolded, the dialogue was not so comfortable after all. It turned out that the group of construction companies, was not light-hearted, but rather sinister. The central issue they raised with Hosoi was this: They wanted, above all, to get me out of Japan. I do not believe there was anything personal in this desire. They simply wanted to eliminate system-A altogether, and uproot any trace of its existence, in Japan.

That was their number-one agenda. The names of the members of this group, were never given to me by Hosoi. Nor was it made clear exactly whom they represented. However, it seemed that they were there on behalf of the bigger construction companies in Japan. And I now know that Taisei (one of the big Five) was involved and present at the time.[2]

As Hosoi told it to me, the contractors' desire to get me out of Japan took the following practical form. He was shown into a room, somewhere in the club. When he arrived there, he was made aware that there was a small suitcase standing against the wall. After some initial discussion, he was told by the men around the table that this suitcase contained twenty million yen in notes (at that time about US$80,000). They intended it to be a gift for Hosoi. He asked what they wanted him to do, in exchange for this money. They told him, "We want you to get Alexander out of Japan." In a joking manner, Hosoi reacted comically, and replied: "I am sorry, the money is not enough."

In the discussion which then followed, they told him that they were aware of the school's intention to use Direct Management, and they — the Five — wanted to give him some advice. Such a thing would be impossible in Japan, and it would never work. He quietly but strongly disagreed. They warned him that if he stayed on this track, he would find it impossible to get cement, or bulldozers for the project: an explicit threat against the project. They again, and repeatedly, offered him the ¥20,000,000 in cash — if he would stop the direct method and get Alexander out of Japan altogether.

Hosoi's impression was that they felt that the possibility of a success by the Direct Management method, had the potential to be damaging to the big construction companies which controlled construction in Japan — so much so, that they were willing to go to considerable lengths to make sure it did not happen.

---

2   At that time the five great companies who more or less controlled construction all over Japan, were Shimizu, Takenaka, Taisei, Obayashi, Kajima (The Big Five). Two companies with whom we had extensive dealings, Fujita and Sumitomo, were also large construction companies, but smaller than the big five.

In order to understand this clearly, it is necessary for a non-Japanese reader to visualize the Japanese construction companies. They are quite unlike any construction companies which exist in the United States or Europe. In Japan, almost nothing is built without the help of the big Five. They have influence in every branch of government, and at that time it was widely believed that they could control the vote on almost any issue in the Japanese Diet.[3] In 1984, they had a virtual monopoly of all construction in Japan. They had overheads and profit margins which were extremely high. And they used these high overheads to maintain their power and influence.

Indeed, they had a very great deal to lose. If it could have been shown in 1984 that even just one large project could be built in Japan without their help, the whole Japanese construction industry, in its then-existing form, would have been seriously compromised. Thus, compared with what the big construction companies had to fear from our project, the offered bribe of $80,000 was a mere trifle.

Two weeks later, the same individual who had originally contacted Hosoi, contacted Hosoi again, and asked him to meet them once again, in the same place in Shinjuku.[4] Reluctantly Hosoi agreed, after making it clear on the telephone that he did not want to hear any further discussions of the bribe that had been offered. When he arrived once again in the Shinjuku meeting room, the same men were there. They asked him if he had had a chance to think about the money, and whether he could agree to their proposal. No longer joking, Hosoi said that he could not continue discussion of this point, and did not want the offer to be repeated.

"In that case," they said, "perhaps you would be interested in this piece of paper." They passed across the table a piece of paper on which dates and times were written. Apparently, as Hosoi relayed

---

3   The National Diet of Japan is the two-house parliament, known in Japanese as *Kokkai*.

4   Unfortunately, even though Hosoi was by now a close friend, in this instance he was very close-mouthed about the details of these events. This is understandable, since any entanglement with the Big Five construction companies, would very likely bring the Yakuza into the picture, too. There is therefore some doubt about the location of the second meeting. It is possible that it took place in Shinjuku. Or it is possible that it took place in Hosoi's office in the Musashino-shi school building, where Hosoi kept his office.

it to me later, these dates and times showed the movements and whereabouts of Hosoi's wife and two daughters, twenty-four hours a day for the previous two weeks! This time the discussion was not an attempt to bribe, but an explicit threat. They made it clear to him, that if the school made any attempt to continue using the Direct Management method, they would break the project. Supplies would become unobtainable. Local bulldozer operators would be told that they would never again work for any company, and would never again be able to buy a bulldozer. And so on. They made it clear that they would simply bring the project to a halt.

They also re-emphasized — "just for his information" — that they had detailed knowledge of Hosoi's movements, hour by hour, every day, for the previous two weeks. To prove it, they gave him details of people he had seen on his last visit to the United States. The threat to him and to his family was clear, it was real, and it was frightening. As if this was not enough, just for a demonstration, and still in the club in Shinjuku, one of them half-playfully began to push him around . . . and then, before going further, simply told him again that this was serious. *They most strongly advised him to change his mind.*

Hosoi was, at first, altogether reluctant to talk to me about all this. He called me to his office, and first just told me that he felt that the Direct Management method could not succeed, and that we should think of some way of using one of the companies we had interviewed. I did not at first accept this comment, because I did not fully understand his line of reasoning. Then Hosoi gave me the details of the threat against his wife and daughters, which he had so far not previously mentioned to me. That was in 1983.

So that we could have face-to-face discussion about the gravity of these severe and dangerous threats, Hosoi asked me to meet a friend of his, an architect named Urabayashi. Hosoi went so far as to arrange a private dinner at which he asked his friend Urabayashi to help me think about these events and their implications. Mr. Urabayashi, a gentle and mature person of great character, and an architect of considerable experience, convinced me that without doubt the threats were realistic and dangerous. He described their connection with the Yakuza, the Japanese mafia, as being at least as dangerous as the mob in the United States.

The men from the cartel meant what they said! Urabayashi asked me, very earnestly, as a personal friend of Hosoi's, to take great care of Hosoi's position, and to behave with the utmost care to protect his vulnerable position in the school, and in the world. He hinted, also, that Hosoi was potentially in danger of being physically damaged, or beaten.

I was affected by Urabayashi's earnestness. He did not seem to be a man who exaggerated. He was sober, and I took him very seriously. Beyond that, I realized that Hosoi, of all people in the world, had given us (CES) the extraordinary chance to do our best to realize a large scale version of system-A in the world, thus to build a very large project. After his great faith in us, I felt that I had, absolutely, to do my utmost to protect him, and to make some kind of balance between the needs of system-A to succeed in the world, and the need to protect Hosoi and his family.

IN BED WITH THE TIGER

I felt, because of what Hosoi had reported to me, and because of Urabayashi's own anxious concern, that I must do everything I could to protect Hosoi and his family.

It was necessary for me to take a very important decision regarding the project and its management. At that moment in May 1983, it was the last day of my then current visit to Japan. What could I do to save the Direct Management method, to save the hopes of system-A, yet also to make sure to protect Hosoi?

Suddenly I had what seemed to me then, an inspired idea. I decided to talk to Kazunori Fujita (the son of the Fujita family, known colloquially as "the Prince"), and asked for his protection. In detail, I proposed to ask Fujita Kogyo (The Fujita Construction Company, of which Kazunori was then Vice-President) to sponsor our project as a demonstration research project — thus leaving the Direct Management method intact, with us in control, but also giving us enough of a relationship to the Japanese construction industry, so that the threats against Hosoi would have to stop.

In retrospect, I realized how naive this was: a classic case of hoping that the fox would guard the chickens. But at the time, it seemed the only possible way to keep going. I felt sure that if the project, with the Direct Management method intact could be placed under Fujita's sponsorship, then no other company would dare to threaten it, or interfere with it.

I invited Kazunori to dinner. During dinner he agreed to my proposal. A few weeks later, he and I jointly wrote the sponsorship agreement which is summarized below.

- The purpose of this memorandum is to confirm an agreement for carrying out work in connection with the construction of the new Eishin school, and to eliminate obstacles in carrying out this work. After signing this agreement, the demands between Gakko Hojin Eishin Gakuen (hereinafter called "the Client"), and Fujita Corporation (hereinafter called "the Sponsor") will be satisfied according to the following articles.
- The client has entrusted the construction of the project to the Center for Environmental Structure (hereinafter called "the Manager").
- It has been agreed that the Sponsor has no responsibility for construction at all, except as requested by the Client or the Manager.
- The Sponsor will appreciate the significance of the whole process of construction which is carried out through the Direct Management method by the Manager, and give the project moral support, as sponsor, and as part of its own study. The Client will pay a certain amount of fee to the sponsor, for the cooperation and goodwill offered by the sponsor.
- As part of the sponsor's moral support, the sponsor will give the Client the following guarantee: In any circumstances, whenever the Manager makes a request, for example, because of some unforeseen problem, the sponsor will be ready to offer his help to meet this unpredictable situation. The Client, Sponsor, and Manager will make decisions about the financial details, each time, through discussion.
- As payment for the sponsorship and moral support, the client will pay the sponsor 44 million yen, corresponding to 2% of the 2.2 billion-yen construction cost, immediately upon signing this memorandum. In being paid for actual tasks, besides the sponsorship, the payments will always be the actual expenses, and the sponsor will never gain any profit.
- In exchange for the base fee of 2%, the Sponsor will not only provide goodwill and moral support, but will also, from time to time, provide certain services free of cost. Exact nature of these services is not yet clear, but this clause is intended to allow the sponsor to back up his basic goodwill with various small concrete expressions of this goodwill, from time to time.

- The Sponsor will provide access to its major suppliers of materials, and arrange for us to obtain items like concrete, steel, and manufactured items, at the same discount that the sponsor normally obtains.
- In dealing with actual tasks, the Manager will be the agent of the Client.
- It has been agreed that requests for work to be performed for the Client, and definition of tasks to be performed by the Sponsor, will be ordered by the Manager, and it is agreed that the sponsor will carry out all requests and directions made by the Manager.
- The chief representative of the Manager is Christopher Alexander. In case of the absence of Mr. Alexander from Tokyo, then whoever is designated by Mr. Alexander will be in charge of requests and direction of the work to be performed by the Sponsor.
- The Client will never request or direct the Sponsor directly, concerning any actual tasks.

The full document was signed on June 15, 1983, by:
Gakko Hojin Eishin Gakuen, Keizo Sakaida, Representative
Fujita Corporation, Akio Fujita, Representative
Center for Environmental Structure, Christopher Alexander,
Representative

This sponsorship agreement clearly stated that the buildings would be built in a Direct Management format, with CES taking responsibility as Manager; and that the process would be done with goodwill, supervision, and cooperation of Fujita Kogyo, so that Fujita could learn and ultimately support the introduction of this new management method. The main practical purpose of Fujita's role, was to protect Hosoi's family and our Direct Construction method from further harm, and to provide certain specialized services if needed.

PREPARING FOR DIRECT MANAGEMENT

At this point we felt sure, once again, that we would be able to proceed with construction, using Direct Management, as we had intended all along. We began preparations for construction. For example, we made contact with our lumber brokers in Oregon, and made arrangements to ship extremely high quality materials to Japan — douglas fir, hemlock, and redwood — at a very low price. We made contact with the wonderful plasterers of Kawagoe, the masters of kura shikkui (polished black plaster), and developed our relationship with these plasterers. We began experiments to create new types of concrete block. We began arrangements with roof tile makers, to make the tiles for the project according to our models.

And — of course — we now began the formal process of preparing a comprehensive legal arrangement for the construction management itself. This was finally signed on September 26, 1984. The type of contract which we proposed to use was a contract type later perfected and used extensively by CES in the United States and elsewhere. In this type of contract, the Architect and Owner agree on the rough size and design of the buildings, and agree on a fixed budget with provisions for management and contingencies. The Architect then commits himself to build these buildings, at this price, while making whatever changes are needed during construction, both to improve the design through changes which become apparent while the building unfolds; and to control cost and hold the fixed cost constant.

The essence of this agreement was a non-profit arrangement. The management which was provided was fixed in price; all financial books were open; and the owner had access to all contracts, bids, and checkbooks. The purpose of the contract was to create the best possible buildings at the fixed price. In order to achieve it the Owner gave the Architect very considerable control over the design, as the buildings were emerging. A mature form of this type of contract has been published in another book in this series.[5]

Once again, it looked as though, after all, our Direct Management method was going to be accepted. Our on-going effort to work within system-A had been given protection by Fujita. And Hosoi's wife and daughters were no longer in danger. At this date, the sun still seemed to be shining on the project.

However, somewhat later, it became clear that the antipathy towards Hosoi had not abated. In 1986, Hosoi and his fellow trustees on the Eishin Board were meeting when, quite suddenly, there was a knock on the door, and a demand by some thugs and

---

5   Copies of the two principal contract types we use are printed in Christopher Alexander, Gary Black, Miyoko Tsutsui, *The Mary Rose Museum*, (Oxford University Press, New York, 1995, Center for Environmental Structure Series) pp. 92-100.

judo students that Hosoi must join them outside. The sounds of the beating could be heard by the Board members in their meeting room, but they did not lift a finger to help, quite possibly out of fear. Hosoi was severely beaten. Hosoi's injuries required a stay in the hospital for broken bones in his face, including a 15 cm crack in his lower jaw. During his hospital stay, I was told that his wife and I were the only two people who knew which hospital he was in. The danger of further physical violence was never far away. It was said that the violent action of these students against Hosoi was instigated by the Yakuza. This remains unproven, but is consistent with the theatrical mock-beating made against Hosoi in 1983.[6]

To add insult to injury, in 1986 two court cases were brought against Hosoi by his fellow Board members Okita and Urago, who alleged in both cases that Hosoi had betrayed his judiciary and managerial responsibilities. In both cases, Hosoi was proven not guilty by the Court on all charges.

In this chapter, I have provided the facts as I understood them in 1983. I began writing down the events in 1983 while they were happening. Throughout the project I kept a written record of what Hosoi told me, and of events that were significant to the process we were following. The manuscript was, in effect, a diary. It bore the provisional title of *Battle: the story of a historic clash between world-system-A and world-system-B*. The first draft was completed in 1985. Hosoi read my early draft of *Battle* (dated 1985) at that time and raised no objection whatever to the details described there. Hajo Neis was still at Eishin working daily on the project, and he remembers having frequent conversations with Hosoi about the manuscript. Hajo was privy to the events as they happened, and during those conversations, there was never any suggestion on Hosoi's part that the events described in the manuscript did not happen.

---

6   See page 287.

HOSOI'S VISIT TO ENGLAND

However, in the year 2009, twenty-six years after the attempted bribe incidents, Hosoi came to see me in England. For the first time, he did raise objections. He wanted me to change this text on a variety of matters in regard to the effort the contractors made to bribe him. He described details which were quite different from the 1985 manuscript, my notes, and my written recollections.

On this occasion in 2009, Hosoi claimed the money was to be paid, not in a cash-filled suitcase, as he had first told me. Instead the same proposed sum of $80,000 was to be paid by credit card or check to Hosoi. Of course, Hosoi did not accept the bribe, and whether the money was to be offered in cash, or in some other vehicle, makes little difference. In his 2009 recollection, Hosoi claimed that his meeting was to be with a single person, not with a group. He named this person, and said this single person initiated the meeting in Shinjuku, and made threats that would be carried out by the Big Five construction companies. He said the second visit with the representatives of the big five contractors did not happen at all. If this were true, this would mean that the paper with Mrs. Hosoi's movements, and the movements of his two daughters, was not presented to him, and therefore the threat against these three women did not take place.

Hosoi now says that veiled threats were indeed made against his family, but that he did not believe he and his family were in danger.

Hosoi's insistence about these details was such that we had to respect his wishes and include them in this account. I cannot explain the differences in these two versions of events, and I do not understand the meaning of Hosoi's recent communications about these matters. I can only say that at the time, in 1983, I was absolutely certain that Hosoi and his family were in danger and I felt that as his close friend, I must do something about it. Further, in 2009 Hosoi explicitly confirmed that the beating of 1986 did take place. Physical danger was undoubtedly an issue that we had to take into account.

———

Hosoi is a brave man. Even today, he insists that he did not give in to threats or violence. Because of his courage, we did manage to build the campus in the way both he and I, and Hajo, felt that it must be built.

What needs to be emphasized though — above all — is the simple fact that several large Japanese corporations did damagingly and actively do their best to interfere with our wishes and the client's wishes, and our intent to build the Eishin campus by the means that we now call system-A. Despite the Japanese construction industry's interference in the Eishin project — an especially virulent form of system-B at work — we remained determined to build the campus using Direct Management and system-A.

We viewed the task in hand, as a dominant obligation to world-wide society, all over the globe, so that the precious environment could be built as a life-support for human beings. It was something we absolutely could not afford to give up.

In our view, *everything* depended on it.

15 Bulldozers, Tea Bushes, Architects, and Carpenters

We must get our hands dirty!

In every work of architecture, the construction details are
the heart of the project, and the true makers of the project
are the ones who make the details, who make the materials
directly, and who are not afraid to get dirt
under their fingernails.

Now we entered the stage of civil works. It was during this period
that the deep incompatibilities of system-A and system-B began
to show themselves in earnest.

Practical and divisive issues of an everyday nature came to the
forefront, in the office, in the workshop, in the field. The further
we went into preparation for actual construction, the more the
practical underpinnings of the two different approaches made
themselves felt in concrete ways. The contrast between the two
was more vivid as each day passed.

Attitudes, preferences of habit, affections for one kind of
work over another kind, became decisive. How to measure, how
to calculate, how to draw even a rough sketch of a joint, how to
make successful experiments in our construction yard, the preference for working with one's own hands — all these differences had
meaning, and were important. The extreme differences in attitude
between people with system-A in their blood, and people with
system-B in theirs, could no longer be avoided.

We began with the working drawings for civil works: the site work, roads, services, and land preparation.[1] We started work on these permission drawings in May of 1983, with the intention that we would then start the actual civil work itself sometime in the late summer or early autumn of the year. At this stage, we still had the full-fledged intention that we ourselves would run *all* construction *directly*, by *direct management*.

We therefore asked Mr. Sumiyoshi, a wonderfully skilled man, seventy-six years old, a master carpenter from Nara whom we had met through Hosoi, to play a big part in our construction management operation. He had agreed, as master carpenter, to be head of our construction works. Mr. Sumiyoshi, in turn, chose Mr. Nishida, as the person to be in charge of civil works. Both of them joined our staff in the middle of 1983.

We also hired Mr. Odagiri, a Japanese architect. He was needed, right away, to begin the process of getting permission for the civil works. In order to do it, he brought with him Mr. Ninomya, another architect, and Mr. Kaneko, a civil engineer. The full fight took its most bitter turn when we found out that Mr. Odagiri and his assistants, on the one hand, and Mr. Sumiyoshi and Mr. Nishida, on the other hand, were deeply incompatible, like chalk and cheese.

THE STORY OF MR. ODAGIRI, ARCHITECT

To explain this disturbance in detail, we have to start with the story of Odagiri. It embodies, in many ways, the heart of the battle between system-A and system-B. It is the most complete case where a person educated, trained, experienced, and faithful to system-B, simply because he knew no other system, came into our project, and then, as the reality of system-A began to assert itself, became our bitter enemy, and betrayed the project.

We have already discussed the case of Mr. Nagashima (the architect I had to let go) in chapter 7. After failing to work well with Nagashima, we had tried various efforts with different Japanese

---

1   In the 1980s Skidmore, Owings and Merrill (known as SOM) was the preeminent architecture firm in the eyes of all the system-B architectural firms in the world, greatly admired, and iconic in its standing.

architects. None of them lasted long. Finally, we talked to Odagiri again. If Yasui had been selected as architect for this project, Odagiri would have been selected by Yasui to do the work. Hosoi considered him a friend. And in our early discussions with him, he seemed very sympathetic. He was also an extremely pleasant person. He was a person who inspired trust. He was friendly, but also solid and reliable.

Further, as Hosoi said, he had the face of a carpenter, and he expressed his own interest in carpentry. After many discussions, we felt we could trust him. He was very interested in the project, and said that he was, in any case, preparing to leave Yasui's company in order to set up his own office, and that he would gladly come and work for us.

He came to work for us in the summer of 1983. At first, he seemed very well-organized. He took charge of getting the permission for civil works. This work went smoothly.

He also helped in the process of getting Mr. Sumiyoshi settled in the work of construction manager. There were delicate issues involved, and at that time Odagiri's attitude was friendly and helpful, and extremely positive in its effect upon the project.

But soon, certain small difficulties began to show themselves. The first happened when he was given the task of getting prices for various typical materials and techniques from contractors. He was extremely reluctant to do this. More accurately, he simply didn't do it. After five or ten requests, he finally began copying prices from the little red book, a Japanese trade compendium of prices for various construction items.

We explained to him that these kinds of compendia were generally useless, and that real prices could only be obtained by getting on the phone, and talking to subcontractors to get actual market prices. He still refused. He argued, roughly speaking, that Japanese craftsmen couldn't give estimates until they had a drawing to look at.

We then explained to him, again, that our cost-control method required that we begin with realistic prices, before doing the design, not after. But he still didn't do it.

We then had a serious session, lasting almost a week, during which we explained our method of cost control to him and to the other Japanese staff in the office, using the prices for civil works as an example. We gave them a breakdown of costs for the civil works, and told them that these were the prices we had to work to, and that we would have to keep modifying the design continuously, until we could actually achieve these prices.

Odagiri was clearly instructed that it would be necessary to do the civil works within this budget, and that we simply could not afford one penny more. I told him that the only answer to any problem of money that occurred, was to simplify the design. After two or three days of this discussion, he, and the others working under him, began addressing this problem enthusiastically. And they seemed to enjoy it. They did prune the budget successfully. One hurdle had been cleared.

But we were surprised to find that they talked about this request as if it was some new method. They even gave it a special name of some kind. It was interesting. The fact that such a simple and obvious thing which any farmer would do almost automatically, seemed like an exotic "method" to them. The methods of system-A, though down-to-earth and ordinary, seemed so unusual when seen within the framework of system-B, that within system-B they needed a special name.

However, the enthusiasm which Odagiri showed for this new method was still highly theoretical. To our surprise, he became quite uncomfortable in any situation which required intimate contact with construction. He told us repeatedly that he was not looking forward to the real construction process, and that he wanted to stay in the Tokyo office, away from the site. His discomfort was also evident in the fact that, although he now had vaguely realistic prices for the civil works, they were still somehow "book" prices, not prices gotten from real people with real bulldozers and real backhoes. In this sense, Odagiri's work was mainly a helpful exercise. His figures had to be drastically revised in order for the project to proceed.

The full reality of our normal approach to cost control did not materialize until Chris and Hajo sat down with Nishida (our head of civil-work construction), several months later. Then, on a level that had everything to do with wearing old clothes and long rubber boots, the reality of the construction process became visible and felt. That was the first time we talked about the real prices, with a sense of practical reality. Then our construction method, and our way of dealing with cost control, began to materialize.

Mr. Odagiri maintained an arm's length distance from such dirty stuff.

EGO PROBLEMS AMONG ARCHITECTS OF SYSTEM-B

In system-A, there is no architect separate from the contractor. We are builders, simply. As builders, we have a direct feeling about construction. We feel it in our fingers, so it is down to earth. One result of this down-to-earth quality is that everything is somewhat experimental. We make experiments all the time. Sometimes we place a piece of wood this way. Another time, we may like to try it that way. Any time something new comes up in the design of a building, we are very likely to try and invent the best way of building it. This is not a great big invention. Just a simple invention, the way we might invent a way of tying a piece of string, to hold a broken toy together. It is just practical.

Of course, there are still right ways and wrong ways of doing things. For example: we know that the mortar for a certain situation has to be mixed about 3:1. When the air is very dry, it may be advisable to put a little extra cement, and extra water. These little bits of knowledge are part of the process of building. There really aren't any fixed rules about the larger things. One simply uses one's knowledge and experience to try and devise the best way of making something.

The architect who works in system-B is in quite a different position. On the level of the mortar (how much water to put in the mix, for instance) he has no knowledge, because this is not part of his trade. As far as the construction details are concerned, these are things which he sees in drawings, and in specifications — and for him, there is a right way and a wrong way. In B, this feeling of a right way and a wrong way is not created by experience. It is created, really, by his excessive ignorance and by what he believes the practice of architecture is expecting him to do. His understanding of how to make buildings comes from glossy magazine photos, catalogs, and detailed specifications manuals. Consequently, his understanding of physical building — especially the process of construction — is theoretical and removed.

Since the architect in system-B doesn't really know the best way to do something, and yet is officially in charge, he is in a very funny position. He has to maintain his authority, since his whole game will collapse if his authority is questioned. But, on the other hand, his actual knowledge of building is very weak, since all he really knows is what he is given by manufacturer's specifications and building regulations. In the worst cases, he is likely to create a fictional aura of certainty about facts, so as to maintain and bolster his authority. But since he fears constantly that his lack of knowledge may be exposed, and he knows that he really knows too little, he can easily be vulnerable to a builder's jokes about his ignorance, or to the collapse of his authority. He may learn to shout loudly, and assert definitively that he knows what to do.

And so, for him, it is very important to distinguish the right way of doing things from the wrong way, and very important to make sure that he is seen, by everyone, as knowing the right answers, and being in charge. And because he rarely does the work himself, the textbook solution is the only correct solution he will ever know. Real life, however, is seldom so simple.

So there is a completely opposite situation for the people in system-A and the people in system-B.

In system-A, they know the very detailed techniques intimately, but are relaxed and experimental about the construction methods. In system-B they know little or nothing about the detailed techniques, but are very rigid about the construction methods.

For people in system-A, who tend to be more relaxed, and

are simply trying to solve the problem, the attitude of a person in system-B, who needs constantly to assert his authority, soon becomes very trying. So the kind of ego-clash that evolves is deeply rooted in the nature of the two systems, not in personality problems. It is almost certain to arise, whenever these two systems meet, regardless of the human personalities involved.

Here is an example which happened when we began discussing construction details. There was always a kind of awkwardness, even a faint unpleasantness involved in talking about construction details with Odagiri. To put it very simply, in these discussions, Odagiri always had to be right, even though in fact he almost never was. And the more he was wrong, the more furious he became internally (underneath his calm professional exterior), and the more one would feel an impossible atmosphere for solving the problem, because he had to be right at all costs. This was not a personal thing, but the direct result of the clash of system-A and system-B. It was a self-image problem.

We ourselves, the group from California, and Mr. Sumiyoshi, the temple carpenter, felt comfortable and relaxed talking about construction details. For us it was enjoyable. But for Odagiri it was a problem of authority. And so, in many cases, he would get into quite ludicrous clashes with Mr. Sumiyoshi, and insist on his own authority, even about carpentry details — cases where Sumiyoshi had a lifetime of experience. In these instances, Mr. Sumiyoshi said nothing. One could see an air of exhaustion in his face. But he was not yet ready to talk. He was far too polite.

While we were discussing the cost breakdown for site improvements, the following important problem came to light. I told Odagiri I wanted to use stone paving in certain places — over a total area that measured out at about 2,000 m². He came back and told me that the cheapest stone would cost about ¥24,000/m² including labor, which made a total of ¥48 million, more than twice what we could afford.

Within the cost-control method we had, I told Odagiri we could only afford ¥24 million for paving stones. But I also told him

I did not want to reduce the quantity of 2,000 square meters, since I felt it was very important to the overall quality of the project. So I asked Odagiri to find a cheaper stone. According to him there was none. I explained the problem, and insisted that we needed something rougher, which would cost less. He insisted that it was impossible.

Now I knew, from other work we had done, of the existence of Oyashi stone — a cheap limestone often used on garden walls. It cost about half as much, ¥12,000/m², including labor. Over lunch one day, I said, why don't we just use Oyashi stone. It is cheap, beautiful, easy to get. I am sure we can use it on the ground.

Odagiri was scornful. "It is impossible to use on the ground," he said. "It is weak. It will crumble. It will break up in the rain. It won't last more than a few months." The stone he had been specifying, something called Mikage stone, the one which cost more than ¥24,000/m², was a kind of granite. I was suspicious of his statements about the Oyashi stone. I didn't believe him. I said, firmly, we will try the Oyashi. I am sure it will work just fine. It will get a bit worn, of course, but then it will be even more beautiful, after a few years when we can see the marks of people's feet in the stone. Don't worry. We will invent a new way of using it that the Japanese haven't tried. So, to test it, I asked Hiro to get a piece of Oyashi stone and put it in the playground at a spot where hundreds of students would walk over it every day. Let's see what happens, I told Hiro.

The next day Hiro and Izumi went to buy a piece of Oyashi stone. One slab, 30 cm x 90 cm, about 12 cm thick.

When they came back, they were ecstatic. "What do you think? What do you think? Do you know what happened? It's amazing. What an extraordinary thing. Listen. Listen."

After a few phone calls, they had found a stonecutter's yard where they could buy some Oyashi. They had driven out there. And to their amazement when they got there, they found that the whole yard was paved in what — in Oyashi stone!

They told the stonecutter, "Isn't it true that it is weak, that it will crumble, that it won't last . . . An architect in our office told us it is quite impossible to use it like this." The stonecutter said: "This stone has been here for about fifty years, with trucks going over it all day long. Whoever said that is a fool."

Since both Hiro and Izumi had suffered under Odagiri's authority, they loved hearing the stonecutter using the word "fool." It may seem silly, but it helped them, and vindicated their belief in system-A, to hear an experienced craftsman speak like this.

A CONVERSATION WITH HOSOI

The most astounding part of this story is still to come. A few weeks later, I was on a plane with Hosoi. We were discussing system-A and system-B, and I said, the trouble is that the architects in system-B have a whole world of images, a series of visual and physical ideals, which remove them totally from reality, and control their thoughts.

As an illustration, I told him the story of the Oyashi stone. How could it have happened, that Odagiri could be so out of touch with reality? I asked Hosoi. He thought it was because Odagiri was a prisoner of a certain kind of physical worldview. To him, only things which look and feel like modern architecture are all right. To be acceptable to him, it had to have the "up-tight" aesthetic typical of Skidmore, Owings and Merrill, a famous architectural firm in the United States.[2]

I believe Odagiri's real reason for rejecting the Oyashi stone, was not the imaginary technical problems he described to us. What he really couldn't stand was the physical character of the Oyashi on the ground. Just the fact that it might crumble, on one corner, the very fact that it can take the marks of people's feet with time, the fact that it is rough, alive, not perfect . . . it is this that he could not stand. In order to be part of good modern architecture, it has to be straight, perfectly smooth, very hard, so that it can conform to the hard-edged images which appear in magazines.

And this image was so deep-seated in his mind, that he was unable to have any real judgment about the practical reality. His

---

2   In the 1980s Skidmore, Owings and Merrill (known as SOM) was the preeminent architecture firm in the eyes of all the system-B architectural firms in the world, greatly admired, and iconic in its standing.

mind is a prisoner of the magazines, and of the images of modern architecture that he aspires to. That is why his judgment about construction details can't be trusted. And this role of the glossy architectural magazines, in the promotion and maintenance of system-B, prevents the most ordinary things which have life, and which have true feeling, from being built.

Hosoi listened in silence to my little lecture.

Finally, he said to me, "Yes, you must be right. But you know what is most amazing of all. The use of Oyashi stone on the ground, as a way of making paving, has been used in Japanese temples for more than a thousand years. I have sat here listening to your story, and asking myself, how it could be possible that an architect like Odagiri could be so completely out of touch with the most ordinary facts."

He went on, "Of course what you say must be a good explanation. And surely the clash of system-A and system-B is part of the story. But the fact that an architect of system-B could be so ignorant, I can't get over that." That was what impressed him most. From that day, he never again had quite the same attitude toward Odagiri. I think, for the first time, he had begun to realize that system-B, whose disadvantages he knew about, was not only dangerous. It was also incredibly foolish.

In summary, we must record once again, that this whole thing, the preference for Mikage stone (granite), the images of SOM's rigid modern architecture, is an example of the way that system-B gets its energy from images rather than reality. This is fundamental to the clash which we experienced. As the project went forward, we saw the clash between image and reality, many, many times again.

STARTING DIRECT MANAGEMENT

It was during this same time, that we began, for the first time, to get Direct Management going for the civil works, which had to be started right away. It was also the first time that Mr. Sumiyoshi was working daily in our Tokyo office, with Mr. Nishida working under him. To help our staff avoid the kind of difficulties we had experienced with the Oyashi stone, I wrote a memo for the young architects who were working for us on the civil works.

A MEMORANDUM TO OUR CES STAFF

THE REAL MEANING OF
THE DIRECT MANAGEMENT METHOD

A few nights ago some of you told me that you were feeling very discouraged, because somehow our work with Mr. Nishida seemed (to some of you) like the normal work of a general contractor, and that you could not see any real meaning in it. It seemed quite different from the direct management method, as you had imagined it would be in practice. I could see that this thought discourages you very much. In order to encourage you, and give you a more positive outlook, I will try to summarize the real meaning of Direct Management.

The essential purpose of Direct Management, as we understand the term, is to create buildings which are *whole*. This means that each part of the building is right in relation to the other parts, and part of the land that makes the buildings and the land more beautiful.

1. THE DESIGN EVOLVES DURING CONSTRUCTION. This means that the form of control, over designs, does not stop when drawings are finished, but goes on, continuously, before, during and after construction. This cannot be done if architect and contractor are separate, or consider their jobs separately. It will only happen if the person who controls the design at the beginning actually controls the construction too.

2. FLEXIBLE COST CONTROL. As we have already seen, cost control requires continuous changing of ideas about what is built, in relation to money that is available, and in relation to what has been done already. This means that the architect must deeply control the most minute aspects of cost, and must continuously modify the construction allocations of cost, in order to get a result that is within the budget.

3. EXPERIENCE WITH ONE'S HANDS. It is also impossible for an architect to have enough knowledge to control the process successfully, unless he has experienced almost every phase of construction with his own hands. This means that the direct management method can only work to the extent that the architect who wishes to control it, has experience as a craftsman, and has himself, managed actual construction, not as a supervising architect, but as chief craftsman, or chief builder. This is fundamental. This control by the architect over the construction process, is meaningless, unless this condition is satisfied.

4. LOVE OF CRAFT AND JOY IN THE PHYSICAL PROCESS OF MAKING.
The fourth condition is a mental one. In the old days, making a building
was clearly understood as a work of making. In this word, designing and
physically building are inseparable. However, in the modern world, design
has become separated from construction. So, today, architects think of their
work as designing, on paper . . . with the idea that the building process is a
separate process. This is not what I call making at all. In fact, within this mental
framework, good buildings can hardly be produced at all. A good building can
only be created, when it is deeply understood as something which is made, by a
direct connection of the act of making, and the act of feeling, with your hands.

If you do not feel anything, during your work, you will get nowhere. The direct
management method is only happening, when all the people involved in it
deeply understand that design and making both come about as an act of feeling,
in your hands. So long as design and construction are considered to be separate,
the direct management method is meaningless, and is not being followed.

With best wishes,
Chris

This memorandum summarized an ordinary way of working that
had existed in various forms for at least five thousand years.

———

After working hard on the preparation of our team, late in
1983 we began the civil works on the site. We used Direct Management in its pure form. We (the architects) ran the construction
job. We arranged the work. We worked directly with the subcontractors and the craftsmen. We paid the subcontractors directly, by
sending the bills to the school, with our seal on them.

We used the backhoes and bulldozers to flatten small areas
where buildings were going to be placed, including the main Great
Hall plaza (a kind of outdoor anteroom to the Great Hall itself);
we had to mark and excavate the lake; and we had to prepare access
roads for construction vehicles to use. It must be emphasized that
this preparation of the ground was entirely unlike the typical
crude cut and burn and grade with bulldozers and blades, which
eliminates all the delicate features of a piece of land.

We also worked out positions for sewer and water lines

accordingly, with the appropriate fall for the sewers. At the same time we were doing these mechanically necessary things, we took enormous care to protect every tree and every bush that did not *have* to be removed. We used the heavy equipment to shape, lovingly, the slope of the ground. We essentially used the bulldozers and backhoes lovingly, to make the land more beautiful, and to leave as much as possible intact. We often rode with the equipment operator, making delicate on-the-spot decisions as we went along, much as one might use a pencil on a portrait sketch.

None of this is possible in a system-B operation, because the overheads are too great. Working in a "speed is money" approach, subtleties are not possible. But, in our way of running a system-A operation, we routinely came in with lower costs for every operation, and could therefore afford the extra care when it was needed.

The process we used is undoubtedly responsible for the present character of the campus.

THE GROUNDBREAKING CEREMONY

The formal beginning of construction came on an auspicious day in December 1983, several months after we had already been running bulldozers and backhoes on the land. It was marked by the traditional Japanese groundbreaking ceremony: a religious ceremony where the good spirit is called to the site by the Shinto priest and the bad spirit, which may inhabit the site, is chased away.

The ceremony was held in a beautiful tent with the traditional red and white colors of happiness and festivity. The tent was placed in the middle of the site, roughly at the location where the Great Hall would later be built. Sitting in front of the Shinto altar and the priest were the guests, the school directors, the officials, the mayor, the congressman, of course the teachers of the school, the architects and construction managers, and also representatives of Fujita Kogyo, the sponsor.

First Mr. Suzuki, the president of the school board, broke the earth with a spade. Then Mr. Neis, representing CES, also moved the earth, confirming the intention of building this project in the Direct Management method.[3] The most important moment of the ceremony, however, was the moment when Mr. Sumiyoshi, our seventy-six-year-old master carpenter and construction manager, moved the earth with the spade in front of all the visitors. It meant that the construction had started with the Direct Management method, working in a pure form of system-A. Also finally Mr. Tsuboichi, a vice president of Fujita, moved the earth to confirm that they would fully support this project in the Direct Management method.

It was a beautiful day. The heavy rainstorm from the early morning had given way to bright sunshine; the site with the red

The Shinto priest blessing the groundbreaking ceremony.

3   I myself was not able to attend the ceremony in Japan, since my second daughter Sophie was born at the very time the opening ceremony occurred, and I flew back to California to be present at her birth. I could not leave her at that moment.

and white tent in the sea of tea fields and hundreds of colored flags looked like the place of a medieval tournament.

The next day, we began construction with the civil works. We enjoyed the work on the site with Mr. Sumiyoshi and with Mr. Nishida, our civil works construction manager. Almost every day we went out there, checking, fine-tuning, and working with our hands. This work was done mostly by Hajo and Hiro, our senior CES staff. First, we enclosed the site with a simple fence, then we started with a relatively minor, but also quite important task, the removal of the tea bushes. We removed tea bushes only where necessary: where the buildings would go, and in areas of public squares, sports fields, streets, paths, and the big lawn in front of the lake. This careful procedure of removing the bushes also helped us to stay inside our budget, because no more work than necessary was done, and the remaining tea bushes themselves would serve as beautiful bushes for the gardens of the school.

Next we started the earthworks. The most important task of the earthworks was the digging of the lake. It was important because the lake, being so big (it covers about 6,000 m² or one tenth of the total site), was going to have a huge impact on the overall feeling of the project. For that reason, the lake had to be placed and shaped correctly — and with great care.

One of the most important aspects of this lake-excavating work is that it was done directly from the flags in the ground, and not only according to a civil engineering plan. The flags marking the buildings and other features remained essential in the process of continuous design and construction; and they stayed in place until they were replaced with something more long-lived.

Another important feature of this work is that it was done incrementally. The earthwork required several months of continuous physical work. We worked amidst the rumbling bulldozers, marking the edges of the lake, cutting portions at a time and checking the shape in reference to the stakeout and the emerging whole. In this way the lake became a real center.

The digging of the lake involved moving about 8000 cubic meters of soil. Since the art of earthwork is to cut and fill inside a given site, in practical terms, what you are doing is looking for the bad parts of the site, which need improvement in landscaping. This work proceeded in accordance with the pattern, "Site Repair" in *A Pattern Language*.[4] in this case referring to earthwork rather than building. In our case, it was the north side of the site with its steep and unwieldy slope which needed considerable improvement. It was the most unpleasant place, where nobody wanted to be. Thus most of the earth of the lake was moved to the north side. We found the right shape with a gradient of terraces leading from the lake up to the north side. With detailed fine-adjustments to exact positioning, height, and sloping, smoothness and roughness, we improved the site to a considerable degree. The north side gradually became a comfortable and rather pleasant area.

During the process of digging out the lake, the lake became more and more visible, its power and overall impact on the site was felt growing ever stronger. Again, a sequential transformation of the site had been achieved, this time with the emergence of a powerful center at the mid-point of the campus site.

In the course of the civil works many other particular works had to be accomplished and refined, including the exact position-ing of buildings; establishing the heights of the plinths of the Great Hall, Gymnasium, and Judo Hall; and the setting of the ground-level heights of the Home Base buildings. Since the levels of the dozen Home Base buildings were set according to the reality and feeling on the site, each one is different. This kind of close in-tegration with the reality of the site could not have been achieved according to standard civil engineering procedures.

Because of the Direct Management method, the civil works went smoothly and helped us create a beautiful place. And doing these works incrementally, in coordination with the site stakeout, thus creating a special quality and feeling that would otherwise have been unobtainable.

---

4   *A Pattern Language* (New York: Oxford University Press, 1977) pp. 508-512.

DYNAMIC COST CONTROL IS ESSENTIAL

To conclude this chapter it will be helpful, once more, to go back to the issue of money.

In system-B, people are fond of saying that system-A pays no attention to money, that it is unrealistic, and so on. Indeed, later in the process, when our full battle with Fujita started, Fujita made statements of this kind very often to the press.

But the truth was very different. The fact was that system-A took a natural, ordinary attitude to money, and puts money, and the sensible use of it, at the very heart of things. System-B had more of tendency to hide talk about money. It starts with ignorance about money from the architect's side, as if it was some kind of mystery, and then opens the door for the general contractor — supposedly the only one who understands the money well — to make gigantic profits, because his mystification of the client is so complete.

The following example will clarify our method of including cost control in the design process. Very early in the design process we made a detailed budget for every building. We always worked, as far as possible, with real costs — so that our design could be precisely tailored, absolutely, to the allocated money, enabling us to do the most possible with the limited money available.

One day Mr. Nishida (our civil works manager) was arranging the construction of some very low retaining walls in the landscape, for tennis courts and so on. I told him the extent of what we needed, how high to make the small retaining walls (about two feet), and so on. A day or two later he came to talk to me about the cost of these walls. The cost he mentioned seemed extraordinarily high. I asked him some detailed questions, and he described the steel forms he proposed using. Then I knew right away that he had not really absorbed the meaning of my request, and I told him that I did not want him to use these kinds of steel forms, which were inherently expensive, and quite unnecessary. "Just use wooden planks of the lowest possible cost."

Then he began to argue. "The quality of the walls will not be good. My workers will be ashamed to make such low-quality work. It will discourage them."

I asked him this question. "Dear Mr. Nishida, suppose that a farmer in this area has to make two-foot-high retaining walls in some place. Will he use steel forms to do it. No, he will not. An ordinary farmer will use steel stakes with holes, double-headed nails, and 25 mm wooden planks. Isn't that true?"

He acknowledged my comment. "Yes, of course."

So I told him, "If a farmer does this, and he does it because it is cheap, simple, and practical, then there is no reason at all for us to use something more elaborate. We want to save every penny possible, where we can, and only spend more money in cases where it really makes a difference to the wholeness of the place. Spending money where it has no benefit to the wholeness is just a waste. Please go and do it as I have asked, and please explain to the workers that it is my request that they understand this kind of economical thinking as a practical matter to be used every day, by all the people working on the construction site. It is just the right path to the kind of life and beauty we hope to get in the campus, as it grows with the Eishin project."

16 THE UGLY CLAWS OF SYSTEM-B

We now come to the blackest chapter in this history.
A sequence of events led to a brief, temporary downfall of
system-A, allowing system-B to assert itself so strongly that
the campus project might have
been destroyed altogether.

At this point, it was beginning to be clear that the campus was really going to be built — a beautiful campus was coming into existence. People began to see that it was going to be beautiful — possibly valuable, too. There were dangers, too, in that different individuals might struggle to achieve control of the campus.

At the same time, there were darker countervailing forces at work. Slowly, during this period, a conspiracy began to show itself.[1] Several unrelated individuals, for different reasons, seemed to have an interest in causing system-A to fail.

The principal parties to the conspiracy were:

- Tsuboichi and Suzuki from the Fujita Corporation.
- Igarashi, the attorney who had been Hosoi's friend, now wanted to be a professor in the college, and a member of the College Committee.
- Adachi, and other professors of the new College Committee.
- Odagiri, the architect from our office was looking for a new position and wanted to get rid of CES and take over the job of campus architect.
- Urago and Okita, Hosoi's enemies on the Board of Directors.

Consciously or unconsciously, these men were pledged to the ideas and social mechanics of system-B. Their interests were diverse. To some degree, we may even say that their coming together was

---

1 The original meaning of the word conspiracy was "breathing together," from the Latin *con-spirare,* to breathe together.

simply an accident, caused by various coincidences of timing. But in a real sense, they *were* related, and they did have a single, deep interest in common. All of them were deeply enmeshed in the conservative world-view of system-B. Also, they shared a suspicious and negative attitude toward system-A. It was this communality of thought and belief which bound them together. This unconscious, subterranean, communality made their actions work together, even when they were not chosen deliberately to be conservative. We thus faced a loosely linked conspiracy of people who did perhaps not really *intend* to conspire, but who acted instinctively to support one another, in similar political directions, because their survival depended on the existence and perpetuation of system-B. The main aim — for all of them — was simply to prove what they had been saying all along. That system-A could not, or *would not*, work.

To justify their statements, to prove themselves right, they took the necessary steps to destroy the operation of system-A in the formation of the Eishin Campus. Once it had been destroyed, everyone would be convinced that system-B was right, because by then it would be the only system which remained.

We (Hosoi and CES) were aware, from the outset, that there would be rocks in the stream, and that the whitewater would be turbulent at times. We thought that if we focused on the principles of system-A, worked hard, and carefully moved through the problems that arose with system-B, we would make our way through the rapids and achieve our collective goal. However, this chapter will demonstrate that there were undermining forces inherent in system-B's machinations — **forces that were at first, invisible**.

———

What was the background of the conspiracy? Towards the end of 1983 and in the first six months of 1984, we experienced a drastic confluence of two, initially, unrelated items. These two items were (1) a political problem which occurred in the context of the establishment of the new college, and (2) a sudden, drastic power play by Fujita, having to do with their monetary greed. Both these items had their origin in factors central to the clash of system-A and system-B.

THE COLLEGE PROBLEM

From the beginning, the Eishin project had been intended to create a new, experimental situation in which a high school and university could coexist on the same campus, under the same administration. The original reason for this premise was the conviction on the part of the directors of Eishin Gakuen, that the college entrance examination process, so fierce in modern Japan, was becoming more and more damaging to the process of education. It was, therefore, the desire of the directors to create a small university which would allow qualified students to proceed smoothly from high school to university, without letting the fear and preparation for the college entrance exam destroy their education during the last two years of high school.

Hosoi himself, personally, had a deeper vision. He imagined a small university entirely dedicated to the establishment of a new form of society, in which community would play a greater part, and in which local decisions by families, neighborhoods, and small towns, would play a decisive role in the political process.

In Hosoi's mind, the new school was not only going to deal with an entirely new subject matter — the social and political process itself — but would also function as a university in an entirely new way. All instruction would take place in small groups and small seminars, governed by informal and highly productive relationships between faculty and students.

We had already agreed that such a university would be most effectively launched by a research institute, where university faculty and visiting scholars could undertake basic research into the nature of such a new form of society. This was the inspiration for the Research Institute which existed in the Eishin pattern language and site plan. It was to be attached to the main library. In 1984 Hosoi wrote a trenchant, brief paper explaining the purpose of the university. Hosoi's ideas were revolutionary. It seemed to us that they might be destined to play a significant role in the future of higher education in Japan. We therefore agreed to to help Hosoi achieve and materialize this idea in the campus layout.

POLITICAL CLASHES EMANATING FROM THE COLLEGE PROBLEM

Hosoi had a brilliant, innovative mind. But he was trained as a high school teacher. He had no PhD. In Japan, the legal requirement for establishing a new university is demanding. There must be a faculty of twenty-six professors, all committed, all qualified by previous experience. It was therefore necessary for Hosoi to find twenty-six established professors, who shared his intellectual vision, and whose joint qualifications could convince the Japanese Ministry of Education about the validity of Hosoi's new university plan. To find such people, Hosoi began a search that lasted almost two years.

Igarashi, the lawyer mentioned in chapter 7, was one of these people. As one of Hosoi's closest friends, and also as a professor qualified by previous teaching experience at Waseda University, he had committed himself to help Hosoi in his struggle. Other people whom Hosoi found during the two years between 1981 and 1983 included Honma, a writer for *Asahi Shimbun*, Professor Isomura, who was considered as the possible dean for the new university, Professor Adachi, and others.

By the middle of 1983 these people had formed a group known as the College Committee. They began preparations to establish a college curriculum, and to launch the new university as a formal venture. Unfortunately, a very fierce ideological struggle now took place, while this process was going on.

First, since the new faculty were established university professors, while Hosoi was not, there was a tendency for the new people to dismiss Hosoi's ideas lightly, and to replace them with their own ideas. Second, this was made easier by the fact that Hosoi, a modest person, was diffident about his lack of formal qualification as an academic. He therefore encouraged the new professors to draft the curriculum, in the hope that through their greater wisdom, they would somehow manage to realize his vision unimpaired, if he only left them alone. Hosoi was naive, and very honorable, and had no idea that lesser teachers would happily steal the academic program that Hosoi had invented.

Third, there was unquestionably a certain lust for power. Some of the new professors, even though they had initially been invited by Hosoi, and even though they had promised to support his ideas, now began to feel the desire to get control of the exciting new university. *They wanted control for themselves*. Disastrously, the group who felt the pull of this kind of greed included Igarashi, Hosoi's best friend.

Fourth, some of the incoming teachers on the new College Committee were simply less mature intellectually, or less well trained or less intelligent than Hosoi himself. This perception might have arisen since he, the Managing Director of the new Eishin campus — as a high school teacher — may have been forced to find lower-ranking professors to help him. But in any case, it certainly became clear that many of the members of the College Committee simply did not understand the depth of Hosoi's ideas. They underestimated the importance of Hosoi's concepts. Although many of them gave lip service to Hosoi's vision, they neither understood the vision deeply, nor did they genuinely support it.

Here we find, once again, at the root of the Eishin project, a clash between system-A and system-B. This time the form of the clash had nothing to do with the specific problems of architecture and construction. But nevertheless the clash had *everything* to do with system-A and system-B. System-B represented the existing order of the universities, the existing mechanistically inspired attitude toward education, the existing attitude toward curricula in general, and the existing attitude towards society.

System-A represented a new academic order, potentially more profound, more deeply rooted in human feeling and human nature, devoted to the creation of a new society, with the capacity to place human feeling and spiritual values at the center of all other issues.

So the clash of A and B now once again made itself felt rather early, during discussion of the physical layout of the College buildings. The college buildings which we designed provided an atmosphere in which students could meet faculty informally, and in which there were many small seminar rooms and few lecture rooms. There was also an ascetic quality, where the professors' rooms were almost monk-like, and where there was sparseness in the quality, and in the space. All this was intentional. It came from Hosoi, and in Hosoi's mind this emotional and intellectual atmosphere was necessary — indeed, it would support the vision Hosoi had always had in mind for the college.

But in the late months of 1983, we became aware that the new professors' committee wanted to change these things, by having fewer and larger professors' rooms, and by replacing the many, small seminar rooms with a number of large lecture rooms. These two points — though subtle — came directly from the professors' allegiance to the conservative approach of educators at that time, from a strongly hierarchical way of teaching. The professors were unaware that, all over the world a new, more radical atmosphere was growing among educators. Ignorance of this new atmosphere, vital to the new view of the Eishin College, came from a deeper ignorance inherent in the attitudes promoted typically by system-B.

TIMING OF CONSTRUCTION

On top of all this, we ran into a serious problem of timing. Our original schedule had been made with the idea of starting construction in January 1984. In order to keep this schedule, we had insisted that no further discussions about building layout could continue beyond July 1983. But the new committee of professors was not formed until toward the end of 1983. Because of this, in June and July we had relied on a very modest group of teachers to help us lay out the college buildings. The participants were Hosoi, Hagiwara, Igarashi who was to be a professor at the college, and a few others.

But of course the professors found this hard to understand. They wanted, naturally, to have their own opinions reflected in the designs as well. We had to refuse, politely, simply because it was impossible to do such a thing, so late in 1983. It would have prevented us from completing the project on schedule. Odagiri, the architect from our CES office, had secretly met with the new college professors without Hosoi's knowledge. He had begun a whispering campaign to the effect that the program of involving users must be fake, since we had not agreed to redesign the college buildings.

Since Odagiri was aware of the construction schedule, and knew there could be no time for such discussion, and since he was also holding these meetings with Igarashi and other professors without our knowledge and without Hosoi's knowledge, there was a very strong indication of a plot, shrouded in secrecy, beneath the surface. But what was going on — quite simply — was that the latent conspiracy between Odagiri and Igarashi to destroy system-A at Eishin had now become an active, dangerous conspiracy in the college and the campus.

Hosoi, himself, as an intellectual, also came under attack. The professors began to argue strongly, against a number of Hosoi's ideas. The idea of a university organized around small seminars came under attack. The curriculum, and the intellectual content of a curriculum directly intended to address the political and social problems of system-A, also came under attack.

THE CONSPIRATORS

Unbelievably, this attack came from the most surprising direction. It came from Igarashi, who had been Hosoi's friend for years. Igarashi began to argue, in public, that Hosoi should step down and leave the managing of the college to himself (Igarashi), and to others more qualified in understanding academic affairs. At first this came masked in the form of concern for Hosoi's health. "He just doesn't have time to do everything . . . we must help to get some of the burden off his shoulders." That sort of thing.

Later, the attack's true meaning became more open, and more ugly. In order to solidify the College Committee, and to give formal authority to their deliberations, several key members of the College Committee were appointed to the Eishin School Board. This happened in November of 1983. Then, unbelievably, in March 1984, a group went to Keizo Sakaida, chairman of the Eishin board, and proposed that Sakaida (Hosoi's former mentor) and Hosoi should both remove themselves from the Board, since Hosoi was incompetent as leader of the new university, and also incompetent to complete the new school project in Iruma-shi.

The group who made this move included four people. Professor Adachi, Igarashi who was Hosoi's lifelong friend, Honma from *Asahi Shimbun*, and Professor Isomura. The group not only made the request, but threatened some kind of scandal in the newspapers if Hosoi and Sakaida did not resign at once. In addition, they demanded that we, the architects, should at once be fired and replaced. To back up their attempted takeover, a poisonous leaflet was distributed in large numbers through the school and the community. Hundreds were circulated during the last days of February. The new group was now doing everything they could, to take over Hosoi's college program.

ANONYMOUS LEAFLET

The Parents and Teachers Association, the Alumni Association and mass media have taken action to oust Hosoi and his clique from Eishin school.

We have filed a complaint against them to the Tokyo Public Prosecutor's Office and Public prosecutor have already started to hear the case and the incumbent managing directors will soon be arrested.

For the cause of rationalization of the school, teachers' union should firmly judge what is right and what is wrong. Lawyer Igarashi, Eiichi Isomura and other main staff have resigned in a body.

All the explanations and statements of the Board of directors are nothing but false. We should like to make school an authentic educational facility. Consider for what purpose the life is and consider in earnest that the prompt ostracism of Hosoi and his clique will lead to the salvation of the school— the sole way of salvation.

System-A was under attack. But on a more concrete level too, there were simple issues of greed, and money, and power. These were issues that went far beyond educational policy; they involved construction and construction money. We may begin to understand fully what was really going on, by simply asking what exactly was being proposed by the Igarashi-Adachi group of conspirators, as the method of construction for the completion of the new campus. They were proposing that the new campus in Iruma-shi, should be taken over and completed by Odagiri and Fujita. The conspiracy had now been broken open.

Such a move could only have been contemplated because of the huge political problem which the school had been experiencing. It suddenly gave Fujita a weapon of great power to use against the school. In order to understand this, we must go back several months in time. During the later part of 1983 (the same period in which the college professors were organizing their attack on Hosoi) two developments occurred.

First, it became clear that obtaining the permission to establish a high school, on the new site, was not as simple as everyone had thought. We are talking, here, not about the building permit, but about land-use permit from the Ministry of Education. For some reason, this had not yet been granted. Second, Okita and Urago — two directors of the Eishin board — suddenly made a surprise move to prevent the school from moving to the new site **at all**.

At first, these directors were simply outvoted, and then removed from the board, by action of the other directors. But Okita and Urago then took legal action against the school. They declared that they had been illegally removed and demanded to be reinstated. Accusations of financial impropriety, and of educational irresponsibility were made. It was a wild conflagration.

Timing was such that all this happened at the very same time that the school was beginning to experience difficulty in getting permission **even to establish a high school**. You can imagine what effect this lawsuit had. The officials in the prefectural government, already slightly doubtful about the new school, found a public dispute confirming their worst fears about the doubtful character of the new school. Their resistance to allowing the new school to be established, stiffened. So, in late 1983, the school suddenly faced the possibility that, because of the scandal in the Board of Directors, they might not get permission to build **any** school. The school faced the possible end of the entire school project, even possible bankruptcy.

What happened next? First, something very surprising. Igarashi, Hosoi's lifelong friend, happened to be the attorney representing the school. He had undertaken the case to protect the school against the attacks of Urago and Okita. But amazingly, on the day when the case opened in the court, Igarashi suddenly revealed a previously hidden sympathy for Urago and Okita. Instead of helping the school to solve their problem, he helped Urago and Okita to solve theirs. The school lost the case. The court decided that Urago and Okita must be reinstated on the board.

Then, at that moment, with the school falling into shambles, Fujita showed their hand. They were very helpful. Fujita had "connections" in the prefectural government. Of course, the new school could not be built, unless the school received permission to establish a high school. Fujita had agreed, to help the school in all permissions matters. They would **need an additional fee**, of course. But they felt sure that they could manage it.

The school, on its knees, said yes. Whatever conditions Fujita wanted to impose, the school would agree. "Only help us to get the permissions, and ask whatever you want." Fujita now began its political efforts on behalf of the school. This lasted from the spring of 1984, until July 3rd. And during that period, the final steps intended to destroy system-A were taken. Fujita made the very same requests that had been proposed to the Board of Directors by Igarashi and the others. They proposed that we — Professor Alexander, the Center for Environmental Structure, Hajo Neis, our whole team — should all be removed. They requested a new contract in which they would build buildings to their own design, and to their own specifications — what, in Japan, is called a package-deal contract. And they proposed that Odagiri should be the architect.

Now Odagiri's relation with Igarashi, his relation with Fujita, and his personal ambition, all came into play. At a meeting of the Eishin School Board of Directors in March

1984, Odagiri made a presentation. He was still working for CES, and was therefore still deeply obligated to us. Treading very carefully, he told the Board of Directors that the Center was incompetent, that the building permits could never be obtained, that the designs were structurally incompetent, that the Center had failed in its obligations to provide adequate drawings of the buildings, and so on and so forth.

The Board was horrified. Odagiri never notified us (CES in California) that this meeting had taken place. He also never notified the members of our office in Tokyo. But he had made his bid for the project. He firmly believed that, at this stage, Alexander would be fired, and that from this moment on, he, Odagiri, would be able to complete the campus by himself, as sole architect in charge. He blatantly betrayed our trust.

Odagiri made one more attempt of this sort. In a private discussion with Hajo, in a restaurant in Kichijoji, Odagiri suggested to Hajo that they (Odagiri and Hajo together) should get rid of me, and do the project together. Hajo made a final mental note about this man's black character.

Interestingly, at about the same time, Igarashi let it be known in legal circles, that he had **"destroyed Chris's project."** This idle boasting reached our attorney's ears when he began to make inquiries about the background of the case, and showed to what extent Igarashi and Odagiri had become allied.

The conspiracy of Odagiri and Igarashi had taken its most dramatic and definitive steps earlier, in November of 1983, at a time when Hosoi was visiting me in California. We were, at that time, discussing certain practical complications of the Direct Management method. Hosoi was already embroiled in the Urago-Okita affair, and in constant touch with Tokyo.

At a certain point, shortly before his departure to return to Tokyo, we had a call from Hiro Nakano (the second-in-command of our Tokyo office). The point of the call was that Odagiri had been visiting Igarashi, for several hours, with a group of other people, and that he had come to the office the next morning with the proposal that Hosoi should be gotten rid of. Hiro was very worried, and felt that Hosoi must be told immediately. I relayed this information to Hosoi. Hosoi refused to believe it, and became angry that anyone should say such things against Igarashi, his friend. He said he knew it must be a misunderstanding, and was upset with Hiro for spreading gossip. Indeed, it took Hosoi more than a year to overcome his discomfort that Hiro had been frank about what was going on. Yet, objectively, Hiro was right. It was less than four months from then that Igarashi finally betrayed his friend Hosoi completely, by speaking against him, and damaging the Eishin school in court (his own client).

WAS THIS A FINAL RUPTURE?

Both we in California and Hajo in Tokyo were unaware how deeply serious things had become. But it was clear that there were some profound problems. In early 1984 I went to Tokyo to make a presentation to the board.

At this stage, we had further talks with Fujita. Initially, I had supposed that Fujita would still be willing to do what they had originally promised (in January 1983); namely, that they would allow us to use some of their professional personnel, on a rent-a-network basis. But it was clear that they were now categorically unwilling to do this. Fujita had only one intention now: to complete the project on a package-deal basis which excluded us completely. A contract of this type was secretly in the process of being negotiated between Fujita and the trustees of the school.

Hosoi was virtually out of power. He told us that he was unable to discuss any further confidential matters with us. He told me that his professional and legal obligations to the school made it impossible for us to have any private friendship, for the time being. I told him that I understood his obligations, and that there might be very hard times ahead, in which we might even, temporarily, become antagonists. I assured him that our private friendship would survive through it, and that when we came out of the trouble, we would be friends again.

My attempts to communicate with the Board of Directors were fruitless. On one occasion they kept me waiting for two hours. Then, when I was called in to talk to them, they listened to me for about thirty seconds, and dismissed me.

The end was coming near. The trustees had no confidence in us, at all. Fujita had gained the upper hand. They now obtained permission for the establishment of the high school, carefully maintaining a certain delay in timing, so that the permission was not finally given until Fujita had exactly what they wanted in the contract for the package deal. System-A had, it seemed, been kicked out. System-B was now in a position to assert itself completely.

THE ANTIQUATED EFFORTS OF FUJITA ENGINEERS

The CES team now began to camp out in our Tokyo office, continued with our work on civil works (our ongoing contract was not yet completed), and decided to get the building permits for the buildings. But as the situation around us deteriorated, more subterfuges came to light.

During the last phases of the college maneuver, one theme which Odagiri and Fujita had used repeatedly, was **their insistence that it would be impossible to obtain building permits** for the buildings in the form we had designed them. This, too, was a direct result of the confrontation of system-A and system-B. Early on we had experienced a lack of understanding of modern structural engineering by Hijikata and Odagiri. Indeed the separation of structural thinking from architectural thinking is typically rooted in the practices of system-B. Hijikata, the chief engineer of Fujita Kogyo, together with Odagiri, had opposed these structures from the time we first showed our designs to them. For example, Hijikata told me solemnly, face to face: "This gymnasium will never be built in Japan." But the engineers of Fujita were mistaken in their opinions. Indeed, they were very profoundly mistaken.

In fact our gymnasium (the largest wooden structure built in Japan since around 1900), was completed a few months later, exactly as we designed it. The real trouble was that Hijikata, Odagiri, and others, did not understand the nature of the engineering structures we had designed. Although simple in conception, many of these structures required a sophisticated and deep understanding of structural behavior. We found out, to our surprise, that Hijikata, Fujita's top engineer, was thinking all the time in terms of bending moment and shear force diagrams — a way of looking at structures that had become obsolete ten or fifteen years earlier in the United States.

The fact that true understanding of structural behavior is only given by a clear picture of the relative motions of all the members and connections under load, was apparently unknown to him. Since this is the way we visualized and analyzed all our structures, it was impossible for us even to talk the same language. The clear picture of structural behavior given by relative motions, which make it easy to judge how stable and efficient different structures are, was not something he understood. The intellectual equipment he was using was just too old-fashioned.

Up until April 1984, we had been assuming that Odagiri and Hijikata, together, provided us with a trustworthy main channel to the building officials. However, instead of supporting us, and helping us to explain the necessary structural concepts to the officials in the Earthquake Center (Kenchiku Center), they had continuously undermined our position by talking negatively to the officials about our structural designs. By April 1984, the possibility of getting a building permit for our structures really was bleak.

I was suddenly aware that Odagiri, the man I had put in charge, had never worked for CES to deliver the project we intended. We had (mistakenly) relied on soldiers of system-B to get the structural permits for system-A. But system-B was only too happy to prove that system-A did not work. They had undermined the communication process with the building officials, at every stage.

We had been aware of the potential for system-B to fight us from within the project. But even knowing this, we had not taken it seriously enough as a clear and present danger. It was a stunning lesson in the care that must be taken when forming the relationships that are necessary to a project.

THE DAMAGE DONE BY CORPORATE GREED AND INTERFERENCE

Our difficulty in getting building permits was not only based on ignorance and resistance.

As soon as Fujita got the upper hand by means of the college maneuver, they began making an attempt to reduce the project drastically, simply so that they could build less for the same money, and so increase their own profit. For example, soon after the college maneuver, we got a message from Fujita saying that they intended to replace all wooden members in the buildings with steel.

Since the wood-concrete combination was fundamental to the project, and since more than three-quarters of the buildings have wood in them, this proposal was comical and absurd. It also flew in the face of our client's (Hosoi's) own love of wood. To him the wooden buildings were the most precious aspect of the Eishin project. Fujita's intention to use steel was created partly by a "we'll show you" attitude; partly by their hope of saving huge sums of money on carpentry work they were not used to; and partly by their genuine ignorance. They had never seen wooden structures as ambitious as these, and their engineers were incapable of analyzing them. They had therefore, during the college maneuver, emphasized repeatedly, that it would be impossible to get building permits for the buildings, and had told the Board of Directors that we would fail. This dire prediction played a huge role in their attempt to take control of the project.

On our side, we were now disheartened by the lack of confidence shown us by the Board, and by Fujita's take-over. However, as a matter of professional responsibility, we decided that we would now reorganize our office in such a way as to get the building permits ourselves, entirely without help from Odagiri or Hijikata.

We had just forty-five days to get the permits for twenty-five buildings, from scratch.

SOME FURTHER COMMON SENSE

Hajo became the hero of the next forty-five days. I decided to make him head of our Japan office, and he agreed. Up until then, we had felt that it was wiser to have a Japanese architect in charge of the Tokyo office. Indeed, Hajo had been reluctant to take charge, and I had been reluctant to appoint a Westerner to be head of our Tokyo office. But now there was no alternative. And there was nothing to lose. We realized that a professional from system-A, even without knowledge of Japanese, and without having standing in the Japanese community, was far more likely to get positive results than a soldier of system-B who was fighting the wrong war.

I dismissed Odagiri and his cohorts. We found our own Japanese engineers, Professor Matsui and his assistant Iwata — the first structural engineers we had met in Japan who spoke the same intellectual language as we did about engineering.[2] We appointed a new set of young Japanese architects, led by Ishikubo. Then, in an amazing effort of intense work, around the clock, for forty-five days, Hajo and Hiro, backed by Gary Black (the excellent structural engineer in our California office), succeeded in doing what everyone in Japan had predicted could not be done — to get the building permits, as we wanted to, and to get the innovative, complicated-seeming buildings into the highly technical channel of the Japan Earthquake Center,[3] with high likelihood of acceptance. All this may seem exaggerated to the reader. However, this effort by Hajo, and by the office staff he hired, was an example of real heroism. It was amazing that it could be done so professionally, in such a short time, and with so many innovations that had to be communicated to the officials. To their credit, the higher ranking officials from the Earthquake Center in Tokyo greatly enjoyed the innovative structures we had made, and enjoyed working on them with us. No one could believe the change of atmosphere.

When we talked to the Japanese officials about the buildings, everything that had seemed hard and impossible in the era of

---

2   These two engineers (Professor Matsui and Mr. Iwata), and Gary Black from California, were a godsend for us. Very fast and quick to calculate, they gave us the intellectual energy and abilty we needed, and they inspired our whole team. Without them we would have failed.
3   The Japan Earthquake Center (nowadays known as the Headquarters for Earthquake Research Promotion) was a single office, based in Tokyo, with the task of dealing with unusual structures outside the normal range of "typical" structures.

Odagiri now became relaxed, workable, possible, and straightforward. Gary had meetings with the officials; I had meetings with them; Hajo had meetings with them. Suddenly we were back to common-sense again. The officials recognized that we knew what we were talking about. They had the same common-sense attitude toward the buildings, that we had ourselves.

The vision of the building officials as monsters, and the fiction of our buildings as impossible to build within the Japanese system, were all stories created by the soldiers of system-B. It was not the building officials who wanted to suppress our buildings and prevent them from being built. It was Fujita, Odagiri with his assistants, and Hijikata who wanted to manipulate the situation. But no matter how hard they tried, they could not succeed. Meanwhile we, the CES group, seized control again by preparing the executed permit documents (for 28 buildings), and by walking the documents through, with the relevant officials in the Earthquake Center, and in the local Saitama government. **On May 15, 1984, we delivered the completed building permits to the school, just as we had promised.**

Now, suddenly, for the first time, the clouds seemed to break. It became clear to Hosoi and to the Directors of the school, that Odagiri and Fujita **really had been creating vicious fictions**. System-B took its first serious defeat.

FUJITA, GREED, AND PROFIT

Because of the college maneuver, for a brief period Fujita still had the upper hand, but only temporarily. Fujita had their package-deal contract, and even though we had defeated them in the matter of the building permits, it seemed as if they had still won a major victory — to build the buildings by their construction method. But not for long. Now there was a ray of light. There was knowledge, by all concerned, that the lies previously spread about the professional inadequacy of CES and system-A had been exposed as fictional inventions.

Fujita had the school under their thumb.[4] The permission to establish a high school was kept ambiguous by Fujita's moves, so that even now the school trustees were afraid to offend Fujita in any way. At this point, Fujita made their boldest calculation. They forced the school to pay approximately nine million dollars for a group of buildings that could have been built, by us, for six to seven million dollars.[5] It is important to establish this clearly. The usual comments made by advocates of system-B who heard about our work in system-A, was something like "Oh, those are idle dreamers ... it is all very well ... but it costs much more money to spend time making all these changes and doing nice things."

The truth is entirely different. The methods of system-B cost more — **much** more, to the client. They were oriented to producing money for the Fujita Corporation by building **fewer** buildings and **smaller** areas, at **lower** specifications. According to the cost estimates we had made, the cost of civil works, site improvements, and buildings of the high school and college, were as follows:

Buildings	¥ 1,098,000,000
Civil Works	¥ 183,000,000
Site Improvements	¥ 142,000,000
TOTAL	¥ 1,423,000,000[6]

Fujita had agreed to work with us, to build whatever was necessary, under the conditions of the Direct Management method. However, having established their power over the school, they now told us that they had made a decision to do the project in the standard building contractor method — for **profit**. We did not, at first, grasp the true significance of this ominous message, but we soon found out. In May we learned that Fujita had negotiated a contract with the school in which they proposed to build the new campus, with much lower specifications. Five of the largest buildings were left out altogether, totaling a **deficit** of roughly 2,864 square

---

4   Note: If the school had not agreed to something, Fujita would simply have removed their political support, and the school would then have faced bankruptcy.
5   The figure of nine million dollars, ran the gamut of 8.3 million to 9.5 million, depending on particular circumstances.
6   The cost estimates we made may be studied and verified in chapter 10.

meters (three major College Buildings, the campus Library, and the Research Institute). Effectively, removal of these five buildings created a reduction of **20% of built value**, while Fujita was to be paid **more money** (an **increase** of **40%**). In numbers this meant:

Total Building Area (plus civil works and site)	13,203 m^2
Direct Management Cost (CES) ¥1,423,000,000 (plus ¥200,000,000	
	contingency)
Fujita Contractor Cost	not given
Reduced Building Area (plus civil works and site)	10,339 m^2
Direct Management Cost (CES) ¥1,114,000,000 (plus ¥200,000,000	
	contingency)
Fujita Contractor Cost	¥2,300,000,000

This proposal was **64% higher** than our own proposal to build 13,203 m^2. Even if we had included all kinds of contingencies, such as ¥200,000,000 for a Direct Management contingency amount, this would still have been an unheard-of percentage.

We protested to Hosoi, but in our position of weakness we had no influence. He told us that it was fair, and that there was no way to do anything about it. The school had to agree to everything Fujita proposed, in order to get the permission to establish a high school at the new site. It was now clear that the whole maneuver Fujita created had been done with one primary objective: to obtain a clear profit of at least ¥ 600 million yen for themselves — a profit of about $US 2.5 million dollars in cash.[7] The actual out-of-pocket costs to Fujita were nominal.

We had no influence. Yet we felt that it was our obligation to make the true cost picture visible to the Eishin Board of Directors. We therefore decided to contact the Sumitomo Corporation, to ask them what they would require to help us build the project. We arranged a private meeting with Mr. Tamura, managing director of Sumitomo's construction division, and asked him if he felt that

---

7   We have to remember that the exchange rate at the time in the mid-1980s, was about ¥230 to the dollar, while today the rate is closer to ¥100 to the dollar. Not including inflation and other cost-increasing numbers, this would mean for today that our proposal would stand at $US 14 million, and Fujita's proposal would stand at $US 23 million.

Sumitomo could work to the figures of our original estimates, under the conditions of the Direct Management method. After three weeks, Mr. Tamura confirmed that he and his construction manager were quite confident the work could be done within the original cost estimate for Direct Management. They then made a formal bid, in which they agreed to work to the figures we had estimated under the conditions of the Direct Management method. The crux of our proposal was that we would build the whole college and high school, by Direct Management, for the original price of ¥1,400 million, working with Sumitomo.

The Eishin board refused our proposal altogether. Instead of being grateful for our work and for the saving of ¥600 million, they were horrified because Sumitomo's bid made explicit what had so far been secret. The bid which Fujita had made was inflated, and possibly illegal. The school and Fujita together were intending to have a fake bidding procedure (with our drawings), to sustain Fujita's high bid. The existence of a lower bid by a better company, was not helpful at all. If made public it would have become a dangerous embarrassment.

The school, at this moment, was so deeply trapped in Fujita's claws that they preferred to stay with the bid of ¥2,300 million made by Fujita. Possibly, the companies who were invited to take part in the bidding had promised to make higher bids than Fujita themselves. The reader will grasp the unusual nature of this bidding procedure, if we say that the bidding contest was organized by Fujita. In order to protect our legal standing, we refused to be associated with it. We could not, legally, or morally, agree to become part of it.

Sumitomo's signed bid of ¥1,400 million yen was ignored. Fujita signed the contract with the school to build the work for ¥2,000 million yen. **Not long afterwards, this sum was once more raised to ¥2,300 million, ¥900 million more than Sumitomo's bid.**

17   THE ANVIL

**To overcome the nearly fatal attack against system-A,
Hosoi and I together, almost by accident, invented a new kind
of contract that would give us massively helpful power.
It enabled us to solve the seemingly unsolvable
problem of construction management, under conditions
of the battle between A and B.**

In effect we built an anvil, on which we could hammer!

The month was May 1984. Eleven months left to go. For us, this was
the lowest point. Fujita had won control over the project. We were
defeated. We had essentially been fired. Even Hosoi had lost his
power. Yet something pushed us — Hosoi and CES — to take an
extraordinary step, to create what we now think of as "a healing
touch" that modified the human dynamics of the project.

———

As Hajo stubbornly continued the process of implementing
the building design and the construction process, we still had no
power to make Fujita do anything. Hajo made request after request, patiently explaining the nature of the project, the nature
of the civil works, the nature of the buildings. The people from
Fujita listened . . . and refused. They listened politely. And refused.
Sometimes they listened less politely, and then again refused.
Hajo's position was near to impossible. He did his best. He dug
his feet in. He took every advantage possible. But he could do very
little, except hang on for dear life.

Even Hosoi's own staff (Nishigori, Yoshida, and Kinogawa)
had turned against Hosoi, and against us. They undermined Hajo's
work at every meeting. They constantly made statements which

were incompatible with our plan and ideology. They gave Fujita permission to do things, which were at odds with our plan. At this stage, our clients had become our enemy — all except Hosoi.[1]

In principle, system-A sounds wonderful. It is after all more profound, more satisfactory in every way, than system-B. But when the client begins to experience the depth of the conflict that occurs when system-A is out of tune with system-B, sooner or later, he may get nervous, or frightened, or finally just give up because in his estimation the issues are too difficult to resolve. This is what happened to Nishigori, and to Hosoi's other assistants. Perhaps, it even happened, in a small degree, to Hosoi himself. After all he, too, had been beaten down by the Yakuza, by his world, and by his colleagues. Perhaps he felt, finally, that system-A was unattainable.

At this stage, no doubt, Hosoi experienced a level of despair which was much greater even than what we experienced. For us, it was a project. Even though it was the most important project we had ever built, still it was a project. For Hosoi, his whole world had collapsed. It was not a group of strangers, but his colleagues, co-directors — even his friends — who had turned against him. We know that he came close to suicide. And even in the later stages, when the tide of battle turned again, Hosoi existed, as he put it, as "a one-man army" — a lone fighter, defeated and abandoned by his friends.

After a few weeks of this, the school told us that we could not be paid. They claimed there was some problem with the Japanese internal revenue service, and that we could receive no further funds. The explanation was transparently false. But it had the opposite effect on me. I was by then (in August) on vacation with my family, 7,000 feet up in the Austrian Alps, in a farm high above the Ötztal valley. We were guests in a solitary farmhouse, a beautiful and peaceful place. Flowers — gentians, edelweiss, brunellen (thousands of tiny, dark chocolate-red, alpine orchids), and tall daisies — were everywhere. The children rolled about in the meadow, and we climbed the hills above us. In the distance were the peaks.

---

1   That the client organization itself should at a key stage become an enemy is not uncommon in the battle of system-A and system-B. We have experienced it more than once.

Then, out of the blue, I had a phone call from Hosoi, speaking from Tokyo. He told me that as a result of the successful poker game played by Fujita, he had now lost his power, and could not influence the process any more. He let me know that as we spoke, the Eishin School Board was making formal plans to fire us. His ability to protect us had run out. He was barely holding on to the cliff-face by his fingernails.

I told Hosoi that I would think about it for a couple of days, and then call him back. Meanwhile, Hajo and I talked about it on the phone. Toward the end of our conversation, I told Hajo, "If they are going to play this kind of game with us, we will take steps to stop the project, and force them to give the project back to our control."

I called Hosoi, and told him about this decision in the following terms: "Unless the school board and Fujita clearly admit that we are in charge of this project, and clearly give us the authority to implement the project as it has been designed, we shall start a lawsuit, against Fujita and the board, claiming theft of copyright, and so force the construction work to be stopped." I explained to him that the purpose of making this threat was that so much time would be lost while such a court case came before a judge, that it would have the effect that the campus could not possibly be finished before the deadline of April 1985. This, in turn, would then lead to the bankruptcy of the school.

Hosoi's answer, on the telephone, was practical and delightful. He laughed and laughed, then said to me, "Chris, that is wonderful. Thank you so much. I will go at once and explain the situation to the school board and to Fujita. Then we shall see what happens next. I think this may work."

A few days afterwards Hosoi called me and told me that we had an answer. The school was willing to consider certain accommodations, and would be willing to meet some of our conditions. Our hand grenade seemed to have worked. The tide of battle had turned.

But there was another surprise in store!

Hosoi talked to me again, and said that there was something I would not like, but "Please don't explode, only listen carefully."

He said, I have thought carefully about the contract which will make this work, and I have found out that there is only one way to make it work. It will sound crazy, and it will sound illogical and unfeasible, but I think it is the only way.

"I propose making a contract," he said, "in which Fujita has total control over the project. And in the same contract it will also say that you, Chris and CES, *also* have total control over the project. Both companies will have total control over the project."

But, I said, this will cause terrible problems, fights, loss of time, deterioration of quality, etc., etc. Nothing will get done.

"I do not think so," was Hosoi's reply. "Both the companies are tough, and both are sincere. Together you will make sure that the project does not collapse, because it will harm each of you very much, if it does collapse. And it will also harm the school very much, if it does collapse."

"I know this sounds paradoxical, even stupid, and probably such a way of thinking would not work in the United States. But this is a very Japanese solution, and in Japan, I believe this one will work." It turned out Hosoi was right.

It took me a few days to calm down. Thinking and writing about it twenty-five years later, it seems almost reasonable. But at that time, my first reaction was that it was foolish and insane, and potentially dangerous in numerous ways. It took me three or four days of continuous reflection to consider it carefully, and see and recognize how well-judged and subtle Hosoi's proposal really was.

This was the anvil on which our project could now be forged. What was it about this proposal that meant so much, and went so deep? It was something far more interesting than a mere forcible bringing together of two parties who seemed to have trouble resolving their differences. Hosoi had created an alchemy in which two opposite forces were made to ignite, creatively. It was not a compromise that was sought, but a creative spark that could lead to a real solution — something almost unimaginable. At the time, I did not understand it as I describe it now, long after the event. I only felt in my bones that something intriguing would come of this. It was one of the most extraordinary things Hosoi had done throughout the five years we had worked together.

And that is what we did. We followed Hosoi's very practical advice, and he negotiated it with all the parties, who also at first had the same objections that I had. Within the next few weeks, with Hosoi in the lead, we managed to negotiate the following new contract, an accompaniment to the Fujita contract that had already been signed. This was the Memorandum of Agreement, which was to re-establish our position in the building works.

This memorandum would be of little interest if we just looked at it as a case of problems between client, contractor, and architect. Such kinds of problems happen often in the ordinary business of architecture and construction. What was dramatic and important here was the power of this memorandum to re-establish system-A. And indeed, paragraphs 1, 2, 3, 4, and 7 of the memorandum demonstrate the vital and significant differences between system-B and system-A (these crucial five paragraphs are printed in boldface italic below).

MEMORANDUM OF AGREEMENT

September 26, 1984

This memorandum of agreement is entered into in order to make the construction work proceed under the direction of Center for Environmental Structure (CES), as Kanrisha (Managing Supervisor) for Eishin School (School).

1. CES shall be party to the construction contracts for both building construction and civil works between School and Fujita Kogyo Co., Ltd (Fujita Kogyo) as Managing Supervisor.
2. Fujita Kogyo shall follow any and all instructions of CES at all times for both building construction and civil works unless they are unreasonable or extreme, in which case Professor Alexander of CES and Mr. Hosoi of School shall consult each other and determine the appropriate instructions to Fujita.
3. All the high school buildings including all the outbuildings and the lake, shall be built absolutely (without exception). The foregoing includes all of the foregoing minor buildings, which do not yet have building permits: bridge house, carpentry shop, boathouse, third gate, and small clubhouse next to the gate.
4. Fujita Kogyo shall follow any and all the designs and specifications absolutely. According to the methods of CES, many details are not yet specified in either drawings or specifications, and will be specified only during discussion of shop drawings, or even during construction, if the work is of critical importance. In all these cases Fujita Kogyo shall accept the wishes of CES.
5. (1) Mr. Neis, as head of the Tokyo office of CES, will continue to keep personnel as necessary for the functioning of the Japan office until June 1985. (2) Mr. Toshimi

Fujita, a construction manager, is a person to whom Mr. Neis has a direct channel of communication.

6. School and CES personnel shall have access to any part of the site or the work being performed at all times.

7. CES will make continuous inspections of the work and will, from time to time, request various modifications in design of portions not yet completed. Fujita Kogyo shall comply with the requested modifications in work, provided that such modifications will not result in any reworking, tearing out or other damage to the completed portions of the work.

8. Checking of shop drawings shall be done directly between Mr. Neis and CES office in California on a daily basis by use of facsimile machines. Final approval of shop drawings shall be given by Mr. Neis in continuous consultation with California office.

9. Fujita Kogyo shall communicate to CES at least two (2) weeks in advance as to any matter which requires approval of CES.

10. All the discussion about problems of design, cost and construction shall be done in the Construction Committee (CC), which is expected to solve these problems on a practical level. The members of CC are Mr. Nodera of School, Mr. Neis (Executive Architect), Mr. Toshimi Fujita (Manager), and Mr. Nishigori. The chairman of the CC shall be Mr. Neis, and Mr. Nishigori shall assist Mr. Neis in the management and operation of CC on any technical matters. Mr. Neis shall be the principal negotiator for the School. Visitors to committee meetings other than Mr. Hosoi and Professor Alexander will be invited at Mr. Neis' request only.

11. Whenever any problem happens, which cannot be solved in CC, the final solution will be made through the discussion between Professor Alexander and Mr. Hosoi.

Signed by: Hosoi for Eishin Gakuen,
Alexander for CES,
Kazunori Fujita for Fujita.

The main effect of the Memorandum of Agreement was, quite simply, to give control of the project back to us. Tsuboichi (chief of construction for Fujita) and Suzuki (his number two) did not want Fujita to sign it. Hosoi forced them to. He was able to do it, partly because of our hand grenade and the very real threat we had posed to the project; and partly because his own power was now coming back.

But since the package-deal contract, with its secret letter of agreement, also still existed, there was an ambiguous and contradictory pair of contracts. This wonderful Japanese ambiguity allowed Fujita to feel that they were in charge, and allowed us to feel that we were in charge. A perfect scenario for a mess, but a highly creative one! In any case, this mess, or contractual ambiguity, was the manifested battleground in which we finally built the project. This anvil, on which a creative spark could now be struck, gave us the last and hardest phase of battle, but also gave us the path to our success.

In order to make this last phase of the battle fully clear, let us once again describe exactly what a builder is trying to do, during construction, if he is working in system-A, and what he is trying to do if he is working in system-B.

In system-A, the builder has a rough mental conception of the buildings which are to be built. He also has a definite fixed budget. As he starts to build, he is constantly paying attention to the evolving structure, asking all the time, how to make it more and more "*whole*" — more deeply connected with the community and buildings next to it. He has a flexible attitude, looking always for signs of weakness, where things have to be improved. Whenever he sees something which is not quite right, or undecided, he starts to make mockups — full life-sized "sketches" in string, paper, cardboard, and thin strips of wood — to see, and evaluate, the right way to make each thing. And, all the time, he is juggling money. The money is fixed. If he has to put more money into one thing, in order to make it just right, then he also has to take money away from another thing, and accept the roughness or informality which follows. *The lack of perfection he accepts in various small ways is the price he pays to achieve wholeness and harmony **in the whole.*** In any case, money only enters into his work as a fixed thing. He has a certain amount of money. He tries to make something as strongly living as possible, with the fixed sum he has. This is our position as the builder.

The building then evolves throughout its construction. As far as timing is concerned, the work follows a normal construction schedule. It is not especially slow. But the emphasis always, every day, by every craftsman, is on the evolving wholeness of the campus, on the satisfaction of the people who are making the buildings, and the fact that they have put their souls in it. It is based on reality.

In system-B, the ground rules are completely different. The builder is building something fixed, from an architect's plans. The architect has made an image. The builder tries to follow this image.

At the same time he is trying to make as much money as possible. Thus, he is trying to build what is on the plans, saving money whenever he can, to make a profit, and meanwhile trying to satisfy the architect and convince the architect that the correct image is being created. In this system the emphasis is on image, and on increasing profits.

This is the difference which caused the final battles on the construction site. Because of the ambiguous situation we were in, and because each of us thought we were in control (and had the paper to prove it), each of us did whatever we could to follow the system we believed in. Fujita followed the dictates of system-B. We followed the dictates of system-A.

They were puzzled, amazed, and continuously in a state of shock, because they found out that we were not made happy at all by their attempt to create what they thought of as "our image." And we became more and more angry as the true substance, the reality, of the buildings was being misunderstood and sacrificed.

We may now begin to understand the true clash of system-A and system-B at its most intense. As we shall see, during the months of the construction process, we were able to do things that we needed to, quite often. But, equally, we were frustrated by an intensely uncooperative and hostile attitude on the part of Fujita.

The reason for this uneven quality in our relationship was rather simple. We tried to follow the dictates of system-A. Fujita followed the dictates of system-B. In the few cases where what system-A required was compatible with the method and process of system-B, we got what we wanted. In the many cases where the two systems required different methods or processes, we did not at once get what we wanted.

But we were ferocious. We did not give in. So even in these cases where Fujita did not want to follow us, often we were able to force them, by the sheer magnitude of our effort, or our anger, and the strength of our desire, and our persistence.

This became the heart of the battle.

A WRESTLING MATCH

The practical relationship between system-A and system–B, as we lived it and experienced it, was graphically and metaphorically depicted in an incident that happened one night. It came at the moment when I first met Toshimi Fujita.[2] He was a burly, powerful man, who had been chosen to be the new overall construction manager for Fujita Kogyo. After polite introductions, he and I decided to go and have some sake in a bar, to get to know each other.

We had a few drinks, exchanged stories, and joked about which of us would actually control the progress of the work. Toshimi was very confident, amused somehow, and at a certain moment I told him that he should be sure to understand that we, CES, were going to control matters. He grinned, and said that this would never happen. Suddenly, without careful thought, I said that I could prove it to him. He asked, "How do you expect to do that?" So, there and then, out of the blue, I said "You and I will have an arm-wrestling match, right now. Then you will find out what happens."

I do not know what possessed me to make such a rash invitation. Toshimi was an enormous man, bigger, beefier, far stronger than I was, and in better physical condition. But somehow, I felt a fire in my blood, and I knew that I had to demonstrate to him, right then, at once, my ability to gain the upper hand.

We sat on two stools at the bar counter, in the usual arm-wrestling position, and someone gave the go-ahead. Toshimi and I began to push, and for a while, we were almost motionless, deadlocked. And then, quite suddenly, I felt a great vigor in my body, and with a huge push forced his arm down to the bar counter very rapidly, almost in a single motion. He was astonished and chagrined. I looked at him, and told him, "I believe that this is what is going to happen in the Eishin project. In the end, Fujita will

---

2   Fujita is a common name in Japan, and even though the Fujita family owned the very large Fujita Kogyo (Fujita Corporation), the person who became the Japanese overall site manager for us, was also named Fujita — Fujita Toshimi — no relation to the Fujita family who owned the construction company. He was a wonderful and fine man, and without his help it would have been very difficult to complete our project. But we did not know this, at that early date.

have to do what our will desires." And indeed, our ability to prevail did materialize, though it took place under arduous conditions of nearly continual, daily confrontation. At a rough guess, in perhaps 50-70% of the cases, we did prevail.

Soon after this event, we discovered that Toshimi was destined to play, next to Hajo, a crucial role in the work on our site. Toshimi made it known that he would like to work very closely with us, since the project was conceived and designed and built by us. And, of course, we were in charge of construction under the Memorandum of Agreement.

We began to hear that it was always Toshimi who supported our key approach to the buildings, materials, and detailed designs. Whereas other members of the Fujita organization would cheerfully argue for various destructive interpretations of the CES shop drawings, Toshimi always came to the rescue, and insisted that it had to be done *right*.

And, in fact, Toshimi made it an article of personal faith, that he would personally see to it that the CES conception of these buildings would be carried out as faithfully as possible. Furthermore, Toshimi (head of the Fujita component on the building site), and Hajo (head of the CES field office in Japan) somehow agreed, as sportsmen, that it would be OK to fight each other during the day, but that they also would go drinking at night and have some fun together.

We owe Toshimi a very great debt.

18 REMAINING BATTLES IN THE FIELD

It is a drama, a tragedy. Nobody outside the site can
imagine what drama is going on here every single day.
-Toshimi Fujita

The atmosphere was tense on the Eishin construction site. To convey the quality of the remarkable discussions and arguments (with lots of shouting) that went on from day to day — *every single day* — in this chapter we describe some of the events that illustrate the differences between system-A and system-B, as we experienced them on site. We also include a few examples which demonstrate the two systems can work together when the effort is made.

Memorandum A (the Memorandum of Agreement described in chapter 17), gave both sides opportunities for guidance — Fujita and CES were given the right and the obligation to fight it out, in order to decide what was to be done on various topics. On the first day of work resumption, we addressed thirty-two items. On this particular day Fujita building construction department had twelve items, Fujita civil works department had seven items, the school representatives wanted to discuss three items, and we (CES) had ten items to discuss.

All of these thirty-two items concerned decisions about the campus that had to be resolved. They ranged from the very small to the very large. In the light of our fragile agreement, neither we nor Fujita had the right or the power to decide anything unilaterally. Even Hosoi as client did not have that right. Every dispute had to be negotiated between CES and Fujita. Occasionally Hosoi acted as an impartial adjudicator to resolve difficult disputes, but only when both parties agreed to this process.

Between November 1, 1984 and March 30, 1985, a total just

short of 3,000 decisions had to be dealt with in five months. This meant that these decisions had to be completed at a rate of 3000 decisions in 5 months or 600 decisions per month. Assume four days of rest per month. This gives Construction Committee (CC) members 26 days per month, working together, to complete decisions in the Committee. The average work day, then, would see 23 decisions dealt with, every day. The members of the CC committee worked as a single unit.

Keep in mind that we had three full crews, each working an eight-hour shift, so that construction was taking place literally around the clock. During any 24-hour period, there were about two hundred men on the site, but at any one time only about seventy men were there — a very intense effort, demanding concentration and causing stress as well. It was fueled by goodwill when the arguments were positive. It was also fueled by bitter heat from time to time.

DAILY CONSTRUCTION-COMMITTEE MEETING

Most days, the problems became rather heavy in the Construction Committee meeting that took place every day in our CES office at 2 pm. The discussion was typically tough. We had to decline almost all of Fujita's requests, or we made instructions for modifications, or we requested time for more checks and mockups according to contract. The Fujita people were quite upset, and accused us of being uncooperative and selfish, and also without understanding the needs of cost and time. It was on one of these occasions that Yuden Tanaka, one of Fujita's site engineers, in a mood of deep frustration, declared: "This is like a scene from a courtroom." However, we had to be strong with regard to our requests and instructions. It was necessary for the good of the project.

It should be noted, also, that during the late sixties, Hajo had been a paratrooper in the German army, and was well able to take care of himself. His wonderful politeness, combined with toughness of character, played a huge role in our ability to stand up to the daily pressure from Fujita.

REFINING POSITION, SHAPE AND LAYOUT OF THE ENTRANCE STREET

The entrance street's direct layout with stakes, strings, and chalk was one of a series of experiments for the final positioning of buildings, open spaces, and their heights, with regard to each other and the site. We had done these layouts already for various places on the campus. This day it was finally time to place the small gate, the main gate, and the entrance street between the two. The main question was, What would make the most harmonious boundary for the entrance street?

Mockup of the entrance street with long stakes, and ropes, provided the opportunity to decide the place where the break in the street should occur. You can see the chalk marks on the ground, representing the position of the small gate, and its tunnel.

We had previously decided this layout at the time of placing stakes (chapter 11 page 194). But by this time, several months later, the context had developed considerably. The Great Hall was by now under construction, and the ideas we had earlier were almost certainly going to need adjustment. Under Hajo's guidance, the team shown in this picture, including Hajo, Hiro, Miyoko, and several others, are estimating the quality of the space the ropes define. The work consisted of subtle adjustments and inspections, until it reached its final form. The essence of this job was to examine the space; imagine that it was made with walls; and test various issues, such as its direction and the height of the walls to see whether the amount of enclosure they provided was comfortable. Most important in this particular case, was the exact spot where the entrance street changed direction. You can see this spot in the picture above. It is marked by the end of the first straight ropes, lying on the ground. They all stop at about the same point. This had taken place, after the dog-leg had been decided.

In the field-drawings (pages 191-2), the portion of the street going from the small gate to the main gate was drawn with actual flags that were recorded. The places where the walls change direction had not yet been settled at the time of the flags in the tea bushes. So a very important issue, now, was how the street narrowed, and where it changed direction. These questions sound abstract, but when you were standing there it was very easy to find the most natural place for the change of direction.

The questions mostly answered themselves of their own accord. For us (CES) this question was essential, because fixing the best place for the street to turn could make the place harmonious, or not. For Fujita's men, we were merely slowing things down and wasting profits. The Fujita crew probably thought it was childish, not worth the expense to be paid out by the company.

CAST CONCRETE COLUMNS FOR HOMEROOM ARCADES

Fujita had earlier requested that we allow them to make the columns and capitals from precast elements, then assemble them on-site. I had refused this because I knew from experience that these kinds of castings are more beautiful if formed and poured in place, having done this on a number of occasions in different projects. Fujita refused to cooperate, and once again asked us for permission to use a precast method. We declined Fujita's request.

Indeed, Hajo and the on-site team had started to experiment with some cardboard column bases and shafts, and had reached a good conclusion with regard to sizes and proportions and relation to the base. These results had been given to Fujita. So, we instructed them to wait a few days, until we had time to come to some equally good conclusions on the column capitals. However, a few days later, Hajo reported to me seeing precast columns all over the site with stiff, mechanical capitals. In other words, Fujita's men had simply gone ahead, without our permission or approval, in flat refusal to honor their agreement with CES.

Fujita went ahead, without our approval, and ordered prefabri-

First precast concrete columns for homeroom arcades, standing temporarily unbraced.

cated columns, based on the early drawings which we had made. *But these early drawings never were intended to be used as final ones.* So, of course all of us became angry, since this was impolite and inconsiderate — by normal professional and contractual standards it was outrageous. It also explicitly violated the written agreement of Memorandum A.

There are two further reasons for pouring the columns in place. First, concrete poured in place always has a more humane character than concrete which is prefabricated. The reason is that slight irregularities of form and surface always develop in relation to the location of each component-piece, and the things therefore take on a slightly organic quality, where variation of form and context are subtly matched. Second, we were still rather unsure about the best shape, size, and character of the column capitals, themselves. We needed to look at this, in place, during the construction process. If we had been fully in charge (without Fujita), we would have poured a sample column, then put a styrofoam or cardboard capital on it, until we felt sure of the shape and size.

But here, once again, we see the basis for a battle between system-A and system-B rather clearly. In our minds, the drawings we had originally made for the columns and capitals were no more than first approximations of the final shapes. In the mind-set we were in (and cherished), we knew that this gave the most harmonious results. We assumed that we would work out the final shapes during construction, and left the inaccurate approximations on our drawings, just for the sake of the building permit. Fujita, used to working with architects in system-B, assumed that whatever was on our drawings *must be what we wanted, and must be implemented as drawn.* Since they had a heavy schedule to meet, they did their best to speed up construction by ordering the columns prefabricated. They were trying to do what they thought we wanted, in such a way as to reduce both time and cost.

In system-B, the image is defined by the drawings. If the contractor does what he can to make the image correctly, he is doing everything right. When Fujita heard that we had refused the prefabrication process, no doubt they thought we were being unreasonable. But from our point of view, the "image" of the columns was not what mattered at all. What did matter was the substance — the actual feel of the poured concrete, as opposed to the slick perfection of the precast ones, the actual correctness of each dimension according to the felt end-result and the psychological feeling created by spacing, shape, detail, lengths and height experienced by people who came in touch with the aggregate of columns as a whole.

There is one strange place on the arts building, where an arcade column has beams coming in at two different heights from one side and the other. When we drew it, we pencilled in a double capital, *only to remind ourselves that some kind of good transition had to be made,* between the two levels. But the actual thing we drew as an image, was never *intended* to be built except as a direction. Yet Fujita built this image exactly as drawn, without paying attention to whether it looked beautiful or harmonious. It was grotesque, of course.

This is the tragedy of system-B. The contractor, and his men, build whatever they are given. They never ask themselves if it is beautiful, or harmonious. They just do it, because this is the way that system-B works.

Anybody who was making those column capitals, if he had seen this "double" capital, and had been free to make something harmonious, would have done it differently. But Fujita's people, in system-B, *did not know how to be* guided by reality. They were guided by "image." In the scrambled-egg world of system-B, they no doubt thought that this weird double capital was an important part of our image. After all, there are plenty of architects in Japan, and everywhere else, intentionally doing the weirdest and most horrible things, just to make a name for themselves.

So Fujita, in this situation, was not free to respond in a natural way to what they saw. They were trapped by the image-making process they were used to. But, because of this, they doomed their own carpenters to a pretentious kind of slavery, producing whatever silly images they were told to do, without being able to ask themselves whether they were beautiful, and unable to use their own sense of reality to make them better. In a case like this, system-B not only failed to do what we wanted. It did not even allow its workers to experience any natural pleasure or common sense.

POURED CONCRETE WALLS FOR THE HOME-BASE BUILDINGS

The construction of the homeroom buildings using poured concrete walls *in situ* was a rather more complicated matter, although the dictates of system-A and the dictates of system-B complemented each other in a happy way that turned out remarkably well. Originally, these buildings were designed to be built from concrete blocks for reasons of cost and simplicity. But ultimately for legal reasons ("no block building with rooms more than 60 square meters"), classrooms could not be built from concrete block.[1] In order to simplify the matter, Fujita proposed and requested that we construct all the buildings in poured concrete. At first we did not quite want to listen to this. Instead, we started to make experiments with a new type of block, in which the block itself serves as a formwork for a poured, concrete shear-wall. But that experiment did not succeed; the walls did not feel harmonious. They just felt wrong. So finally we followed Fujita's proposal. We redesigned the buildings as poured concrete buildings, and in fact they became simpler, and much better — even though they also became somewhat more difficult to build.

---

1 This had been missed by Mr. Odagiri, from the CES office; we had to deal with the topic once again.

We owe it to Fujita to acknowledge that the simple thing they proposed was the right thing to do, which made the homeroom buildings sturdier, more elegant, and to our surprise, cheaper. In this case, both sides reached a very positive, mutual understanding because both sides worked to improve the buildings through a cyclical process of repeated design and construction. That gave the opportunity for evolution of better costs and better techniques. And this gave *really* good results after building fifteen homeroom buildings in a row. It was a highly successful result that was based on excellent cooperation between system-A and system-B approaches.

ORNAMENTAL BLOCKS FOR THE HOMEROOM BUILDINGS

Whenever Fujita could do something in fast, cheap production, they were eager to do so. The ornamental blocks, which divide the first floor from the second floor, are an example of this kind. We had developed one ornament for each homeroom building, so that each building could get its own identity. This meant that Fujita had to make fifteen different types of ornamental blocks. They were only willing to do three to five. Finally we settled for eight types, sometimes using the same block in two buildings. This worked out semi-okay. However, what did not work out was the dead quality of the blocks, because of their mechanical production. If we had known ahead of time, we would have worked on the blocks with experiments until they were really good.

However, Fujita started to produce them while we were in the middle of experimentation without informing us. The absence of refinement has the effect that there are only a few isolated cases where the ornamental blocks work really well.

REFUSAL TO CORRECT THE HOMEROOM STAIRCASE HANDRAILS ACCORDING TO CES INSTRUCTIONS

Let us now follow more carefully, and more slowly, the dramatic unfolding of conflict between Fujita and CES during later phases of our work together. As we shall see, further misunderstandings caused by the enormous gap between A and B, aggravated matters. Much of the time, Fujita willfully denied and damaged what was necessary. Fujita was still working within the package-deal contract, trying to build cheap replicas of our buildings, so that they could walk away with the largest profit, and feel that they had done the minimum to satisfy CES and the client.

This example is a rather small point, in itself, but we mention it in detail, because the human elements of the case help to pinpoint, accurately, the attitude which Fujita took. During my visit in February 1985, we chose to single out the homeroom handrail for discussion and inspection. Fujita had purchased handrail material for the homerooms, without approval from me, and proposed to install them. I felt that the handrail cross-section Fujita had chosen was too heavy, and very uncomfortable for the human hand. We therefore asked that a sample piece of wood (about 60 cm long) be cut down to a smaller cross-section, to check the idea that the stock already bought for the handrails could be cut down to a better shape and size.

Morishige Tanaka asked the carpenter to make the cut, and five minutes later I examined it. The result of this first cut was better, but still not satisfactory. I then sketched another slightly more complex section, and asked Mr. Tanaka to have the carpenter cut a second sample to *that* shape. Mr. Tanaka refused. I told him it could easily be done on a table saw, like the first cut, and explained how to do it. Mr. Tanaka still refused. From a purely technical standpoint the cut was very easy to make. It therefore appeared that Mr. Tanaka's refusal was merely an excuse, and that he simply did not want to satisfy me. His statement that the cut could not be made was a polite but clumsy lie.

A few days later, since the sample had still not been made, I asked permission to use the table saw myself, so that I could demonstrate the cuts and the shape I wanted. For about 24 hours Fujita made various excuses. Then finally, Morishige Tanaka said that this request had *also* been refused. Shortly thereafter, Fujita installed their original crude handrails (left), in flagrant

A massive, ungainly stair rail, uncomfortable to put your hand on, or to hold on to it. These inappropriate and clumsy staircase handrails were quite out of keeping with the delicate garden walls and fences.

disregard for CES's clearly expressed wishes. Without further discussion. Fujita had wilfully abused our request.

Our requests and instructions to build all the platforms, walls, benches, flower beds, bushes, and trees in the home-base street, to make it a nice and comfortable place, were also neglected by Fujita. The system-B crew simply claimed cost and time was a problem, and went off, without any negotiation or friendly goodbye.

FOUR MAJOR MISTAKES MADE INTENTIONALLY BY FUJITA'S MEN ACTING UNDER ORDERS FROM FUJITA KOGYO (THE FUJITA COMPANY)

We have given a few examples of non-cooperation between Fujita and CES, and, lamentably, only a relatively small number of examples where we had positive cooperation. Having experienced this, we decided that we had to confront Fujita with a legal document, in order to get better cooperation.

On October 15, 1984, an eighty-page Memorandum of Complaint was submitted to formally oppose and expose Fujita's practices. The four examples which follow from the memo demonstrate the lengths to which Fujita was willing to go to maintain control, undermine our efforts, and save money. They are numbered as they stand in the complaint.

COMPLAINT 1. THE FALSE SUBSTANCE OF THE GREAT HALL STRUCTURAL COLUMNS (FUJITA'S USE OF CALCIUM BOARD VOLUMES INSTEAD OF REINFORCED CONCRETE IN THE STRUCTURE OF THE GREAT HALL).
In the permissions drawings for the Great Hall, it was defined as a steel building, with PC (precast) or RC (reinforced concrete) on all columns, capitals, and beams. These drawings and specifications formed the basis of the contract negotiation. The actual structure, as presently built, is SRC for the base of the main columns. But all other columns, beams and capitals have been carried out in some kind of cheap plasterboard work, using calcium board or plywood, with light gauge mesh and plaster surface.

This specification is strongly in violation of the contract, and must be torn out and replaced with PC or RC. The present construction is estimated by us, to have an expected lifetime of 20-30 years at the most.

The CES original drawings clearly specify RC or SRC, for all columns, beams and capitals. The permission drawings made by CES clearly specify PC. Most important, the client himself (Mr. Hosoi) also made it clear to Fujita, on a large number of occasions, that he wished all the buildings to be built of excellent materials, with a long lifetime "of at least 200 years."

COMPLAINT 2. REFUSAL TO PLACE GREAT HALL INTERIOR COLOR AND SHIKKUI.

CES specified, from the beginning, that the interior of the Great Hall would be finished in colored shikkui. It was made clear to Fujita that Professor Alexander would come to Japan, personally, in order to specify the exact colors, after the building shell was complete, at a time when the quality of the interior light could be clearly experienced. This matter, together with emphasis on its importance, was again explained to Fujita in writing on January 17, 1985. At that time Mr. Neis warned Fujita, three weeks ahead of Professor Alexander's next visit to Japan, that it would be necessary for him to work in the Great Hall for several days without lights, and without noise, and asked Fujita to prepare the necessary arrangements.

Fujita neatly ignored the intention and purpose of this visit. By the time of Professor Alexander's arrival, they had already begun to plaster the interior of the great hall in white shikkui, which was a waste of money for the school, and a serious failure to pay attention to CES's instructions.

In a further attempt to continue their disregard for CES's instructions, after his arrival in Japan, Fujita again and again refused to meet his request, and tried to force a compromise allowing him to extend the lunch hour by one hour, to do his work. After this arrangement began, Fujita spread a rumor to the effect that he had closed down all work on the Great Hall. The existence of this rumor greatly affected CES, since it gave a clear indication of the tactics and lies which Fujita was using.

The unpleasantness reached such a level that Mr. Hosoi himself, who had on the previous night already obtained absolute guarantee of the matter from Mr. Toshimi Fujita CM, was forced to come to the site office of Fujita and fight almost physically in order to make the Fujita corporation meet his request which they had already agreed to. The whole incident merely showed, by example, the extreme level of disrespect which Fujita repeatedly showed to the client and to CES, throughout this project.

At this date Fujita had failed even to begin the work of interior colored shikkui according to specifications, and hinted that they will try to seek extra compensation for this part of the work. Yet it is clear that the use of colored shikkui in the interior, was part of the design from the beginning. Fujita's attempt to plaster the interior in white, and their attempt to keep Professor Alexander out of the Great Hall in spite of three weeks of warnings, was understood by us as a deliberate attempt by Fujita, to avoid their obligation for the color work according to the contract.

COMPLAINT 6. FAILURE TO USE KNOT-FREE REDWOOD AS SPECIFIED FOR THE STRUCTURAL COLUMNS OF THE JUDO HALL, THE EXTERIOR COLUMNS OF THE GYMNASIUM, IN THE EXTERIOR OF THE CENTRAL BUILDING, AND IN MANY OTHER PLACES.

The use of redwood was made completely clear, in the construction specifications. In addition, to help Fujita, Professor Alexander made extensive arrangements to buy high-quality redwood at a low price. However, when the initial lumber list for redwood was presented to a lumber mill in California, and checked by Professor Alexander, he noticed that certain items, and most conspicuously, the columns for the Judo Hall, were not included on the lumber list. The lumber list had been retyped by Fujita, to leave out the beautiful and massive columns.

We immediately pointed this out, and drew Fujita's attention to the omission, and asked them to correct it. However, Professor Alexander had a suspicion, even at that time, that the omission was intentional. This suspicion was recorded in the memorandum of October 15, 1984. Later, Fujita bought their redwood in log form, and then at some time even later explained to the supervisor, that "most unfortunately" they did not have enough redwood to finish all the jobs, including the redwood columns in the Judo Hall, the exterior columns of the Gymnasium, and the exterior siding of the Central Building.

At the time, Professor Alexander immediately suggested that if they had bought short they should simply buy more redwood. They refused to do so. But the Judo Hall columns are extremely conspicuous items. There are 34 columns, almost 7 meters long, and 240 x 240 cm in cross-section. These are very large pieces of wood, and immediately noticeable to anyone experienced in lumber purchase. The fact that these items had already been left off the lumber list several months earlier, and that there was no other lumber in that early lumber list from which the Judo Hall columns could have been cut out, clearly proves that Fujita had the intention, to substitute Douglas fir columns for the redwood columns. This is not merely an intentional violation of the contract specifications. It will also severely damage the structure of the Judo Hall. CES had specified redwood in all cases where lumber was directly exposed to the weather, so as to guarantee a long life to all the buildings. Douglas fir cannot tolerate long exposure to the weather. By using Douglas fir for columns of the Judo Hall, and for the exterior columns of the gymnasium, and for the siding of the Central Building, Fujita has drastically reduced the structural life of the buildings, in a way which cannot be remedied. The same thing has happened in other parts of the project.

COMPLAINT 39. SUBSTITUTION OF INFERIOR MATERIAL AND INFERIOR LEVEL OF FINISH WHERE FINE EXTERIOR SHIKKUI WAS SPECIFIED ON THE GREAT HALL, MAIN GATE AND GYMNASIUM.

In the original contract specifications, CES clearly specified the use of old style shikkui, trowelled 8-10 times, on several important buildings, including the Great Hall, Gymnasium, and Main Gate. This specification was also clearly recorded in the form of the price. On the exterior plaster work of those buildings, and on the interior plaster work of the great hall, all shikkui was calculated at 6000 yen/m^2 for colored, and 8000 yen/m^2 for black. These prices are contained in the detailed price sheets, which we gave Fujita, as part of the contract specifications. The high price which was specified for this plaster work, makes it impossible for Fujita to claim that they misunderstood the instruction. There is no other kind of plaster work which has such a high price per square meter, and there can only be one interpretation of these numbers.

However, in an effort to lower the level of quality during the construction of the project, Fujita made various excuses. For example, they made various technical excuses about the difficulty of obtaining workers who knew how to do the old-style shikkui. They also made various excuses about the weather, and the fact that the cold would make it difficult to use the high grade plaster.

However, at a formal CC meeting, Mr. Neis explicitly refused to sign Fujita's request to substitute new-style shikkui for old-style shikkui. In addition, even if technical reasons later made Fujita use new-style shikkui, instead of the old style, the surface has still only been trowelled 2-3 times. The original specification, and the high price of 6000-8000 yen per square meter originally specified, clearly indicate the level of mirror finish which can only be obtained by trowelling 8-10 times.

A POSITIVE EXAMPLE OF TWO ORNAMENTS ON THE STUDENTS' DINING HALL

On the ornaments of the Dining Hall front wall, we had first drawn in the ornaments freehand, knowing that it would be extremely difficult to get the balance of positive space and negative space just right. The white on brown design was not satisfactory, when we saw the building nearly complete. We then made an experiment reversing the brown and white with a series of mockups on-site, and made the surprising discovery that, in order to get the negative and positive feeling just right, white and brown had to be reversed.

Since this mockup was made before the carpenters began to cut the pieces, and before the plasterers went to work, Fujita built what we told them, without argument. An unusual but happy outcome!

White on brown. Original design for the Dining Hall front wall, as first drawn on paper (not very successful color balance).

Brown on white. Revised and final design for the Dining Hall front wall, after mockups, reversing the colors (much better color balance).

BEGINNING OF THE THREE-PAGE SECTION, 356-358
REAL SUBSTANCE versus IMAGE OF SUBSTANCE

The greatest difficulty we had with Fujita throughout the project arose because we were always concerned with the material substance of the buildings, while Fujita made a practice of creating only an image of the substance, and doing it with inferior materials.

In every building, we had conceived the building as a definite kind of structure, which was made in a certain definite way, with materials which had a certain definite emotional quality, and cost, relative to one another. To us, building the exterior cardboard shell of the buildings, meant nothing at all. The buildings were imagined as living things, with certain definite emotional and substantial reality. The details needed to be the ones we had invented, or the life of the buildings would be destroyed. Of course this caused an immense series of conflicts, a few of which are listed here.

On the homeroom buildings, we wanted an ornament in which the white shikkui was poured into the ornamental block, because we had found in our own experiments that this created the most beautiful result. We had even found the mixture of portland cement and shikkui which gave the best white, and the most beautiful surface. Fujita ignored our request, refused to listen to our detailed explanations of the necessary construction method, and simply placed a piece of white calcium board behind the block, in the ugliest possible fashion. The workman who did this, should never have been allowed to do it; it was barely better than trash, and should never have been allowed on a professional building site.

We wanted wood, not only in many visible places, but also in the roof trusses of the homeroom buildings, where they are invisible. Fujita wanted to replace the invisible trusses with steel trusses. They could not understand the idea that it was the actual substance — even though not visible — which would control the feeling of the thing.

We had invented a beautiful structural system for the administration building — a system in which diagonal steel wires, encased in a shot concrete grid, provided the shear panels for the exterior walls. White plaster inside the gray diagonals, made a beautiful effect. Fujita wanted to create an image of this reality, by using a wooden lattice over the plaster. The fact that it had an entirely different structural meaning, and that the lifetime would be drastically reduced, seemed to mean nothing to them.

We (and the client) wanted the Great Hall built of solid material. Fujita tried to cheat the client by building a steel structure, which then had a fake surface of calcium board, plasterboard and plywood built out to form the structural members. Instead of creating a building that would last two hundred years, as we had promised the client, Fujita tried to get away with a building whose lifetime might be less than forty years.

The reader must bear in mind, as he/she reads these stories, that we had gone to very great trouble in our original designs and budgets, to make sure that all these things would be possible.

We had specified some things at a very high level, and compensated with others that could be made at a very low price, in order to balance out the budget. Thus, when we heard about Fujita using a 12 cm structural slab on the bed of the lake, we were not only horrified by the inappropriate hardness of the substance, we also saw it, immediately, as a ridiculous way to spend money. A slab of 5,000 m^2 would cost about 25,000 yen/m^2. In other words, on this one decision about the lake bed, Fujita had just spent about 140 million yen, or close to $700,000. We could have done the job our way, using the traditional method of making a bentonite clay bed, for less than half the money, about 40 million yen. In this one incident, Fujita wasted close to 100 million yen, or about half a million dollars.

They did it, because in system-B, it made financial sense to do it. System-B is not concerned with the wholeness of the thing, only with money, liability, and engineering. Fujita apparently felt it was worth wasting close to 100 million yen, or half a million dollars, to protect themselves against future troubles with the school. But what they were doing, of course, was taking 500 million yen away from all the other places where it really needed to be spent, to make things whole, according to system-A.

Because of this waste, we lost the right kind of beautiful plaster on the Great Hall; we lost the fences on the homeroom street; we lost all kinds of beautiful and necessary materials that were essential to the project.

For example, we had gone to great trouble, in our original cost calculations, to make it possible to use real old-style shikkui, on certain crucial surfaces. This old-style shikkui was to be trowelled ten times, to a mirror finish. Fujita replaced it with a surface of dolomite, a crude surface, trowelled twice. It is entirely different in its emotional experience. But to Fujita it was the same, because they were concerned with **image** (only the way it **looked**).

How may "image" be defined, then? Very simply. It may be defined as that which will show up in a photograph in an architectural magazine. In system-B, this is the crux. In system-A, the crux is the actual experience of being close to the materials, touching the buildings, and sensing their spirit, and breathing it in.

A major point of dispute between ourselves and Fujita lay in the issue of on-site changes. From the very beginning of our work, we had made it clear to Fujita that subtle construction could only be undertaken under conditions where the design was continually reviewed while it was being built. Thus changes in construction would be made continuously, as part of the construction process. We guaranteed that this process would be kept strictly within the existing cost structure, and that changes would always be made before construction, and that cost would not be increased. In essence, we described to them the process of making a continuous series of mockups, which would generate the actual construction work.

This idea is fundamental to system-A. It is quite impossible to produce any work of value, unless this process is going on. In chapter 12, we described how we used this method successfully, in the early stages of civil works, when the construction work was under our own management. However, Fujita repeatedly misunderstood this idea throughout the project — or, perhaps, intentionally ignored it.

ENDING OF THE THREE-PAGE SECTION, 356-358
REAL SUBSTANCE versus **IMAGE OF SUBSTANCE**

———

THE LIGHTS OF THE GREAT HALL AND
THE CONSTRUCTION OF THE LAMPS

Lamps are extremely important for the correct feeling of space, because that is simply where we get our light from in the dark. Unfortunately lamps have become abundant in catalogues, but we hardly can find lamps which fit to a particular space. In most cases, it would be advisable to design and build the lamps, but lamp design and special order manufacturing adds to the cost. Fujita had proposed some catalogue lamps which were completely wrong in feeling, and emitted too much light. We advised Fujita of our desire to do this work by ourselves. Surprisingly, they fully agreed. We had to do this work inside the given cost of what Fujita had set aside for lamps.

At the time the problem came up, I proposed a very simple circle, with lamps standing on the ring, as the only thing simple enough to hold its own inside the hall (visible on page 361). The mockup was tested in the Great Hall, and with a few modifications, the lamps were built. They were very beautiful. The final arrangement had a feeling of festivity. The character of the Great Hall was highlighted. Most impressive, we did this work for far less money than the cost Fujita had proposed. We saved US$50,000, on the lamps, money we could then use for other parts of the project: a small example of the typical cost-effectiveness of the procedures of system-A.

The lamp on the right, was our earliest prototype. The simplicity is so straightforward, that it did not need any special tricks to make people like it. It is beautiful, like a crown, or a corona. Working in our own shop, we designed and built the lamps by ourselves in the Direct Management method.

Almost the ugliest lamp imagineable. A proposal suggested to us by Fujita Kogyo, and rejected by us.

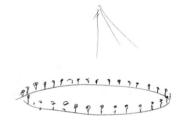

A very simple lamp, that we made in our own workshops. This lamp is almost naive in its simplicity, and very ordinary. Yet it is beautiful, and reaches the heart.

As part of the design process, the prototype lamp, when first made, was sitting on the floor of the Great Hall where it was built. Then when we felt that it was safe, we rigged it in the air. The engineer who rigged it was Miyoko Taneda, a former student of Professor Alexander. On page 360, you can see her on the scaffolding.

Our first prototype lamp, which was hung and rigged up to see how people received it. It was immediately popular.

Hajo made a more detailed design of these lamps, working together with a Japanese lamp manufacturer. We also built a mockup, checking the size of the ring, the section and the details of the individual lamp holders. You see the result on the left, and then on page 361 a photograph shows the actual lamps functioning, and the character of the illumination which they produce.

GREAT HALL CONSTRUCTION AND ORNAMENTATION

The Great Hall was the first structure which went up on the site. Its influence on the whole campus could be understood and realized rather early; a majestic building, even in its pure steel frame. We felt very happy about it because the presence of its real scale, size, and position was very helpful for many decisions we had taken and others to be taken in the process of construction. However, this was the best part of it. After the initial positive phase, the real battle around the Great Hall started.

The first trouble happened when Fujita did not want to cover the steel with con-

Next page: finishing touches to the black shikkui, red-chevron ornaments, floral ornaments on the frieze, w panelling, and the ring-shaped lamps installed. Some beams and columns, and some ornaments are not yet con

crete, mainly because of cost, so they claimed. They wanted to cover all columns and beams with calcium board, which meant that the columns were hollow, and when you knocked on them you heard a hollow sound. When we noticed the matter, angrily we wrote a letter to the Fujita construction manager, asking him if he wanted to do Hollywood architecture instead of real buildings. In the construction meetings we exchanged angry words. Finally, the only thing Fujita was willing to do, was to pour the first seven meters of the main columns in concrete, so that they are structural, and solid, but everything above, including the capitals were to be made cheaply, despite our strong objections.

Still, even under these very unpleasant conditions, we managed to do a beautiful color arrangement for the interior plastering of the Great Hall, including a final design for the stage part. Over a period of two weeks, we developed the design, with the help of large-scale experiments. Parts of the Great Hall were covered with colors and ornaments, painted with poster color. According to the color principles and principles for the direct decisions on the spot, a color arrangement was found, with the main columns dark reddish black, and the capitals the same dark, reddish black with a red ornament in the middle. The main beam over the capitals was worked with a running dog ornament, gray-and-white and dark gray. The top columns were gray, the main ceiling purple, and the side ceilings in the galleries bluish green. The Great Hall suddenly had its living character.

However, Fujita staff completely ignored the results of this work, and disregarded the instructions to color the interior of the Great Hall in real shikkui. They just covered the whole interior with some artificial plaster in white, and walked off the job.

Fortunately, we were later able to force Fujita to meet its obligations with regard to contractual specifications. Some months later, it was decided by the Eishin School (our client), that US$800,000 of the construction fee would be held back, and that CES could use all that money to undertake the many works abandoned by Fujita. CES would then be able to make up the money that had been spent on Fujita's defaults, and the $800,000 would make up for the work

Fujita should have completed. Fujita should have made the campus whole, and acted honorably on their debts to Eishin.

THE LAKE BED AND REVETMENT WALLS

The lake, so hugely important to the overall feeling of the campus, needed to be laid out exactly for its final construction. Also the details of the lake needed to be finalized: its revetment walls, bridges, its base and connection to the outer precinct.

The final layout emerged over an extended period, in many day-to-day experiments on the site, as a matter of fine-adjustment. The revetment walls had to be developed afresh, since our first idea of simple concrete block structure all around the lake was not accepted by the authorities, because some of the walls were too high and needed to be engineered as retaining walls.

Mr. Tanaka of Fujita proposed some horrible blocks, which not only felt cheap, but which would have completely destroyed the feeling of the lake. We refused and looked for better ones. Of the various types of block, the gray split blocks felt most like stone (some visitors, still today, believe it is granite). Finally we emphasized the lake wall along the main public square with some white stones in between. This felt solid, calm and comfortable.[2]

Revetment built of inexpensive split blocks, yet creating a natural and grand effect in the retaining walls around the lake.

As a further key part of the lake, Chris designed the curved wooden bridge (page 489). Hajo added the other three smaller bridges next to the gymnasium. All four were detailed by Mr. Sumiyoshi..

Night was coming up and it was very hard to see. In addition, on these two pages we see the magnificent v

...najor campus buildings, standing stark against the snow-laden sky, expecting a powerful thunderstorm.

THE VOLUMES OF THE BUILDINGS RISING FROM THE LAND

The battle between system-A and system-B was difficult every day. It was so painful, that I did not visit Japan between October 1984 and February 1985. All the modifications and discussions, during day-to-day work, were done by telephone and fax. Hajo and I spoke every day for half an hour or more. We exchanged drawings, photographs, and talked over every detail, as it evolved.

I did not go to Japan during those months, because I feared the worst. The attitude of Fujita was so hostile, so uncooperative, that I assumed the physical buildings would be ruined in their feeling, no more than a shell of what we had intended. I could not bear to see that.

When, in February I did finally go back to Japan, to do the color work for the inside of the Great Hall, and to take care of many other details, I could not avoid it any longer. After arriving at Narita (Tokyo International airport), I took a taxi directly to the site. I could not even go to our office. I was so afraid, so painful were my feelings, that I did not even want to meet our office staff. I remember the moment very well. It was pouring rain. Hajo, Ingrid and I drove to our field office in Nihongi. I left them in the car, and went out to the site alone in the pouring rain.

I walked up and down. Then some more! And then, suddenly, I felt alright. Because I saw that the magnificent being-nature, which we had tried to realize, was there in the buildings after all. The huge forms of the buildings, the way they stood together, the rain pouring off the roofs, the gray hulks in the gray rain . . . the "being" we had seen in our dreams, was there. The living thing had been preserved. Its feeling was unmistakable. The being was there.

19 APPEARANCE OF A GENUINE AND LIVING ATMOSPHERE

How shall we judge a new community?
The proof of the pudding — in any place we come to —
must always be how people treat each other, and what they
experience there.

If you are lucky enough to live in such a place, then you may
bless your good fortune and can safely say, "This is a
wonderful place."

The following comments and behaviors
were a measure of our success.

In April of 1985, on the day the school opened, members of Eishin school bought ten ducks and put them on the lake. They did this without being told, entirely on their own. It shows that this place was theirs, completely, and that they knew that it was theirs. They treated the school the same way that one treats one's own garden, or one's own farm. Even the first day, the school called out for life.

Dear Chris,

I am looking forward to sharing an indescribable pleasure about our success in this project with you on April 11th. Please let me say to you, "We've succeeded at last."

I've been waiting for this day since I visited you for the first time, when I felt I found the true architect whom I had been looking for at last after my long journey I had traced until that day. It's confirmed by the actual result after experiencing many painful and serious situations we've got over together. And spring has come.

Please let me say to you again, "We've succeeded at last."
Very sincerely yours,
Hosoi
March 16, 1985

———

Dear Chris,
Please enjoy one good information. I forgot to tell you it on the phone.
Three days ago, I experienced a wonderful night view from the lakeside near the bridge at night. The lighted gym, homeroom buildings, arcade, the administration building were reflected on the water. It was an indescribable one. It was much more beautiful than I expected.
More than that, ten ducks have started swimming in the lake very gracefully. Mr. Kojima got them four days ago. It shows how deeply they appreciated and started enjoying this lake.
I'm very much pleased to confirm the very important meaning of the lake by these matters. The lake has started breathing. Let's enjoy it tomorrow together.
Hosoi
April 9, 1985

———

It is very surprising that none of the teachers are complaining about the buildings and spaces of this school. — *Comment by a journalist.*

You have done what everybody somehow wanted to do, but nobody could do it so far. — *Comment by a visitor.*

These buildings remind me of childhood, as if I had seen these buildings somewhere in my earlier life. — *Comment by a visitor.*

Probably I will never have a chance again to construct such a beautiful environment. — *Mr. Tanaka, chief of civil works of Fujita.*

———

Another fact which sheds enormous light on the students' feelings when they were first introduced to the new campus, is that they did not want to go home at night.

In Japan many students have to commute. They go to school by bus, and come home at night by bus. Many schools, like the Eishin Gakuen, provide their own buses for the students, or they have a contract with a bus company to provide the needed buses. After construction of the new campus, students liked it there so much, and wanted to be there so much, that they did not want to leave the campus at the end of the day. Very often when evening came, school officials and the authorities could not persuade them to leave.

Mr. Tada, school administrator, provided this analysis. Buses left at 3:30, 4:30, and 5:30 pm to take the students home and to the train. At the old school, the 3:30 buses were full because students wanted to leave. At the Eishin campus the 3:30pm buses were always empty. The 4:30pm buses were nearly empty. The 5:30pm buses were full because students wanted to stay on campus as long as possible, and avoided going home until the last possible minute.

———

In 1985, two awards were given. The Japanese Association of Architectural Journalists designated Eishin as the Most Interesting Building Project. And the second prize for Best Building in Japan prize was awarded by the Japan Institute of Architects. In 1987, the Silver Medal for Best Building and Landscape was awarded to Eishin by the Prefecture of Saitama.

———

Student enrollment increased to 400% of what it was before the move. The old school was more than fifty miles from the new site. The new school therefore has a completely different population base from the old one. Before the move, school administrators were very worried about the financial future of the school, and about the uncertainty of enrollment. Application for enrollment began at the end of 1984, while the new school was still under construction. Even then, with scaffolding everywhere and mud on the ground, visitors came in droves, every day, to see what it was like. Hundreds of new students applied for admission.

———

Mockups and improvements of the Home Base street were begun almost as soon as the school opened. This work was followed almost at once by the new construction of a series of stepped terraces. As soon as the campus was occupied, preparations were made for new construction. Our CES team undertook the job of making full-size mockups for the character of the homeroom street, and we prepared for construction as the first increment of improvement. There was an air of excitement and participation. The school community recognized, with us, that this campus was not merely a sterile group of buildings, built according to a design, but was a living breathing place with a life of its own. Since Fujita had not cooperated with us, as far as the good environment of the homeroom street was concerned, people who taught there and studied there had the good sense, and the initiative, to press us for those features of the homeroom street that would make it come to life as an environment.

———

Sasha Shamszad, owner of the ZIBA photographic laboratory in San Francisco, processed the photographs of the Eishin campus for a public exhibition in 1985-86. When he saw these pictures for the first time, he seemed dumbfounded and said: "It seems incredible that a group of people built these buildings. This is just entirely different — an entirely different level, from what is being built today."

———

In 1986, we completed the color works in the interior of the Great Hall. They were intended to be a highlight of our construction, something like a final touch, to give the feeling of completion in the most satisfactory way. During March 1985 Chris had already made the essential design with color experiments in 1:20 scale models as well as at full scale 1:1 inside the Great Hall itself. The experiments were done with painted paper using poster color, and then putting them on columns, capitals, beams, and ceilings (pages 372, 410).

After accomplishing that task, we then developed the whole interior into a beautiful hall, based on these original color designs. The first thing we did, was to try to find a way to do this work within a cost ceiling of 31 million yen. Fujita had made a preliminary bid of about 40 million yen for these works. However, in our budgeting, we decided that the cost must not be more than 31 million. This was very difficult. After many attempts to come to grips with this problem, we decided to leave out the invisible or hardly visible parts, concentrating on the most visible parts. Even then it was difficult to get the work done.

In the winter evenings of 1985-86 we visited master plasterer Ishiguro quite frequently at his home to find a way of getting the works done inside the cost and within the Direct Management method, with no general contractor in-between. But Fujita also made a bid, and they also wanted Ishiguro to do this work, using the general contractor method. Hearing that, Mr. Ishiguro strictly refused to do this work. He said, "Mr. Alexander is one of the few people who appreciates traditional craftsmanship deeply, and for him I can try to do this work, even with a very low cost. But I cannot do this work with a general contractor."

When Toshimi Fujita got to know Mr. Ishiguro's feeling about the color works, he admitted that it would be better to use the Direct Management method. The school signed the contract, and we happily started our work. The first practical thing we did was to make a lot of samples, a lot of experiments with actual colored paper and shikkui plaster techniques in the hall itself, which soon felt like a Renaissance palace space. Our CES team then built an exact full-size column, using steel scaffolding, cardboard surfaces and paint. This work was done by Miyoko Tsutsui, climbing, painting, and hanging colored materials.

Later, we heard from Mr. Emoto, a goldsmith, "The Great Hall color shikkui works look like a piece of art, similar to the old Italian types of frescos."

———

At some point in 1986 the school suddenly became known as the "school of lovers." At first this surprised us, though we were amused. Talking to some students, we were told the following:

"The school has so many very small spaces that one can hide in many of them, one can enjoy oneself in peace and even hold hands, without necessarily being detected. It's a great place. Many of the buildings contain small elements for relief and privacy, such as the large alcoves in the homerooms, or the various-sized alcoves in the cafeteria. Even the main gate has some mysterious spaces."

Hosoi and other teachers commented: "We consider this a wonderful compliment from the students, because it adds to a feeling of freedom in the school."

————

The atmosphere of the students is the most palpable thing. As soon as you walk into the school, you feel the life of the students. You feel an easygoing, ordinary life. It does not feel like a "school,"

Left: A preliminary mockup of size, arrangement, color, and feeling for the Great Hall columns.

Right: The mockup showing detail golden chevrons and the range of sc the details.

but like a place. The feeling that it is a place, with its own life, is so strong that, sometime in 1987, the faculty and students decided to abolish the title of "headmaster" which the school principal had always been called in the old school. From that moment on, on the new campus, the principal teacher was affectionately, but formally known as the "Mayor of Higashino" — a designation used by teachers, parents, and students to indicate the fact that they feel the school is a community, like a beautiful village, and not an institution in the normal ugly sense. This change came about because of the environment.

————

In 1987, the school Board of Directors took an extraordinary decision, consistent with the previous philosophy of the Eishin Foundation, but still revolutionary. From then on, there would be no more school rules, except the constitution of Japan.

————

At the time of my visit to the Eishin Campus, to celebrate the coming of age of the campus, I was very delighted and honored, when Mr. Murakoshi and I were sitting on the veranda of the Faculty Building, looking out at the garden. He told me he wanted to give me a special thank you, on behalf of all the faculty. I was delighted to hear this news, but did not know what reason there might be for a special thank you. However, I did have the impression that Mr. Murakoshi gave me this gift not only on behalf of his faculty, but also on his own behalf, as a private and personal matter.

Then Murakoshi-san spoke to me in these words: "Dear Professor Alexander, when we asked you, in 1981, to favor us by building our new campus, we also asked that if possible, you could create for us a new way of life, an entirely new and whole way of life. We meant to say to you that we wanted not only buildings from you, but a culture, a spiritual, and academic, and intellectual way of life, which would transform our feeling about the meaning of life, and enable us to live life in a new way.

"At the time we said it, we did not place too much emphasis on this request, and we realized it was an almost impossible request, and that it would be a miracle if you could do this for us. We see now, years later, as we are living here, we see the gardens, and we see the buildings, bearing in them the meaning of life. I want you to know that this is the most precious gift that we have received from you, and we are, all of us, deeply affected in our hearts."

I bowed deeply to Murakoshi-san, and gave him my thanks for his great, great kindness in treating me so well.

———

Hiroshi Ichikawa, professor of philosophy and aesthetic criticism at Kyoto University, wrote a book in 1998, in which he gave a lengthy assessment of the Eishin Campus. "When I first visited the campus, I found it rather strange and uncomfortable; I left soon after seeing it. The next day, I kept on thinking about what I had seen, and went back to see the campus again. A few days later,

After a few months, a CES team built the terraces seen here, to make the Home-base street a really pleasant place, where students could sit, and talk, and play ball, and relax.

still having the picture of the campus in my mind, I could not let it go, and went back to see it once again.

"During the next months, I found myself drawn back to it, again and again and again. The place and the buildings have a hidden depth, not present in contemporary, 20th-century works of architecture. Finally I realized that in the last two hundred years, no one has attempted what these architects have attempted. What has been accomplished here, on this campus, is something which has not been achieved anywhere so far, in the twentieth century."

———

Hosoi was still hopeful that a college would be built, and that research done there would show that a living environment would bring about changes needed in society. Following is an excerpt from Hosoi's plan for establishing the new college and the Research Institute for Construction of Environment Institute.

> In the Eishin Project we proposed "Japan Autonomy College," the main purpose of which was to study the coming new society.
> The process in which technological civilization and pollution as twins of progress have been providing many problems may be called "The history of continuous failure in creating environment." The trial to study how to create a desirable environment for human beings, preserving an ecological system of nature, has become one of the most important themes of the day, especially in the case of Japan where we are facing the revival stream of development. Such a trial, will, of course, include studying the "coming new society." For, the study on the relation between progress of civilization and creation of culture is one of the leading topics in the later half of the 20th century. It is the reason why I would like to use the phrase "creating environment" in the name of our new college.
>
> *Hisae Hosoi*
> *December 15, 1988*

———

In spite of the unbelievable struggle, the day-to-day battle which was necessary to build this project, and in spite of the tremendous compromises which were made during the process of its construction, in the end it worked, and gave great happiness.

This was not obvious immediately after the campus was finished. At that moment, we only had the buildings. The buildings are physically beautiful. But there was no way to know if they had actual life in them. Human life, a feeling of life and inner freedom in the people. Did we succeed on that level? Did we manage, with our great hopes for the power and value of system-A, to make any real difference to the almost universal deadness of 20th-century construction projects? It was very hard to say.

Even after the completion of construction, the battle went on. At first Hosoi was virtually fired. The school suffered lawsuits. We were unable to make the small changes and improvements we wanted to do. The restless struggle continued for about three years.

The situation did not come to order until 1988. In June of 1988, I received a letter from Mr. Hagiwara who was then chairman of the board: "I am very happy to be able to say to you: There is not a cloud in the sky. At last we can say thank you to you and your family. Please come to Japan, to be our guest, so that we may thank you for what you have done for us."

A Fall Festival was held at the school. My family was invited to help celebrate. It was a very happy time.

A homemade boat, made by students, sailing on the campus lake. A nice continuation of ordinary life and education.

———

An architect, sitting in a group of thirty architects in Nagoya, discussing new housing work in Chikusadai, having dinner together, and discussing the Eishin project, told this story (rough memory of his words): "When I first visited the Eishin Campus, I came through the little village of Nihongi, and then walked up the road, to the main entrance. It was quiet and peaceful.

"Then as I came through the small gate, a student walked up to me, in very friendly words, greeting me, and asking me if I needed any help. I told her 'no thank you, it is not necessary, I am just visiting.'

"A little further along, I came to another gate, and the view of the lake. There another person greeted me, in a friendly way, saying 'good morning.'

"Then another person I met, also spoke with me, something I don't remember, but friendly kind words, just ordinary talking. After a while she also asked me if I needed any help. I thanked her, and she said goodbye to me.

"Later I came to the gymnasium and wandered in. Inside, students were practicing. A teacher saw me coming in, standing shyly by the door, and asked me to come in, invited me to please come in and be with them. He said: 'How are you. Please, just come in and make yourself comfortable. Please watch us if you would like, and stay as long as you want.'"

Altogether, I was almost in tears from hearing this explanation. It was just a beautiful picture of human society. The architect's description of the place was not about the buildings or about their form, just about the human feeling that is being created there.

———

In 1991, Japanese television NHK ran a one-hour special program, on the fiftieth anniversary of Pearl Harbor. They chose six cases, which they considered the most significant examples of Japanese-American cooperation since World War II. One of the six projects was the Eishin School and Campus.

———

An art student was interviewed by Mr. Ozawa, director of a 1991 feature film made by Japan Television on the Eishin Campus. Ozawa asked the student, "What do you think of the school?"

The student said, "All my life I have lived behind bars. When I came to this school, it was the first time in my life, that I felt free."

His detailed words, translated from Japanese, were like this:

"After having experienced the world at Eishin, I now look at the world from a different perspective from the one I was used to. Not that it is different per se, but somehow my world got broadened, or something like that . . . I don't know how to say it clearly.

"Just like wolves or lions in the cage at the zoo. I don't know how to put it. But they go on living and eating from what their keeper feeds them. They don't need to think.

"But once the cage is broken, they have to think and live their lives on their own. That is what I mentioned earlier that true hardship means. I am saying that once free out of the cage, they will face the hardship of life. They must think where they should go or where they should be heading to."

"That is what this place has done for me."

———

Finally, the most recent bit of evidence came to us in 2009.

In December of 2009, *Nikkei Architecture*, a Japanese journal, reviewed the history of the project and pronounced that, unlike what one would typically expect of a 25-year-old project, these buildings are more beautiful. They quoted their opinion in these words, "25 years of time raised the incomplete to the 'great work.'"[1]

After these many years, the architecture and the community of the Eishin Campus continues to attract attention.

---

1   Two commentators, Tatsuo Iso, Hiroshi Miyazawa, wrote a pungent article in *Nikkei Architecture*, December 12, 2009.

PART FOUR

GROUNDWORK FOR A NEW CREATION SYSTEM

2011 and beyond

CHAPTERS 20-25

PART FOUR

After the partial completion of the Eishin Campus in 1987,
we began to ask ourselves how the new production system we
had put in place at Eishin might be developed and expanded,
so that similar methods could be put in place in every country
and every place. In the intervening years, we have seen more and
more people around the world become aware of the terrible
mess we all have made of our environment, and in these people
we sense a genuine desire to repair that damage. All the more
reason to make as explicit as possible the basic tenets of
the production system we used
on the Eishin campus.

So now, in Part Four, having built Eishin,
we shall describe the elements of process
that are necessary to create any living building complex,
place, community, or settlement.
Unity, connectedness, and wholeness-extending transformations
are the keys to making this great shift
in consciousness.

The creation system we envisage, however, goes further and
deeper. We may say that a creation system is something like a
conventional production system, but one that also has within it
the elements of art, feeling, and inspiration.
This is a conception which embraces the aspects of production,
and simultaneously embraces aspects that will ultimately make it
more significant — one that engenders meaning, one that
emphasizes its significance, one that even hints at the
mystery of creation.

If we can understand this creation system, learn to respect it,
cooperate with it, and learn to use it well,
we should be able to create environments
that touch the soul,
and we may have the opportunity
to unite our work and craft with the depth of our own selves.

20 AWAKENING OUR CREATION SYSTEM

Hosoi was astonished to find out after we
began our work together, that the fundamental battle
between system-A and system-B, which all of us had been
fighting all our lives as social or political activists,
had never been as vivid, or as openly and fiercely fought,
as in this case of
the construction of the Eishin Campus,
where the issues so directly and concretely revolved around
the making of space and buildings.

Architecture — often thought of as a relatively unimportant social phenomenon — turned out to be the battlefield *where the most serious social and political battles between systems A and B, came to be fought*. Because of its concreteness, because the visible forms of space and buildings tell us so directly what these places do to help (or hinder) human interaction and discourse, because society as a whole is felt and experienced most directly within space, and as a product of space — and because these issues can be felt and understood so clearly and so intuitively in space — this domain of physical space above all, then seems to be the domain where the confrontations of system-A and system-B occur most sharply and most decisively.

Since the industrial revolution (roughly speaking, the time when system-B began to function and to grow), political dialogue and the daily kinds of discussion about politics and social order, have rarely, if ever, confronted this issue. It would perhaps be more accurate to say that they do not confront it now, and have never confronted it. For reasons not entirely clear, during the last hundred years there has been an unintended blindness to this issue of the generating system. It is this blindness which we need to rectify.[1]

The colossal importance of the generating system is that it is precisely this which makes us creative. Through the ordering of space it enables us to be creative. In our general behavior in society, it creates and makes possible a coherent, practical, and harmonious arrangement in the world around us. The generative system does this for us in a vast range of different versions.

Throughout the world, the order which exists in space, indoors and outdoors, in the city and in the countryside, dominates the kinds of social actions which emerge. Our well-being originates in large part in the spatial order of the world. But this important insight is not, today, acknowledged. With only the tiniest exceptions, it has never yet been adopted as part of the construction of the physical world around us.

———

Of course, for centuries there have been various kinds of environmental legislation, attempting to regulate the shape, form, size, and position of roads and buildings. But these constraints are indeed only constraints. They are at best punitive or restrictive. They are not, and have rarely been, creative. *Yet it is the creative force which we, as human beings collectively possess, that is the most powerful well-spring for the improvement of society.*

Consider the creation myths that many, if not all, cultures and societies have or had, in one form or another. The south sea island cultures of Melanesia have a picture of the world, how it was made, and how it is continually made again. The African culture of Mali, has its own legends and ways of portraying the way that the world was made. We, in the West, have one of our own creation myths, that appears in a famous painting by Michelangelo, on the

---

1   The concept of a "generating system," known in architecture as a generative code, has sprung from the earlier concept of a pattern language. The paper by Alexander, Schmidt, Mehaffy, Hanson and Alexander, "Generative Codes," in *New Urbanism and Beyond: Designing Cities for the Future,* edited by Tigran Haas, Rizzoli, New York, 2008, pages 14-29, provides one reference for such a conception.

Michelangelo — the panel from the ceiling of the Sistine Chapel, showing God breathing life into Adam.

ceiling of the Sistine Chapel. The essence of the painting lies in the injection of energy, passing from the pointed finger of God, injecting energy, life, and soul, into the body of Adam.

This is fanciful, to be sure, but it does convey the emotional depth and meaning which needs to be recognized, and somehow is activated and objectified by this depicted action. We are not interested in discussing this painting as a philosophical subject. Nor are we inviting the reader to contemplate the possible religious or theological meaning it might have. We introduce this painting because it has inspired millions, and is by widespread acclaim regarded as a great work of art. But, in particular, we choose to illustrate this painting, because it conveys the awe and mystery of the phenomenon of creation.

We introduce the example to underline the fact that the very subject of creation *itself* is of absorbing interest to almost all people. And, beyond that, lies the question of *how* things are created. What it is about creation that is so profound, which touches us, inspires us, and animates us?

Michelangelo's painting shows the finger of God causing creation (of some possibly unknown kind) to occur. It summarizes and enhances and enlightens our understanding, and our overall subconscious passion for this subject. Perhaps we do not know exactly why it is so fascinating and so moving. But that it is moving and fascinating — of that there can be little doubt. In some form, which we certainly do not yet understand fully, when living flesh or living art is created, this is for us a central, emotional, and spiritual event. If the production system that we have been describing in this book is necessarily a creation system, and if we are able to draw some understanding from the creation myth and metaphor — perhaps going beyond metaphor — then the metaphor may provide us with a deeper level of awareness and respect for the production system itself.

The closer we may come to understanding, or accepting, such a creation story, the more valid and the more profound the spiritual meaning becomes — coupled and sewn back-to-back, with the seemingly, more mundane idea of a production system.

———

The production of our habitat, and its physical interweaving with our own bodies — this process is an unavoidable basis and foundation of the life all human beings lead.

However, the production system of our present time, as our present society has configured it in the last hundred years, is something largely mechanical. We have fallen into the habit of referring to the factory universe we now inhabit as "production," because we have come to think of the association of factories and mechanical processes as the natural basis of our everyday life.

But in doing this, we have distorted the reality of what happens when things — artifacts, objects, buildings — are made in the world. Making, when conceived properly, and with its true meaning intact, *is* creation. The act of making, when properly understood, is the act of creating. It will help us keep our focus, if we acknowledge to ourselves, as often as possible, that our production system needs to be thought of as a creation system. It is not merely an economic system. It should not be reduced, merely, to that technical status. Nor should it ever be regarded as a technical system that exists merely for our use or convenience.

Here, in the material of this book, where we look at the issue of production as an overall and necessary theme, we have the sketch of a creation myth, and a sketch of a creation system. It is a rational, reasonable, and sensible view of the production process — one which puts our relation with the production process, in its full psychological dimension. We then have, finally, the wherewithal to create the living tissue of a community.

Surely this is a momentous theme. It is not only inspiring. We also receive the impression that what this book says about creation, and the way it works, is artistically fascinating, poetically fascinating, and technically fascinating. One has the strong impression that the use of this creation system, and respect for it, will create living environments, help to create beauty, and help create harmony.

The production system which has been described in many

Two CES staff members making experiments in the yard at Eishin, in the old Musashino school. These were to become prototypes for ornaments on the homeroom buildings.

chapters of this book is not merely technically adept and sophisticated. It is a new kind of system, a new kind of process, which seems almost to breathe fire into the world. The system can reawaken us, and it can give us a hint of what such a creation system is actually doing in the world.

And even that is not yet all. The achievement of this creation system is not merely practical. It is also symbolic. The activities depicted on these pages are engaged in joy — as you can see in the picture below. It is the joy of making. And this joy is of the essence, in our work together.

The symbolic, fire-breathing dragon, mobilized by the acts of building, carving, shaping, pouring, fitting, smoothing, and cutting is not merely the result or the production of thought. It is art itself, shaping the world on a modest level, which takes inanimate clay, and breathes life into that clay, making those buildings which are the very offspring of the creation system.

Being A Maker, Builder, Contractor, Artist, Working with Your Hands

The underpinning of this new creation system is our capacity for making. When our process of making is connected to our hearts, not our egos, creative energy flows through our minds and our hands, and we can achieve what may now seem unachievable. If the emotional quality of a building is to be alive, and seen and understood and felt by the people who live and work there, the process of building it must have this energy. The life and magnificence of the building will come to fruition only if the architect, builder, artist, craftperson, or apprentice engages the task of shaping it as a sacred act. If the maker is prevented from this sacred task, by a developer for instance, the work will not succeed.

Buildings can be made with depth of feeling and insight, when craftsmen and craftswomen have their responsibility clear in their own minds. The job is to make wholeness. We have the knowledge in our hearts to do just what is needed, and not push beyond our abilities, to experiment and learn gradually, depending on the results in the work itself as our teacher. The teacher is the feedback you gain with experience.

Years ago, I used to judge my apprentices by the extent they were joyfully willing to sweep the floor. Some people cannot do that, because they may think they are too fine. But the person who enjoys sweeping the floor, because it needs to be done, and knows it must be done beautifully . . . that person will, with great likelihood of success, gradually and slowly climb up the ladder.

My own learning about making began early in my life, and my passion for it has endured throughout my life. As a boy of eleven, I made in our garden a concrete model of the famous Brooklands automobile racetrack at Weybridge in Surrey, England (the first racing circuit built in the world, 1907). Mine was complete with small model Maseratis. I built the forms and poured the concrete, smoothed the cambered surfaces, and then raced the cars. My simple curiosity about how to make such a racetrack, led me into discoveries that were joyful and confidence building. In

Metalworking craftsman in Bali.

high school, my classmates and I were taught how to work with
a steel-cutting lathe, how to make cylindrical rods and threaded
rods with different pitch and diameter. We made bronze figures
using wooden patterns and then placing the wooden model into
tightly packed casting sand, replacing it with molten bronze, and
finishing the casting to a smooth finish. I made a wooden vice
in dense maple, where the slider had to be perfect. I hammered
sheet copper to make a roasting pan for chestnuts, plus a lid with a
hinge which made it possible to close the pan while the chestnuts
were being roasted. These tasks, and many more, were taught and
supervised by master craftsmen in our school.[2] We had access to
them in a variety of circumstances, and we were required to spend
a full week with them during each twelve-week semester.

When I began to teach students how to make buildings

2   I was very fortunate to go to Oundle School, near Peterborough in England. Under the great
headmaster, Sanderson, Oundle was the first school in England to teach science. And this tradition
also extended to the habit that each term, each pupil took an entire week, to have the opportunity
to experience training in any one of many possible trades, or crafts. They formed the backbone of an
ability to create things, almost anything, with their own hands.

Small, locally operated bulldozers and backhoes allow simple earth moving and shaping to be done. Seventy-six families in Santa Rosa de Cabal, Colombia, working with CES, built a neighborhood for themselves. Each house was different, and each was built by the family members themselves (1985-90).

in the University, I taught them how to make tiles of different kinds, glazed and unglazed; how to pour concrete under various conditions; how to prepare earth that was suitable for use in making clay; how to fire clay and bricks of different kinds. Later we taught ourselves how to make lightweight concrete vaults with thin shells; and how to cast prefabricated columns, beams, and corbels as supports in a wall.

One semester at the University of California, Berkeley, I had each architecture student in my class making a full-size building, at real scale, with walls, columns, roofs, etc. I do not mean a scale *model* of a building. I mean that each student was asked to make a real building, but small, so that one could grasp the nature of a real building, even though tiny, and also cheap so as not to waste money.

The upper photograph shows four craftsmen having lunch lying on the curved truss bents, before the bents were erected inside the building. When those bents were erected, one could see the wonderful shape of the interior space. See the finished interior of the Central building, on pages 30–31.

Eishin Campus: the Central Building, under construction in 1984. As we see here, although this building is relatively large, it is being put together in a way of working which allows individual craftsmen to work piecemeal, keeping their individual tasks at their own scale, yet allowing people, cooperatively, to create a relative large and complex whole.

Each building was perhaps no more than nine feet by eight feet. It was designed so that each student could define a set of construction details (invented by the student), and it was completed. One of the buildings was even a two-story structure, made by Carl Lindberg, a very enterprising student. All the buildings in my class stood for a few weeks in the open area in front of Wurster Hall (the building that houses the architecture department). I am afraid that those architecture professors who were inclined to make their buildings by CAD or drawing, were not amused. But my students never forgot this task and the huge impression it made on all the students

MAKING THINGS

There is no other way to come to terms with architecture and what it means to us. Imagine groups of people who come together to make buildings and neighborhoods with this kind of sensibility, working with their hands, and from their common sense, and helped by carefully learned manual skills. In such a creation system, we had a new conception of the built environment; a residuum which grew progressively. It intensified its own life, and it intensified the life of its inhabitants.

There is something else. During the 20th century, there was a tendency for architects and craftsmen, men and women, to focus more on the technical aspects of their crafts, and less on how they contributed to the whole. In those days they had little experience of wholeness, or the whole. They also viewed the larger tools and equipment — cranes, bulldozers, backhoes — as mundane, with little artistic content. For these larger and more massive tools — crude sometimes, heavy certainly — there was a tendency to use such heavy equipment only in order to get results. Even the people who use the equipment take the tools for granted. They do not always remember that a bulldozer is a piece of equipment which is central to the creative work of the human groups who use it.

We must not forget that in the wholeness of the world, the bulldozer and the people who use it together form one system. It is the presence of the human beings, and the presence of many, many human beings in the context of nature, that makes this wholeness work.

OVERVIEW OF THE CREATION SYSTEM

It is the humanity of our work that governs everything. The nine guidelines outlined in the preface (pages 7-8), ultimately form the basis of creation and production. In every effort to make buildings that respect, honor, and delight the people who move through them, we find that all of them are governed by their humanity.

In Part Four we shall now explore the creation system to be set in place, one that is capable of endowing our actions and their results with meaning and significance. It enables all of us, collectively, to take up the process of creation — thus giving to ordinary people the stage on which they can use their capacities to fill our built works and buildings with meaning.

Such a creation system will grow with each generation — generation after generation. As a production system, it has the capacity to generate real wholeness in the world, thus encouraging further wholeness to be generated. Then, once we have the understanding of what creation really *is*, we may then think out the overall approach to a workable large-scale, society-wide production system, which views production and creation as tasks of human creation, done by people, for people.

Understanding the geometry of wholeness is a first step. In the next chapters, we endeavor to lay the groundwork for a new creation system by clarifying how wholeness is to be attained — both in architecture and in society. With this understanding we may be able to change course for an improved world.

————

Beyond that, it will also help to generate power in seven billion human beings, most of whom have not yet fully recognized that they are ready to exercise this power.

In this chapter we must now put forward the consequences and the powerful argument for the necessity that buildings **must** be **made** (**m-a-d-e**) by the people who are shaping them, by the people who do shape them, by people who want to shape them. It can *not* be done by first drawing (as an old-fashioned architect would do), and then having the drawing assembled by a technician (an old-fashioned builder).

In a nutshell, what all this means, is that the emotional energy of a building can be achieved, only if the artists who make and shape the building, are *genuinely* responsible for the way the building gets its shape. To put this another way around, it means that if we fail to take the practical responsibility for the acts of shaping, the emotional energy of the building will almost certainly be false. If the emotional quality of the building is to be alive, and is to be seen, understood, and felt by the people who live there or work there, then this task must not be handed on to someone else. The life and magnificence of the buildings will come to fruition only if we architects, or master builders, or artists — or for that matter, lay people — any of us — take on the task of shaping as a practical and sacred act.

This is an entirely different process from the present process followed by architects if they are working within system-B. For those who aspire to be members of the American Institute of Architects or of the Royal Institute of British Architects, it is unlikely that they will be able to make a thing which is truly beautiful. That is because these institutes are bureaucratic in nature; as a result, the liberty and skill with hands and materials cannot be supported adequately. As a result the trainees will be taught how to make designs on paper, and their ability to be truly creative will inevitably be constrained. In short, if the artist is prevented from the sacred task of **making**, the work will not succeed. Of course it also depends on the artist's level of ability. It requires the ability to help a conception of a great work to come to fruition. This requires that the artist is able to forget his or her own ego. There is, also, the necessity that the artist, in the process of maturing, must be able to gauge and carry such a responsibility. It means that this artist has the knowledge in his heart or her's, to do just what is needed.

The capacity to undertake this work — even if only in a minor way — is an enormous responsibility. The apprentice, whether man, woman, or child will achieve this only to that extent that they have the ability to work in an egoless fashion.

We have inserted this short passage in the book, because it is vital for the readers to be aware of the direction in which this story is going. At the same time, we caution that a university degree does not automatically mean success, nor is success achieved in the earliest days of engaging with the process described. That capacity can grow only through work with your *hands*. That kind of work can be encouraged from the earliest days of apprenticeship.

We need people to learn, under conditions of apprenticeship, in the hope that they will grow up from earliest stages of learning. We hope that students and possible apprentices will eagerly demonstrate their wish to undertake this magnificent endeavor — that of building towns and villages and cities on the Earth, on the platform of wholeness, as far as we can grasp it and understand it.

And we anticipate, too, that these eager apprentices will soon come to know in a humble, not exaggerated fashion, that this path can be accomplished, so long as they work with pure hearts.

Be patient, and take this in slowly. The course of study we are advocating is, effectively, all that is outlined in this book, all that is taken together. The twenty-five chapters — all of them, when taken together — describe the profession of making living environments. This is the most direct, and most effective way of training architect-makers. And of course, this course of study will need to include five years of apprenticeship; and it will cover the practical, earthy art of making — training people who want to **make** buildings.

On the basis of this training, young apprentices will have a chance, and can develop the aptitude to use their hands and fingers, to make something truly beautiful, any thing that has life. Then there is chance, even a powerful likelihood, that people who emerge from this kind of training will be able to help make the Earth beautiful once more.

21 THE GEOMETRY OF LIVING REALITY AND BEAUTY

How Wholeness Comes About From Nested and Overlapping Wholes

Nature, of course, has its own geometry.
But this is not Euclid's or Descartes' geometry.
Rather, this geometry follows the rules, constraints, and
contingent conditions that are, inevitably, encountered in
the real world.
This geometry is made up of elements pushing and pulling
on each other, elements that give way to complex
conditions that are not shaped by prescribed
configurations, but by reality.
Hence the phrase "living reality."
In order to make a great building — or equally, a tiny
ornament — profound, powerful, significant,
something truly wonderful — we need to learn how
wholes, nested and overlapping, can reach the
highest levels of harmony and wholeness.

We shall now try to describe the complexities and intricacies that lie in wholeness. Wholeness is a geometrical structure.[1] And further, it is a geometrical nesting of wholes. We may call this higher level of geometry *a geometry of living reality*. What I mean by this phrase is a kind of geometry which is concrete and *real*. It is not theoretical. But it is found throughout nature, and throughout buildings, too — especially in those architectural eras that were more relaxed than our own.

---

1   See the first ten pages of David Bohm and Basil J. Hiley, *The Undivided Universe*, (New York and London: Routledge, 1993). Bohm and Hiley emphasize, from the very beginning of their massive work, that wholeness is not a casual, airy-fairy 'something,' that can be discarded at will. Instead it is an objective structure, which plays a serious and decisive role in the world and of the universe. The authors have laid out a highly analytical analysis of wholeness and its nature. It is fair to say that the next few decades, perhaps even the next century, will be spent in bringing this objective structure into common usage, and clarifying well-understood notions of wholeness and its attributes.

At school, geometry we learn in mathematical texts is essentially abstract. It concerns itself with lines, planes, with exact angles, with perfect symmetrical figures and volumes, and with curves, for instance, which follow pure mathematical rules. This has been understood as "geometry" since the time of Euclid, more than two thousand years ago.

The Two-Dimensional Nature of Carpet Ornament

I have studied ancient carpets throughout my career as an architect, because the makers of the old carpets understood the intricacies of wholeness, and the structures that made the carpets vibrate with this living geometry.[2] The reality of observations of nature, shape, and form are serious, cannot be set aside, and accommodations must be made to allow the irregular facts as they are. These must be permitted by the mathematical process.

Although nature sometimes follows figures, or lines, or arithmetically ordered figures, these arithmetically defined figures do not occur exactly in nature. The figures which really occur in nature are only approximations to these ideal forms.

Look at the 16th-century carpet shown opposite, from the district of Tabriz in Persia. The compartments and cartouches, varying with bright color and shape, are filled with the smaller dazzling ornaments that occupy the spaces of the design. This carpet might almost be regarded as an embodiment of the Sanskrit vision of the Avatamsaka Sutra — regal, fitting as an emblem of the universe, dazzling and endless in its scope and fascination: a model to be copied in every building; not literally, but metaphorically, showing us the spirit of all living reality.[3]

What are the marks of this unending pattern? In some cases, hundreds of borders, thousands of nested centers, together forming

2   Christopher Alexander, *A Foreshadowing of Twenty-first Century Art: A Study of Very Early Turkish Carpets* (Oxford University Press, 1994).
3   The vision of these endless wholes and beings is most magnificently expressed in *The Avatamsaka Sutra* (The Flower Ornament Sutra), one of the great, possibly the greatest, of the Vedic scriptures. Edited and translated by Thomas Cleary, published by Shambala, 1994.

In this photograph, we see just slightly more than the upper half of this magnificent carpet. The great medallion, seen at the bottom of the photograph, is actually in the middle of the carpet. Below this central medallion, there is another large area containing elements, medallions and cartouches, in a roughly similar arrangement not visible in this picture, but BELOW *the central medallion.*

still larger, and more intricate centers. Some centers share parts of other centers, or the wholes overlap each other. The elements are ambiguously overlaid together. Each one can be seen as combining with this one, or that one, most often having any one of half a dozen partners. Each is surrounding other elements, and each one is surrounded by other elements. Each one is shaped by its neighbors.

Look carefully at the geometric shapes in the carpet. They were drawn by an artist, and each line has been shaped by the conditions in which it finds itself. Look, for example, at the eight white figures which surround the central dark blue star. These white forms appear, at first, to be more or less identical. But when we examine them carefully, we see that each one is squashed, or squished, to fit into its immediate surroundings.

The upper two are narrow. The two below them, are fatter, with resulting distortions of the white shape, each one slightly skewed, with the result that the smaller details are also skewed, to make them fit into the white outline. We see, then, that the shapes of the various figures and elements in the carpet *appear* to be similar. But they are not. Instead, they are guided by the surrounding elements, and each one is shaped according to the particular details of its context.

Plainly, the carpet has carefully executed details. It has order, certainly. But the order cannot be well described by using Euclidean geometry to specify the curves and details. The rules of the game come from fifteen properties, which will be described in detail in chapter 22.[4] These might be regarded as loose specifications of rough mathematical ideas and relationships. But they do not lend themselves to exact numerical specifications as we know mathematics today. If you seek ways of shaping the lines, figures, even the colors, you will find that all of these are inspired by the fifteen properties. These properties set the framework in which these subtle and profound shapes, lines, curves and areas are created.

Let us now try to understand the extraordinary depth of the effect that living reality and its geometry can have on the observer or the maker. Overall, the whole may be seen as a dense packing

---

4   See chapter 22, pages 426 and pages 431-438.

of wholes, with no gaps between them and hundreds of elements with overlapping smaller or larger elements.

Imagine, even more powerfully, the intense activity, the excitement of the act of arranging geometric elements, lines and forms and planes, shapes, and, above all, *centers*. This intensity and excitement in your heart is released by the geometry. In general, if you really want to make a living thing, one that has true depth, you must focus on this geometry — the living geometry — of what you are doing.

THE ESSENCE OF WORKING WITH CREATION

Let's talk about what this means. If you want to make a building, or a part of a building, a window, anything that is mainly built of lines, sticks, straights, a curve now and then, a focal point that is intensified, a rhythm, a repetition beating against another repetition, then ... this excitement in your heart, will tell you when you are seeing it and hearing it correctly.

The entities which are formed, or generated, or created, are always in some form, centers. This does not mean that the geometric figures you create will be center-like, in a stilted *mathematical* sense. But what it does mean is that these centers — the component figures that appear in your creation — are shaped to appeal to your human mind and are connected to your own heart, to the inner knowledge and inner emotions that you experience.[5] All this inner structure, which appears as a matter of typical and beautiful autonomous activity, is dependent on these centers.

You will find that your own self, and your own *knowledge* of your self, are supported by these centers as they appear in your mind. They are the elements which arise spontaneously in your mind, and they activate the creative forces that arise in your thoughts.

The more freely you are able to marshal these configurations, the more your work, as a painter, or as an artist, or as a builder, a maker, will produce, through your hands, these beautiful and

---

5 For example, these configurations which have direct sensuous appeal to color, to shape, to simplicity of shape, simplicity of juxtapositions of complementary colors: African flags and cloths, Greek sense of design in ceramic tiles, Chinese and Japanese flags of different countries, eyes as they might be drawn on a flag, a cross of some kind etched into the drawing of the flag ... the Union Jack, and so on, and so on.

Eight-lobed star.

Black Maltese cross with two yellow lobes and two red lobes.

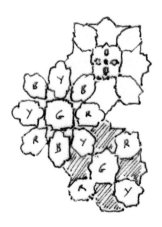

heartfelt, exotic structures which are precious and tuned to our human nature.

And you will find that these autonomous creations are the most beautiful things that you have ever seen come out of you. You can rely on them. They will only rarely let you down.

GROUPING, OVERLAPPING, AND THE FUNDAMENTAL IMPORTANCE OF OVERLAPPING CONFIGURATIONS

In the middle of the carpet on page 397, we see a brightly colored eight-lobed star. There are three yellow lobes at 9 o'clock, 12, and 4 o'clock. There are two red lobes at 3 o'clock and 7 o'clock. There are three blue lobes at 6 o'clock, 10 o'clock, and 1 o'clock. Eight lobes in all. And there is a green squarish figure in the center of the eight-lobed star. The same eight-lobed star is shown on *this* page. This upper detail (top left) shows the eight-lobed star in isolation.

In the middle detail (center left), we see a star-octagon, with a similar green square in the middle, surrounded by four black figures, forming the arms of a cross. You now see the same yellow lobe that you saw previously, at the 10 o'clock position, and in the 4 o'clock position you see an apricot-colored lobe.

Futher, below the two colored snapshots, on the left you see a black-and-white pencil sketch which shows how the three colored elements fit together. You see a diagram of the eight-lobed star (left), surrounded by two of the black Maltese-cross figures nestling against the eight-lobed star octagon (right). The Maltese cross appears twice, one to the right and above, the other, shaded in pencil shading, is in position below it, located N, S, E, and W.

The most important feature of this configuration *is the overlap that occurs,* between the eight-lobed star and the Maltese cross that appears twice. The yellow lobe that appears in both figures, is marked with a Y in the pencil sketch. This is the point of overlap. This yellow lobe occurs three times around the eight-lobed star, as you can see on the topmost illustration on the left.

The principal features of a complex configuration are always created by overlap. Although this overlap may seem trivial, when we examine the overall design of the Persian carpet on page 397, you will see that this kind of overlap, and ambiguity, is essential and pervasive. It is happening everywhere.

This is the glue in any system of wholes. Wholeness *itself* is directly created by this apparent overlap, or ambiguity. The greater the number of overlapping wholes, the more tightly bound the configuration is, and the more deeply the wholeness of the object shows itself to be. To drive this point home, we will now show larger and larger systems of overlapping wholes. The wholes, in this example, are all made coherent, either by the regularity of arrangement, or by the fact that certain elements are picked out by their shape or color, like the four black figures that form the Maltese cross in the star octagons.

If you return to the carpet as a whole, you may see many different overlapping figures and configurations. Just the arrangement of the eight gray-green squares creates such a grid of these squares, placed diagonally, and present as an almost unnoticeable arrangement of 45-degree positions. You may see this in the adjacent diagram. Note the handwritten labels "green", to identify gray-green squares.

As the rings ripple outwards, the elements repeat again and again. These rings are actually octagon-shaped. Inside

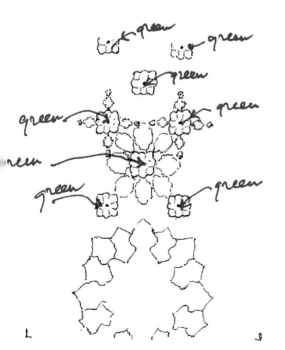

In the adjacent illustration, we see the eight-lobed star. This star is surrounded by four Maltese-cross figures. The eight-lobed star is surrounded, tightly, by eight of the black figures, now forming a black octagon. And then, outside the black octagon, there is a complex figure of green squares, laid out to form a large square which can be seen as a diamond, or square standing on its diagonal. Alternating with the green squares, are eight cartouche shapes, two yellow, two apricot, two blue, and two red.

the outermost ring, is a ring composed of the eight black figures, immediately adjacent to the innermost multicolored, eight-lobed star.

Outside the outer ring, there is yet another ring, only partially visible, because it collides with the narrow white border on the left and right. At the bottom end, it collides with a glimpse of the massive star medallion. And at the top end, there are five colored cartouches, and these sit next to a configuration of two black, Maltese-cross figures, side by side.

The principle is simple. The figures group themselves by similarity: similarity of shape; similarity of color; continuity of curvature. These grouped entities are the wholes which dominate the form.

The wholeness of the carpet is primarily formed by the wholes, of many different sizes, which overlap, and join, and articulate themselves, creating the glue from which the wholeness of this carpet is made!

The Three-Dimensional Nature of Buildings

Now let us embark on a discussion regarding the nature of **buildings,** as opposed to the two-dimensional nature of a carpet pattern. We want to recognize the weight and substance of the built material. We ask ourselves how we can (and *should*) feel the weight of a building, feel how the maximum interior feeling of the building comes into play, and how we cherish, carve, and shape the members of the building, as we build them and join them. When we succeed in this effort, then we feel it all around us. It is wholeness that we will feel.

We start with the fact that any part of a building, to be valuable emotionally, must bring the human being to the fore. The inner feeling anyone has will be visible, manifest, in the shape, size, bulk, surface, space, and shaped volumes of space of the elements we are considering.

STAVE CHURCHES AND NORWEGIAN STOREHOUSES

The stave churches, mostly built from 900 to 1200 AD or CE, have a few dominant elements. Columns; capitals; arches springing from capitals; open galleries; wooden tiles or shakes, very large, on steep roofs enabling heavy snowfall to slide off; dragons or other carved creatures standing up from the steep roofs; the hierarchy of volumes sharply delineated, and gracefully proportioned in the ratios of one volume to another; very steep spires, clad in wooden shakes.

The staves themselves have broad wooden planks, deeply carved to depict snakes, dragons, or other shapes of unidentifiable origin, but very plainly recognizable, sometimes resembling knotted or interlacing ropes, or vegetable creepers (see page 404).

The scale of the spaces is very small, yet there are many, many overlapping and nested wholes, elaborated by the overlapping and nesting.

Rodven Stave Church, Norway.

Church galleries on an upper floor, Gol Stave Church, in Heritage Park, Minot, North Dakota.

Elements are painstakingly fitted together on a larger scale, but still many wholes are nested together and overlapping to compose wholeness that is palpable when you look at this picture. Just imagine what it would feel like to stand in this passageway!

Zoomorphic carvings on the planks of the Urnes Stave Church.

Borgund Stave Church with carved dragons on the roof extremities, built around 1180. Thousands of hand-cut wooden roof tiles create a shimmering effect of beings or wholes, covering the whole roof surface, and showing an arrangement, carefully placed, so that the alternation of in and out is dramatic and continuous, seemingly endless.

Ancient stave church capital, with carved, knotted ropes, reminiscent of early knotted interlace carpets, circa 1200. The upper right image shows detail of the same interlace, at a larger scale.

Julian Street Inn, shelter for the homeless, San Jose, built 1981. Colonnade, with capitals cast in a rubber mold, and cut and glazed red tile inset into casting.

The ancient stave church capital seen here (left), with its chaste and beautiful ornamentation, establishes and identifies a key focal point in this part of the auditorium (carved wood, 11th century). A similar note is struck in a series of capitals we at CES made a few years ago, for a colonnade in the Julian Street Inn (San Jose, California, 1981). The capitals were cast, in a rubber mold, with fragments of red tile attached during the pour, making an integral concrete+tile material, for the capitals and column shafts (right).

FRANK LLOYD WRIGHT'S ENNIS HOUSE, IN LOS ANGELES

Here is another example of a different sort, but still with many overlapping and nested wholes that form the larger wholeness of the interiors of Frank Lloyd Wright's Ennis House. The density of wholes is what draws us in, eager to touch and experience the space on a visceral level.

Wright made many buildings in the Southwest and West of the United States, especially

the Southwest. The most
characteristic types of uniform
decoration are heavily etched
ornamentation, cut into stone, or
cast in other concrete and other
materials.

The three-dimensional quality of the surfaces gives them a
way of engaging the person's body,
and attention, and the incessant
patterning, cut into the surface,
causes visitors to put their fingers
to the deep etches, cuts, and
angles in the surface and the volume of the solid elements.

AN EXAMPLE FROM EISHIN: WHOLENES IN THE MAKING

A The Great Hall interior, uppermost lery, as finished in the winter of 1984- Here we already see the scale and rich of the columns, beams, and capitals they were first built in calcium board.

B The *shapes* of the columns, capitals, beams were first made with calcium bo also using steel sections and reinfor inside the shell, prior to pouring conc The final pouring of the concrete work done two years later, in 1987.

B

C

C The "white" structures of (B) were covered in painted paper to try different experiments and determine the best combination of colors and patterns for the Great Hall interior. When we were satisfied with the designs and colors, the structures covered in painted paper then became full-size mockups, later to be executed in high-polish, lustrous shikkui.

D Finally, two years later, the outer shell of colored shikkui was actually applied and polished. The final plastering was done in black, highly polished shikkui, nine coats of trowelled layers. The floral frieze above the capitals is, at the time of this photograph, a full-scale painting, on paper, awaiting the final plaster work. The red and black emblem on the capitals, and the chevrons, also red, on the column shafts, are in the state provided by the finished surface. The work was done by Mr. Ishiguro, the legendary master plasterer from the small town of Kawagoe, in Saitama prefecture, not far from the Eishin Campus.

D

Geometric Wholeness of a Group of Buildings, and Its Consequences for the Human Community

THE UNBROKEN WHOLENESS OF THE CAMPUS AND COMMUNITY

Looking at the picture of the great carpet on page 397, we have learned to see the endlessly interlocking and overlapping elements, working together to form a coherent whole.

Now we have to learn to see the Eishin Campus, *also*, as a *single, unbroken whole*. When we are actually physically present on the campus, we will experience all the buildings together, all at once. But when we have been looking at pictures, as in this book, we do not automatically see or feel the interconnectedness. Instead we see the buildings as individual parts.

In order to give the reader an experience of the campus as an unbroken whole, we have devoted the next seven pages to the experience of the campus as one single whole. To come close to this reality, please look at the pages that follow, and do your best to focus on the task of welding all the photographs together, as one single thing and a single experience.

We hope that the photographs on the next seven pages, coupled with the others throughout the book, will enable you to see the wholeness that is there.

CONCLUSION

What, then, is this whole that has arisen from the buildings we have built, working together with the students and teachers and visitors who come there, working with craftspeople, walking in silent pleasure, and taking in the atmosphere. It enlarges them all. And why does it enlarge them? Why does it deepen their experience?

It happens because the structure of the place forms strands, connections, interlocking elements, human connections too, and the matter which also comes through the soul, from the mind, and from the poetic substance which exists there.

Text continues on page 419.

When a state of wholeness is reached, we almost inevitably embrace the structure of the actual place. And it embraces us. The elements, centers, and properties are part of that embrace. The wholeness consists of a multistranded chain of interlocking properties and interlocking elements, forming one whole, and being nourished by that one whole. The place has something positive to give, and it nourishes people to be there. And the place has the power to help create life within the people themselves, and their interactions with one another.

Text on this page continues from page 412.

Looking at these small photographs, we see many parts of the Campus, just as we see many parts of the Persian carpet. We see a great number of interlocking relationships, built from the fifteen properties described in chapter 22. But without a very special effort, we do not see the shimmering, flowing, and continuous whole. To see this whole, you must stand back, deliberately make your eyes and mind go out of focus, so that you do not see the parts, only the flowing and connections of the endless whole. We may say that we can see the structure in its completeness. How does this happen? What is the difference between seeing all the parts, and seeing them as a whole?

- In the shimmering carpet, the various areas are all very softly calibrated, none is too strong; and each piece of the campus, too, plays a soft, not overwhelming role. Then the wholeness blinks as it comes to the fore.

- When we look at the many parts, we see that the similarities between parts create linkages. They create a tissue of similarities, forming thousands of connections of varying degrees between the different elements.

- These similarities alone, also create unity — simply by virtue of the fact that they are more or less, at one, in their resemblances.

- Contrasts between places also create senses of connection.

- Physical pathways and bridges literally form links. These, too, help to form unity by binding things which seem too far apart or separate.

- Similarities of colors, forms, connections; similarity of dark and shade form connections. Smoothness and jaggedness, too, may be connected, especially if they are placed in alternating rhythms.

As these multiple phenomena occur within the whole, they bind the whole more and more deeply.

———

In the next chapter, will shall describe how the fifteen properties of wholeness have guided us in making living structure. Once we succeeded in making wholeness — in the rich mixture of formal geometry and intuition that we followed by instinct — the fifteen properties became evident all the way throughout the structures we had made.[6]

6 The properties are defined in chapter 22, and they are discussed at length in *The Nature of Order*, first in Book One, *The Phenomenon of Life*, on pages 143-242, and then again further in Book Two, *The Process of Creating Life*, on pages 65-80.

22 THE FIFTEEN GEOMETRIC PROPERTIES OF WHOLENESS

In addition to *seeing* the nature of wholeness differently (as proposed in chapter 21), our relationship to the work of *creating* wholeness itself needs consideration.

The regimented task orientation that drives the procedures and rules of system-B must give way to more subtle processes capable of generating living structure.

In system-A, the focus on wholeness is paramount.

We may then recognize that this intentional, ongoing, creation of wholeness in the world will open an altogether fresh, new discipline in the realm of architecture.

As a result, chapters 22 to 24 describe a practical starting point in the work of creating wholeness. New terms will have to be invented that are very different from the usual way of handling architectural planning, design, creation, or production.

EVERY LIVING ENTITY, EVERY ARTIFACT THAT HAS LIFE, AND EVERY LIVING CREATURE, HAS, AS ITS MOST BASIC QUALITY, THE FACT THAT IT IS SOMEHOW "GLUED TOGETHER."

The parts belong together; they are cemented by physical ligaments, by processes, by various kinds of functional interdependence. This functional interdependence comes about obviously, and is usually visible. We see that when one part of the system is in trouble, or is damaged, other parts which depend on that damaged part themselves become vulnerable. Gradually — and sometimes suddenly — the larger part begins to crumble. They cannot survive without the health of the parts that they depend upon. The unity of the thing, depends on a pervasive pattern of linkages and structural interdependencies.

The really important linkages, connections, and interdependencies, are those which occur *within space itself*, and which rely primarily on space — those one might call "the in-space connections." This is a subject which is much less well understood by 20th-century people. The structure and nature of these "in-space" connections is better understood by artists than by scientists. It was well understood in primitive cultures, by cultures such as the aborigines and the cave dwellers from long-past eras, where people were more profoundly visual, and less profoundly verbal. A number of examples of this kind have been given in chapter 4 (pages 65-68). Modern young people of the present era will, in all likelihood, have more difficulty.

IN-SPACE CONNECTIONS

Let us contrast active, physical connections with the more subtle connections. If two billiard balls come in contact, they affect one another, and affect the way these two balls move. If a gate in a fence is built, the gate can be opened or closed, and the gate therefore has the power to influence events; a big influence on the way that relationships can arise there. In both these cases, the *space* which lies between the balls, or the gate and the fence and their surroundings is a passive medium, *which itself becomes active.*

There are other more subtle kinds of relationships which can arise in space, *where space itself becomes filled with relationships*. If, for example, two triangles are lying in space, the shape of the space between these two triangles may *itself* become *active*. In this case, the space is not merely a passive medium where other more solid objects move and interact.

Look at the following example of two triangles lying in the plane (next page). The triangles in the upper example induce a square-shaped space, which I have colored light blue. If, in addition, we add the light gray lumps shown in the second picture, the squareness of the blue space becomes stronger. So we see that

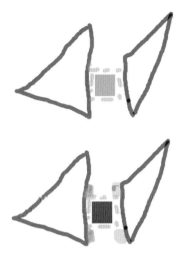

When these two triangles are placed together (first drawing), they induce a square of space. If four larger gray blobs are added (second drawing), the gray dots make the blue square much stronger.

space, in this way of thinking, is now an active medium, and may be active in various different degrees, according to the arrangement they are in.

As these more subtle effects occur in space, *unity (or wholeness) begins to appear*. Depending on the configurations, space can create greater and lesser degrees of unity. The richness, number, and complexity of these spatial relationships is far greater and more subtle than the purely mechanical effects that come about from the two billiard balls hitting, or the gate opening and closing. If we begin to focus on these subtle spatial relationships, we shall find that a marvelous and dazzling world may be created by them. It is the production of these spatial relationships, and the way they interact, that creates unity and life.

HELPING UNITY TO OCCUR

How, in general, does such unity come about? Many informal geometric metaphors link the idea of geometrical connection with the idea of life and unity. Take for instance two interlocking hooks. Braids, where twisted yarns or cables physically connect the yarns and make a larger yarn. Flat bricks can use their flat sides to make two bricks connect. Electrons in the shell around an atomic nucleus are bound by their quantum number. Planets and galaxies are connected by gravitational attraction. Vortices join configurations through dynamic flow. Phyllotaxis — the growing and intertwining of stems and leaves — has biological effects that bind cells and molecules together.

The history of science from about 1600 to about 1950 favored models in which such mechanical forces (magnetic, chemical bonds, gravitational attraction, and so on) were the commonly accepted mechanisms considered responsible for the binding that occurs, and then form larger and more complex structures. However, since Einstein's work in 1905, more subtle, purely geometric arrangements have been accepted as the origin of binding, or attraction. The force of gravity is now understood to have a purely geometric origin; as does phyllotaxis in biology; as do tessellations in three-dimensional arrays of atoms; as do the varying densities in roaming herds of deer and cattle; as do lightning strikes when viewed as shortest paths.

In this light, let us consider the subtle configuration of the two triangles a little more carefully. When the two triangles are placed near each other they induce a rough square of space in the gap between the two. If very small gray lumps are added, the gray lumps are likely to make the square much stronger.

A wholeness is an arrangement of shapes together with the various spaces that lie between them. In addition to shapes and spaces creating wholenesses, they can also induce changes in other nearby wholenesses.

This complex phenomenon is, effectively, the basis of all art, all painting, all sculpture — and of course, the basis of all architecture. Small shapes frequently modify the wholeness of configurations, merely by being near them. Even the smallest configurations influence and affect the wholeness of other configurations, reaching out from a distance, without any direct physical contact.

GEOMETRICAL CONFIGURATIONS OF LIFE

Let us now turn to the actual geometry of a small portion of the architecture in the Eishin campus. The life of buildings that we have observed throughout this book, in many examples, has arisen because of the geometrical configurations in what we built.

Facing: Long college arcade,
hundred meters in length, connec
three major college build

The extent to which a configuration has life or unity within itself, is caused by the geometrical connections among its elements, and also by its relation to its immediate surroundings.

Consider, for example, this major arcade in the college buildings on the south side of the college (pictured on the previous page). The fifteen properties defined in *The Nature of Order* give the underpinning of the geometrical organization and connections in the arcade in the photograph.[1] We shall see, presently, that the geometric structure of any "living" building is dependent on certain repeated features, or characteristics, or "properties." The quality of any building is, to a much deeper degree than we have understood, so far, caused by combinations of these properties that are purely geometric. The properties have been discussed extensively in all four books of *The Nature of Order*, and the discussions and examples run to some four-hundred pages in *Books One* and *Two*, alone.[2]

To start with, let us introduce some preliminary terminology. More detail on each of the properties will be provided later in this chapter. This arcade that we built on the Eishin Campus has a solidity and robustness, which arises because of the **POSITIVE SPACE** that is formed between the columns, and the beams and walls. The size of the massive volumes, the size of the spaces, follow the prescription of **LEVELS OF SCALE**. If the ratio of volumes and voids was less definite, the coherence of the configuration would be weaker. When we look down the length of this arcade, we see it (and experience it) as a single very strong center, thus following the prescription of **STRONG CENTERS**, because the nature of the big center that is formed, is composed of dozens of smaller centers formed by the individual bays in space. Further we see the configuration of columns and the spaces between columns as an almost solid substance (all together), thus allowing the arcade itself to form a **THICK BOUNDARY** which bounds the inside volume of the building itself, and again bounds the exterior volume of space that

---

1   *The Nature of Order*, Book One, *The Phenomenon of Life*, chapters 5 and 6, pp. 143-296.
2   *The Nature of Order*, Book Two, *The Process of Creating Life*, Author's Note, pp. xiv-xviii, and chapters 1 to 7, pp. 1-228, including especially chapter 1, "The Principle of Unfolding Wholeness," chapter 2, "Structure-Preserving Transformations," chapter 6, "Generated Structures," and chapter 7, "A Fundamental Differentiating Process."

makes the college green (outside the colonnade). Thus, once again we get one of the prescribed fifteen properties in its strongest form. In addition, the rhythm of the columns alternating with the rhythm of the open spaces between the columns (which also repeat), create a syncopated rhythm that may be called the repetition of the columns alternating with the repetition of the space between the columns — all together then forming ALTERNATING REPETITION.

A further aspect of the connectedness and unity that appears in the arcade, lies in the way the stepped or feathered arrangement of the two pairs of column capitals are on each column, one on top of the other. These flat rectangular capitals, create GRADIENTS from the shaft of the column to the underside of the ceiling. The two stepped capitals, together, form a curve that comes about from the gradient of the different stepping of the upper and the lower capital. This connects the column to the ceiling, and makes the unity of shaft and capital and ceiling.

The more densely these properties appear in a given part of space, the more likely it is that this part of space will be alive! The arcade gets its visible and palpable unity from the presence of these fifteen properties, in differing degrees.

We have, so far, mentioned six of the fifteen properties. The remaining nine properties (listed below), are not explicitly discussed above, but they, too, are part and parcel of the wholeness of the arcade. Please look for them in the picture on page 425!

LOCAL SYMMETRIES
ROUGHNESS
GOOD SHAPE
CONTRAST
INNER CALM
ECHOES
DEEP INTERLOCK AND AMBIGUITY
THE VOID
NOT SEPARATENESS

We may expand the range of scales that have unity and connectedness. The connections of a purely geometric nature jump from one scale to another, and these kinds of connections, reliant on the fifteen properties, will create bridges between all scales, and allow a great hierarchy of connections, active at different LEVELS OF SCALE, and spanning continuously from the largest regional connections (at the scale of kilometers), to the smallest wooden fibers and details of crystals and molecules (at the scale of nanometers).

In each case, and in each size or type of connection, the density of overlapping connections can grow thicker and more dense. Then life, beauty, and satisfaction will have the opportunity to show themselves.

A REVELATION

The first time I started thinking about structure-preserving transformations,[3] or *wholeness-extending transformations*, as my colleagues and I now call them — was when I was standing on the Eishin site outside Tokyo, in 1982. I was looking at the ridge which runs along the south edge of the site, and I began to have an intuition that whatever we were going to do there would have to expand, or reinforce, the structure of that ridge and the way the ridge site exists, and sits in the landscape.

This was the first time I had a hazy intuition, or feeling, about the forward movement of any dynamical system (in time), which must, at any point in its history, obey the law that every step forward taken by the system, will enhance, or preserve, the deep structure that it and its surroundings already have.

This was many years after I first identified the fifteen properties, which took place just after I left Harvard, in 1963 and began work at the University of California. During the late sixties I found, in my mind, a growing list of things I simply identified as "geometric properties." I knew these properties were useful, and I

---

3 See discussion in *The Nature of Order*, Book Two, *The Process of Creating Life*, pp. 51-84. In the first edition of *The Nature of Order*, these transformations were called structure-preserving transformations. This term was derived from a mathematical concept that plays an important role in topology. However, in our work, these transformations are now called "wholeness-extending transformations," because it suggests something more important — namely the idea that wholeness can always give rise to further wholeness, thus creating a direction toward an open-ended growth and development of wholeness, without limit.

felt them to be very, very important. Reflecting on my experience of the Eishin landscape, and thinking about it again and again in the following years, yielded increasingly articulate formulations of how these fifteen properties might give a coherent basis in which spatial geometry contributes to, and generates life. Now, twenty-five years after the experience, I can be more precise about what was happening there.

DEGREES OF UNITY

Earlier in this chapter we saw that coherence (the quality we also call "life" or "unity") ultimately comes from the interactive and mutual support of a small number of interacting geometric centers, and the properties that bind them. The relative degree of coherence in a building, or an arcade, or a garden or a park, depends on the number of properties which overlap, and the degree to which they are packed together.

These tightly packed systems of centers and properties occur *both* in man-made artefacts, *and* in naturally occurring physical systems of various kinds. What governs the geometric properties which provide the underpinning of a given system? And what governs the order or sequence in which these properties are introduced into an evolving or growing structure over time?

This topic has, of course, attracted a great deal of attention in many fields. Every spatial system has some degree of unity. Some have more unity than others. This may also be called relative degrees of coherence, or relative degrees of life, or beauty. It will be useful if we take some time here in this chapter, to summarize what has been written about at great length in *The Nature of Order*. Conscious use of the principles that follow makes a place come alive.

THE UNITY OF ANY SPATIAL SYSTEM IS GENERATED BY THE RECURSIVE INTERACTION OF THESE FIFTEEN GEOMETRIC PROPERTIES, INTERACTING AT DIFFERENT SCALES.

Extensive research has shown that coherent geometry arises from morphogenesis, because of deep-seated causal links that link coherent centers.[4] To some degree each center[5] gets its coherence from other centers with which it is associated, and it is this cooperative helping which generates more and more coherence or *unity*. Otherwise stated, each center is (recursively) dependent on other coherent centers for its own coherence. Its coherence arises because of its relationships with other coherent centers. To understand this idea, it is helpful to regard a center as a physical manifestation of coherence in space, and to define all centers in this way, as *the fundamental primary entities*.

A center is any zone of coherence that occurs in space. There is no other more elementary quality or substance from which centers may be made. Centers can only be made from other centers.

A center may arise, initially, as a minor non-homogeneity in space, through differentiation. Thus, a speck of dust in a vacuum might be such an non-homogeneity; or a line in space which is different from all that surrounds it is a non-homogeneity; indeed any spatial zone which is internally homogeneous in character, and surrounded by different material of different character, would qualify as a non-homogeneity. All these are configurations which act as seeds to morphogenesis. The ridge on the Eishin site is still a seed of this kind, but is rather larger than the previous examples. Others are much larger still.

Morphogenesis then occurs by the repeated application of the fifteen transformations on the centers in a configuration.[6] We call them transformations from now on, not properties, because each one is expressed as an instruction — an action or transformation — which can be applied to a configuration, then giving a concrete geometric result, thus transforming the overall wholeness. Each transformation can be applied to any of the centers in a given configuration, and can thus transform the configuration in

4 The relationship between the geometric transformations and the step-by-step process of morphogenesis, was first explored at length by Christopher Alexander, The Schumacher Lecture, Bristol, England, 2004. It is later to be published as *Sustainability and Morphogenesis*.
5 The concept of a center is defined on page 131 in chapter 9.
6 These fifteen transformations are described at length in *The Nature of Order*, Book 1, *The Phenomenon of Life*, chapters 5 and 6; and again, in their dynamic aspect they are described in *The Nature of Order*, Book 2, *The Process of Creating Life*, chapter 2.

a huge number of different ways. The fundamental and important generic idea at the core of what follows is that taking these actions continuously extends the wholeness of the structure.

THE BASIS FROM WHICH WE BEGIN

In any living system or living process, there is, at any given moment, a structure we may identify as "the" wholeness of the system at that moment. This structure is an approximate picture. It is, in fact, a map of all the most powerful centers (large and small), in a given configuration. It should be borne in mind that some centers are very large indeed, and the centers which occur there are nested spatially inside one another.[7] That is what I saw when I viewed the Eishin site.

Whenever a spatial configuration has a particular form, one or more of the properties will enhance or strengthen the system of centers that form the wholeness of that configuration. In order to grasp this system in a practical way, one focuses on a limited number of centers at the core of one's range of observation. This may be very limited, but still has enough "clout" to get realistic and useful results, when trying to decide what to do.

————

From this point, then, having identified the wholeness of a system — a site, a ridge, a garden, a path, a window, all related to larger wholes — one can consider which steps to take, experiments to try, explorations to pursue.

Here are the fifteen properties, now expressed as fifteen transformations that generate life. These provide the active juice with which a living system provides the range of possibilities with which we may work. Every living system uses these transformations. They are the active elements which go to work.

---

7   In addition, the definition of the wholeness, as including all possible centers that there are, implies that there is an infinite number of centers, most of them so far away that some have little practical effect. However, this wholeness, which *always* contains an infinite number of centers, is the only accurate way to visualize the wholeness as a "something."

1. The **STRONG-CENTER** transformation. This is a generic transformation which simply makes the coherence of a center stronger, by making it more "center-like." It does so by calling on any combination of the other transformations. For example, if a center is embellished by a **THICK BOUNDARY**, additional centers are created, and the original center will (in most cases) become stronger. If a center is embellished by a **LEVELS-OF-SCALE** transformation which creates new centers inside the original center, the center will, once again, become stronger — provided the placement of the smaller centers was chosen to have this effect. If the smaller centers are placed so that the sizes of the smaller centers create one or more **GRADIENTS,** supporting the orientation of the original center, and thus strengthening it, the same thing happens, but in a different way. Each of these transformations then spawns (or generates) new centers, which fit in a natural way into the system of centers already in existence, and supports the wholeness which was there initially.

2. The **THICK-BOUNDARY** transformation. This transformation places a thick boundary around or partly around the zone occupied by a weak center, thus helping to make that center more coherent. The radial thickness of the boundary is large, sometimes of the same order of magnitude as the diameter of the original center being surrounded. It is large enough, anyway, so that smaller second-magnitude centers can populate this boundary, meaning that the thickness is at least one-quarter the diameter of the original center, and sometimes one-half of the original diameter, thus forming a thick band around the circle, where the band has the same thickness as the diameter that it now surrounds.

3. The **LEVELS-OF-SCALE** transformation. This transformation modifies the given center, by embellishing it with smaller centers. These smaller centers are typically one-half to one-third the diameter of the original center, but sometimes smaller. They may be created within the original center, or in the space adjacent to it.

4. The **ALTERNATING-REPETITION** transformation. This transformation repeats centers to form a local array. This may happen in one, or two, or three dimensions. The key effect of the transformation is that it typically then creates a second system of centers between the loose-packed array of the first centers, in such a way that the first centers and the second centers are made strongly distinct, by shape or material or color, and become more coherent, by virtue of the alternation. In the course of the operation, the transformation often changes the shape of the first centers, to make the in-between, second centers well-shaped.

5. The **LOCAL-SYMMETRIES** transformation. This transformation strengthens a given center by introducing one or more local symmetries — most often a bilateral symmetry. If the center already has a natural axis of orientation, the symmetry is made to coincide with it. Otherwise, it orients the symmetry to make it as congruent as possible with the field induced by other nearby centers (i.e. where it seems natural). It is best to apply the symmetry to a center that is already nearly symmetrical.

6. The **POSITIVE-SPACE** transformation. This transformation is one of the most important and profound, but it is one of the hardest to define. It may be applied to any center, and helps to shape some of the so-called "empty" spaces which fill out the interstices within the original center. The "positiveness" of space comes from a combination of good shape, local symmetries, boundedness and above all from the appropriateness of the space for human purposes. This transformation is applied most typically to the latent centers formed in the spaces between other centers, thus giving these otherwise leftover spaces definite and recognizable form.

7. The **ROUGHNESS** transformation. In the course of unfolding, as the wholeness-enhancing transformations push and shove to make various things happen, as required by the detail of the

transformations, it happens, very often, that something does not quite fit neatly. Instead of creating a perfect or pristine shape, it is then necessary — absolutely necessary — to relax certain conditions, in order to make the configuration work successfully. For example, a putative rectangular building, when put on a difficult site, may need one corner to be slightly off — 90 degrees (perhaps 88 degrees or 95 degrees in one corner) — simply because of a tree that is in the way. In another instance, a doorway may need to be crowded under a roof, requiring the doorframe (and its door) to have one of the upper corners cut off, so that the door can be put there at all. For a similar reason, one wall in an exterior envelope of a building may need to be gently curved, and if left straight will fail to adapt itself to some recognizable and important geometric feature of the site.

In all these cases, the roughness that is introduced is created *of necessity*, because some aspect of the building's fitness for the site is more important than a perfectionist desire for Cartesian regularity. So this transformation gives the unfolding process permission to be rough and ready, when this serves larger and highly important aspects of an ongoing adaptation.

8. The **GRADIENT** transformation. This transformation creates gradients that point toward or away from a given center. Some common gradients are gradients of size, gradients of contrast, gradients of spacing, gradients of orientation. The gradients are implemented through smaller centers that have the above-mentioned characteristics, varying with position, magnitude, and orientation toward the parent center.

9. The **CONTRAST** transformation. The coherence of a proto-center is enhanced by contrast — whether of color, or material, or gradient, or density. The contrast transformation increases the contrast between the inside and the outside of the center, or provides some other differentiation which makes the center stand out more strongly from the field.

10. The **DEEP-INTERLOCK AND AMBIGUITY** transformation. This transformation is used at an interface between two adjacent centers. Its purpose is to create a zone, usually an ambiguous zone, forming a third center between the two original centers. It is made ambiguous, in the sense that there are ties from one side, and ties from the other, with the result that there is a visible ambiguity about which of the two outer centers this new center belongs to.

Since the belonging of the third center, to the two centers adjacent to it, is ambiguous, this is often accomplished by mutually interlocking "peninsulas," which penetrate the ambiguous zone, first from one side, then from the other side, creating an interlocking configuration.

11. The **ECHOES** transformation. This transformation has mainly to do with angles and curves and ratios. As the collection of centers grows, there will be certain predominant angles, or curves, or ratios or proportions, in the shapes that have been created. The **ECHOES** transformation then uses the statistics of these angles, curves, and ratios that so far dominate the configuration as a whole, and introduces this statistic as a default in the drawing of subsequent centers that are created nearby, thus slowly giving the whole system of centers a family resemblance shared by many of them.

12. The **GOOD-SHAPE** transformation. This transformation directly influences shape. If some rough outline of a shape has been generated, this transformation examines the overall convex pieces of the shape, and tries, as far as possible, to strengthen or emphasize these pieces, within the segments of the curved boundary, in such a way that makes the overall shape more distinct, more recognizable.

13. The **INNER-CALM** transformation. This transformation is a clean-up tool working along the lines of Occam's razor. It simplifies a configuration. It removes, as far as possible, all superfluous structure. Any aspect of the configuration that is experienced as

chaotic or complicated, instead of calm, is questioned as to whether it belongs there.

14. THE **VOID** transformation. This is a pervasive transformation, working at many levels of scale. The basic idea of the transformation is that at the core of any center, there is always some undisturbed and perfectly peaceful area which lacks busy-ness or excessive structure. It is very important that each serious center, has, within its boundary, some area or volume like this. Often this area is large in extent, compared with all the other elements that have a great deal of structure. This transformation can probably be expressed arithmetically, as a statistic on the whole configuration.

15. The **NOT-SEPARATENESS** transformation. This transformation comes into play after the majority of centers have been established. The purpose is to overcome any separation that is caused between the configuration and its environment, or between any individual center and *its* immediate environment. To mobilize this transformation, wherever a boundary is too sharp, bridges should be formed, by chains of centers, which cross that boundary, thus creating a softer and more permeable edge. In successful applications of the transformation, the chains of centers which it generates sometimes have considerable length and are anchored in the space on either side of the original "hard" edge by gradients of size, color, contrast, or other variables that vary with distance from the edge.

This transformation acts as an instruction to soften the hardness of an edge that defines a center. It can sometimes be very complicated. This transformation does not have a particular outcome: it rather defines a range of possible actions, which may all have the effect described above.

THE OVERALL QUALITY OF A CREATION SYSTEM

These fifteen wholeness-extending transformations were used thousands of times, over and over again, to create the design of the

An ordinary, but beautiful spot, on the Eishin Campus. Here wildflowers, big trees, and the carpentry building — all of them are centers. They seem to belong together. And if we study this picture, it also helps to give us a glimpse of the basis for deepening comprehension of wholes and wholeness in the universe.

Eishin Campus and build it. Chapter 11 (Flags: The Reality of the Land) and chapter 12 (Symmetry, Simplicity and Grace) describe some of the many decisions that were made to implement the life-giving qualities and properties needed in creating any part of the structure of the campus. They are a means to the creation system we can use on a grand scale, throughout the world.

In the next chapters, we shall see just what actually happens, when we apply the wholeness-extending transformations to a part of the world, and what happens after that. Although the present chapter has been written in an analytical tone (and is of necessity, therefore, rather dry), the next chapter (chapter 23) will show us how this procedure deals, above all, with feelings and intuition, and shows us a grand vista of process that is carried by the emotions and connects us, mentally and intellectually, with phenomena that are like dreams. The dreams go to work for us on the holistic level, and speak to us as artists — thus opening a vista which is exciting and inspiring. We finally experience what it means to connect with the wholeness of the world *directly*.

IN CONCLUSION, THERE IS AN IMPORTANT POINT THAT IS ESSENTIAL AS A BASIS FOR DEEPENING COMPREHENSION OF WHOLES AND WHOLENESS

If I say that a wristwatch is largely made of a spring, a number of gear wheels, and other small devices, no one will be astonished. On the other hand, if someone said that a watch could be made of *watches*, that would sound like nonsense!

We usually think of one thing as made up of smaller things. For example, molecules are made of atoms. Then, in normal speech, we assume that atoms are entities of a different sort from molecules. As in the case of watches, it would be very funny to say that atoms are made of atoms. If we did so, it would be puzzling, and affect the clarity of our thought.

But when it comes to centers, we do encounter precisely this sort of apparent anomaly. When one says that centers are themselves made of other centers, it seems as though a mistake of logic is being made. How could centers be made of centers? It almost sounds like nonsense. But the very nature of wholeness stems from this enigma. The idea that there is only one kind of "stuff" in the universe, is the enigma created by self-reference. Centers are not only sometimes made of other centers. They are *always* made of other centers.

Although this is puzzling, you will find that this loop-like, self-referring quality among the entities which exist in space, is closely related to the very origin of wholeness. It is this which makes it possible for centers to exist as configurations in an endless sea of homogeneous material. This sea (and by "sea," I mean the universe, or the endless space of which the universe is made) is made only of centers. This gives us a glimpse of the very deeply surprising quality of space as a single material, which allows itself to be formed, reformed, and reformed without end, into an endless variety of matter configurations at different scales and in different guises.[8,9]

In chapters 21 and 24, we see how configurations become more significant and more profound — and one might also say, *more powerful* — as the number, relative coherence, and density of centers in a given volume of space increase. As the centers become more significant, more meaningful, more alive — possibly even conscious, or capable of communication — the significance suggests something of considerable gravity. Essentially it tells us that space itself, far from being "dead matter," could have the capability of being alive and conscious. We may find that where space is most dense in centers, it is just possibly endowed with spirit.

There is one further, very important point. In *The Phenomenon of Life,* there is a matrix which shows the interdependencies of the fifteen properties, with a brief discussion.[10] What does this matrix mean? Broadly stated, the interdependency matrix shows that each one of the properties depends on about half a dozen of the other properties — different in each case. Clearly, then, the properties cannot be considered to be independent of one another. We have the observation that these properties are distinct, yet they are also interwoven. It is curious, too, that there are just fifteen of these properties, suggesting, further, that each of these properties is somehow a *facet* of wholeness, not an independent quality. This suggests that the properties are interdependent in some probabilistic fashion.[11]

---

8   David Bohm and Basil Hiley, *The Undivided Universe,* (Routledge, London and New York, 1993).
9   Steve Talbott, "Getting Over the Code Delusion," *The New Atlantis,* no. 28, Summer 2010, pp. 3-27.
10   *The Nature of Order,* Book One, *The Phenomenon of Life,* pp. 237-242. The interactions in this matrix are not always symmetrical, since a link may go one way, but not necessarily both ways.
11   What exactly do we mean by an interdependency between two of the fifteen properties? What kind of interactions should we expect between two properties? Consider, for example, LEVELS OF SCALE and ALTERNATING REPETITION. If we have a case of a real physical system, where levels of scale are plainly visible, will it be likely that alternating repetition is also going to be found in the configuration? Not very likely, I would say. It could happen, but it is not worth betting on it.
    If we take the two properties the other way around, we have a physical system which clearly displays alternating repetition. The two types of entity creating the alternation are likely to be of different sizes, so levels of scale will arise with the alternation. The alternation actually gets better when there is a distinct difference in the sizes of the two entities.

I have thought about this remarkable fact for years. It seems to me, now, after several decades of thinking further, that the fifteen properties must be directly expressing linkages to the existence of wholeness itself. Each whole is an undivided and indivisible whole, that can be viewed as a single phenomenon. Yet each whole is a cascade of smaller wholes, going down in scale endlessly. And large wholes also display an *upward* graduation in scale, which has the effect that they are leaning on still larger wholes and contributing to still larger scales above them.

Furthermore, the cascade of wholes is somehow fractal, or recursive. This comes about from the mere fact that each entity comes at a certain scale, and then, by way of the recursions, makes an endless chain of the fifteen properties, making the entities or centers repeat the scaling relationships again and again.

In summary, all wholes have the following qualities. No whole has a hard edge. The boundary defining a whole is always fuzzy or indeterminate. The wholes are usually placed in such a way that smaller wholes appear near edge zones. And they often have gaps between them.

This cannot mean that the wholes are limited. Nor are they finite entities. It must mean that the open-ended, infinite wholes always get their life from every scale, and from their participation in the larger wholeness.

23 How Wholeness is Generated, Continuously Following the Golden Glow

Nature is created continuously, day by day. Animals, fishes,
shellfish, oak trees, even geological formations that take shape
over millennia, are created stepwise.
Wholeness, all wholeness, comes into being gradually.

We have become aware, by now, that wholeness can only be
built up, action upon action, piece by piece, over aeons.
This means, of course, that we have to view the
ongoing creation of wholeness as something that happens
over time. It means that it can ONLY be done gradually.
This presents us with an entirely different scenario for the
accomplishment and maintenance of wholeness,
in any system, of any kind.

The golden glow is a felt vision which guides the makers,
step by step. Each step transforms the previous stage, and
gradually, stepwise, the deep structure of new wholeness
emerges continuously —
daily growing more subtle, more and more profound.

When I first thought of the phrase 'a golden glow,' it came to me
out of frustration. As I was trying to explain the thoughts boiling
in my mind, in a conversation with Maggie, I said to her that
the vision which came into our eyes, or minds, was something
autonomous, something that rises up involuntarily, and helps to
guide us, just because it **IS** involuntary. Some of my colleagues
found the expression "*a golden glow*" almost dubious, perhaps not
a respectable concept in a serious book. But the more I dwelt on it,
and the more I compared it with the actual experiences I had had,
in allowing myself to be guided by the inner visions that arrived in
my mind when studying a piece of land — rural or urban — the
more I became sure that this is a practical, intelligent, realistic,

and necessary concept which allows us to see truth, via a path of intuition. It is something which comes of its own accord, and it is the phrase which has most accurately described my experience. I became more and more sure that this concept was a reliable form of truth, which could not be ignored.

It arrives of its own accord, and it is a gestalt, something whole, which exists as a voice, a result of inner reflection that arises directly from looking at the land, and allowing it to form a coherent whole — approximate perhaps, not necessarily precise, but nevertheless reliable, practical, and true. It is something which has to be heard, respected, and followed. It is something necessary and useful. It is something **real**!

OUR STARTING POINT

It is time, now, to come to the *emotional* core of wholeness-enhancing actions, and to describe the way that such actions can be understood, felt, and undertaken practically. In chapters 21 and 22, we have seen examples of wholeness-enhancing transformations — and we have seen these examples as fundamental changes in the system of building and settlement production. But now we want to give examples which are not merely analytical, like those in chapter 22, but also emotionally compelling and easy to grasp from a *feeling* point of view. We wish, in short, to give examples which will make clear what kinds of positive emotional sensations a person is likely to experience when contemplating a wholeness-expanding plan of action.

Great harm has been done in the last half-century because modern societies have been paying attention to money, greed, and politics. They have **not** been concerned with expanding and preserving wholeness. The build-up to this most recent half-century of havoc, was preceded by one to two centuries of the same thing in milder form. Many acts that are performed every day, especially in cities, are performed without this awareness. They generate more damage, until damage is all we see around us. The damage continues to build up, cumulatively, and we experience it daily. All this is happening as a result of actions which are *not* wholeness-enhancing.

If we pay attention, carefully and slowly, place by place, to every aspect of the possible steps forward, we will notice that — in spite of good intentions — the steps nearly all contain some element which is stiff and dead, which cauterize the soul. Then at last, we must agree that the focus and direction of this growing cascade of mis-steps needs to be — *must be* — changed. Sickness of plants, sunshine taken away by smog, and a million other maladies of similar effect, must all be healed.

This requires cultivation of a new attitude that both seeks out wholeness-enhancing transformations and recognizes destructive actions. Mentally, it requires a scalpel, which will prune out the smallest dead feeling in the contemplated place, or in the contemplated action. This in turn will require intuitive seeking for what is most wholesome, for what is beautiful, or for what is emotionally true. In order to see this, feel it, and understand it realistically, we must learn to see each **not**-wholeness-enhancing action (even if minor) as a bomb blast to the world. If it is a smaller action, yet is **not**-wholeness-expanding, it is a hand grenade, which still maims and kills on a small scale. If it is a large action and is **not**-wholeness-enhancing, it will then typically maim and kill and disrupt and twist and unravel the *larger* part of the world to which this act has been applied.

In order to understand and grasp fully the nature of the harm which is done when actions are not wholeness-enhancing, we first have to grasp that the consequences that flow out from **NOT**-wholeness-extending actions are *genuinely* harmful. They are charged with destructive events, creating further destructive tissue in the social body. So long as this is going on, the energy people have for making positive environments around themselves is dissipated, and the harm perpetuates.

In short, if this kind of harm is done *at all*, then people, animals, and plants will be compromised. Worms, bees, and butterflies will be compromised. Beauty in the world will be compromised, also. The social tissue will be compromised. The vague feeling that ugliness makes us feel less well, is not vague at all. It spreads, it multiplies.

Let us therefore focus strongly, determinedly, on the positive.

CREATION OF A CLARIFIED GESTALT, THAT FLOWS DIRECTLY FROM FORMS ALREADY LATENT IN THE LAND

To make a wholeness-enhancing impact on the world, on any part of the world, large or small, we must always start with a limited whole — *a gestalt within the whole* — and on this day, **now**, this whole must be endowed with an increase of life-giving atmosphere and quality.

This will often require starting again, starting afresh, so that the outline of the form — a shadowy but glowing vision of the positive — comes into the picture from the outset. Unless this is the first step, the contemplated transformation is virtually doomed. It is better to start again.

In particular, the successful starting point for a wholeness-enhancing transformation will always be a concrete vision of some whole that already exists. It demands that we examine the places that are most precious, pull them out mentally and give them new shape — always making sure it is a continuation of the deep structure that was there already. A slight mental glow, containing a hopeful future, then hovers over the better qualities of the place, even if they are embedded in a sea of ugliness. The constructive gestalt that is detected can then be made *more* positive. Some correction is a starting point, but somehow one then succeeds in transforming something not-so-good, into something that grows *out of* the present circumstance. This circumstance — a heart-felt gesture in the landscape, or an accidental configuration of buildings or paths or roads or trees which is the most positive thing visible — **this** is almost always the element which can most likely be made to give rise to the newly transformed land.

In general, the way to begin is by settling your gaze on the most positive aspects of the place. Look for the inner structure of the place that is composed — a gentle curve, a striking color, a quality that begs to be elaborated in the area where the transformation is to take place. As your mind appreciates what is there, it will take on warmth in your imagination, a subtle, patient light. You can see in your mind's eye the land and buildings, and the town, that may grow from those precious details that seek completion.

Some are beautiful. Others are not, in themselves, beautiful. But, like the features of the ridge, they are natural, and they belong there. Conjure in your mind a metaphorical, golden light that is consistent with what is there — one that erases the negative influences there now. Sketch (in your mind's eye) a few major points that will be consistent with that light — things that seem to belong there. Somehow make something that is the offspring of that light. That is what sets the whole thing on its feet. If you make something consistent with the vision you now begin to see, it will take you in the right direction.

FIRST GESTALT: FORMATION OF THE LAKE

Here were our thoughts with regard to the lake. It was first mentioned on page 137 of the pattern language chapter, which explicitly called for the creation of a lake. Then, naturally, when it came to the real land, we had to find an area of low-lying land. A swampy bit of land, where the farmers used to grow vegetables, was just right kind of place. In the map on the next page, the thin blue line shows the first low contour that drops 50 centimeters. And then inside that contour, we see the next low contour line — the edge of the aquamarine area on the diagram.

That became the lake that emerged from the land. Indeed, the lake became the most remarked on and most loved part of the campus. After everything was built, many students told us that the lake was their favorite place on the campus; and their second favorite was the curving bridge that crossed the lake. And the curving bridge, in a graceful arc over the water, connected the plaza formed by the position of the Great Hall, with the far side of the lake, the position of the students' Dining Hall. The relationships between land, built form, and emotional content are reciprocal. *Recognize that the overall geometry of the place embodies the emotional atmosphere which is needed, in order to make the newly created place embody the feelings that are needed to fill out the land. When built, the place engenders feelings of connection and affection in our inhabitants.*

At first we could see a golden light in the position where you now see the gently dug out soil, shown as aquamarine on the drawing.

446

Then, again, we could imagine a glow in the place where the bridge was to cross the water, and this was manifested in a slender arc crossing the lake. This is indicated in the second drawing on the next page, where the bridge extends the wholeness that was started with the lake. Once seen in the mind's eye, then actually and actively, that light could transform itself into a physical and fleshed out vision of a place that, when built, would maintain the wholeness which was there. And then in the bulb of the lake, we could imagine the gymnasium as an island in the water, connected to the island by smaller bridges — once more a golden light that gradually, in the mind's eye, became an island.

This aspect — the light which stands for a vision not yet quite fully formed — is a major tool in the process of actualizing a wholeness-enhancing transformation. And

The lake, pedestrian bridge, and Dining Hall, wh first built in 1984.

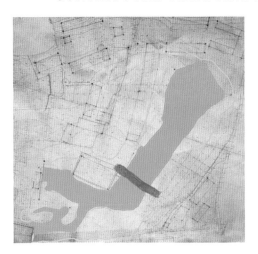

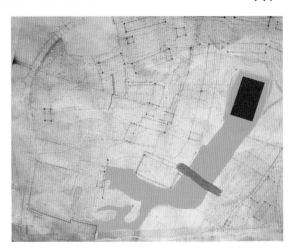

Step 2: The bridge placed at the neck in the lake that invites it as the most natural crossing.

Step 3: The dark red rectangle shows the position of the gymnasium which is to be — the gymnasium will literally be an island, fully surrounded by water.

The gymnasium, surrounded by the lake, in front, and by a narrow channel of water on the other three sides. Small bridges give access to the building.

this simple tool, if honestly and literally followed as a guide, will usually lead to the appropriate results. But it is essential that these simple, human, dreamlike processes are followed with great seriousness.

SECOND GESTALT: ENHANCING THE RIDGE

Let us transfer our attention to a second example: the ridge! Our most basic orientation to this campus started with the ridge on the Eishin property. We returned to the ridge again and again as a place we could embellish. The drawing we have placed below is a very old drawing (we are using because it is too arduous to redraw the contour lines). In the upper part of the drawing (which is the direction of south, not north), you see the gradual contour lines showing the slope leading up to the ridge, and down again on the other, steeper side. See plan below.

For us, the ridge was an iconic place, and gave us a strong reason for returning. We kept on seeing the product of the ridge, as it might be, in order for it to be emphasized and captured, as one now sees it in the place of the Tanoji center. It is the three-

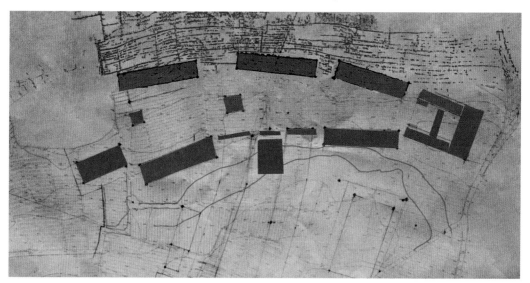

The ridge. The space between the positions marked for buildings, corresponds, almost exactly, to the place we experience as the ridge. And at the top of the drawing, we see the steeper slope visible in the closer spacing of the contour lines. South is at the very top of the drawing. Preliminary sketch layout of the ridge contours and its buildings shows five college buildings: the Judo Hall, the Central Building, the Library and Research Center, and in the very center of the college green, the Student House, three stories high.

dimensional, volumetric center that maintains the feeling of the ridge, in built form. The emerging form leaves gaps between the beautiful long buildings, and is held by the two end places, that were emphasizing the length, and the bent axis of the ridgetop. At one end (to the left) was the physical Judo Hall with its bare, almost stark form (page 417, bottom right). At the other end (to the right) was the Library and Research Center with its cloister. But this was not yet built ... The library exists, so far, only in the mind's eye. The Library itself, strongly decorated with large green and white diamonds, will stand high, with its great windows looking out over the entire ridge top in a single view. So far, we see it only in as a model (page 249).

The structure of the ridge is reflected, and "reborn" and extended, in the arrangement of the first college buildings on the ridge, shown on page 196. The form of the buildings reflects the structure of the ridge, and has already intensified that structure, because of the south-lying college buildings that run the length of the ridge.

THIRD GESTALT: A NET OF ARCADES CONNECTING TO EACH OTHER

Now we will examine a third example of larger wholes being created — this time, at a slightly smaller scale.

The campus is crisscrossed with arcades, larger ones in the college parts of the campus, narrower ones in the high-school areas. A person can walk all over the campus, staying mainly in the arcades, without getting wet or muddy in rainy weather, or snow. As you can see, all these arcades are social gathering places, and, at almost any time of day, people are enjoying them, talking in small groups, leaning against a column, arguing, chatting.

And this is, indeed, what we imagined. It was a natural extension of the flow of the buildings — the flow of people interacting with them. The land and the pattern language guided what was created there, and this is what they generated. The same practice went on to generate wholes on smaller levels of scale. Many examples of smaller levels of scale, and the detailed nature of steps that would be wholeness-enhancing, are given in chapter 12.

The arcades are built, of course, along the edges of buildings. Each edge is a potential meeting ground between indoors and outdoors. And in this sense we may recognize each edge, or arcade, as a boundary between indoors and outdoors. The injection of such a physical boundary, along a building edge, forms a zone which looks both ways. X+Y forms one unit. Y+Z forms another unit. These two composite units overlap in Y, the arcade, which therefore knits the indoor space and the outdoor space together. This boundary is therefore a zone which can extend the wholeness of the place where it occurs.

By building such an arcade, X,Y,Z forms a complex entity, made from X+Y and Y+Z. The building X, and the outdoor space Z, together, extend the wholeness, because the arcade Y then cements the three entities (X, Y, Z), and extends and further unifies what has been made whole.

Y is the intermediary, ambiguous structure which joins X and Z, and makes of them, a unity whole.

The smaller, narrower arcades in the high school buildings.

The larger arcades of the college buildings.

These three elements — lake, ridge, and arcades — are just a few examples that demonstrate how the work of creation combines the use of the wholeness-enhancing transformations of chapter 22, with the visionary orientation described in this chapter. This is the means by which the whole campus was created, as far as it is completed so far. **It is the means by which the larger wholes of ANY project must be gradually formed and built.**

Wholeness-enhancing transformations are *felt*. It is this feeling which engages our senses, and takes us beyond the structure, to a new structure which emerges from it and follows from it. We must learn to experience, see, and describe the feeling of extending, continuing, and enhancing wholeness, wherever it is felt to be necessary. Even when we cannot perfectly *define* the wholeness, we can distinguish those continuations which are most apt, and most true. Judging whether a transformation is reliably wholeness-enhancing or not, can be applied empirically, and can even be done under laboratory conditions.[1]

This puts us in a new relation to the future. In the old Newtonian world, we could not mechanically extrapolate from the present to the "what is to be" of the future. The Newtonian world demanded that we accept that we are on our own, there are no sources of inspiration, and no threads which link our dreams and visions to the past that has existed, or to the present — the now that exists today.

In the new scheme of things we have described, we are able to see and extract new and future realities from our present reality. That means we are able to see beyond the definable reality of what is, and can hold on to ropes that guide us into the future. The vision of what to do is not a feat that one is expected to do by arbitrary, artistic invention. Instead, we can use these ropes from the present, and climb up the ropes, hanging, if you will, from heaven.

Our knowledge of the present structure of things, opens doors for us — and leads us directly to the shining visions that we can extrapolate from the deep structure of the present, to things that come into being as if by themselves.

They come from us. Yet they do not come from the inventions of our minds. They come mainly from the workings of the world around us. And further, they come from the workings of the deep structure of the present, that shows us what to do, as if through the autonomous working of our visionary souls.

This is the mysterious nature of creation!!

---

1   Discussion of these experiments is to be found in *The Nature of Order, Book Two, The Process of Creating Life*, chapters 2-3.

24

THE BEAUTY
OF DAILY LIFE

In this chapter we have a glimpse of ordinary life as you and
I might like to live it. Simple beauty and wholeness in the
environment heals, supports, and engages life.

On the pages of this chapter, we give examples of some
beautiful and tranquil pictures where we can see physically,
and point to the underlying nets and arrays of living space.
This helps our story to come full circle, and verifies — in
part — the structure of the wholeness which has been
deliberately created.

Humorous, relaxed, waiting for a class to start.

The daily life on this campus is beautiful in an ordinary, down-to-earth, and spiritual sense. Accompanying this quality, there is also the physical beauty of the buildings, and their material details.

The interaction of the two aspects — the physical, geometric beauty, and the spiritual beauty — comes from the fact that successful buildings have an inner "glow." Perhaps this is too strongly stated — but this glow reflects, or makes to shine, the expressions on people's faces when they are present in this place.

We may equally say that people who are studying or working on this campus feel happy or contented more than is usual in contemporary high school and university campuses. It comes from the way the buildings have an effect on them.

Teacher walking in the arcade of what used to be the old teachers' common room, late summer 2011.

One of the students' favorite places, on a roof outside the Central Building.

To some degree it must be admitted that the Eishin Campus is beautiful. The beauty is not skin deep. The beauty is not a coat of lipstick that beautifies an otherwise ordinary structure. But if we want to use the word beauty, we must be careful about how we use it. It has been misused and distorted, especially during the last hundred and fifty years. It is not a word to be used casually or lightly. It cannot be properly used by applying a template of taste or preference against a thing, or a face, or a tree. Rather, what we see and experience as beauty is a quality in which the world around us is profoundly integrated, deeply interwoven with the feeling of the whole, with some health, and, of course, with the deep well-being of people — men, women, infants, children, students, and the elderly — and with animals and trees, and ducks, and birds and flowers. And, too, with rockfaces, ice-sheets, rushing water, and purifying forest fires.

The small Music School, attached to the Great Hall, which lies to the right in the background.

A music teacher in the Music School, leading a class.

*Gathering in one
of the alcoves of the
Central Building.*

*Below: The Music School,
showing the clear beauty
of its diamond frieze.*

I do imagine, and hope, that the steps we took in Japan may set out the first stones of a new path that can lead us there. Gradually then, we shall fathom a greater truth: that it is in the making of our world that we become alive, and it is in the making of the world that we can at last infuse it with ordinary life. Not with some artificial life, but with the very ordinary stuff of a hamburger, eaten from a paper bag, sitting on a wall, gazing at the river. If we understand it, permanently, and recognize it as the permanent stuff of life, embrace it, don't make too much of it, but do not make too little of it, either, then we shall find ourselves right in the midst of life. The beauty of life is then directly linked to the living beauty of the buildings.

If we reach such a very ordinary state of daily life, and then back it up with building and construction that comes from the depths in us, that gradually accumulates our value in the world, all of us together as a whole. Later, then, perhaps hundreds of years later, people will look back at our stones and say to themselves, "My word, those people way back then — they certainly knew how to live," and they would say this because they could see the lingering whispers in the walls and mosses, and could read them, and could treasure them, and would learn from these traces how to live like that again.

We may view this totality as an ecological totality, one that cares for trees and grasses, insects, and fish. We may view it as a totality that supports the health of people, creating opportunities for physical exercise, and opportunities for mental and emotional exercise. We may view it as an ordered social system which permits and preserves the health and welfare of its citizens. In short, if we are prepared to recognize that a successful, living environment is at once physical and social in its beauty, and embodies the interweaving of these many aspects all at once, and all together, then our view of the world will suddenly and dramatically be changed.

What is the path to such a construction? Is it possible to aim, deliberately, at a social system, or at social structures which have these qualities? The Eishin Campus does have qualities as a physi-

*The Home Base street, in the first stage of construction,
when terraces had not yet been built.*

cal structure, and also qualities as a structure that supports human
activities. The beauty of one interacts with the beauty of the other.

So is it possible that the physical beauty of the environment, as
displayed on the Eishin Campus, is necessarily part of such a social
healing? And may we then argue that the healing qualities of the
physical and social environments are of necessity bound together?
Have we succeeded in a way of looking at cities, neighborhoods,
streets, so that the nourishing physical beauty of these places is the
underpinning of emotional and social health?

If that has indeed become possible, it will give us a way of regarding the quality of an environment in social terms, in ecological

terms, and in human and emotional terms of personal well-being. And if there were a way of conceiving the physical beauty of such a world, as a necessary ingredient of the whole, this would lead to a new and non-arbitrary kind of aesthetics, one that follows from the joy and well-being of the people, plants, and insects, that live together.

That would be remarkable — an entirely new goal for our lives and our society. A new achievement, which would lead us to understand the physical environment, architecture, building, and planning, in an altogether revolutionary way, a way that could open doors to a new age of architecture.

We may dare to hope for a future era — not too far in the future — when we have a natural awareness of these many living things interacting, playing together. And the playground — our environment — will be playing, too: a world that enjoys itself.

The result of thirty years of growth. Students and visitors wander among the forest of well-grown trees. Yet the Great Hall and the Administration building, at the core of the Campus, are just by the forest.

In that day, we shall understand that there is no such thing as architecture separated mentally from how we live, but rather that there is a new kind of structure made of our hopes and aspirations, coupled with our daily caring for the physical fabric. All this comes to life with the architecture. **In this form it is all one living thing.**

The Judo Hall, in snow, glows in the early morning sunlight. The photograph was taken very early, and the two college arcades, making a frame for the Judo Hall, are in darkness.

Students gathering in front of the lake and the bridge that crosses the lake.

The recently appointed new headmaster, Mr. Susumu Nakagawa, greets the students as they arrive on campus every morning. The headmaster does this every day to welcome them as they start their day.

left and immediately above: Students helping to plant out seedlings, as they all do to maintain the campus environment.

Main picture, left: The student clubhouse, donated by the students and their families, under a canopy of cherry blossoms. The boat landing stage is a little old, and worse for wear. But the idyllic quality of the place remains. Next year, we hope the landing stage will be repaired.

Above: The clubhouse itself, as it looked when first built.

A student standing casually in a small boat, paddles as he passes by the clubhouse. You can almost see him whistling by himself.

The Judo Hall, standing at the west end of the ridge, looking out almost like a castle at the highest point.

he Art Studio, next to the Central building. Drawings and sculptures fill the place, create an intense atmosphere, and yet the place is both calm and intense and quiet.

Laundry drying on a clothes line stretched across one of the minor streets.

: This arched passage with students ing through it, has a charming bination of the formal and informal. nior student leads three younger boys heir first day on the Campus.

basketball, in the Gymnasium.

Above, an exciting relay race on Campus.

Below, the bridge over the lake, crowded with students and visitors watching the finals of the annual canoe races.

A shrine made by students in 2003. It continues to
be looked after by the students.

Wild purple spring flowers, at the edge of the campus.

In the half-dark, the audience relaxes during an interval in a Great Hall performance. Please forgive the camera shake, but I had to take a one-second, hand-held exposure with my old black Leica. It was taken from the gallery pictured below. I love the colorful, informal postures and the clothing of the audience.

Gallery in the Great

Festival Day in bright sunshine 1987.

Evening performance in the Great Hall.

Sunset on the Campus.

25 RECOVERY OF HUMAN NATURE AND REBIRTH OF CIVILIZATION

The creation process in chapter 20, and the kinds of actions described in chapters 21-24, present us with a disarming and powerful potential. Using the comprehensive paradigm of conceptual tools and stepwise actions, and taking the great care that has been described, it is within our power to recover the deeper aspects of human nature and work our way toward a compassionate and ethical civilization. It is possible to recover ourselves, our world, and a future for our children and their children — one that is rooted in profound and lasting values.

Knowing that our devastated civilization cannot be repaired in a hurry, we may assume it can be rebuilt and reaffirmed only if we go very deep into the foundations of this new potential civilization. That requires, as underpinning, a renewed physical world, together with a new way of building and looking after land.

We can begin now. We can lay out a new way of thinking which is, perhaps, deep enough to give us the stepping stones we need to replace the disastrous errors we made during the last century.

If we have sufficient courage, we can make a difference in our lifetimes. In a couple of hundred years we may have recovered our selves, our wits, our common sense, together with a newly inspired framework, giving us back real architecture as the locus of our new life and our recovery.

One thing we can be quite sure about. The foundations of this new civilization must be rooted in its *architecture*. It requires an architecture for real life — a new physical structure. That means a new arrangement of physical forms, spaces, buildings, the shapes of buildings and the shapes of spaces, and, above all, a new and realistic philosophy of arranging gardens and streets, and a new philosophy of building them.

You may say to yourself, isn't this exactly what we have been discussing all along, throughout this book, demonstrating, and explaining, and showing how it may be done? Well, yes, that is true! But so far in this book, as it stands, it has not yet gone far enough to be unmistakably clear. People can talk about these things. But doing it, and making it — making these shapes and spaces come to life as a civilization — that is something else again. And it is just *this*, which is so important.

To be successful, and to deliver the goods, it is the making of the spaces and the buildings which is the crux. And within this great task of making, **it is the way or manner in which we make the buildings and the spaces between them that matter most**.

THE STRUCTURE OF REAL ARCHITECTURE

So now I shall do my best to make it clear — as clear as I am able — to describe and define the difference between the current professional conception of architecture (those buildings whose pictures are typically paraded in the glossy magazines and books, including the work of so-called star-architects) and real architecture — an entirely different group of buildings: the buildings which contain deep feeling and carefully considered soul, that deserve our respect in a different way, at an entirely different level, and for different reasons.

The "high" architecture of our time — the architecture put forward by famous, or pretentious architects — consists of shapes which are dominating and simple, often stark, and often making a "statement." The starkness of these buildings makes it almost impossible for them to be good buildings, because goodness, in buildings, depends on the subtlety and minutely careful adaptations which are present throughout, to give them life. The very existence of a good building is by its nature at odds with the schematic, rigid forms that were so much copied by the attention-seeking architects of our present-day era.

The simplified, stark, attention-seeking forms of many modern buildings — especially those that are considered notable — are at odds with the very nature of any good building in which there are necessarily thousand-fold layers of subtle adaptations.

In chapter 2, we have given examples of subtle, local adaptations that occur at every level of scale, and with almost infinite finesse, to make human beings comfortable. In many other chapters, we have discussed the critical nature of small subtleties in length, width, and height, which occur as a result of these practical and functional, adaptations.

The forms which come about, as a result of these thousand-fold adaptations, are carefully, minutely shaped and proportioned. Architecture that is built for real life contains a near infinity of large and small adaptations and harmonies, which bind together into heretofore unknown form.

The infinitely varying dimensions and proportions, all occurring at dozens of different levels of scale, create a new family of forms, an entirely different class of shapes and concepts. The example of the Eishin Campus has already demonstrated this case, and proves that it is possible in practice.

The buildings which we designate as real, are precisely and necessarily those which cannot be captured in any simple formula, or in any drawing, or schematic.

So by dealing, realistically, with the forms of building that are necessary, we enter, collectively, a new landscape, a new architecture of forms, a previously unknown kind of buildings and landscapes, rooms, windows, passages, roads, paths, and terraces. On the surface, for an observer with a tired or lazy mind, these entities may look like others they have seen. But that is an illusion. These unknown forms are the necessary result of biological thinking, when it is applied in a natural way, to architecture. This is why I said earlier that we shall move into unknown territory, and into a land of unknown forms. The morphological characteristics of these new buildings cannot be replaced, or created, by the mechanical techniques of present-day architectural procedure.

What we have done at Eishin, and in other projects, enters new ground. The buildings created come from new realms of thought, and allow us to generate hitherto unreachable forms.

There are an infinite number of these forms, created by adaptation and direct making. As a class, they are surprisingly different from the simplified and more gross forms of the recent past.[1]

This truly is a revolution — not as a matter of rhetoric, but as a matter of fact. It will change the art, and the profession, of architecture. And these are the only kinds of forms, which will bring the life that people need, to the task of building and the task of making habitable new environments for the future.

DISTINGUISHING REAL ARCHITECTURE FROM CONTEMPORARY ARCHITECTURE

Another way of describing the artificial design quality of many late 20th-century buildings is that in most buildings, the architect used to focus attention on a few strongly defined elements. Usually, the way the building stood out in its surroundings was very sharp, and intentionally separated from the buildings that surround it.

Real architecture comes about in a different way. If the architecture is real, there will be thousands of living centers; many of them modest, all of them having direct impact on human beings. In this condition, there is an overall wholeness in the building and the zones nearby, but this quality is not aggressive not too sharp. It rather creates a condition where the building melts into the town, or street, or garden where it is placed. The overall feeling it creates is gentle comfort. Whenever you find a building with such an easy-

---

1   The infinity of new kinds of forms, lying outside what can be reached by conventional graphic techniques, is discussed at length, in *The Nature of Order*, Book Three, *A Vision of a Living World*, Appendix on Number: "The Class of Living Structures," pp. 687-693.

going quality, you find it difficult to separate such a building from its context.

THE RESULTING POTENTIAL FOR BATTLE

In the five hundred pages of our book, there are, on almost every page, examples of the subtle ways in which human feeling — people's feelings — depend on the subtle arrangement of the surroundings in which people seek to *be* themselves. Well-being, happiness, comfort, joy, physical health, emotional health — all depend on the kinds of adaptations that have been described, and they are seen in virtually all the illustrations we have given.

The subtlety of these connections between human beings and buildings is not obvious, although they come from the most ordinary experiences, shared by millions. Architects and planners are rarely aware of these subtle connections and causal links. That has happened because the culture of "professional architecture" — the so-called modern architecture we inherited from the 20th century — deliberately confused the issues, deliberately created a climate and a style, in which connections between human beings and buildings have been trampled and destroyed. Key facts have been hidden, obscured, and made inaccessible. Architectural students have not been taught the nature of these facts; nor have they been given opportunity to learn, study, and encompass these facts with their own common sense.

When you think about it, this situation creates an inevitable battle. It has become a battle because people have deliberately disregarded the subtle underpinnings of person-to-building interactions. When these people also gain power in such institutions as the American Institute of Architects or the Royal Institute of British Architects, of course there will be a considerable amount of bad feeling in society, together with negative competitiveness, which grows more and more serious, and uglier and uglier — even at the same time that it is masked with hyped-up, shiny, flash and falseness.

To rescue the planet, to rescue our habitat, to rescue the living character of the environment, we, as a society, might want to look to the experts. But the context in which the experts are presently taught to make architecture — as disconnected from real life, as egotistical statements, as construction for hire driven by the market — means that sooner or later, millions of ordinary people will have to take to the streets and metaphorically pull out their guns, make demands, and make public demonstrations. People who are not professionals may feel they don't know enough about what is required, or how to defend themselves against these confusions and these outrages. But we now see growing numbers of people taking stands against developers who are proposing projects that will cause destruction in their communities.

So we begin to see the origin of a great battle. We see the need to defend the planet, and the human rights of ordinary people to protect themselves against the vitriol which has been thrown into our cities because of the present idea of architecture.

THE PHYSICAL ORIGIN OF THE BATTLE

The battle we have been describing really *is* a battle between system-A and system-B. If we look back at the story of the last five hundred pages, and at the nature of the conflicts which erupted, in one form or another, we can easily confirm that the conflicts, each time they occurred, were conflicts about deeper questions than architecture. They were conflicts about how to behave, how to conceive of society, how to deal with money, how people participate in society, how to judge what is important and what is not, how to place the all-important matter of health and our own wholeness in the context of our daily actions. These conflicts are embedded in history, in social philosophy, in the changing ways we regard the worlds of animals and plants, in the changing ways that we regard issues of human rights. And now we see that they are also embedded in the creative actions we take on.

This deeper battle was, without doubt, one of the main debates of political and social life in the 20th century. It is continuing into the 21st century, and will continue further. As a political issue, it has been written about since the time of Marx, and up until the present day. It has been discussed endlessly, in intellectual magazines, in journals, in coffee houses, in political tracts, in the context of ethics, and in the context of what are called matters of the spirit.

Yet, so far, it only rarely reaches the stage of *real* battle where damage can be felt and understood explicitly for what it is — a ferocious conflict, as it was felt continually throughout the construction of the Eishin Campus. The same battle, the same struggle, is experienced indirectly by most of us, longing to find a worthwhile daily life.

But what is perhaps most astonishing about the battle this book has recorded, is that the very large matter that touches society so deeply, this battle so fundamental to the history of the modern era, has finally been fought out, not in a civil war, not in some political clash between two political parties, *but in the realm of architecture.*

Although we do experience the conflicts between A and B every day in our own lives, in few other contexts are the conflicts so visible, or the choices available to us so limited. This Eishin project, its conception, its construction and production, created a major confrontation about society and politics and ecology — not only about buildings. We might say that architecture — the entire making of the campus — provided the stage on which the confrontation could take place and could be witnessed. The massive and disturbing confrontation between system-A and system-B took place, essentially, over the issue of *what architecture means to society.*

My colleagues did not know that this would happen when we began the Eishin project. Such a thing had not initially occurred to us. The fact that architecture — "little" architecture, that had always been thought to be a minor player on the stage of history — was to provide the opportunity, the stage where this titanic battle occurred, was completely surprising. When we discovered this connection, simply as a result of doing what we found we needed to do in order to build the Eishin Campus well, we were thunderstruck.

We now understand that even in the building of something small, when system-A is used it will have a large impact on the people who are involved in it, and they themselves will be changed. In a significant way, it will contribute to changing the world. When a group of people make their environment for themselves, this has massive consequences. Because they are bringing forth the real content of their own existence, becoming aware of what their bodies know, this activity allows their instincts to reveal previously undreamt-of knowledge about themselves. This has a liberating and transforming effect on their consciousness, and ours.

How this social process works is not yet well understood. What we do know is that when people are given an environment built by others, and built for quite different motives (profit, for instance, or prestige), such a transforming, healing process does not take place. People's consciousness is not stimulated positively. Rather, they become passive and are likely to find themselves diminished and oppressed.

This massive opportunity for human growth is a necessary part of awakening. But in the modern world, such a process cannot now happen of its own accord. Things are too complicated. A social structure which allows it to happen must first be put in place. This is precisely the meaning of system-A, as we have described it. It is a kind of building process which allows a people's consciousness to come into being. It helps self-awareness to arise, and freedom to exist. It also helps people's awareness of their connection to the Earth. That is a fundamental human need, experienced by everyone. But when houses, offices, and apartments are abstract and impersonal, there is no way that people can connect themselves, and establish that necessary bridge to Earth.

People today do not usually think about these things. Nor do they typically know these things about themselves. But for some reason — also not yet well understood — the making of the world, the brute *making* and *placing* and *shaping* of our physical space brings these issues to the fore as almost nothing else can do. The social and economic revolutions — revolutions that have been debated for the last 250 years or more — suddenly come into clear focus when we find ourselves dealing with the actual making of the world, in concrete terms. That is when we begin waking up, if we have the opportunity to find ourselves, our true spirits.

The provision of hospitals, houses, offices, schools, roads, and parks — made by others, not by ourselves — seems benign. But it is, in both cause and effect, more likely to stifle us and to suppress our human qualities, as we have all experienced. Indeed, although we have these gifts of many kinds, we are not *really* blessed with gifts in the houses, apartments, offices and so on, whether these are provided by the welfare state, or by the profit-seeking developer! These artificial environments do not help us to regain our humanity.

This is the struggle in which we find ourselves. We find the stakes are higher as the conflict becomes more explicit, and more clear.

HEALING THE DAMAGE INFLICTED ON SOCIETY

A hundred years ago, writers like Dostoevsky, Kafka, Orwell, and Solzhenitsyn were drawing attention to a profound form of damage to society — so difficult to describe that in some cases it seemed mysterious or inexplicable, occasionally even entirely beyond comprehension; so far beyond comprehension that it could only be grasped through indecipherable feeling.

It is now the nature of our modern age that these hurts and wounds, these wastelands, are caged in a system of impenetrable rules and laws. We do not know how to extricate ourselves, and remain human. We can only grasp the painful reality as it is presented to us. This inscribes it and engraves it in our breasts. But as for what to do about it, no one knows the answer, and we continue living in the cage, while glimmers of comprehension slowly grow in us. Only slowly, slowly, we may hope that we are making our way toward the light.

The field of architecture — the art of making our homes, neighborhoods, shopping-centers, factories, and other buildings — perpetuates the morass. Up until now, architects of our centuries have aligned themselves with system-B, which makes things worse. In the case of literary artists, most revolutionary writers are on our side. They are shining light on the morass, deciphering the cruel cage for us, helping us to see it. In the case of architecture, however, many of the architects of our era, by standing with system-B, became prisoners of the morass themselves, and had little clear idea of the horrors they themselves created. So of course, they did not shine light to allow us to decipher the situation. They consciously worked hard to prevent themselves — and us, too — from seeing how things really stood, when it was in their interest to do so.

So the extreme contrast of the two systems, A and B, and the battle between the two, existing in society and in the present world of architecture and construction, now became as deeply problematic as were the widespread social ills encountered by the social crusaders of the 19th and 20th centuries (e.g. child labor and inhumane prisons). We will not be able to extricate ourselves from the ills of the 21st-century environment until we explicitly disentangle the conflicting and confusing architecture of system-A and system-B.

OPENING A NEW DOOR TO COMPASSION, AND TO RECOVERY OF THE CONNECTION THAT PEOPLE NEED TO HAVE WITH EARTH

We must find a way of seeing and knowing the role of architecture, which allows us, consciously and emotionally, to recognize that the material beauty of the buildings and physical material details we build, can convey the qualities of compassion and happiness. But even more profound than this communication is the fact that such buildings do not only communicate such qualities, but actually contain — *have in them* — the qualities of compassion and happiness. These feelings are comparable to the behavior we call kindness; they elicit and call out compassion in the social and spatial situations which are called forth by this architecture.

Years ago, the beauty of a building, then, would have in it a broad sense of humanity that was manifest in the windows, in the doors and steps, in the roofs, in the plants which accompany the buildings, and in the animals and insects which surround the building that was made. In the future, it is hoped that building will also create a broad sense of kindness and compassion in human beings, spreading out sometimes even to animals and insects.

THE NEW ARCHITECTURE

To characterize, fully, the nature of this coming architecture, and to allow us all to grasp why this new architecture will be, and must be, quite different from the thing we have been calling "architecture" today. I expect the following.

The new architecture that I envisage is geometrically different — deep, deep down to its very roots. The shapes, and spaces will be different. The foundations will be different. The character of the buildings will be entirely different. All of it will be different, and when this transformation comes — as it must come — the world will be physically different. In this sense, what is coming is literally another world, a world that is physically and emotionally different, its shapes, and colors and materials will all be different — an extraordinary marvel, which will be rooted in some humanity so deep, that animals, and plants, and trees and flowers, fish and birds will all be at home, with us, in this living place.

It will be almost unrecognizable to those of us who think they know what architecture is, and what architecture looks like.

It is, and will be, a huge revolution!! The multiplicity of human beings — language, music that is particular, clothes that are particular, these things, too, will reveal and support a rich variety of human beings — children, adults, older people doing things they have never done before.

Within the creation system described in this book, people are capable of making buildings with new geometry which comes from that part of our hearts, just as the feeling of human sympathy also comes from our hearts.

When we deliberately embody — as far as we are able — this kind of compassion in such a way that it shines out from our buildings, then the people of our coming society will be making buildings and cities which have, in some literal sense, a goodness which floods over us, affects us, and makes us aware of the very *quality* of goodness *itself.*

GOODNESS

If it is true that the kind of environment we have built (and have now partially described) can stimulate the recovery of human nature, this implies that the shaping of goodness as an attribute of society, morals, law, possibly even religion — all have the capacity to help us rebuild what we probably think of as the vaguely defined but positive archetype of human nature. It is, perhaps, a model of goodness, or a possible inbuilt source of goodness, capable of going forward, capable of getting better, capable of giving each one of us the ability and the desire, to mend ourselves, and help others, in some way, by going forward toward enlightenment and wisdom — even if it occurs only in very small steps, and we are swallowing very tiny doses of improvement at any one time.

We have said that the environment (its physical structure) is linked in some way with the social and mental discovery, and maintenance, of the structure of a social good — a self-guiding, autonomously developing, moral structure that has the capacity to regulate itself, and improve morally, by the gradual learning of a broad association between moral values and the shapes of buildings and the spaces between them. This means that the deep structure implanted in us, of an environment which is "whole," interacts with individual minds, and groups, slowly improving, cultivating the wisdom that grows in individual beings, as a result of the interaction with the world.

A CIVILIZING INFLUENCE

The civilizing influence of real architecture contributes, hugely, to all humanity. And the civilization itself, in which people behave with patience and affection, is itself subject to the influence of the battle between system-A and system-B.

In the regimen of system-A, it is not only the buildings which are able to create goodness and civility. The patterns of civility itself, even leaving the buildings to one side, are given their quality by a force that comes from within. It is this coming from within that is the ultimate richness of civilization; and it is this richness that is likely to be the force of something beyond food, sex, and money.

It is important that this force comes from within. In the materialistic times of the last century, our willingness to adapt to the rules of culture and society has too often been held, by 20th-century social science, to be a mechanical artifact, a mechanism. No more!

The core of the human being lies deep. It is no artifact or

mechanism. The scheme of things which has been displayed in the action of system-A, and the effect of the architecture that contributes to comfort, wisdom, and small niceties between people, this is the profound and mysterious interlocking web that exists between human beings, and between people and animals, and insects, and birds and fish, and the world as a whole.

The usefulness of the web of action is part of the much larger human culture, and of the wisdom that recognizes and bows down to the very subtle bonds that are part of the social and spiritual architecture of our human species.

When we reflect on the issues that have been raised in this book, we must give thanks for that, and use it as a means by which to find ourselves again.

COMPASSION AND LOVE

Again and again we are confronted daily by decisions, by the question, "What should I do, what path should I take, how should I approach this problem?"

There is no human being who does not, in some form, encounter this kind of self-doubt. Every one of us needs help or guidance in doing the best possible thing, in so far as what is available and practical, on the day when you encounter this question, in yourself.

Gandhi-ji, Christ, the Buddha, Aung San Suu Kyi in Burma, and the man down the street at the gas station. They did it for love. I can do it for love. Any one of us can do it because of love, and because love is simple and so powerful.[3]

Love *itself*! Not love for this person or that person — but love for a small spider who has fallen into a tin can, love for the field which nourishes, and the individual grasses that sway as the breeze comes gently across.

The ecology of humankind is created by the fabric of buildings, by the human fabric of affection, and by the powerful force of our love for our Earth — love, even for the smallest pebble.

---

3   Aung San Suu Kyi, the democratic leader of the Burmese people, has been kept in prison for nearly twenty years, uncomplaining, quiet, reasonable, but until recently (November 2010) remained imprisoned by the generals. She lost her husband to cancer while she was imprisoned. Her calm face and kindness are an inspiration to all who see her. For her biography, please see Wikipedia.

Try to be aware, every waking day and every minute, of the love that lies in your heart. The most tender wakefulness lies in your heart, and gives you the only realistic picture of the world. It can give you access to the ultimate reality. At every moment, remain wakeful and aware of your love for the Earth and for the Universe around you.

It does not need effort. It is already there, in your heart. If you look gently, you will see it in every corner of your heart.

This keeps our humankind afloat. It is a body of thought, a fortress of love and reason, which is the most powerful bond we have to the Earth, to our fellow-beings on the Earth, and ultimately to ourselves.

Our inner life is the product of our civilization, our dreams, our physical built world. But the present urban structure separates us from each other and separates us from ourselves. We must stop building and rebuilding this horribly familiar structure (usually called "development"), which fragments us socially and keeps us apart. If we wish to be united, to exist and live as a worldwide community, then we must endeavor to build the kinds of deeply adapted structures which have been described.

This expanding, living structure, if we have the nerve to build it and to keep on building it, will unite us with each other, with all our fellow beings — people, animals, and plants and trees and insects — all of us together, with the buildings where we live.

APPENDIX OF SELECTED DRAWINGS

A FEW CHOSEN DRAWINGS OF THE BUILDINGS
ON THE CAMPUS

PEDESTRIAN BRIDGE

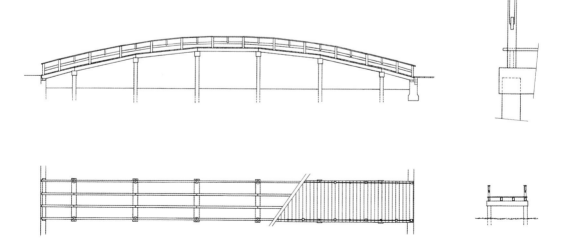

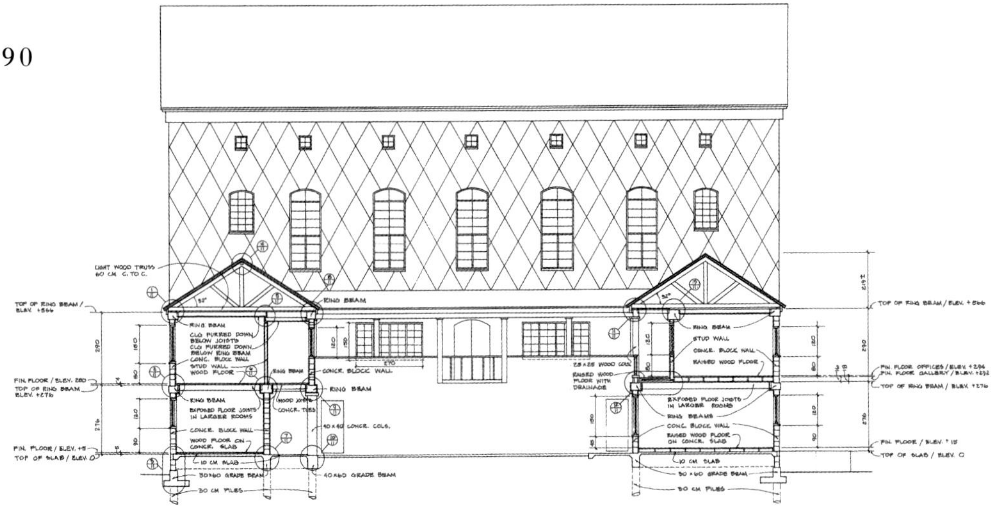
LIGHT WOOD TRUSS
60 CM C. TO C.
TOP OF RING BEAM / ELEV. +566
RING BEAM
RING BEAM
CLG FURRED DOWN BELOW JOISTS
CLG FURRED DOWN BELOW RING BEAM
CONC. BLOCK WALL
STUD WALL
WOOD FLOOR
RING BEAM
CONCR. BLOCK WALL
RING BEAM
FIN. FLOOR / ELEV. 280
TOP OF RING BEAM ELEV. +276
RING BEAM
EXPOSED FLOOR JOISTS IN LARGER ROOMS
WOOD JOISTS
CONCR. TIES
40 x 40 CONCR. COLS.
CONCR. BLOCK WALL
WOOD FLOOR ON CONCR. SLAB
FIN. FLOOR / ELEV. +5
TOP OF SLAB / ELEV. 0
10 CM SLAB
30 x 60 GRADE BEAM
40 x 60 GRADE BEAM
30 CM PILES
25 x 25 WOOD COL.
RAISED WOOD FLOOR WITH DRAINAGE
RING BEAM
STUD WALL
CONCR. BLOCK WALL
RAISED WOOD FLOOR
EXPOSED FLOOR JOISTS IN LARGER ROOMS
RING BEAMS
CONC. BLOCK WALL
RAISED WOOD FLOOR ON CONCR. SLAB
10 CM SLAB
30 x 60 GRADE BEAM
30 CM PILES
TOP OF RING BEAM / ELEV. +566
FIN. FLOOR OFFICES / ELEV. +294
FIN. FLOOR GALLERY / ELEV. +292
TOP OF RING BEAM / ELEV. +276
FIN. FLOOR / ELEV. +15
TOP OF SLAB / ELEV. 0

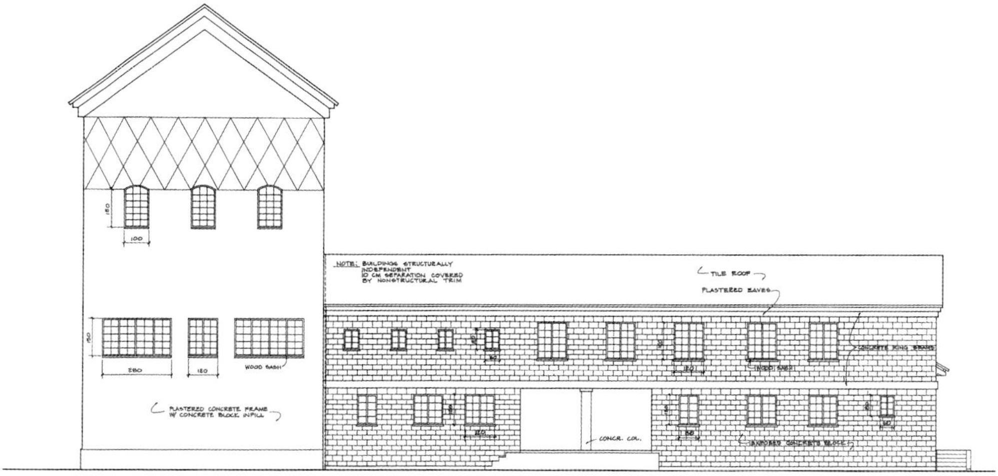
NOTE: BUILDINGS STRUCTURALLY INDEPENDENT
10 CM SEPARATION COVERED BY NONSTRUCTURAL TRIM
TILE ROOF
PLASTERED EAVES
CONCRETE RING BEAMS
WOOD SASH
WOOD SASH
PLASTERED CONCRETE FRAME W/ CONCRETE BLOCK INFILL
CONCR. COL.
EXPOSED CONCRETE BLOCK

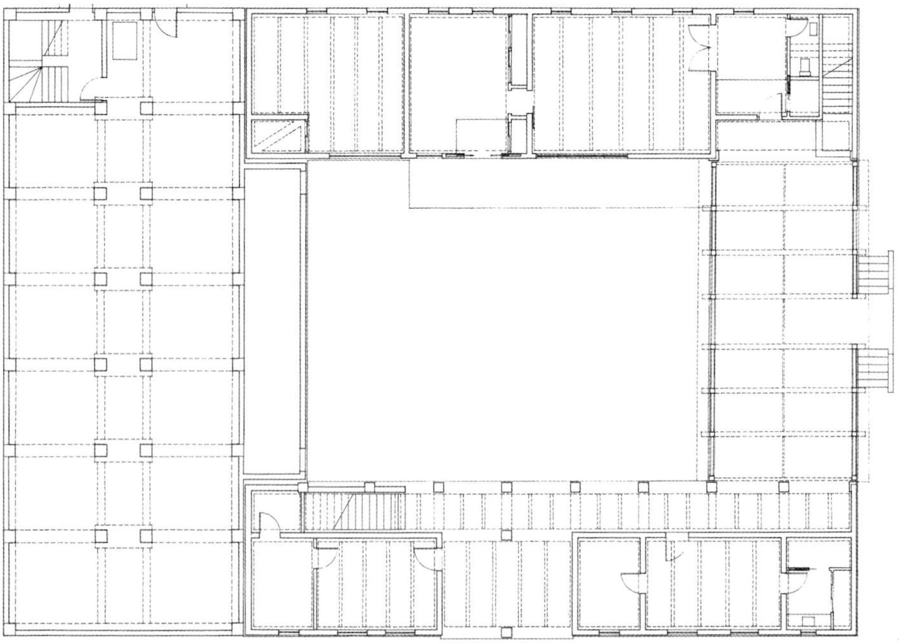

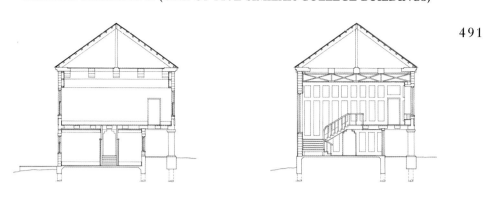

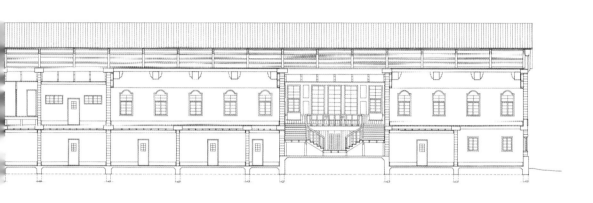

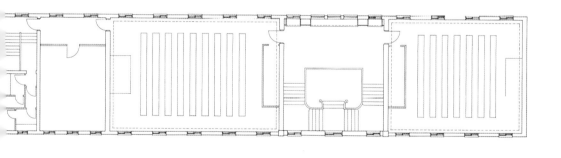

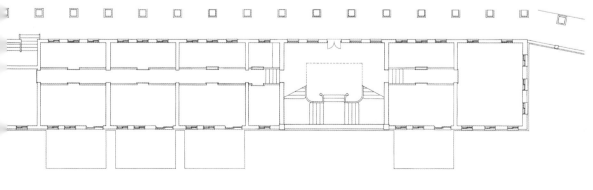

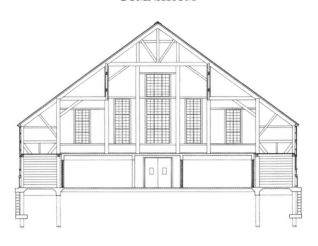

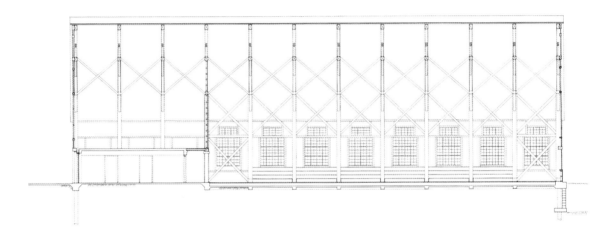

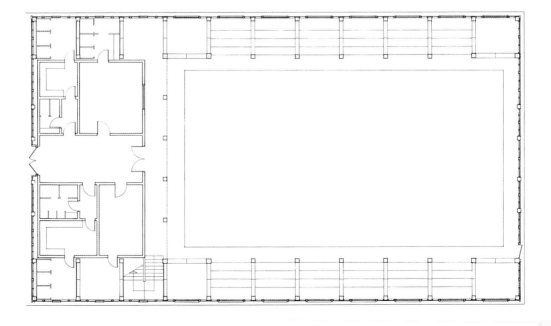

CENTRAL BUILDING

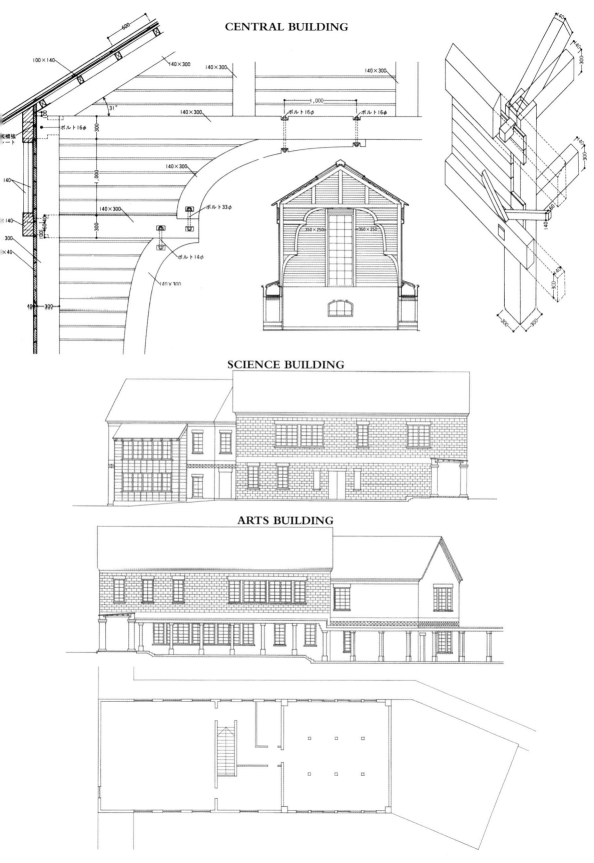

SCIENCE BUILDING

ARTS BUILDING

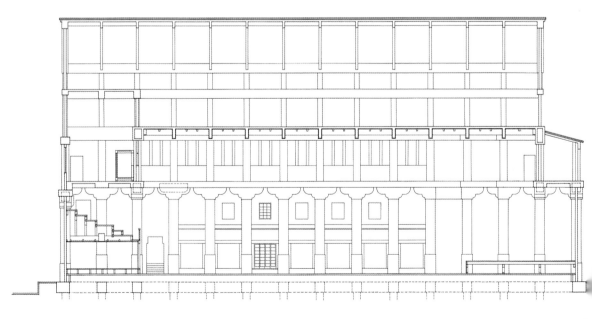

Drawings of floor plan and exterior elevation are on page 227.

MAIN GATE

495

SMALL GATE

STUDENT HOUSE

MUSIC SCHOOL

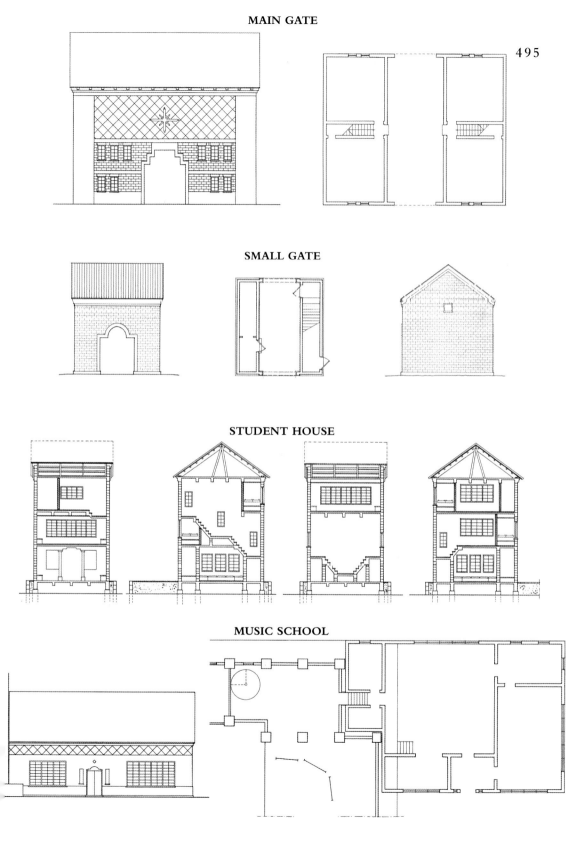

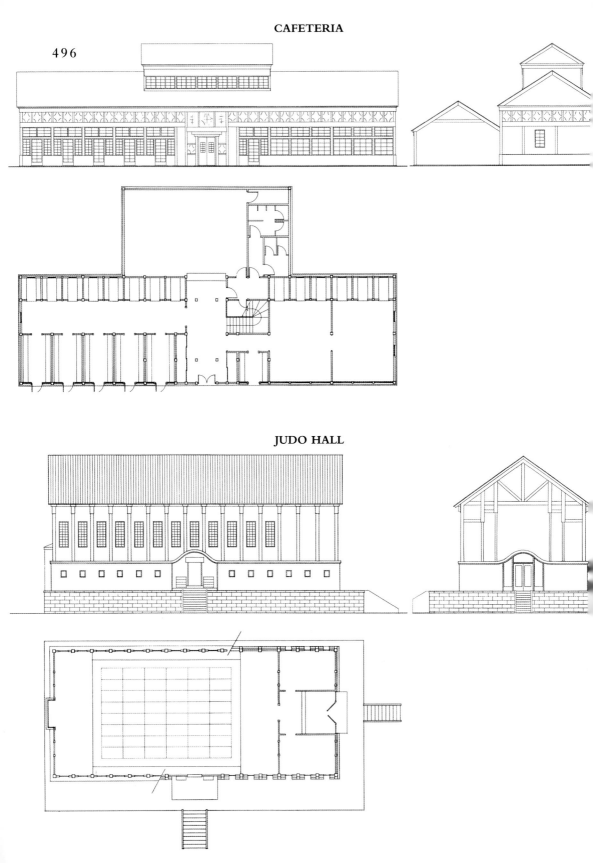

CAFETERIA

496

JUDO HALL

ADMINISTRATION BUILDING

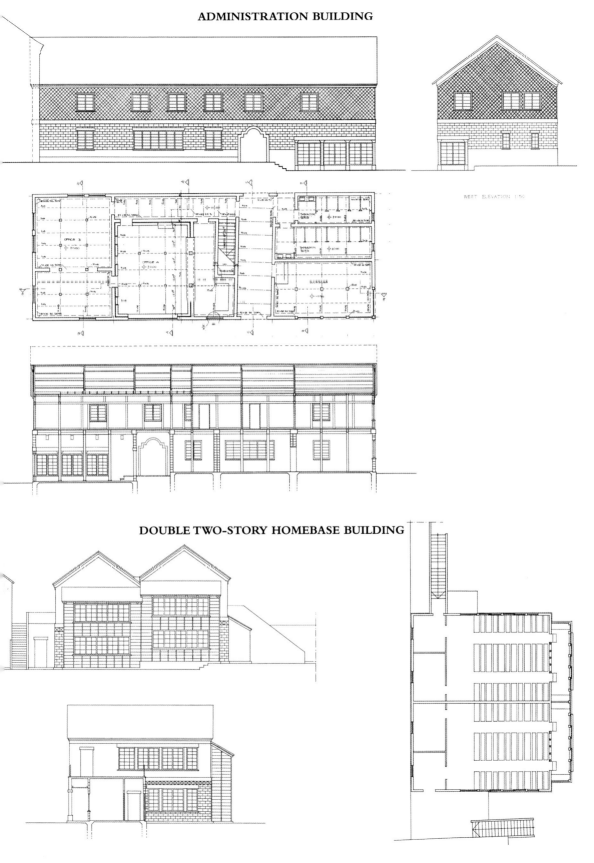

WEST ELEVATION 1:50

DOUBLE TWO-STORY HOMEBASE BUILDING

AUTHORS OF PICTURES, DRAWINGS, AND PHOTOGRAPHS

Several staff members of the Center for Environmental Structure have photographed the Eishin Campus over the years. We are grateful for their skill, as well as their affection for the place. That is evident in their photos. In particular, we wish to express appreciation for the pictures that Christopher Alexander, Hajo Neis, Hiro Nakano, Miyoko Takeda, Sara Ishikawa, and Jeraldene Lovell-Cole have all contributed throughout the construction of the campus. They have also contributed greatly to the CES archive and to this book.

Additional photographs have been contributed by:

Chapter 3
p. 44 ©Anthony Potter Collection/Getty Images

Chapter 4
p. 65 French Ministry of Culture
p. 67 Bradshaw Foundation, Geneva
p. 74 David Liaudet

Chapter 6
p. 93 Philip T. Dixon Cocking Church
p. 95 Anders Pearson

Chapter 21
p. 404 Berge Hjörungnes
p. 405 Jennifer L. Jeunger
p. 406 Samuel Rosset
pp. 407-408 Christin Markmann/Tim Street-Porter

Although every effort has been made to trace and contact copyright holders before publication, this has not been possible in a few cases. If notified, we will be pleased to rectify any errors or omissions at the earliest opportunity.

INDEX